M A Griffith

The Office of Speaker
in the Parliaments
of the Commonwealth

Dedication

To the Speakers of the Parliaments of the Commonwealth

The Office of Speaker in the Parliaments of the Commonwealth

PHILIP LAUNDY

Forewords by The Rt. Hon. Bernard Weatherill, MP
and Viscount Tonypandy

QUILLER PRESS
LONDON

First published 1984
by Quiller Press Limited,
50 Albemarle Street,
London W1X 4BD.

Copyright © 1984 Philip Laundy

All rights reserved. No part of this book may be reproduced or transmitted, in any form or by any means, without permission of the publishers.

ISBN 0·907621 31 7

Design and production in association with Book Production Consultants, Cambridge.

Typeset by
Macmillan India Ltd, Bangalore.

Printed in UK by The Alden Press, Osney Mead, Oxford.

Contents

	pages
Forewords by The Rt. Hon. Bernard Weatherill, MP, and Viscount Tonypandy	ix
Author's Preface	xiii

Part One

The Speakership – Background, Origins and History

		pages
Chapter 1	Introduction	3
Chapter 2	The History of the Speakership	11

Part Two

The Speaker in the Parliaments of the Commonwealth

Chapter 3	The British Speakership in the Twentieth Century	62
Chapter 4	The Speakership in Canada	103
Chapter 5	The Speakership in Australia	143
Chapter 6	The Speakership in New Zealand	164
Chapter 7	The Speakership in India	175
Chapter 8	The Speakership in the African Parliaments of the Commonwealth	193
Chapter 9	The Speakership in Sri Lanka, Malaysia and Singapore	218
Chapter 10	The Speakership in the Smaller Nations of the Commonwealth	236
Bibliography		261
Index		270

List of Illustrations

(between pages 144 and 145)

Viscount Tonypandy
The Speakers Procession
The Presentation of the Speaker to Queen Elizabeth I.
The Speaker admonishing a prisoner
Disraeli as Chancellor of the Exchequer, 1867
Cromwell Dismissing the Long Parliament
The Speakers Chair, Westminster
(*The above pictures are by permission of the Controller of Her Majesty's Stationery Office*)
The First Woman Speaker of Canada, Jeanne Sauve
Speaker Harrison
Speaker Forrest
Speaker Jenkins
Speaker Jakhar of Lok Sabha
Speaker Datuk Mohamed Zahir Haji Ismaili
Speaker Tomasi R. Vakatora
Speaker Nabulyato
Speaker Kolane
The Speakers and Presiding Officers of the Commonwealth, 1981

The jacket illustration – a stained glass window in St. Leonard's Church, Farleigh, Hungerford – is reproduced by permission of the Controller of Her Majesty's Stationery Office.

Foreword
The Right Honourable Bernard Weatherill, MP
Speaker of the House of Commons, Westminster

It is a great pleasure for me to respond to the author's invitation to contribute a foreword to this wide-ranging review of the Speakership in Commonwealth Parliaments. Mr. Laundy has already put all occupants of, and aspirants to, the Chair in his debt by his analysis of the historical development of the office of Speaker.

This new work will be of great value in permitting comparisons to be made of the various ways in which the office has evolved in the widely differing soils into which it has been transplanted. Just as each Speaker will perform his role in a way best suited to his own temperament and the mood of his House, so the powers and influence of his office will vary according to the requirements and traditions of the Constitution he serves. There is, therefore, no 'ideal' Speakership, but there are sufficient common elements, in the responsibility every Speaker bears for maintaining the health of the institution of Parliament, to make a comparative study of this kind enormously worthwhile. The regular Conferences of Commonwealth Speakers have, I am aware, already established this fact.

Mr. Laundy's book will serve as a standing reference work to all students of government and an invaluable source of information, anecdote and advice to those of us whose privilege it is to maintain the traditions of democratic Parliaments.

Bernard Weatherill,
House of Commons, Westminster,
1983

Foreword

*Viscount Tonypandy**

In his earlier work, *The Office of Speaker,* Mr. Laundy provided both the student of the British Constitution and the practitioner with an invaluable insight into the development of the ancient office that it was my privilege to hold. Readers of that book will be aware that its final section was a review of the Speakership overseas. I am delighted that Mr. Laundy has now produced a book devoted to the evolution and status of the Speakership in the Commonwealth as a whole, and I am equally delighted that he has done me the honour of inviting me to contribute this foreword.

I am sure that the author would agree that the primary purpose of a comparative study of this kind is not to advocate a uniform 'ideal' type of Speakership. Each Parliament will inevitably evolve according to the requirements of its own circumstances. Nevertheless, I consider that the deeper and wider understanding of the nature of the Speakership that this book provides can be of enormous benefit to developing Constitutions – and all Constitutions, whatever their seniority, are constantly developing. In particular, I commend Mr. Laundy's conclusion that, even in those Parliaments where Mr. Speaker remains a member of a Party, his impartiality in the Chair 'will ever remain an essential feature of any political system which permits free men and women to air honest differences of opinion in open debate'. It is no secret that the complete withdrawal from party affairs of the Speaker at Westminster has allowed him to be entrusted with total discretion in whom to call in debate, in the selection of amendments, and in the acceptance or refusal of the Closure. These are extremely important powers for any Speaker in the discharge of his most delicate and vital task – the protection and balancing of the rights of minorities and the rights of majorities.

My colleagues and I in the Chairs of the Parliaments of the Commonwealth may not all be able (or wish) to match the requirements set out by Mr.

---

* The Rt. Hon. George Thomas was elevated to the House of Lords as Viscount Tonypandy after leaving the Speakership (which he had held since 1976) and the Commons at the June 1983 general election.

Foreword

Speaker-elect Yelverton in 1597 when he said, 'Your Speaker ought to be a man big and comely, stately and well spoken; his voice great, his carriage majestical, his nature haughty, and his purse plentiful.' But we are all aware of the solemn trust placed upon us to ensure that we pass on our great office to our successors with its powers, dignity and status preserved, and, if possible, enhanced. By bringing together the experience of the whole Commonwealth in this field, Mr. Laundy's book can only contribute to that purpose.

Viscount Tonypandy,
House of Lords, Westminster,
1983

Author's Preface

In 1964 Cassell and Company Ltd. published a book of mine entitled *The Office of Speaker*. It was essentially a study of the Speakership in the British House of Commons, although it also contained a section dealing with the office in certain other Parliaments.

The present book is substantially a new work which attempts to survey the office of Speaker throughout the Parliaments of the Commonwealth. Although the British Speakership is included in the coverage – one could hardly overlook the country which gave birth to the institution – it does not dominate the book. Eight of the ten chapters deal with the office in the other countries of the Commonwealth and consist almost exclusively of new material. The only chapter which draws heavily on the previous work is that dealing with the history of the Speakership, chapter 2 being largely a condensation of the historical section of the book which was published in 1964. The other chapters incorporate the many and varied developments affecting the Speakership in the Parliaments of the Commonwealth which have taken place over the past twenty years and every effort has been made to produce a book which is as up-to-date as possible.

I am indebted to the Commonwealth Parliamentary Association for contributing to the costs of this book and thus enabling it to be published. Finance was in fact provided by the Association's Working Capital Fund, to which seventy-seven branches have so far contributed. I owe a particular debt to the Canadian Branch of the C.P.A. for financing my attendance at a number of conferences and other parliamentary occasions which have given me the opportunity to pursue a great deal of original research.

I am grateful to my employers, the Canadian House of Commons, and in particular to the former Speaker, Hon. Jeanne Sauvé, and to the Clerk of the House, Mr. C. B. Koester, for providing me with other opportunities to undertake essential research. As the secretary to the Standing Committee of the Conference of Speakers and Presiding Officers of Commonwealth Parliaments, I have enjoyed unique opportunities since the inauguration of the Conference in 1969 to familiarise myself with the nature and functions of the office of Speaker in the many Parliaments of the Commonwealth. The financing of these secretarial activities has been borne by the Canadian House of Commons as its contribution to the success of an important Commonwealth institution. I am grateful also to the many Commonwealth

Author's Preface

Speakers, past and present, who have accepted and placed their confidence in me as the element of continuity in the ongoing activities of their Conference.

To Rt. Hon. Bernard Weatherill, Speaker of the British House of Commons, and his predecessor in office, Rt. Hon. Viscount Tonypandy, I wish to express my deep sense of the honour they have accorded me in contributing forewords to this book. Both have given their unstinted support to this project and have made the author aware of their continuing interest throughout its preparation.

The others to whom I owe a debt of gratitude are so numerous that I would not venture to prepare an exhaustive list. They include many occupants of the Chair and colleagues, in both Canada and other Commonwealth countries, who have encouraged me in this work, provided valuable information and advice, and made available the photographs which illustrate this book. Such merits as this work may possess are due in large part to the co-operation I have received, while its shortcomings are purely my own. I sincerely hope that this collective acknowledgement will prove acceptable to those many friends of mine who serve the Parliaments of the Commonwealth and have placed their wisdom and experience at my disposal.

I wish, however, to make special mention of certain courtesies I have received which have involved financial considerations. In the course of my researches, I have visited a number of Commonwealth Parliaments, and in some cases my expenses were paid by the host branch of the Commonwealth Parliamentary Association. I acknowledge with gratitude the special invitations that I received from the Hon. R. M. Nabulyato and Mr. Mwelwa Chibesakunda, Speaker and Clerk respectively of the National Assembly of Zambia; Mr. M. T. Puna, Clerk of Parliament of the Cook Islands; Mr. Mosese Qionibaravi, former Speaker, and Mrs. Lavinia Ah Koy, Clerk to the Parliament, of Fiji; Datuk Azizul Rahman bin Abdul Aziz, Clerk of the House of Representatives of Malaysia; and the Hon. F. M. G. Mati and Mr. Leonard Ngugi, Speaker and Clerk respectively of the National Assembly of Kenya.

The extracts I have quoted from the late Lord Selwyn-Lloyd's book, *Mr. Speaker, Sir*, are reproduced by permission of Curtis Brown Ltd., London, on behalf of the estate of Lord Selwyn-Lloyd. Permission to quote from the late Sir Ivor Jenning's *Parliament* was granted by the Cambridge University Press. The quotation from *Government and Parliament* by the late Lord Morrison of Lambeth is reproduced by permission of the Oxford University Press. Extracts from *Orders of the Day* by the late Earl Winterton, published by Cassell and Company Ltd., are quoted by permission of Macmillan Publishing Company Inc., New York, who hold the contract for this title. Permission to quote from Mr. H. B. N. Gicheru's *Parliamentary Practice in Kenya* was granted by the author. Permission to quote from the 1958 BBC radio broadcast by Charles Pannell is granted by the British Broadcasting Corporation. All quotations from British government publications are reproduced with the permission of the Controller of Her Majesty's Stationary Office. Blanket permission to quote from *The*

Parliamentarian and other C.P.A. publications was granted by the Commonwealth Parliamentary Association.

In the preparation of a manuscript one is dependent on competent secretarial assistance, and I acknowledge the contributions of Miss Madeleine Tapp, Mrs. Mariette Renaud, and Miss Pauline Ladouceur, the three secretaries who at various times typed and re-typed the copy for the printers. Finally, I express my gratitude to my wife for her invaluable help in editing the final version of the manuscript.

P. A. C. Laundy
OTTAWA, 1984

Part One

The Speakership Background, Origins and History

Chapter One

Introduction

The parliamentary system seems to be infinitely adaptable. It has been retained, in one form or another, in the majority of the countries of the Commonwealth. It is one of the unifying factors underlying that unique association of nations, as evidenced by the existence of the Commonwealth Parliamentary Association and the wide range of activities which take place beneath its umbrella. It is a system of government which has undergone many refinements and modifications in order to meet local needs. Every country requires a system which reflects its own customs and traditions. The institutions of government need to be meaningful to the society they govern and the people should be able to identify with them.

Although colonisation represented alien government, the parliamentary system established by Great Britain in its former colonies was generally found to be acceptable by them when they attained independence. Its evolution in these widely scattered nations has demonstrated its 'geographical' adaptability. Its 'historical' adaptability had already been proven by its centuries of growth in Great Britain.

One of the features common to the parliamentary system wherever it is to be found is the speakership. Every Commonwealth Parliament has its Speaker. Except in Cyprus, where the presiding officer of the House of Representatives is styled the President, the designation 'Speaker' has been retained in every other unicameral assembly and in the lower House of every bicameral Parliament. In the case of Canada the presiding officer of the upper House is also styled the 'Speaker'. In Great Britain the Lord Chancellor is the Speaker of the House of Lords in addition to being a cabinet minister and the head of the judiciary. Elsewhere the term 'President' is more commonly used to describe the presiding officer of an upper House. In those Parliaments where languages other than English are employed, these designations have their equivalents in the languages concerned, but the use of the terms described above holds good throughout the Commonwealth from the point of view of English language usage.

This book does not deal with the presiding officers of upper Houses, a subject that could well be pursued in a separate study. There is a considerable diversity of upper Houses in the Commonwealth and this is reflected in the nature of their presiding officers. Seventeen Commonwealth nations have bicameral Parliaments, ranging from the sub-continent of India to the tiny island of St. Lucia.* In addition some of the Indian States and all the Australian States except Queensland have bicameral Parliaments. The difficulty of making comparisons among the presiding officers of the upper Houses of these Parliaments may perhaps be illustrated by making a short digression from the main theme of this study.

In Great Britain the Lord Chancellor, although *ex officio* the Speaker of the House of Lords, plays no part in the regulation of debate. His most important functions are discharged as a member of the government and head of the judiciary, his duties when presiding on the woolsack being much subordinate to his other responsibilities. Unlike the Speaker of the House of Commons, he is not responsible for maintaining decorum, he does not decide points of order, he has no casting vote in the event of a tied vote and he does not even call on members to speak. If more than one peer seeks the floor at the same time the House itself decides whom it wishes to hear. His duties are confined to formal proceedings and to putting the question at the conclusion of a debate. In the event of an equality of votes the question may be decided in the affirmative or the negative, depending on the circumstances. As a member of the government the Lord Chancellor votes in divisions and participates in debate, simply standing aside from the woolsack should he wish to speak.

The Senate of Canada, although none of its members occupy their places by hereditary right, resembles the House of Lords in that senators are appointed on a permanent basis. Until 1965, when a compulsory retirement age of 75 was introduced, they were appointed for life. The Speaker of the Senate is appointed on the advice of the Prime Minister from among the senators and normally changes with each Parliament. The rules of the Senate equip the Speaker with the power to regulate debate, decide points of order and maintain decorum although his disciplinary powers do not equate with those of the Speaker of the House of Commons. He has a deliberative vote, should he choose to exercise it, but no casting vote in the event of a tie.

The Australian Senate is an elected chamber and it elects its President from among its own number. He has similar powers to those of the Speaker of the House of Representatives, including the power to 'name' a member for disorderly conduct. Like the Speaker of the Canadian Senate he has a deliberative vote but no casting vote. As the elected President of an elective chamber, he is likely to be more assertive in the use of his powers than his Canadian counterpart. He has been known to take important initiatives. For example, Sir Condor Laucke, who retired as President of the Senate in 1981, instituted the practice of drawing the attention of the Senate to cases where the government had failed to respond to criticisms or requests for explanations contained in the reports of Senate committees.

The upper House of the Indian Parliament, Rajya Sabha, is largely elected by the Legislative Assemblies of the States by means of proportional representation and also includes twelve nominated members. The Chairman

---

* The full list is Antigua and Barbuda, Australia, Bahamas, Barbados, Belize, Bermuda, Canada, Fiji, Great Britain, India, Jamaica, Malaysia, Nigeria, St. Lucia, Swaziland, Trinidad and Tobago, Zimbabwe.

of Rajya Sabha is the Vice-President of the Republic. He is elected by an electoral college consisting of both Houses of Parliament. In regard to the chairmanship of the upper House, India followed the example of the United States where the Vice-President is President of the Senate. There is, however, an important difference between the two offices in that the principal function of the Vice-President of India is to preside over the upper House, whereas the executive duties of the Vice-President of the United States occupy the greater part of his time. The role in government of the Vice-President of India is not very significant except when he is acting in the absence or incapacity of the President, in which case he may not perform the duties of Chairman of Rajya Sabha. As Chairman he is vested with wide powers. He rules on points of order, maintains discipline, and protects the privileges of the House. He ensures that the proceedings of the House are conducted in accordance with the constitution, and to this end he may be called upon to interpret the constitution and statutes as well as the rules and practice of the House. His decisions are binding and may not be challenged. He has a casting vote in the event of a tie but no deliberative vote. He discharges his functions with complete impartiality although he is expected not to speak or act in any way which is inconsistent with government policy. Rajya Sabha also elects a Deputy Chairman from among its own members and he shares the duties of the Chair with the Chairman.

The Senate of Nigeria is a popularly-elected House, five members being elected from each State. The President of the Senate is elected by the senators from among their own number. Malaysia's upper House, Dewan Negara, consists of two members elected by the legislature of each State and 32 nominated members, the President being himself a senator elected by his colleagues. Zimbabwe's Senate of 40 members is a mix of four separate groups comprising ten chiefs, six nominated members, ten elected by the white members of the House of Assembly and 14 elected by the other members. The President is a senator elected by his colleagues and the constitution provides that he shall act as head of state in the absence or incapacity of the President of the Republic.

Jamaica, Trinidad and Tobago, Barbados, Bahamas, Antigua and Barbuda, St. Lucia, Belize and Fiji have appointed Senates, the President in each case being elected by the House. In Belize the constitution provides that a non-senator may be elected as President. In Trinidad and Tobago the President acts as head of state in the absence or incapacity of the President of the Republic. In Barbados the President may act for the Governor-General in similar circumstances if the Chief Justice is not available. Swaziland has a Senate of 20 members, half of whom are elected by the House of Assembly, the other half being appointed by the King. Both the President and Deputy President may be either senators or non-senators. They are elected by the Senate and if elected from outside the Senate they become senators in addition to the other twenty.

Although this book does not propose to deal any further with the presiding officers of upper Houses, it should be emphasized that they, together with their colleagues the Speakers, are equally members of the Conference of

Speakers and Presiding Officers of Commonwealth Parliaments which has met periodically since 1969. This conference held its inaugural meetings in Canada and has since met in India (1970), Zambia (1973), Great Britain (1976), Australia (1978) and Canada again (1981). The next conference takes place in New Zealand in 1984. The matters discussed at these conferences relate to the duties and functions of the Chair, parliamentary procedure and practice, and the various problems encountered by presiding officers. The conference provides them with their only opportunity to come together on a regular basis in a forum which is not overshadowed by any other activity. It has enabled the participants to exchange information and express views on matters of common concern to the fraternity. It has promoted a sense of unity among the presiding officers and has, perhaps, helped to ease the burden of loneliness and isolation which tends to be their common lot. It is certainly one of the numerous organised activities which serve to stimulate the family spirit of the Commonwealth. Continuity is maintained by a standing committee of Speakers and presiding officers representative of the various regions of the Commonwealth, which meets between conferences and determines the arrangements, including venue and agenda, for the forthcoming conference.

The Speakers and presiding officers of the Commonwealth had come together on at least three occasions prior to 1969, although in each case their meetings were incidental to another event. In 1950 they were among the guests who attended the ceremony at Westminster opening the new House of Commons Chamber, rebuilt after its destruction by German bombs in 1941. Advantage was taken of the occasion to hold a conference which appears to have been confined to the Speakers of the Parliaments of those countries which at the time were fully independent, plus the Speaker from Southern Rhodesia (now Zimbabwe) which, although not fully sovereign, enjoyed responsible government. In 1965 another ceremonial event, the celebration of the 700th. anniversary of the Parliament of Simon de Montfort, brought the Speakers and presiding officers together in London and a conference was held which included all the Speakers present. The presiding officers of upper Houses met separately. In 1966 the Commonwealth Parliamentary Association Conference was held in Ottawa and the Canadian Speaker called an informal conference of all the Speakers and presiding officers who were present as delegates.

In addition to the main conference, which now takes place on a regular basis, similar conferences are also held in the various regions of the Commonwealth. A conference of federal and state Speakers and presiding officers of India has been meeting regularly since 1921. A conference of Malaysian Speakers is held annually under the chairmanship of the Speaker of Dewan Rakyat. In the Australasian and Caribbean regions the conference is extended to include Clerks-at-the-Table. In Canada the federal and provincial Speakers form the Council of the Canadian Region of the Commonwealth Parliamentary Association. They meet once a year to plan the Regional C.P.A. Conference and also take advantage of the occasion to discuss matters of common concern to them as Speakers.[1]

The Office of Speaker

In order to trace the evolution of the speakership outside Great Britain, it is necessary to go back to the 17th century when the first colonial legislatures were established.

Representative legislatures were established in England's earliest colonies. The first colonial representative assembly was set up in Virginia in 1619, and in the following year another was established in Bermuda. But it was not until 1689 that the general pattern for colonial legislatures was set under what became known as the old representative system. These early colonial legislatures resembled the Mother of Parliaments much more closely than those of more recent origin. They were, in fact, miniature versions of the Parliament at Westminster. They were bicameral, the lower House being an elected assembly like the House of Commons, and the upper House being a permanently appointed council, comparable to the House of Lords, the theory being that the latter should serve as a restraining influence upon any impulsive tendencies of the former. The colonial Governor took the place of the Sovereign and was similarly equipped with the power to veto legislation. The three traditional branches of the legislature were thus reproduced to provide a model of the English Parliament. Examples of the old representative system survived until comparatively recently in Bermuda, Barbados and the Bahamas, while the Canadian Senate, whose Members are still appointed on a virtually permanent basis, is a survival of the early colonial upper Chamber.

The system, however, was not a success, for although it conceded the principle of popular representation, it did not incorporate the cabinet system. There was no ministerial responsibility to Parliament, and therefore no bridge between the legislature and the executive. Executive authority was concentrated exclusively and absolutely in the hands of the Governor, and as most of the early colonial Governors were, at best, tactless and, at worst, tyrannical, colonial grievances multiplied and the elective House of the legislature was permanently at variance with the administration. The colonists became highly resentful of external control, and through their elected representatives they never ceased to press for the right to control their own affairs, while the colonial Governors, pledged to uphold the Royal Prerogative, stubbornly resisted all demands for political reform. This conflict, which was to lead to the loss of the American colonies, was no less bitter in the smaller island colonies. In 1710, for example, the Governor of the Leeward Islands was killed in the course of a violent clash between his soldiers and the Antigua House of Assembly, which had defied his authority by continuing to sit after he had issued a proclamation dissolving it.

Under the old representative system the lower House of the legislature, like the House of Commons, elected its own Speaker, and it is hardly surprising that he was normally a Member who stood in the forefront of the opposition to the Government. He was, in fact, a popular spokesman in the truest House of Commons tradition, and some of the early colonial Speakers were rebels of the most militant kind. At least one was publicly whipped at the cart's tail, according to a complaint lodged in London by the agents of Barbados in 1700. In the same year the Speaker of the Bahamas House of Assembly forced his way into the Governor's presence and attempted to shoot him. His pistol was brushed aside as he fired and the bullet wounded one of his own supporters instead, whereupon he brought the butt of the weapon down on the Governor's head. This outrage apparently went unpunished. Nor was this the only instance of a Speaker having murderous designs against a Governor, for in 1750 the Speaker of the Bermuda House of Assembly endeavoured to hire an assassin for a similar purpose. While these incidents may not have been exactly typical of the manner in which the colonists conducted their disputes with established authority, they nevertheless illustrate the discontent and unrest which England's early colonial policies aroused.[2]

The old representative system was introduced into Canada in the latter half of the eighteenth century, where it proved equally unsuccessful. It was largely due to the difficulties experienced in this part of the Empire that Britain was induced to reappraise her colonial policy and apply the principle of responsible government in her overseas possessions. Canada's political grievances were comparable to those which had incited the American colonists to rebel, and it was in Lower Canada, the stronghold of the French-Canadian population, where the peace was most seriously menaced. An insurrection broke out in 1837, and it is notable that the leader of the popular cause during the period which led to this rising was the Speaker of the Lower Canada House of Assembly, Louis-Joseph Papineau. He was first elected to the Chair in 1815 and remained in office until the year of the insurrection when the Assembly was suspended. His party carried every election which took place during this period, and under his leadership the House of Assembly became the spearhead of French-Canadian resistance to external authority. In 1827 the Assembly was dissolved for refusing to vote supply, and the election campaign which followed was so bitter that when Papineau, having triumphed at the polls and been re-elected Speaker, presented himself for the formal approval of the Governor, the latter declined to confirm his appointment. The Assembly flatly refused to elect another Speaker and the constitutional machine ground to a halt in consequence. In the following year he was confirmed in office by a new Governor, and thus secured a moral victory which added further to his strength. In 1834 he sponsored, in the form of ninety-two resolutions which he brought before the Assembly, a far-reaching scheme of reform which would have brought the Government under the absolute control of the House of Assembly and made the Speaker the most powerful executive officer. But from this point on his influence began to decline. He gave offence to the Roman Catholic Church by promoting a Bill which would have lessened its authority in the province, and when the rebellion broke out he fled to the United States in order to avoid arrest. When he subsequently returned from exile he had virtually ceased to count as a political leader.

In 1838 the Earl of Durham was appointed Governor-General of the Canadian provinces and devoted himself to the achievement of a settlement of their problems. When the Home Government failed to support his proposals he resigned office, but in 1839 he published his famous 'Report on the Affairs of British North America' in which he advocated the introduction of responsible government in the Canadian colonies. In the same year it was decided to go some way towards implementing Lord Durham's scheme, and in 1841 Upper and Lower Canada were united into a single province for the purpose. But it was not until 1848 that Nova Scotia, New Brunswick and the Province of Canada became the first British possessions to be granted responsible government, and the success of Lord Durham's scheme in Canada led to its application elsewhere in the colonial Empire.

The reforms initiated by Lord Durham changed the character of the British Empire, and henceforward the bicameral legislature came to be associated more with the system of responsible government than with the system of colonial representative government. Thus, in the colonies without responsible government the old representative system began to give way to the new representative system, taking the form of a Legislative Council in which elected Members sat together with officials and nominated Members. The changing balance between them reflected the measure of constitutional progress of the territory. Commencing with an official majority, the Legislative Council advanced to an elected majority as a prior step to the achievement of internal self-government and ultimately total independence.

One of the characteristic features of the colonial Legislative Council in the days when the elected majority was comparatively rare, was the fact that the Governor presided over its debates. It is easier to comprehend how this seeming anomaly came about when one recalls that the colonial Legislative Council evolved in the first place from the Governor's Advisory Council. But since he was also the representative of the Crown and the president of the Executive Council it meant that he combined in his one person the functions of Sovereign, Prime Minister and Speaker. It was not uncommon, either, to equip the Governor with both an original and a casting vote in the Legislative Council. Martin Wight points out that this was a necessary consequence of the principle of the official majority, but as one of the reasons for the official majority was to shield the Governor from the invidiousness of a sole responsibility for overruling the unofficials, the dependence on his double vote for a majority, should such a situation arise, would defeat this purpose. In Van Diemen's Land (now Tasmania) it was the passing of controversial estimates by the use of the Governor's double vote that precipitated the constitutional conflict of 1844.[3] The inherent danger in this situation was foreshadowed in 1927 in a memorandum submitted to the Colonial Office Conference by Mr. Bryen Fell, a Senior Clerk in the House of Commons. Writing of colonial legislatures he observed:

> ... they have in the Presidency of the Governor a more direct contact with (the Crown) than is enjoyed by the British House of Commons. The relationship is indeed close enough to be pregnant with future danger. At the moment the Governor's position as President may seem indispensable and the danger, if any, sufficiently remote. But, as the advancement and the political education of the non-European races of the Empire and their inter-relationship with the Colonial communities living among them proceed, they will inevitably carry in their train the

need of a perhaps slow, but steady, increase in the responsibility of Colonial Assemblies for the conduct of their own public business. Simultaneously the position of the Governor will be enhanced. In such circumstances suspicion is easily generated: House of Commons procedure still bears traces of it, and it is easy to imagine incidents arising, which, occurring to the representative of the Sovereign, would render his position difficult. It is not suggested that the time is ripe for a universal separation of the offices of Governor and Speaker or President, and it may be that the intermediate stage of an appointed official (such as the Chief Justice) is necessary, but the position in every Colony might well be reviewed and a general scheme agreed upon whereby, in due course, a transition from the present system to that of the freely elected Speaker can be achieved.[4]

Nevertheless the Conference recommended that 'it was essential in present circumstances that the Governor should retain his position as President and continue to participate in the proceedings of the Legislative Council'. But after the second World War the Colonial Office view changed, and the appointment of a Speaker to preside over the debates of a colonial legislature came to be symbolic of an advance in the direction of self-government. The Kenya and Northern Rhodesia Legislative Councils acquired Speakers with their first unofficial majorities in 1948. In the former colony of the Gold Coast, now Ghana, the speakership was instituted in 1949. The appointment was a notable landmark in the history of the colonial speakership, as the chosen Speaker was an African, the first to preside over a British colonial legislature. In the case of Nigeria, the constitution of 1951 provided that the Governor should be the President of the Central Legislature, but he was empowered to appoint in his discretion any person not a member of the House of Representatives to discharge the functions of President. In the exercise of this power he appointed Mr. Edward Fellowes, then Clerk Assistant of the House of Commons at Westminster, as President during the initial period of the 1951 constitution. In 1954, when the new House of Representatives met under Nigeria's first federal constitution, the retired Clerk of the House of Commons, Sir Frederic Metcalfe, accepted appointment as Speaker. Tanganyika's first Speaker was appointed in 1953 when an official majority still controlled the legislature, a precedent which was followed in Nyasaland (now Malawi) in 1956. Uganda's first Speaker was not appointed until 1958, and the country achieved independence shortly afterwards. The colonial Speaker was normally appointed by the Governor from outside the legislature until the stage of constitutional advance was reached at which the Legislative Council was wholly or predominantly elected, when the right to elect the Speaker was conceded to the Council itself.

There remain a few colonial territories, the vestiges of the former British Empire, scattered over the globe, and there are still at least four legislatures – those of Hong Kong, the Cayman Islands, the Falkland Islands and St. Helena – where the Governor presides. There are other colonial legislatures, including those of the British Virgin Islands, Gibraltar, Montserrat, Niue,

Anguilla and the Turks and Caicos Islands, which have a Speaker.[5]

The rapid transition from colonial to independent status which has taken place in the Commonwealth in recent decades has greatly accelerated the evolution of parliamentary institutions in the countries concerned. The process has not always been easy. Parliamentary institutions have been under stress in many parts of the world and the countries of the Commonwealth have not been immune from these pressures. In some of them great difficulties have been encountered in adapting the parliamentary system to their particular needs. Coups d'états and military take-overs have occurred or been attempted in some Commonwealth countries, and at the time of writing parliamentary government has been suspended in four of them — Bangladesh, Ghana, The Seychelles and Grenada. There are others where it has been interrupted and subsequently restored, and it is to be hoped that it will be restored in the four countries mentioned. It is only realistic to recognize that in some countries the parliamentary system rests on fragile foundations, but overall the process of its transplantation and adaptation in the far-flung countries of the Commonwealth has been impressive and encouraging. It has become a common denominator in an association of nations where there are few common denominators which can be defined.

At the heart of the system lies the speakership, 'the linch-pin of the whole chariot' as it was once described. A Speaker is, or should be, one of the trustees of a nation's liberties. On his fair interpretation of the rules of procedure depends the protection of the rights of members. In protecting these rights he is protecting the political freedom of the people as a whole. One of the issues addressed in this book is the political status of the Speaker. The fact that he himself may have political attachments is not in itself important, provided he is able to distinguish between a party allegiance and his duty to Parliament. The impartial presiding officer will ever remain an essential feature of any political system which permits free men and women to air honest differences of opinion in open debate.

Notes to Chapter One: Introduction

1. For further information concerning the evolution of Speakers' Conferences see Philip Laundy, Conferences of Speakers and Presiding Officers, The Parliamentarian, Vol. LII, No. 4, October 1971, pages 264–270.
2. See Sir Alan Burns, *History of the British West Indies*, Allen & Unwin, 1954.
3. Martin Wight, *The Development of the Legislative Council*, Faber & Faber, 1946.
4. Cmd. 2884, pp. 85–6.
5. At the time of writing St. Christopher and Nevis has just become independent.

Chapter Two

The History of the Speakership

From its Origins to the Reign of Mary I

The office of Speaker is almost as old as Parliament itself. The first Speaker to be so designated was appointed in 1377, some years after the separation of the two Houses became finally established in or near 1341. But the origin of the speakership can be traced back to a considerably earlier date. The principal function of the early Speakers was to communicate the resolutions of the Commons to the King, and it may be presumed that some kind of intermediary between Parliament and the King came into existence when the English Parliament first assumed its rudimentary form. The names of some of the first Speaker's precursors have come down to us from the mists of mediaeval obscurity, although little is known about them. They were variously styled 'Parlour', 'Prolocutor' or 'Procurator', and the first of whom we have a record is Peter de Montfort, who apparently presided over the so-called 'Mad Parliament' which met at Oxford on 11 June 1258. It has been suggested that he was the son of the great Simon but no evidence exists to support this theory. The 'Mad Parliament' was in no sense a popular assembly—in fact seven years were to elapse before Simon de Montfort's famous Parliament of 1265 introduced the principle of popular representation for the first time. It consisted only of barons and prelates, but it set itself against the tyranny of the Court, and owes its derogatory appellation to those whose abuses it sought to check. Peter de Montfort himself belonged to the faction which was in opposition to the Court, and he became a member of the commission appointed by this Parliament which prepared the plan of reform known as 'the Provisions of Oxford'.

Mr. Enoch Powell in an article entitled 'A Speaker before "The First"' drew attention to the probability that Henry de Keighley acted as joint spokesman for the Lords and Commons at the Parliament which met at Lincoln in 1301. He incurred the displeasure of the King by presenting a remonstrance under the heading: 'a bill of the prelates and magnates presented to the King on behalf of the whole community'. The remonstrance was clearly drawn up by both Houses jointly as it contained an offer of taxation and the words 'on behalf of the whole community' imply that the two Houses were acting in concert. Henry de Keighley had in all probability been elected by the Commons as their 'porte-parole' and should therefore be taken into account as one of the Speakers' predecessors.[1]

The records shed no further light on the Speakers' predecessors until 1327 when William Trussell appears as the spokesman of the joint assembly of Lords and Commons which deposed Edward II. In 1332 two further names emerge—Henry Beaumont and Sir Geoffrey Le Scrope (who was Chief Justice), both of whom appear to have acted as spokesman of the Lords and Commons jointly. In 1340 William Trussell makes another appearance, and again in 1343 when he speaks on behalf of the Commons alone in reply to a communication from the Pope. Next we come upon the names of William de Thorpe, William de Shareshull and Henry Green, all of whom held the office of Chief Justice. It seems that the practice had arisen whereby the Chief Justice declared the cause of summons when a Parliament was called, but to what extent these gentlemen also acted as the mouthpiece of the Parliament is a matter of some doubt.

The first record of the Commons selecting one of their own number to be their spokesman dates from 1376. On 28 April of that year the assembly which has become known to history as the 'Good Parliament' met in the Painted Chamber of the Palace of Westminster where those present answered to their names. On the following day the Parliament assembled again in the presence of John of Gaunt, whose influence was in the ascendancy and who presided in the absence of the ageing King Edward III and his stricken son, the Black Prince. The cause of summons was declared by the Chancellor, Sir John Knyvet, and in accordance with the custom which by then had become fully established the Commons separated from the Lords and deliberated apart in the Chapter House of Westminster Abbey. They appointed their most prominent Member, Sir Peter de la Mare, a knight of the shire for Hereford and an opponent of John of Gaunt, as their spokesman, and he became in all but name the first in the long line of Speakers of the House of Commons. From what is known of him he was certainly a worthy man to found a great office, and a fitting leader of an assembly bent on the elimination of corruption at Court. The old King had become the prey of evil influences, foremost among whom was his mistress, Alice Perrers, whose favours brought profitable rewards to ambitious courtiers and who was responsible for much of the extravagances of the Court. John of Gaunt had espoused this woman's cause in the face of the hostility of the Black Prince. Parliament was greatly concerned at the abuses in the administration which were threatening the welfare of the realm, and encouraged by the support of the Black Prince it set itself to the task of correcting them. After lengthy debates, during the course of which the brazen Mistress Perrers had put in a personal appearance and presumed to lecture Sir Peter de la Mare on his duties, the Lords and Commons again assembled in the Painted Chamber before John of Gaunt to give answer to the financial demands which had been made of them. Speaking on behalf of the Commons Sir Peter de la Mare boldly refused to grant supplies until the nation's grievances were redressed. He took the opportunity to deliver a homily on the required reforms and in a forthright speech he condemned the abuses in Court expenditure, calling for an enquiry and the removal of corrupt ministers. These demands were granted. Alice Perrers was banished from the Court, and the Chamberlain, Lord Latimer, was impeached and dismissed from office, earning in the process the distinction of becoming the first Minister of the Crown to be impeached by the Commons before the Lords.

Unfortunately the Black Prince died while the work of reform was at its height, and John of Gaunt immediately regained his influence. Alice Perrers returned to Court, Latimer was restored to office, and Sir Peter de la Mare was imprisoned in Nottingham Castle. The Parliament which assembled on 27 January 1377, commonly called the 'Bad Parliament' in contrast to its predecessor, was packed with John of Gaunt's supporters, and it proceeded to undo the good work of the previous year, one of its first acts being to reverse the sentence of banishment against Alice Perrers. Yet from the point of view of the history of the speakership the 'Bad Parliament', the last of the reign of Edward III, was a memorable assembly, for from it emerged the first Speaker to be so styled—Sir Thomas Hungerford, a knight of the shire for Wiltshire. Although a supporter of John of Gaunt, Hungerford was not completely unmindful of his duties. At the close of the session he drew attention to certain grievances and at the same time presented seven 'Billes' to the Clerk of the Parliaments, of which, apparently, nothing further was heard.

Edward III died on 21 June 1377 and was succeeded by his grandson, the son of the Black Prince, who became Richard II. With his accession the power of John of Gaunt suffered a decline. The first Parliament of the reign met on 13 October 1377 and included many of the Members who had sat in the 'Good Parliament', among them Sir Peter de la Mare, who had been released from his imprisonment by order of the young King. De la Mare was again called by the Commons to be their Speaker, and on this occasion he was thus designated. In his speech at the opening of the Parliament he made various proposals for the administration of the state during the King's minority, the care of the King's education and the proper observance of the law. A petition which he presented, relating to the composition of a council to administer the affairs of the state, was implemented—an indication of the growing influence of the Commons. He declared that he spoke on behalf of the whole body of the Commons, and should he happen to speak anything without their consent it should be amended after he had done. He added that should he inadvertently fall into error the blame should be imputed to his ignorance alone, and thus set a precedent which has endured to this day.

The Speaker of the next Parliament, which met on 20 October 1378 at Gloucester, was Sir James Pickering, a knight of the shire for Westmorland. His speech on the occasion of the opening of this Parliament was the first such oration to be recorded in the Rolls of Parliament. He began with a protestation of loyalty which foreshadowed the request, later to become customary, for a favourable construction to be placed on the deliberations of the Commons.

Richard II's third Parliament met at Westminster in April 1379 but the Speaker is unknown. The Speaker of the two succeeding Parliaments which met respectively at Westminster on 16 January 1380 and at Northampton on 5 November 1380 was Sir John Guildesborough, a knight of the shire for Essex. It was this Speaker who first asserted the right of the Commons to approve public expenditure. He demanded a statement showing the manner in which the supplies were to be appropriated, thus foreshadowing the Queen's annual message to the Commons in her speech opening the parliamentary session: 'Members of the House of Commons: Estimates for the public service will be laid before you in due course.'

Guildesborough was succeeded in the Parliament of 1381 by Sir Richard Waldegrave, who was the first Speaker to attempt to excuse himself from taking office. In all probability he anticipated a dispute between the King and the Commons which could result in embarrassment for himself. Little could he have known that in expressing his own genuine reluctance to serve as Speaker he was founding a tradition which was to endure for centuries, long after it had become completely meaningless. The King declined to release him from the appointment, charging him on his allegiance to fulfill his duties since the Commons had placed their confidence in him. Waldegrave may have served as Speaker again but the records become defective at this period.

It was in the Parliament of 1384 that the Commons were for the first time specifically instructed to go and elect a Speaker. However, it is not until 27 January 1394, when the twenty-second Parliament of Richard II met at Westminster, that the Speaker can again be definitely established. The Speaker in this and the three succeeding Parliaments was Sir John Bussy, a knight of the shire for Lincolnshire.* He was the last and most prominent of the Plantagenet Speakers, and a leading advocate in the cause of the King in the last days of Richard's ill-starred reign. He figures in Shakespeare's play as Bushy, a creature of the King, whom Bolingbroke described as 'a caterpillar of this Commonwealth which I have sworn to weed and pluck away'. Certainly he was too close an adherent of the Court to enable him to discharge his trust as the spokesman of the Commons, and the fact that he was four times elected Speaker suggests that the influence of the King over the appointment had by this time become considerable. During Bussy's third term of office there arose the famous case of Thomas Haxey. Presenting himself before the King on the occasion of his election as Speaker for the third time Bussy submitted a petition from the Commons requesting a curtailment of Court extravagances. The petition aroused the wrath of the King, who condemned it as an assault on his rightful prerogatives, and demanded to know the name of its instigator. The Commons became faint-hearted and appearing before the King in the Painted Chamber they besought him on their knees for pardon. Bussy attempted to excuse them and disclosed the fact that Thomas Haxey had initiated the petition. The King consented to pardon the Commons but insisted that an example be made of Haxey, who was tried for treason before the Lords and condemned to death. His life was subsequently spared, but it was not until the succeeding reign that the judgment against him was reversed and the Commons' claim to the privilege of free speech thereby vindicated. So much for Bussy as the guardian of the Commons' privileges!

The Haxey case is illustrative of the despotic and unconstitutional course

---

* It is not definitely established that Bussy was Speaker during the twenty-third Parliament of the reign, but it seems likely on the basis of the evidence available.

which Richard embarked upon in the later years of his reign. The climax was reached on 28 January 1398 when the fourth Parliament in which Bussy served as Speaker adjourned to Shrewsbury where, after sitting for only three days it resigned its authority to a committee of Court minions comprising twelve peers and six commoners of whom Bussy was one. This subservient act confirmed Richard as an absolute despot, but his rule was destined to be short-lived. Returning from a visit to Ireland in 1399 he found that John of Gaunt's son Henry Bolingbroke, whom he had banished, had returned to England where a large army awaited his command to march against the King. Emboldened by his enthusiastic reception Bolingbroke claimed the throne, and Richard, finding himself abandoned, had no alternative but to yield. Bussy, who with other adherents of the King had fled to Bristol and taken possession of the castle, was captured when the city surrendered to the combined armies of Bolingbroke and his uncle the Duke of York. He was beheaded without trial on 29 July 1399 and thus became the first Speaker to meet with a violent end. He was not to be the last.

On 30 September 1399 there assembled at Westminster the shortest Parliament in England's history. It met for the purpose of deposing Richard II and sat for only one day. No Speaker was appointed. The deposition of two monarchs in the course of a century is a significant testimony to the power which had accrued to Parliament since the Model Parliament of 1295 had set the pattern for future Parliaments. The Lords, however, were by far the more powerful of the two Houses. At this stage in history the Commons were little more than a body of petitioners. Their principal weapon was their power to withhold the subsidies required by the King until their grievances had received satisfactory attention. But the King exercised an absolute control over the sittings of Parliament. He alone could summon a Parliament and issue the necessary writs for the election of the Commons. He could dissolve a Parliament at will and could suspend its sittings. It is likely also that he exerted a powerful influence over the appointment of the Speaker. Sir John Bussy was undoubtedly a royal nominee, and while no other mediaeval Speaker was as slavishly devoted to the royal interests as Bussy, it can be assumed that the man selected by the Commons to be their spokesman had to be acceptable to the King. The earliest record of the leave of the King being sought in relation to the election of the Speaker occurs in 1401, but it seems more likely that an established precedent was being observed rather than a new one introduced.

The Speaker's function in those early days was not to preside over debate with a view to keeping order, but to listen to all that was said and to collect the views of the House as a whole. It is not even certain that he sat as a chairman; he may well have taken his place in the body of the assembly with the other Members. No doubt a number of matters were discussed at the same time. Discussion of one grievance probably led to consideration of another, and each knight, citizen and burgess probably had a point to raise in connection with the interests of his own particular community. Presumably the Commons first satisfied themselves that the Speaker understood their mind before allowing him to petition the King on their behalf. But it seems they never relied too implicitly on him as they invariably attended him when he appeared before the King or the Lords, probably to ensure that in expressing their will he did not alter the sense they had intended to convey, either by addition, omission or distortion.

The Speaker was thus originally a mouthpiece, as his designation implies, and it was probably as much his function to communicate the will of the King to the Commons as that of the Commons to the King. His presidential role evolved as Parliament itself evolved. The speakership was not created to a deliberate pattern. In its original form it was a natural product of the dim and distant age in which it first emerged, and it has been shaped and adapted according to the changing character of the popular assembly through successive centuries.

The advent of the fifteenth century heralded the dawn of a new parliamentary era. Henry Bolingbroke's dubious claim to the throne rested entirely upon popular consent, and he was wise enough to base his rule on constitutional methods and govern with the support of Parliament. He lost no time in securing himself in the position he had usurped, and his first Parliament, comprising the same Members who had deposed Richard, was summoned to meet on 6 October 1399. One week later—on 13 October—he was crowned Henry IV in Westminster Abbey. The first Speaker of the reign was Sir John Cheyne or Cheney, a knight of the shire for Gloucester, who was confirmed in office on the day following the coronation. His tenure of office was, however, short-lived—two days to be precise—for he pleaded a sudden infirmity and begged to be discharged. In fact he was a supporter of John Wycliffe, and it is more than likely that his resignation was forced by pressure from Archbishop Arundel. The Commons selected John Dorewood, a knight of the shire for Essex, in his place. Dorewood was probably the first lawyer to fill the office of Speaker, although Dasent accords the distinction to Roger Flower, who became Speaker sixteen years later.[2]

The first prominent Speaker of the reign was Sir Arnold Savage, a knight of the shire for Kent, who was first elected on 20 January 1401. He seems to have been the right man to assert the growing authority of the Commons. Although he was careful to address the King with a deferential respect, he was the boldest Speaker since Sir Peter de la Mare, and he seems to have made the most of his opportunities for oratory. On the occasion of his first election he prefaced his speech to the King with a somewhat elaborate personal eulogy, but if Henry thought that the Speaker had come merely to lavish compliments upon him he was disabused as the speech continued. Having pointed out that the hearts and goodwill of his subjects were a King's greatest riches Savage went on to demand that the Commons should be given plenty of time in which to consider the matters referred to them and not be called upon to make important decisions with insufficient notice right at the end of a session—a significant indication of the tactics which Kings had been wont to employ in the past. Henry, in reply, gave the required undertaking. A few days later Savage was complaining that reports of the Commons' deliberations were reaching the King's ears before decisions had been finally arrived at and he begged the King to pay no heed to such untrustworthy accounts. Henry assured the Speaker that he would listen to nothing concerning the proceedings of the Commons which did not issue from the Speaker's own lips. Shortly afterwards Savage was again claiming audience of the King, who had by this time grown impatient of the Speaker's importunities, it seems, for he abruptly demanded that all future petitions should be submitted in writing. Savage's apparent delight in his own oratory led to the establishment of the custom, which endured well into the nineteenth century, whereby the Speaker upon the prorogation of Parliament delivered a speech to the Sovereign reviewing the work of the session.

Sir Henry Redford of Lincolnshire became Speaker in the Parliament of 1402, but in January 1404 Savage was again the Commons' spokesman. In this Parliament he reiterated the right of the Commons to demand redress of their grievances before granting the supplies, and he introduced another new precedent by petitioning for the immunity of the Commons from arrest for debt or trespass. The petition was confirmed by a statute conferring the required immunity not only on Members themselves but on their servants also, and covering the journeys to and from Parliament as well as the actual sittings. Thus was established one of the basic privileges of the Commons, and one that is claimed by the Speaker as a matter of course at the beginning of every Parliament, although it was not until 1543 that it was finally conceded as a permanent right.

Sir William Sturmy, or Esturmy, of Devonshire, a royal councillor in intimate association with the King, became the Speaker in the Parliament which was summoned to meet at Coventry on 6 October 1404. This assembly was subsequently stigmatized as the 'Unlearned Parliament' by the legal profession as lawyers had been excluded from it on the ground that they had in the past used their influence as Members to advance the interests of their clients.

Sir John Tiptoft of Huntingdonshire succeeded Sturmy in the Parliament which met at Westminster on 1 March 1406. He was extremely modest about taking office, protesting not only that he was too young but that he lacked sufficient sense! However, he proved to be an even bolder Speaker than Savage, and on one occasion he went so far as to admonish the King on his extravagance, protesting that in spite of his doubtful claim to the Crown his household expenses exceeded those of any of his predecessors! Several testimonies exist as to Tiptoft's independence as a Speaker, yet there is no doubt that he was also devoted to the service of the King, as his subsequent advancement goes to prove. The Parliament of 1406 was an important one from Henry's point of view, the succession to the Crown and the formation of a new Council being among the business it was due to consider. It was the task of the Speaker to manage these matters in the House of Commons on the King's behalf, and the appointment of the youthful Tiptoft was probably due to the need for a man of vigour and stamina to undertake the arduous duties of the difficult session ahead. It proved to be one of the longest Parliaments ever to have been held. At its prorogation Tiptoft, like Savage before him, begged the King to disbelieve the rumours which had been circulating concerning the Commons' proceedings, Henry responding with his customary magnanimity. Tiptoft was created a baron in 1426, thus becoming the first ex-Speaker to be raised to the peerage.

Tiptoft's successor was Thomas Chaucer of Oxfordshire, reputedly the son of the poet, who was successively Speaker in the next three Parliaments, and who was appointed on two subsequent occasions in the following reign. He began by maintaining the bold tradition of Savage and Tiptoft. The first Parliament in which he represented the Commons, which met at Gloucester on 20 October 1407, was notable for an important constitutional advance. The King, having conferred unilaterally with the Lords as to his financial necessities, formulated proposals involving a heavy increase in taxation without prior consultation with the Commons. When the Speaker and his deputation reported back to the House, the Commons protested that their privileges had been infringed. Since the main burden of taxation fell upon themselves it had been agreed some years previously that they should be conceded precedence in matters of finance, and a formula to this effect had first been adopted in 1395. A declaration was accordingly made and entered upon the Rolls deploring the intervention of the King and the peers and reasserting the Commons' claim that the financial initiative rested solely with themselves, that no grant should be reported to the King unless both Houses had agreed to it, and that the report should then be made by the Speaker of the House of Commons and no other. The King conceded the claim, and thus established a financial procedure which to this day incorporates these traditional formalities.

The Commons had come a long way since the deposition of Richard II, and it became evident that Henry, at least, considered that they had come a little too far. At all events, when Chaucer embarked upon his third term of office in November 1411 the King appears to have decided that it was time his boldness received a salutary check. When the Speaker asked for permission to make the customary protestations he was sharply informed that he might speak as others had done before him but must introduce no novelties. Chaucer had not been expecting this rebuke for he asked for three days in order that he might consider what he should say. The Commons seem to have viewed with some alarm this hardening in the King's attitude, for when they reappeared in the Painted Chamber Chaucer assured the King that he desired to make no other protestation than that which other Speakers had made before him, and continued with the customary plea that should he say anything which incurred the King's displeasure it should be imputed to his own ignorance alone.

The first Parliament of Henry V met at Westminster on 14 May 1413 and William Stourton of Dorset was appointed Speaker. He appears to have exceeded his authority, for having been commanded by the King to deliver certain complaints in writing he submitted a petition without consulting his colleagues. The Commons thereupon sought an audience with the King with another spokesman at their head—John Dorewood, who had served as Speaker in the preceding reign—and repudiated Stourton's action. Shortly afterwards they reported that Stourton had fallen ill and presented Dorewood as their new Speaker. Stourton's dismissal—for such it must have been—provides an interesting indication of the extent of the Commons' independence at this period. However powerful the influence of the Court might have been in the appointment of the Speaker it is clear that the Commons reserved the right to reject an unacceptable candidate and to replace him with one who was more in accord with their own views.

The second Parliament of the reign was summoned to meet at Leicester on 30 April 1414, the Speaker being Sir Walter Hungerford of Wiltshire and the son of the man commonly recognized as the first Speaker. This was a notable Parliament for it established the Commons as a body of legislators rather than mere petitioners. In a memorable petition, the first in which the English language was employed, the Commons prayed that 'from this time forward there never be no law made and engrossed as statute and law, neither by addition nor diminution, by no manner of term or terms, the which would change the sentence and the intent asked'. This was a concession for which the Commons had been repeatedly pressing. The statutes arising from their petitions had not always in the past corresponded with the wishes they had expressed. On this occasion they were successful in extracting the required undertaking from the King, who promised that 'from henceforth nothing be enacted to the petition of the Commons contrary to their asking, whereby they should be bound without their assent'. Thenceforward the practice arose of sending petitions to the King in the form of ready-drafted statutes which the King could either accept or reject but not amend. By the end of the succeeding reign the two Houses were on an equal footing in matters of legislation and the fact was recognized in a new enacting formula whereby a law was made with the 'advice and consent' of the Lords and Commons, to which was later added the significant words 'and by the authority of the same'.

By the end of the warrior King's reign a sufficient number of Speakers had held office to reveal quite clearly the sort of man whom the Commons tended to choose as their spokesman. He was always a knight of the shire, for the Commons required their Speaker to be of a standing to which no burgess could in those days hope to attain. It was not until 1533 that a borough Member was first called to the Chair. He was invariably a man who was close to the Court, but although in favour with the King he was the Commons' own, and not an imposed, choice. He was removable at the instance of higher authority, as we have seen in the case of Sir John Cheyne, but equally he could be displaced by the Commons themselves if they found him unsatisfactory, as in the case of William Stourton. Parliamentary experience was naturally regarded as an important qualification and most of the Speakers of this period had represented their counties in a number of successive Parliaments.

England was now to enter a disastrous period of its history, an era in which constitutional progress was brought to a standstill and government was virtually to collapse. The supreme misfortune was the long minority of Henry VI, coupled with the fact that his dynasty had been founded by a usurper, for it allowed hostile factions to develop which erupted eventually into the bloody conflict which was to reduce the nation to chaos and Parliament to nullity. With the outbreak of the Wars of the Roses Parliament became the instrument of whichever faction happened to be in the ascendancy, and the Speaker was inevitably a partisan of the controlling faction. However, it is an indication of the high standing enjoyed by Speakers at the outset of the reign that of the four knights appointed to the council by the first Parliament of Henry VI three had held the speakership – Sir Walter Hungerford, Sir John Tiptoft and Sir Walter Beauchamp. The value placed on parliamentary experience as an attribute of the Speaker, then as now, is also indicated by the election of Sir Thomas Walton or Wauton, a Member of some 30 years' standing, as Speaker in the Parliament of 1425. Twenty-five years later we find the Commons electing as their Speaker one, William Oldhall, in the year of his first entry into Parliament. This astonishing departure from the practice of selecting an experienced Member to fill the Chair was perhaps symptomatic of the general chaos into which the affairs of the realm were falling.

A number of Speakers met a violent end during this turbulent period, not, as is sometimes supposed, in consequence of their activities as Speakers but because of their involvement either as Yorkists or Lancastrians in the Wars of the Roses. William Tresham, who was four times Speaker, was the first to die at the hands of his opponents, a fate he was to share with Thomas Thorpe, Sir John Wenlock, his own son Thomas Tresham and William Catesby, Speaker in the only Parliament of the reign of Richard III. In the course of the next 50 years following the beheading of Catesby in 1485 three others who had held office as Speaker were to die by the axe, in each case for reasons totally unconnected with their occupancy of the Chair. Sir Richard Empson, Speaker in the Parliament of 1491, and Edmund Dudley, Speaker in the Parliament of 1504, were both executed on the same day in 1510. Empson and Dudley had been instrumental in the implementation of Henry VII's extortionate fiscal policy and were sacrificed as a concession to popular feeling by his son Henry VIII on a trumped-up charge of constructive treason. Sir Thomas More, Speaker in the Parliament of 1523 and a man of incomparably nobler character, died a martyr's death in circumstances which belong to the broader course of history.

With the accession of Henry VII Parliament was to enter an era of subservience to the Crown. His claim to the throne was disputable to say the least but he restored stable government to the country and set about re-establishing the monarchy on the strongest basis possible. Parliaments were summoned as they were needed and became little more than instruments of the royal will. The Speakers naturally reflected the subservience of the Parliaments. They became the direct nominees of the Crown and their election nothing more than an endorsement of a royal appointment. With certain notable exceptions, whose fame derives from spheres other than the speakership, it is a servile procession of court lackeys which passed to and from the Chair of the House of Commons during the reigns of the Tudor monarchs. The fact that men such as Empson and Dudley could have held the office suggests the inglorious depths to which it was degraded during this era.

One who stood apart from the rest was Sir Thomas More who was called to the Chair in the fourth Parliament of Henry VIII which met in 1523. More's fame does not, of course, rest upon his brief tenure of the Chair of the House of Commons. Like every other Tudor Speaker he was appointed because he was a faithful servant of the Crown—yet he, almost alone among the Speakers of this period, was not unmindful of his duties as the protector of the Commons' privileges. It is the measure of More's calibre that his brief appearance on the parliamentary stage is one which cannot be glossed over. He sat as a knight of the shire for Middlesex, and was appointed Speaker on the recommendation of Wolsey, who was then Lord Chancellor and the most powerful man in the land next to the King. The Parliament had been called because an enormous subsidy was required of the Commons for the prosecution of war with France, and Wolsey no doubt felt that the exaction of this demand called for the co-operation of a Speaker of a rather different order from the undistinguished gentry who normally sufficed to fill the office. At his election, More made the traditional protestation of his inadequacy and begged to be discharged, to which the King returned the customary courteous refusal. He then made two petitions. The first was the usual plea on his own behalf, requesting that if he 'for lack of good utterance, by my misreporting, pervert or impair (The Commons') prudent instructions, it may then please your most noble Majesty of your abundant grace to pardon my simplicity' in which case he asked leave 'to repair again to the Commons House, and there to confer with them, and to take their substantial advice what thing and in what wise I shall on their behalf utter and speak before your noble Grace'. The second was on behalf of Members individually, and in this he set a new precedent. He did not claim that the privilege of free speech belonged to the Commons as of right, but he certainly argued that debate could not be properly conducted without it.

The petitions were graciously granted, and shortly afterwards More was called upon to defend the rights for which he had successfully pleaded. On 29 April 1523 Wolsey came to the House of Commons to declare the reasons for the war with France and to demand the prodigious sum of £800,000 towards its prosecution, to be raised by a tax of four shillings in the pound on every man's goods and lands. More urged the Commons to accede to the demand but it was stoutly resisted, and a deputation of the Commons waited upon Wolsey requesting that he pray the King 'to be content with a more easier sum'. The Lord Chancellor dismissed the request abruptly and discourteously, and seeking to force the Commons' hand by intimidation he came again to their Chamber in a wholly unconstitutional manner, complete with his retinue, and arrayed in all the pomp and might of his great offices. The House listened to Wolsey in sullen silence. He demanded an immediate answer, and when no one spoke he addressed himself to individual Members. Continuing to meet with 'a marvellous obstinate silence' he demanded an answer of the Speaker. More rose to the occasion. He did not openly condemn the Lord Chancellor's flagrant violation of the Commons' privileges, but while cloaking his defiance in a subtle deference he met the outrage with an unmistakable rebuke. Falling on his knees he excused the silence of the Commons on the ground that they were 'abashed at the presence of so noble a personage, able to amaze the wisest and best learned in a realm'. He then reminded Wolsey that for the House to return an answer without an opportunity for unhindered debate was 'neither expedient nor agreeable with the ancient liberty of the House' and as for himself 'except every one of them could put into his one head all their several wits, he alone in so weighty a matter was unmeet to make his Grace answer'. Speaker Lenthall's memorable

The Office of Speaker

rebuke to Charles I over a century later was surely foreshadowed on this occasion by Sir Thomas More.

Wolsey departed, baffled and angry, and is alleged at a later encounter with More to have exclaimed: 'Would to God you had been at Rome, Master More, when I made you Speaker!' Nevertheless the subsidy was granted and More was instrumental in obtaining it. It would thus be mistaken to read too great a significance into the incident. It would be false to regard Sir Thomas More as a champion of the independence of the Commons. He was the servant of a King who regarded Parliament as an instrument which existed to do his bidding. But the Commons were possessed of certain recognized privileges, one of which was the right to debate in private and without interference and to deliver their answers to the King's demands through their Speaker. More, while acknowledging his duty to the Crown, recognized that he also had a duty to the Commons. He was a just and honourable man, and no doubt he intensely disliked Wolsey's bullying methods. He must have realized also that a subsidy freely given would serve the interests of the King far better than one extorted under duress. His speech on his election as Speaker is indicative of his enlightened conviction that the King would be likely to gain rather than lose the loyal co-operation of the Commons by showing them tolerance. Thus it was that he did not hesitate to uphold the Commons in their rights and prestige, even at the cost of offending the King's most powerful minister.

The most important Parliament of the reign of Henry VIII was his fifth, which ran from 1529 to 1536. Known to history as the Reformation Parliament it gave legislative effect to the great religious revolution whereby England severed its ties with the Church of Rome. The Commons emerged as the dominant Chamber and the bills which were eventually to bring the Church of England under the King's personal control were initiated in the lower House, the Lords being obliged to endorse them in the face of the combined determination of King and Commons. By the time this Parliament was dissolved the influence of the House of Lords had been severely curtailed and its majority of spiritual peers destroyed by the expulsion of the abbots. The Speaker at the outset of this Parliament was Sir Thomas Audley and he was as compliant a tool as Henry could wish for. He was at the spearhead of the Commons attack on the Church during the first four years of the Parliament, resigning the speakership when he was appointed Lord Chancellor in succession to Sir Thomas More. His successor in the Chair was Sir Humphrey Wingfield, who sat for the borough of Great Yarmouth, thus becoming the first burgess to be appointed Speaker. During his speakership the major work of the Reformation was accomplished and as the manager of the King's business in the Commons he would have played a leading part in conducting the crucial legislation through the House.

The Speaker in the Parliament summoned in 1536, two months after the dissolution of the Reformation Parliament, was Sir Richard Rich, probably the most infamous in the long catalogue. Like Wingfield he represented a borough constituency, having been returned as the burgess for Colchester. The basest of Henry's many catspaws, he was implicated in the ruin of many of his contemporaries and is largely remembered for his perjured evidence which led to the conviction of Sir Thomas More and his personal participation in the torture on the rack of the Protestant martyr, Anne Askew. Sir Nicholas Hare of Norfolk became Speaker in the Parliament which met on 28 April 1539. Undistinguished and compliant, he was a typical Tudor Speaker. If he has any claim to fame at all in connection with the speakership it is that he spent a part of his term of office as a prisoner in the Tower! He was committed by order of the Star Chamber for violating the Royal Prerogative in that he had advised Sir John Skelton how to evade certain provisions of the law in making his will. He was released shortly afterwards and on making humble submission was permitted to resume the Chair. The fact that this gross infringement of their privileges was suffered by the Commons to pass without protest is an eloquent commentary upon the impotence to which they were reduced under Henry VIII.

Hare was succeeded in the Parliament meeting on 19 January 1542 by Sir Thomas Moyle who sat for Kent. He was the first Speaker to include a definite claim for freedom of speech on behalf of the Commons when presenting himself for the royal approval. The King replied by granting *honestam dicendi libertatem*, and in reply to the claim for freedom of access to his person he said that the Commons should not approach him in a body but should send delegates. It was in this Parliament that the Bill of Attainder against Catherine Howard was passed, and a precedent was set, in order to spare the royal feelings, whereby the King gave his assent by Letters Patent under the Great Seal instead of in person. This Parliament is also notable for the case of George Ferrers on which is based the Commons' privilege of freedom from arrest in civil actions. Ferrers had stood surety for a debt and was arrested at the instance of the creditor. Hearing of this the Commons sent the Serjeant-at-Arms with the Mace to demand Ferrers' release, and on his being roughly turned away by the Sheriffs of London, they and the creditor were summoned to the Bar of the House and committed to prison. The King upheld the Commons' action, not because he had suddenly developed a fervour in the cause of the liberties of his subjects, but because it was in his own interests to uphold the supremacy of the High Court of Parliament over all other courts in the land. Of Sir Thomas Moyle it can be said that having supported the Reformation he did not deviate from his principles, and in the reign of Mary he resigned his seat rather than support the reconciliation with Rome.

The Journals of the House of Commons commence with the first Parliament of the reign of Edward VI which met on 4 November 1547 although the election of the Speaker, Sir John Baker, is not recorded. The first Speaker whose election is recorded in the Journals was Sir James Dyer who was called to the Chair on 1 March 1553, the day of the first meeting of Edward VI's second and last Parliament. The journal entry indicates that he was nominated by 'Mr. Treasurer of the King's House', from which we learn that the Speaker in those days was not only a royal nominee but that the motion for his election was actually made by a royal officer.[3] The only notable event concerning the speakership during the reign of Mary I occurred at the outset of her third Parliament which met on 12 November 1554. On presenting himself for the royal approval three days after his election the Speaker, Sir Clement Heigham or Higham, distinguished himself by becoming the first Speaker to make the formal claim on behalf of the Commons to three basic privileges simultaneously – freedom of speech, freedom from arrest and freedom of access to the Sovereign.[4]

By the end of Mary's reign the tradition that the Chair of the House of Commons should be occupied by a man of law had become firmly established. Sir Nicholas Hare was the first in an unbroken line of lawyers which extended through the following five reigns and the Cromwellian era, and from the end of Mary's reign the speakership came to be regarded as an important stepping-stone from which an ambitious lawyer could expect to rise to the highest judicial offices in the land. The catalogue of Speakers to the end of the seventeenth century abounds in names which later (and occasionally simultaneously) were associated with the offices of Lord Chancellor, Chief Justice of the Queen's (or King's) Bench, Chief Justice of Common Pleas, Attorney General, Master of the Rolls, Recorder of London or Baron of the Exchequer. It could be that lawyers were found to adapt themselves easily to the duties of the speakership through their knowledge of legal and constitutional procedures. But it is equally likely that among the legal profession it was easier to find a candidate susceptible to royal influences since the higher appointments which they sought were in all cases dependent on the Crown. The first break with tradition came in 1673 with the appointment of Sir Edward Seymour as Speaker, and it is coincidental that this was the very Speaker from whose subsequent appointment the royal confirmation was withheld. More remarkable probably is the fact that after such a length of time any departure from tradition occurred at all.

From the Reign of Elizabeth I to the Cromwellian Era

Elizabeth I continued the Tudor tradition of personal monarchy but her Parliaments became something rather more than the mere tools of her policy. If they were compliant in comparison with those of the two succeeding reigns it was on account of her great personal prestige and the fact that she embodied the fulfilment of the English Reformation. Thus, although her faithful Commons were to become the bane of her life it was never their aim to undermine her authority or the security of her throne. The later Parliaments of Mary had shown strong signs of intractability, and these, the first stirrings of the new parliamentary independence, were to manifest themselves stubbornly and consistently throughout the Parliaments of Elizabeth. But there is an important difference to note. Mary had not been a popular monarch and her religious policies had incurred a widespread odium. The opposition to her government had come from the Protestants, and from the anti-papal feeling which the excesses of her reign had engendered there had emerged the Puritan movement, a radical Protestant faction which was fanatical in its hatred of the Roman Church and resolved on nothing less than its total extirpation in England. When Elizabeth came to the throne every Protestant heaved a deep sigh of relief. With her accession the Protestant revolution was confirmed and she came to be regarded as the very personification of Protestant England. But she was a conservative Protestant while her Parliaments were strongly Puritan. From the ranks of the Puritans emerged the boldest spirits among the Commons. Although devoted to the Queen they were anxious for the implementation of church reforms far more radical than the Queen was prepared to concede. She was their bulwark against the hated Church of Rome and they were eager to reinforce that bulwark. They wanted to settle the succession to the throne, to initiate legislation of their own, to revolutionize the Church even further. Elizabeth regarded any interference in religious affairs as an encroachment on her own prerogative and was forever commanding the Commons to cease their meddling. But cease they never did. They persisted in their opposition, although, as Sir J. E. Neale so felicitously expresses it, 'the contest went on in a kind of romance that excluded any thought of divorce'.[5]

The appointment of the Speaker remained in the control of the Crown, and as the Commons' recalcitrance became increasingly manifest it was no doubt considered more than ever necessary that he should be first and foremost a royal servant. Elizabeth's Speakers certainly showed her no defiance, although on the whole they compared very favourably with the previous Tudor Speakers. The election of the first Speaker of the reign, Sir Thomas Gargrave, on 25 January 1559, provides the first evidence that it was customary for the candidate to attempt to disable himself on being nominated as well as on being confirmed in his appointment by the Sovereign. He petitioned for four privileges – freedom of speech, freedom from arrest, freedom of access to the Queen and permission to amend any mistakes he might make in reporting the decisions of the Commons. His successor, Thomas Williams, elected on 12 January 1563, petitioned for the same privileges 'according to the old ancient order'. In fact the privilege of freedom of speech had been formally claimed for the first time little more than twenty years previously. Sir Thomas More's notable speech in defence of freedom of debate had been made but forty years earlier. Perhaps Williams was harking back in his own mind to Henry IV's reversal of the judgment against Thomas Haxey, although this could hardly have been considered as ancient history by the citizen of the sixteenth century! The petition was duly granted with the usual precautionary admonitions. Thomas Williams was the first Speaker to die while in office, and he was succeeded by Richard Onslow, who held office as Solicitor-General and whose family was to provide the House of Commons with three Speakers altogether, including the greatest of them all. In accordance with custom he did his best to disqualify himself, and he must have been convincing, for his proved to be the first contested election on record. His nomination was carried by the narrow majority of 82 votes to 70, a significant indication indeed of the Commons' growing independence. It is probable that the opposition to Onslow was inspired by an objection to having an official in the Chair, and a growing belief that it would serve the Commons' interests better to appoint as Speaker someone less dependent than heretofore on the patronage of the Court.

The Speakers of the Elizabethan Parliaments frequently found themselves caught between the Queen's displeasure and the insistence of the Commons in discussing matters relating to the Church and the succession. In 1566 Paul Wentworth, one of the bolder spirits in the Commons, enquired whether the Queen's commandment to cease discussion of the question of her marriage was not an infringement of the liberties of the House. A long debate ensued on the matter which resulted in the Queen sending for Onslow and instructing him to permit no further argument. The Commons reacted by drawing up a petition asserting their privileges although it was not actually presented.

The Commons gave further offence to the Queen during this session by attempting to legislate for further church reforms. When she overruled them they retaliated by employing dilatory tactics in dealing with government business. Altogether the session of 1566 was a notable landmark in the history of Parliament. Never before had the Commons displayed such resolution in the face of royal displeasure. Onslow's speech on the occasion of the dissolution of this Parliament on 2 January 1567 is also of particular interest. He spoke for two hours, and although he was a royal official it was as a true mouthpiece of the Commons that he addressed the Queen. He discoursed, *inter alia*, on the duties of a Sovereign and the limitations on the Royal Prerogative, and ended by dropping a broad hint to the Queen that she should not be unmindful of her promise to marry.

At the outset of the following Parliament, which met on 2 April 1571, the Speaker, Sir Christopher Wray, when making the customary petition for privileges at the Bar of the House of Lords, was warned that the Commons would do well to meddle with no matters of state which were not referred to them, an instruction which was not heeded. The appointment of the Speaker in the fourth Parliament of the reign, which was summoned on 8 May 1572, involved an astonishing departure from tradition. His name was Robert Bell and he had been one of the outstanding radical leaders in the previous Parliament. The motive behind his nomination is not difficult to appreciate. Lord Burghley and his fellow privy councillors, whose influence in the choice of Speaker was crucial, had long been pressing the Queen to proceed against Mary, Queen of Scots, and in this matter at least they knew they could count on the support of the radicals. Bell's oration when presenting himself for the Queen's approval dwelt at length on the conspiracies involving the Scottish Queen and when Parliament was prorogued on 30 June 1572 he strongly urged the necessity of proceeding against her. In this matter the Queen stood alone against Lords, Commons and even her own ministers and for years she resisted their concerted pressure.

Bell died before Elizabeth's fourth Parliament had run its course and he was succeeded by John Popham, a compliant Speaker who was soon in trouble with the Queen for permitting a debate on a motion by Paul Wentworth calling for a fast. The next Speaker of the reign was Sir John Puckering who served two consecutive terms of office and was nominated to the Chair in spite of the fact that he was a newcomer to the House of Commons. A compliant tool of the court, he delivered a lengthy rebuke to the Commons on behalf of the Queen on 2 March 1585 which provoked great resentment among his colleagues. Already, it seems, there was a growing feeling that it was not the Speaker's place to be too subservient to the Crown. Puckering again found himself in trouble in the ensuing Parliament when the Puritan Members again launched a campaign to revolutionize the Church. Although he reminded the House that it had been instructed not to meddle in matters of religion he found himself unable to prevent a debate on an extremely radical bill for the abolition of the existing ecclesiastical laws, which was accompanied by a book in which was set down a proposed revision of the form of common prayer. Before the debate could resume on the following day the Queen sent for the Speaker and had both the bill and the book delivered to her. The Puritans responded by treating the matter as one of privilege and Peter Wentworth, the brother of Paul, formulated a series of questions relating to the liberties of the House which he presented to the Speaker with the demand that they be read. Wentworth asked, *inter alia*, whether the House was not a place where any Member could debate freely any matter 'touching the service of God, the safety of the Prince and this noble Realm', whether the Speaker might interrupt any Member in his speech, whether the Speaker might rise when he will without the consent of the House, whether the Speaker might overrule the House, and whether it was not a breach of privilege to disclose to the Queen any proceeding of the House without its consent. Seeking to worm his way out of an embarrassing situation Puckering pocketed the questions with the promise that he would peruse them. Before the House met again the Speaker had been summoned to the royal presence and Peter Wentworth in company with some of the other Members involved had been committed to the Tower. Reporting back to the Commons Puckering informed them that he had been rebuked for permitting the proceedings of the previous sitting and warned them afresh that no more should be said in relation to matters of religion. The Puritans were thus frustrated for the time being, although the imprisoned Members were released at the dissolution three weeks later.

The Speaker in Elizabeth's eighth Parliament, which met on 19 February 1593, was the great lawyer, Sir Edward Coke, who, like Sir Thomas More before him, made a brief appearance in the Chair of the House of Commons before finding greater fame in other spheres. He was a typical Tudor Speaker, and his conduct in the Chair gave no promise of his later parliamentary career, when he emerged in his old age as a stout defender of parliamentary liberty and one of the sponsors of the Petition of Right. Unlike Sir Thomas More, whose nobility of character added lustre to every office with which he was associated, Coke did little to enhance the speakership during his tenure of it. He showed himself a docile servant of the Crown, and his ornate oration on being presented for the royal approval outdid those of most of his predecessors in its terms of fulsome praise of the Queen and denigration of himself. The royal reply in response to the request for freedom of speech was even more grudging than usual. The Lord Keeper of the Great Seal, whose duty it was to act as the mouth of the Queen on these occasions, was none other than Sir John Puckering, who had so recently himself been Speaker. It is an ironic commentary that his response to Coke's petition amounted to an expression of contempt for the body of which he had once been a Member.

Coke's tenure of the speakership lasted a mere seven weeks and from the Queen's point of view he must have seemed the ideal Speaker. He seems to have mastered the difficult art of serving two masters, and showed a remarkable dexterity in the manipulation of procedure and precedent in order to expedite business and comply with the wishes of the Queen. The Speaker was, of course, the manager of business. He decided on the order in which Bills should be taken, and Coke was particularly adept at taking advantage of a sparse attendance in order to push through a government measure. It was probably in this manner that, towards the end of the Parliament, a Bill extending the penalties imposed upon Catholic recusants to Protestant nonconformists secured a successful passage. The Speaker was also responsible for the framing of the question, and Coke excelled in the art of securing the acceptance or rejection of a measure by means of cunning phraseology when putting it to the vote. Even the actual voting left room for strategy. If the Speaker was unable to decide whether the 'Ayes' or the 'Noes' were the louder chorus he could call for a division, in which case the 'Ayes' walked into a lobby and the 'Noes' remained in their seats. The Chamber being small there was insufficient seating accommodation for all Members when the House was crowded, and standing Members were often quick to seize the seats vacated by the 'Ayes' when a division was called. Coke did not hesitate to make use of the stratagem which this situation invited when he wanted to secure the defeat of a measure. During the subsidy debate this practice was angrily challenged. Why, asked some Members, could not the 'Ayes' remain in their places and the'Noes' go into the lobby for a change? But Coke, the master of precedent, was ready with his answer: 'The inventor that will have a new law is to go out and bring it in; and they that are for the law in possession must keep the House, for they sit to continue it'.

Coke probably introduced a rule empowering the Chair to enquire, when two or more Members rose to speak at the same time, which side of the argument each intended to support, and then to accord the floor to a Member intending to oppose the arguments of the last speaker. Although the framework of parliamentary practice had long been established, the House of Commons was at this stage still developing its rules of procedure as it went along, and there is no doubt that a Speaker such as Coke, with his great legal knowledge, his genius for argument, and his sensitive nose for an obscure precedent, must have played an influential part in the process. It is unlikely that any other Member could have bested him in a procedural dispute.

The last Speakers of the reign were Christopher Yelverton and John Croke. The former had started his parliamentary career as a leading radical but thirty years later had found sufficient favour with the Court to be nominated for the Chair. John Croke's tenure of office is notable for the precedent which established that the Speaker has no deliberative vote but a casting vote only.[6]

With the accession of James I to the throne of England the Crown and the Commons came into open conflict. It had been impending during the reign of Elizabeth but thanks to her immense popularity, skilful diplomacy and understanding of the temper of her people, she had always managed to avert it. James was a monarch of a completely different stripe and he lost no time in asserting his view that the right of a king to rule was based on the divine will of God, that his authority was absolute and that the privileges of his subjects were not enjoyed as of right but by his grace alone. To the politically conscious and strongly Puritan Commons no doctrine could have been more repugnant.

The first Speaker of the reign was Sir Edward Phelips and it appears that some discussion preceded his election. Perhaps there were those among the Commons who were no longer prepared to accept the nomination of the Court as a matter of course. Phelips's tenure of office was notable for his conscientious regard for the Commons' privileges although he did not allow this to obscure his strong sense of duty to the King. One of the Speaker's functions at that time was to keep the King informed of the bills which were being introduced and to suppress those which touched on his prerogative. There is evidence that Phelips fulfilled this duty over the objections of the Commons and it would be incorrect to assume that the speakership underwent any change of character during his period in office. It is during his tenure of the Chair that the first record appears of the House equipping the Speaker with powers to counter obstruction and irrelevance in debate,[7] which suggests that he nevertheless managed to win the confidence of his colleagues.

James's first Parliament spanned a period of seven years and by the end of it his relations with the Commons had greatly deteriorated. He had antagonized them with his claim to absolute power, his unconstitutional exactions and his habit of proclaiming new offences without regard for the existing law. Religious differences had become aggravated by the activities of the ecclesiastical courts and the adherence of the Anglican clergy to the doctrine of the Divine Right of Kings. The Commons, for their part, had been dilatory in granting supplies and shown no enthusiasm for the project which was dearest to the King's heart, a legislative union between England and Scotland. In these circumstances it is not surprising that James delayed the calling of his second Parliament until he was driven to it by sheer financial necessity. It met on 5 April 1614 and proved as unyielding as its predecessor, in spite of an attempt on the part of the King to influence the elections. It sat for only two months, passed no Bills and granted no supply, and has thus become known to history as the 'Addled Parliament'. The distinction of presiding over the Commons during this abortive Parliament fell to Randolph Crewe who was not an experienced parliamentarian, having served in only one previous Parliament and that as far back as 1597. The failure of the 'Addled Parliament' may well have been due in no small measure to the inexperience of the Speaker and his consequent inability to manage a factious and angry House of Commons.

For seven years James governed without Parliaments, relieving his financial necessities by various unconstitutional methods. Thus by the time the third Parliament of the reign met on 30 January 1621 the nation was smarting under a considerable sense of grievance. Sir Thomas Richardson was appointed Speaker, but although the Parliament in which he served was of the greatest constitutional importance his own impact on it was slight. His was no doubt the plight of the small man caught up in the tide of great events. His office demanded that he should serve two masters, and with both of them locked in an irreconcilable ideological conflict he found the task beyond his capacity. His compliant attitude more than once earned him the censure of the House, which objected to his habit of vacating the Chair as a means of preventing or terminating debates likely to give offence to the court. On 4 June, in obedience to the command of the King and over the objections of the Commons, Richardson adjourned the House without putting the question. When they reassembled on 20 November the Commons immediately began to attack the King's unpopular foreign policy and drew up a petition urging him to abandon the Spanish marriage he was anxious to promote for his son Charles. The King wrote an angry letter to the Speaker ordering the Commons to cease their meddling in matters of state, in reply to which they drew up a second petition complaining that the letter seemed to abridge them of the ancient liberties of Parliament. The King rejected the complaint, and on 18 December the Commons recorded their famous Protestation in vindication of their liberties which the King tore from the journal with his own hand. On the same day the King again commanded this refractory Parliament to adjourn and on 8 February 1622 he dissolved it.

James's fourth and last Parliament met on 12 February 1624 and was presided over by Sir Thomas Crewe, brother of him who had been Speaker in the 'Addled Parliament'. By all accounts the Commons were reasonably satisfied with him as he was re-elected to the Chair in the first Parliament of the reign of Charles I which met on 18 June 1625. Charles came to the throne a firm adherent of his father's theory of government and his first encounter with Parliament was not very encouraging. The Commons were as grimly determined as ever to abolish the abuses of the royal prerogative and they greatly incensed the new King by voting the most meagre subsidies and granting the taxes known as tonnage and poundage for one year only instead of for life as had been customary. Charles dissolved his first Parliament after less than two months but was driven by his need of money to call another on 6 February 1626 which was no more productive than the first. The third Parliament of the reign was the memorable assembly from which emerged the Petition of Right. It met on 17 March 1628 and its Speaker, Sir John Finch, in no way reflected the lustre of the Parliament. He was a royal minion whose unfortunate tenure of office demonstrated conclusively that a Speaker who served the court interests had become an anachronism.

The Commons lost no time in addressing themselves to their grievances, principal among which was their objection to the King's favourite counsellor, the Duke of Buckingham. On 5 June 1628, while Sir John Eliot was speaking on the King's evasive reply to the Petition of Right, the Speaker, fearing he was about to launch an attack on the Duke of Buckingham, intervened to command him not to proceed. The House responded by resolving itself into a committee to prepare a remonstrance. However, the King, being desperate for money, decided it would be wise to take a conciliatory approach and in the presence of both Lords and Commons he gave his assent to the Petition of Right. But harmony was not to be preserved for long. The Commons had no intention of abandoning their remonstrance which was largely directed against the hated Duke of Buckingham. Speaker Finch joined with the other courtiers in the House in making an unavailing appeal to the Commons not to name the Duke in the remonstrance and it was with the greatest reluctance that he complied with the order of the House to present it to the King. The King reacted by proroguing Parliament on 26 June 1628 and when it reassembled for its second session on 20 January 1629 much had happened to aggravate further the relations between the King and the Commons. Although they had only been granted for one year at a time the King had continued to receive the revenues from tonnage and poundage without prior parliamentary approval in contravention of the Petition of Right to which he had so recently assented. These illegal exactions coupled with his anti-Puritan church policy combined to bring matters to a head on 2 March 1629, a day which witnessed one of the most extraordinary scenes in the long history of the House of Commons.

The House had reassembled following an adjournment when the Speaker arose after prayers to inform the House that the King had ordered a further adjournment until 10 March. Immediately there were protests and Sir John Eliot rose to speak, upon which the Speaker indicated that he intended to leave the Chair. For the long-suffering Commons this was too much and as Finch made to move away two Members grabbed him and thrust him back into the Chair, remaining at his side for the remainder of the proceedings. Vainly did he point out that the Commons had always obeyed a royal command to adjourn. The Commons remained adamant and insisted that the declaration prepared by Sir John Eliot should be read. Neither threats nor entreaties were able to persuade the Speaker to remain in the Chair of his own volition. By this time Finch was thoroughly demoralised and abjectly begging to be released. One Member in exasperation asked him whether he was not the servant of the Commons to which Finch returned the significant reply, 'I am not less the King's servant for being yours!'

Realising that nothing would move the Speaker to resist his fear of royal displeasure, Sir John Eliot addressed the House at length on the grievances of the Commons. In the course of the debate the Speaker was reviled and denounced, one example after another being cited of how he had failed in his duty to the Commons. Finally, the resolutions contained in Eliot's declaration were put to the vote and the House resolved to adjourn for a week. But it did not meet again a week later. It did not, in fact, meet for another eleven years. On 10 March the King dissolved the Parliament and committed a number of the radical leaders to prison including Sir John Eliot, who remained in the Tower for the rest of his life.

Before proceeding to the great climacteric in the history of the speakership, reference should be made to an important procedural development of the early seventeenth century. It has often been alleged that the practice whereby the Speaker leaves the Chair when the House resolves itself into a Committee of the Whole House owes its origin to the mistrust with which he was regarded as the nominee of the Court. When the House wished to debate freely (so the theory runs) it was first necessary to get rid of the Speaker so that he could not report the proceedings to the King. This explanation does not seem to be supported by the evidence, however. It ignores the fact that the Speaker, like any other Member, had a perfect right to attend debates in

Committee of the Whole House if he wished, and to speak and vote in them. It also disregards the fact that there were other courtiers in the House who were equally capable of carrying tales to the King, so that the removal of the Speaker would not have removed the danger.

The committee organization of the House of Commons can be traced back to a very early date but the 'grand' or 'general' committee, consisting of all the Members of the House, developed during the reigns of James I and Charles I. Such committees, where discussion could be more informal and less restricted, became forums for debating weighty matters of church and state, and when they were appointed the House would resolve that all who attended should have voices. In 1621 the meaning of this proviso was the subject of some discussion, and it was resolved 'that, when limited, all, that will come, shall have voice, that they, in that case, if they come, are committees, as well as those nominated.'[8] In 1628 all standing committees save the Committee of Privileges were made Committees of the Whole House which, being too large to adjourn to a smaller room, took to meeting in the chamber itself. Thus it was only necessary for the Speaker to leave the Chair, for a chairman to be appointed and for the committee to proceed to business.

The Speaker, of course, had no control over debate while the House was in committee, and this may well have been a reason why the Commons preferred him to be out of the Chair when they were debating matters of national importance. In the House they were liable to find their will frustrated by enforced adjournments and manipulations of procedure; in committee they were less vulnerable to these tactics. Their opportunities for free and unrestricted discussion were infinitely wider in committee than in the House itself.

Eleven years were to elapse before another Parliament was called and the abuses during this period of Charles I's personal government were flagrant and numerous. The enforced payment of tonnage and poundage, the exaction of ship money and other illegal methods of raising revenue, together with the oppressive religious policies of Archbishop Laud, had caused the popular grievances to mount. The attempt to extend Laud's policies to Scotland led to war with the northern kingdom in 1639 and also to the summoning of the fourth Parliament of the reign on 13 April 1640. It lasted but three weeks, and since it immediately preceded the historic Long Parliament which met later in the same year, it became known to history as the Short Parliament. The Speaker, Sir John Glanville, had been a prominent radical in previous Parliaments, and it is known he was appointed Speaker with the King's prior consent. It is therefore fair to assume that the King, anticipating the temper of the Commons, was seeking to conciliate them by accepting as Speaker one who enjoyed their confidence. If he hoped in this way to induce their complaisance he was destined for disappointment. They were in sympathy with the Scots and smarting under their grievances, which they insisted should be redressed before any supplies were voted. The King reacted by dissolving this unproductive Parliament and appealing for financial support to the peers whom he called together at a Great Council in York. When they failed him his financial dilemma left him with no alternative but to call another Parliament, his longest and his last.

The Long Parliament met for the first time on 3 November 1640 and was finally dissolved some 20 years later, thus enduring through some of the most momentous events and revolutionary transformations that England has ever witnessed. The Speaker was William Lenthall, an unspectacular lawyer who was to win himself a place among the lesser immortals in the annals of English history thanks to one incident which proved to be the climacteric in the history of the speakership. During the Short Parliament he had presided as chairman over some of the most important debates in Committee of the Whole House and this experience no doubt influenced his selection as Speaker. His speech when presenting himself for the King's approbation was the usual mixture of abject humility and honeyed flattery, but it included two significant references to the constitutional disputes which had long bedevilled the relationship between the King and the Commons. Acknowledging that a King's exchequer was his subjects' purse, he added: 'Subtle inventions may pick the purse, but nothing can open it but a Parliament.' He went on to say that the Commons would strive for two things: the continuance of their liberties and the honour of His Majesty at home and abroad. He concluded with the usual claim for privileges.

As a Speaker it is fair to assume that Lenthall proved himself capable. Once assembled the Commons applied themselves with a grim determination to the removal of their grievances, and the momentous issues which occupied their attention at the very outset of the Parliament give some indication of the tasks which must have confronted Lenthall in the management of such business. The imposition of ship money and all other irregular exactions were declared illegal. The principle of parliamentary consent to taxation was reasserted together with the right of the Commons to appropriate the supplies. The Court of Star Chamber and other ecclesiastical courts with arbitrary powers were abolished by statute. A Triennial Bill provided that the interval between Parliaments should never exceed three years, and a further bill required the consent of Parliament to a dissolution – a thoroughly unconstitutional infringement of the royal prerogative although one can sympathise with the motives which prompted it. Concurrently with these measures the Commons proceeded to impeach the Earl of Strafford and Archbishop Laud, the principal instruments of the King's policy. Lenthall introduced various rules for the preservation of order without which many a sitting would have collapsed in chaos and uproar. One of the procedural innovations dating from his speakership is the quorum of 40 members, introduced by resolution of the House on 5 January 1640.[9]

Lenthall's supreme moment came on 4 January 1642, the King having determined on a showdown with the parliamentary leaders. Matters had come to a head with the passing of the Grand Remonstrance and the subsequent resolution that it should be printed, thus turning it into a direct appeal to the people against the policies of the King. The Commons were by no means at one over this issue. The Remonstrance had been carried by a majority of eleven votes only, and the motion for its publication had been carried only at the second attempt. Religious differences were dividing the House of Commons, many of whose Members were alarmed at the extreme anti-Royalist and anti-Church tendencies of the radicals. By no means all of those who had opposed the King's unconstitutional rule were republican in sentiment, neither did they seek any but moderate church reforms. Had Charles stayed his hand the way for negotiation might yet have remained open. But instead he succumbed to the evil counsel of his wife and to his own fatally erroneous judgment. He determined to come in person and at the head of an armed escort to the House of Commons to seize the five leading opponents of his government—Pym, Hampden, Holles, Hazelrig and Strode—whose arrest on charges of high treason he had ordered on the previous day. Thus he dared what no other Sovereign before or since has ever attempted—an assault upon the privileges of the Commons by a direct invasion of their very citadel.

On the previous day a message had been delivered to the Speaker from the King requiring the surrender of the five members. On receipt of the message the five were ordered to remain in daily attendance, and on the following morning, while the House was considering the King's message in committee, notice was taken of the fact that armed men were assembling in the neighbourhood of the Palace of Westminster. It was clear that the King was preparing to use force and as news reached the Commons of his design the five members were given leave to absent themselves. In its record of what followed the Journal of the House of Commons is brevity itself, stating only that the King entered the chamber and took the Speaker's Chair. The following account is based on the records left by two eye-witnesses, Sir Simonds D'Ewes, a member of the Long Parliament whose journal is considered to be the best authority for the proceedings of its early years; and John Rushworth, the Clerk-Assistant, who made notes of what took place.

A loud knock announced the arrival of the King at the door of the Commons Chamber. Halting his followers outside he crossed the Bar of the House, the only sovereign ever to have done so, and informed the Speaker that he needed to borrow his Chair. Standing before the Speaker's Chair, he cast his eyes around the members, all of whom were standing in silence, and failed to discern the five he had come to arrest. After briefly addressing the Commons in justification of his action, he asked if Mr. Pym were present. On receiving no answer he asked if Mr. Holles were present and, continuing to be met with a stony silence, he turned to the Speaker and asked him where the five members were. Lenthall's reply was historic, for in a few well-chosen words it expressed unequivocally and for all time where the Speaker's first duty lay. Dropping to his knees he said:

> May it please Your Majesty, I have neither eyes to see, nor tongue to speak in this place, but as the House is pleased to direct me, whose servant I am here; and I humbly beg Your Majesty's pardon that I cannot give any other answer than this to what Your Majesty is pleased to demand of me.

Whatever Lenthall's deficiencies might have been, on this occasion he rose to the greatness of the moment. For the first time the Speaker of the House of

Commons had declared his allegiance to the cause of parliamentary liberty. Speaker Finch had been faced with a similar challenge and had collapsed under it. But much had transpired since Finch's occupation of the Chair. It was inconceivable during his speakership that within a short space of time the power of the King would have become so diminished and that of the Commons so formidably augmented. Little more than a dozen years had elapsed between Finch's 'I am not less the King's servant for being yours!' and Lenthall's 'I have neither eyes to see nor tongue to speak . . .' but there is a century of difference between them. But even if we concede that Lenthall's stand was not a completely disinterested one, that he judged he had less to gain from serving the King than from serving the Commons, he is nevertheless entitled to his measure of honour and glory. For as he knelt before the King in that tense and silent House he had a spontaneous and irrevocable decision to take with only his own judgment to guide him. That he did not fail or falter in the face of it is greatly to his credit. In spite of all that had gone before it was still no light matter to incur the Sovereign's displeasure. The Commons, angry as they were, still held the King sufficiently in awe to refrain from demonstrating against his intrusion while in his presence. Yet Lenthall's words, cloaked in humility and respect though they were, were words of unambiguous defiance—a repudiation of the authority which the King claimed in respect of the privileges of the Commons.

Charles departed frustrated in his design, having brought a temporary unity to the Commons by his outrageous violation of their privilege, and having made the final rupture between Parliament and himself inevitable. He left the Chamber with angry cries of 'Privilege!' ringing in his ears, the bounds of restraint having been broken with his departure. On 11 January the five members returned in triumph to Westminster and by August the civil war had broken out.

Lenthall's resistance to the King greatly enhanced his prestige in the eyes of the Commons, but in 1647, following the victory of the parliamentary forces, he became embroiled in the struggle for power between Parliament and the army and he fled to the army for protection. He was brought back to Westminster and reinstalled in the Chair, and it fell to him to put the question on the various stages of the bill constituting the House of Commons a High Court of Justice for the purpose of bringing Charles I to trial. It was a much-depleted House of Commons which adopted this proceeding, the majority of the members having been forcibly excluded by the army because they were opposed to bringing the King to trial. Lenthall is not recorded as having registered any objection to this unconstitutional outrage. Following the death of the King and the abolition of the monarchy and the House of Lords, Lenthall continued to preside over the rump of the Long Parliament and as the symbol of the sovereignty of the Commons he was accorded the honour and precedence normally due to a King. However, effective power resided with Cromwell and the Council of State, as was dramatically demonstrated on 20 April 1653 when the Parliament, which had become corrupt and self-perpetuating, was dismissed by Cromwell in person, Lenthall, according to some accounts, being plucked from the Speaker's Chair.

This was not the end of Lenthall's parliamentary career, however. Following Cromwell's unsuccessful attempt to govern through a Parliament of nominees — the so-called 'Barebones Parliament', named after one of its members who rejoiced in the name of Praise-God Barebone — a new constitution known as the Instrument of Government was adopted providing for a Lord Protector as head of state, a Council of State and an elected single-chamber Parliament. Lenthall secured election to this Parliament and was again called to the Chair. The Parliament was dissolved after only five months, having failed to address itself to the urgent needs of the nation, and it was eighteen months before Cromwell decided to call another one. Lenthall was again elected to the Parliament which met on 17 September 1656 but was not on this occasion elected Speaker. With the dissolution of this Parliament on 4 February 1658 and the death of Cromwell seven months later, the regime immediately began to crumble. One Parliament, consisting of two Houses, was called during the brief tenure of office of Cromwell's successor as Protector, his son Richard; it lasted but three months and produced as many Speakers. The record of the election of the first, Chaloner Chute, is of particular interest as it reveals for the first time the part played in the proceedings by the Clerk and the Mace. The Clerk directed the proceedings until the Speaker was installed in the Chair, at which point the Mace was brought in to signify that the Speaker was now invested with his full authority.[10]

Richard Cromwell's short-lived Parliament having been dissolved under pressure from the army leaders, the latter decided to recall the rump of the Long Parliament which had never been legally dissolved. Lenthall was approached on 6 May 1659 and persuaded to return to the Speaker's Chair, and on the following day he proceeded once more to Westminster, the Mace before him, and with 42 other members once more took his seat. But the rump did not prove as compliant as the army leaders expected, one of its first acts being to bring the army under parliamentary control. The army reacted in characteristic fashion and on 13 October troops were stationed around Westminster to prevent members from entering the House. Dissatisfaction with the army leaders was nevertheless mounting. The nation was in a virtual state of chaos—taxes remained uncollected and the wheels of the administration were grinding to a halt. A new initiative came at this time from General Monk, who wrote to Speaker Lenthall from Edinburgh affirming his adherence to parliamentary government. The army leaders who comprised the Committee of Safety attempted to negotiate with Monk, but on 24 December they were faced with a new revolution. The soldiery of London assembled in Lincoln's Inn Fields and determined to restore the Parliament. They marched to the Speaker's house, acclaimed him as their general and the father of their country, and on his orders they took possession of the Tower. Two days later Lenthall was back in the Speaker's Chair, and on the 29th he received from the House a resolution of thanks to him 'for his very good service done for the Commonwealth'.

It is likely that Lenthall and Monk had resolved at this stage to work together towards a restoration of the monarchy. The rump, however, continued to exclude those members who had been turned away by the army many years before because they were opposed to bringing the King to trial. It refused to fix a time for its own dissolution and issue writs for new elections, but instead passed an act providing for the filling of the vacant seats under conditions which would have enabled it to cling to power. But the Speaker flatly refused to sign the necessary warrants. On 13 February 1660 at Monk's invitation a large number of those members who had been excluded since 1648 returned to the House and took their seats. They immediately found themselves in the majority and began to pave the way for the restoration of the monarchy. On 16 March 1660 the Long Parliament at long last dissolved itself, having spanned 20 of the most momentous years of English history.

Lenthall thus played his part in restoring Charles II to his inheritance. Although not a great man in himself he rose to the challenge of the great events in which he found himself involved. His conception of the speakership was an advanced one for an age of powerful monarchy and his resistance to royal tyranny raised the office to a higher dignity than it had ever reached before. Not only did he define the Speaker's first duty, and thus set the example for the future evolution of the office, but he preserved its continuity through a period of turmoil and revolution during which every institution of government, including the monarchy itself, underwent an interruption.

From the Restoration to the end of the 18th Century

The first Parliament of Charles II began its life as a Convention, its first business being the restoration of the monarchy. The Lords assembled as of right and declared that the government should consist of King, Lords and Commons in accordance with the ancient constitution. Since only the King could constitutionally summon a Parliament, the Convention was not strictly speaking a Parliament until the restored monarch recognized it as a legally constituted authority. It was not deterred from observing the customary preliminaries, however. The Speaker, Sir Harbottle Grimston, was called to the Chair in the traditional manner, having pleaded the usual excuses. Although it restored the monarchy, the Convention Parliament placed very definite limits on the royal prerogative, disbanded the army, and reaffirmed parliamentary control of the purse, the privileges of Parliament, Magna Carta, the Petition of Right and other statutes guaranteeing popular rights and liberties. When it turned its attention to religious questions Charles decided to dissolve it.

The second Parliament of the reign lasted seventeen years, running from 8 May 1661 to 30 December 1678. At its outset it was strongly royalist but by the end of its long life it had reasserted the popular cause and witnessed the beginnings of the party system. The choice of Speaker reflected the royalist trend. Once again the office came within the gift of the Court, and we find the familiar process of nomination by a royal officer, the sham expressions of humility by the candidate and his ornate flattery of the monarch being repeated. This Parliament's first Speaker was Sir Edward Turnour who held the office for ten years. His successor, Sir Job Charlton, held it only for ten days before succumbing to ill health. He in turn was succeeded by Sir Edward Seymour who broke the long tradition which had virtually secured to the legal profession a prescriptive right to the office. Seymour was very much a 'King's man' whose influence at Court had already secured for him the office of Treasurer of the Navy which he retained on his appointment to the Chair. Shortly after becoming Speaker he was appointed a privy councillor and this gave rise to a debate in which a number of Members voiced objections to the conflict of interest thus created.[11] Among those objecting were two who subsequently became Speakers themselves, Sir Thomas Littleton and Henry Powle. This debate affords interesting evidence of the growth of a new parliamentary outlook. It was becoming recognised that no man can be expected to serve two masters and that the Commons' representative had to be independent of the Court if he was to fulfil his functions effectively.

Seymour gave great dissatisfaction to the Commons through his insistence that the House was bound to adjourn in obedience to a royal command. On several occasions in 1677 he forcibly adjourned the House, refusing to hear Members who rose to speak. When a parliamentary session was eventually opened on 28 January 1678 the Commons, incensed by the repeated adjournments of the House in the face of their objections, declined to consider the King's speech until they had debated the irregular behaviour of the Speaker. Seymour, who was not lacking in strength of character, strongly defended his actions, citing precedents of his own in refutation of those of his critics. The outcome of the debate was inconclusive but the independent Members of the Commons had registered a challenge to the royal authority the impact of which was to prove significant.[12]

The third Parliament of the reign met on 6 March 1679, the opposition, or Country Party, having been returned in great strength. The election of the Speaker is of particular interest because it was the only occasion in the history of the office on which the King declined to confirm the Commons' choice. Edward Seymour was again proposed for the Chair, not by a minister but by a private Member. It is perhaps remarkable that such a strongly independent House of Commons should have been prepared to countenance a candidate who had proved himself such a staunch adherent of the Court. Seymour had, however, shown himself to be a strong and able Speaker, very mindful of the dignity of the House and the prestige of his office, and it so happened that he had fallen from the favour of the Court on account of some amorous intrigue. He probably knew that the King had decided not to confirm his election because his speech on presenting himself for the royal approval was audaciously short and the traditional plea of unfitness for the office was pointedly omitted. The Lord Chancellor, speaking on behalf of the King, informed Seymour and his colleagues of His Majesty's pleasure and commanded the Commons to make another choice. The unprecedented situation was debated by the House for five days. They rejected an alternative candidate proposed by the Court and made a representation to the King, insisting that it was the undoubted right of the Commons to choose their Speaker and again submitting Edward Seymour as their choice. The representation was curtly dismissed and the indignation aroused thereby led the King to prorogue Parliament.

How the impasse was finally resolved is rather obscure, but when Parliament met again on 15 March the Commons again received their formal instruction to choose a Speaker as though nothing untoward had happened. The candidate proposed was William Gregory and he was nominated and seconded by independent Members, suggesting that the Court as a part of the compromise had conceded the principle that the choice of Speaker belonged to the Commons. Gregory was elected without opposition, although one dissenting voice was raised on behalf of Seymour, and His Majesty graciously confirmed the Commons' choice, albeit their second choice. His tenure of office lasted but four months, the King having decided to bring an early end to a Parliament whose works he found displeasing.

If he hoped that fresh elections would produce a more complaisant Parliament he was destined for disappointment. The Country Party, or Whigs as they were coming to be called, were again returned in strength and the Speaker, Sir William Williams, was one of their own number. He was the first Welshman to occupy the Chair and as an outspoken critic of the Court it is safe to assume that he was not its nominee (the Journal does not record the names of his proposer and seconder). His election was indicative of the trend, now beginning to manifest itself, towards an isolation of the office of Speaker from the influences of the Court. A radical to the core, Williams celebrated his election to the Chair with a bold departure from tradition. He disdained to mouth meaningless expressions of humility and self-abasement and declared that if the Commons had elected him to this trust he must be supposed worthy and fit for it. It was during Williams' speakership that the House first resolved, on 30 October 1680, that its votes should be printed.[13] He was re-elected Speaker in the last Parliament of the reign which met at Oxford and which, like its predecessor, was extremely short-lived.

Another Welshman was elected Speaker in the one and only Parliament of James II which met on 19 May 1685. He was Sir John Trevor and his portrait reveals him as having had a pronounced squint which must have complicated even further the traditional pursuit of catching the Speaker's eye. His election was notable for an important constitutional departure as it took place before the cause of summoning Parliament had been declared, thus establishing a practice which has since persisted. The accession of the new King swiftly precipitated a constitutional crisis because of his violations of the law and the constitution which were aimed at the restoration of the Roman Catholic faith in England. His only Parliament, which met for the last time on 20 November 1685 although it was not dissolved until 4 July 1687, was succeeded by a Convention following his abdication and the landing of William of Orange at Torbay on 5 November 1688. The Convention, which chose a leading Whig, Henry Powle, as its Speaker, prepared the celebrated Declaration of Right on the basis of which the Crown of England was offered jointly to William and Mary. Powle stood at the head of the Commons at the ceremony at which the offer was made and on 16 December 1689 it became his privilege to present the Bill of Rights, which gave legislative effect to the Declaration, for the royal assent.

One of the Acts to pass through Parliament during the first year of the reign of William and Mary was that which established the Speaker's precedence as the first commoner in the land. He ranked immediately after the peers in the order of precedence, a status which remained unaltered until 1919. Thus 1689 is a notable year in the annals of the speakership as being that in which Parliament first defined and recognized the national, as distinct from the parliamentary, eminence of the office. It was, like Parliament itself, entering upon a new phase.

In the second Parliament of the reign which met on 20 March 1690, Sir John Trevor again found himself Speaker. It is surprising, perhaps, that James II's one and only Speaker should have been favoured at the outset of this new era of parliamentary government. His reappointment may have been actuated by a desire to preserve every possible thread of continuity in order to minimize the effects of revolutionary change, for the Cromwellian era was still very much a living memory. His second tenure of office lasted for five years but it came to an ignominious end. He accepted a bribe from the Corporation of the City of London for assisting the passage of a bill it was anxious to promote and the House of Commons appointed a committee to investigate the charge. The committee adjudged the Speaker to be guilty and after a debate in the House, during which Trevor was himself in the Chair, the committee's report was endorsed and it was subsequently resolved that he be expelled from the House.

The election of Trevor's successor on 14 March 1694 is of particular interest as it was a contested election and the Journal of the House of Commons gives a particularly descriptive account of it.[14] Sir Thomas Littleton was proposed as the Whig nominee of the Court but Paul Foley, the choice of the Tory majority, was elected in his stead by a majority of 179 to 146. Foley's election was an important step forward in the separation of the speakership from the influence of the Court. But if the Speaker ceased to be a nominee of the Crown it was only to become the nominee of a party. At this stage in the evolution of the office the Speaker was expected to be partisan and to use his position to advance the interests of the party to which he owed his appointment. The speakership was now to become the legitimate prize of the party controlling a majority in the House of Commons.

Littleton was compensated for his defeat by his election to the Chair in William III's fourth Parliament. He again faced a contest although the Journal does not name an opponent. The first non-lawyer to occupy the Chair since Edward Seymour, he was a staunch Whig who made no secret of the fact that his actions in the House were guided by party considerations. He was succeeded by the eminent Tory statesman, Robert Harley, who served three terms of office as Speaker before finding fame through ministerial office. He was in fact appointed a privy councillor and a secretary of state one year before he finally relinquished the speakership. He faced a contest for the speakership on at least two occasions, the second time winning by the narrow majority of 216 to 212, the closest contest for the speakership on record. His second tenure of office extended into the reign of Queen Anne in consequence of an act providing for the continuation of Parliament for a period of six months following the demise of the Crown. Previously a Parliament had automatically ceased to exist with the death of the sovereign.

The elections of 1705 returned a Whig majority to the House of Commons, and the election of the Speaker became the occasion of a bitter party contest. The Whigs carried their candidate, a gentleman bearing the unpretentious name of John Smith, by 248 votes to 205. To him fell the distinction of presiding over the first Parliament of Great Britain following the union of England with Scotland. It was in fact the existing English Parliament with the Scottish members added to it, but the ceremony of re-electing the Speaker was nevertheless observed and on this occasion Smith was called to the Chair unanimously. He was subsequently appointed Chancellor of the Exchequer while still Speaker. The third Parliament of the reign met on 16 November 1708 and another Whig, Sir Richard Onslow, was elected unanimously. Unlike his distinguished nephew Arthur, who was to be called to the Chair twenty years later, he was not a successful Speaker. He was intensely partisan and mainly notable for a choleric disposition and for his vindication of the right of the Commons to carry their Mace to the Bar of the House of Lords when seeking a judgment following an impeachment.[15] The next two Speakers were Tories: William Bromley, who had been John Smith's opponent in 1705, and Thomas Hanmer, a Shakespearian scholar and the last Speaker of the reign of Queen Anne. Hanmer, who together with Harley favoured the Hanoverian succession, was able to frustrate a procedural manoeuvre by those ministers who favoured a Stuart restoration, and thus established himself as the leader of the Hanoverian Tories.

The accession of George I introduced a long period of Whig ascendancy and the Speaker throughout his reign was Sir Spencer Compton who was later to attain high ministerial office, although his subsequent career as a statesman was hardly impressive. Compton was the first Speaker to be re-elected in an ensuing Parliament in the interests of the continuity of the office. The speakership was now acquiring a dignity commensurate with an office whose occupant ranked as the first commoner. It was no longer a stepping-stone to higher legal preferment, and Compton, in common with other early eighteenth-century Speakers, was not himself a lawyer. He was a man of limited abilities, and his inadequate grasp of the procedure and practice of the House led him astray in some of his rulings. On one occasion he informed a member who was being shouted down that the House was under no obligation to give him a hearing. It appears, nevertheless, that he was well regarded as a Speaker, and his occupancy of the Chair marked an important step forward in the establishment of the continuity of the office and the promotion of its dignity.

With the election of Arthur Onslow as Speaker on 23 January 1728 the speakership was to attain its highest eminence. His tenure of office was of immeasurable importance, not only to the evolution of the speakership itself, but also to the broader course of parliamentary history. Onslow was a man of rare integrity in an age of corruption – in fact his rectitude must have made him appear something of an oddity in the eyes of his contemporaries. In his day elections were decided by bribery and intimidation, votes were bought and sold, friendships and loyalties were betrayed according to the demands of expediency and personal interest. The system was designed to perpetuate the concentration of power in the hands of an oligarchy, and it was tolerated and even condoned at the highest levels of society.

Arthur Onslow came to the Chair at a crucial period. He realized that the honour and stability of Parliament as an institution were threatened by the political system. He saw that if its dignity were to be maintained and its foundations protected it was necessary to place the Chair beyond reach of contamination by the sordid intrigues and disreputable rivalries which were the essence of contemporary politics. His greatness rests upon the fact that he succeeded in his object. He was the first Speaker to appreciate the supreme importance of preserving the independence and impartiality of the Chair, and it was he who set the high standards which have since come to be associated with it. He brought a permanent lustre to the office which had only once before been matched, and matched but fleetingly, by Lenthall in his own historic moment of greatness. Eminent men had occupied the Chair before but none had approached the example set by Onslow. For thirty-three years he maintained a strict and impartial control over the proceedings of the House of Commons at a time when a stabilizing influence was vital to the preservation of its historic continuity. It was a task for which Onslow was eminently suited. If ever the right man was in the right place at the right time it was Arthur Onslow. The speakership might have been tailormade for him. And it is on his greatness as a Speaker that his renown exclusively rests.

Onslow set the pattern for the impartiality of the Chair but although he removed it from partisan influence it would be misleading to assert that he completely stood aside from politics. He saw his role as one of leadership in protecting the institution of Parliament from being undermined by political corruption and intriguing factions. The party system as we know it today had yet to develop and he would not have been able to fulfil the duties he set for himself through total political detachment. A Whig himself, he regularly spoke in committee on controversial issues and was known to attend ministerial meetings. But the motivation behind his political activity was his dedication to the protection of the constitution, as declared and established by the revolution of 1688. His aim was to preserve a balance. He was equally suspicious of overbearing ministers and disruptive opposition. He was a great upholder of the rights of minorities, representing as they did the independent element in the House, those beyond the influence of faction. To achieve what Onslow was able to achieve the Speaker had to exercise not only a moderating influence but frequently a dominant one.

Onslow realised that the forms and practices of the House could be a most effective curb against the assaults of power and the intrigues of factions. He therefore insisted on their strict observance. He would lay great stress on the most trivial procedural details and he reinforced the edifice of parliamentary precedent with innumerable rulings. His manuscripts reveal voluminous commentaries, notes and annotations relating to every conceivable application of rule and practice. They amount to a massive codification of contemporary procedure and demonstrate that no detail was too insignificant to merit his attention. This obsession with procedure was entirely consistent with Onslow's view of the Speaker's role as the guardian of the parliamentary institution. John Hatsell, who came to the Table of the House during Onslow's tenure of office, confirmed the great Speaker's belief that nothing tended more to inflate the powers of ministers than neglect of the rules of procedure; 'that the forms of proceedings, as instituted by our ancestors, operated as a check and a controul on the actions of ministers; and that they were, in many instances, a shelter and protection to the minority, against the attempts of power.'[16] The severe view which he took of breaches of order and precedent probably explains his reactionary stand in the matter of the reporting of parliamentary debates. The practice, although widespread, had long been regarded as a breach of privilege, a view in which Onslow concurred, and on 13 April 1738 he brought the matter to the attention of the House. A debate ensued which led to a resolution condemning the practice.[17]

Also consistent with Onslow's view of the Speaker's functions was his concern for his personal prestige, for he regarded the dignity of the Speaker as inseparable from that of the House. Hatsell records that he 'never permitted a member to come in, or go out of the House, whilst he was in the Chair, without calling to him, if he observed, that the member did not make his obeysance to the Chair.'[18] He was equally assertive of his dignity in his relations with the House of Lords and was an inflexible champion against attempted encroachments on the part of the upper House. He did not hesitate to sacrifice financial advantage in order to safeguard his independence. On 20 April 1734 he was appointed to the lucrative office of Treasurer of the Navy, but he resigned it eight years later, the day after giving his casting vote on a highly political issue, in order to discount scurrilous assertions that he held it only for personal interest. Thenceforward he contented himself with the emoluments accruing to the speakership itself.* He took a great interest in the clerical organization of the House and introduced a number of improvements, notably with regard to the keeping of records. It was due to his influence that the House, in 1742, first ordered its journals to be printed.[19]

Onslow was five times elected to the Chair, each time without opposition, and his tenure of office spanned the entire reign of George II. It would be difficult to exaggerate the importance of the impact he made on the modern evolution of Parliament. He transformed the speakership and set the pattern for its later development. He exalted the rules and usages of Parliament as a hallowed part of the constitution and thereby protected the House of Commons from being dominated by factions. He introduced administrative reforms which laid the foundations for the modern administrative organisation of the House of Commons. He gave to Parliament a new kind of leadership, a leadership unsullied by the temptations of power but dedicated

---

* The emoluments and perquisites at that time included five pounds a day while the House was in session, the fees from private bills, a 1,000 pounds 'equipment money' at the beginning of each new Parliament, an official residence, a service of plate, a claret allowance, a stationery allowance and possession of the Speaker's Chair at the end of each Parliament over which he presided.

The Office of Speaker

unswervingly to the integrity of the institution itself. He retired on 18 March 1761, honoured by his fellow parliamentarians, and in a simple and moving speech he expressed all that his life's work had meant to him.[20]

Onslow set a standard for future Speakers which was not easy to emulate and his immediate successors cannot perhaps be blamed entirely for their failure to do so. Sir John Cust, who was elected to the Chair unopposed on 3 November 1761 at the outset of George III's first Parliament, certainly did his best to discharge his duties conscientiously. But he was blessed neither with Onslow's strength of character nor with good health, and it is generally believed that the strains and stresses of the office led to his untimely death. As a Speaker he was impartial, but he gave no leadership as Onslow had done. He was unable to control disorder or enforce his rulings and the interminable debates, particularly during the stormy and protracted sittings which arose from the exploits of the notorious John Wilkes, overwhelmed him physically and morally. It must be remembered that in Cust's day there was no provision for a Deputy Speaker and the long hours in the Chair must have been a gruelling ordeal for a man in poor health.

Cust's successor, Sir Fletcher Norton, was a man of a very different stamp. A Tory, he was elected on 22 January 1770 in the first contested election for the speakership which had taken place in many a long year. His principal attributes were an uncompromising toughness and a fiercely independent spirit. Otherwise he seems to have had none of the qualities required of a good Speaker. He was coarse and unrefined, possessed of a violent temper and offensive in his use of language. Tact and discretion were alien to him, but he was bold and shrewd, and during his tenure of office he demonstrated that he was nobody's lackey. He had been in office less than a month when he found himself at the centre of a heated and undignified wrangle over some words he had used. Since nothing could induce the Speaker to apologize or acknowledge any error, the matter was debated for some six hours before a way was found of disposing of it.[21]

Norton did not care to whom he gave offence. On 20 March 1772 he fell foul of the Court as the result of a speech he made in committee on the Royal Marriage Bill. He was later to offend the King even more gravely, winning the approbation of the Whigs in the process and losing the favour of his own party. He was unanimously re-elected Speaker on 29 November 1774 – an indication of his rising popularity with the Whigs – and during his second tenure of office he became identified to an ever-increasing extent with the opposition to the government. The crisis was reached on 7 May 1777 when, on the occasion of presenting a money bill for the royal assent, he addressed the King with an extraordinary outspokenness, declaring that the grants of the Commons were 'great beyond example; great beyond your Majesty's highest expense'.[22] The King took great exception to the speech and in the House of Commons the Speaker was violently attacked by the Tories for his conduct. But the Whigs rallied to his support and a motion in vindication of the speech was carried without a division. On 6 April 1780 Norton supported John Dunning's famous resolution that 'the influence of the Crown has increased, is increasing, and ought to be diminished', and on 1 May be denounced a government bill for the appointment of commissioners to examine the public accounts on the ground that the commissioners would simply be placemen nominated by the ministry. Small wonder that the government seized the first opportunity of getting rid of this bold, blunt, abrasive Speaker. It occurred with the opening of a new Parliament on 31 October when Charles Wolfran Cornwall was proposed as Speaker on behalf of the ministry. Their excuse for supplanting Norton was the state of his health. But the Whigs were not prepared to allow their champion to be so easily dismissed. They proposed him for re-election and in the ensuing division Cornwall was elected by 203 votes to 134.

Cornwall, whose tenure of office was not particularly notable, died in office, and his two immediate successors were men of considerably greater calibre. William Wyndham Grenville, elected to the Chair on 5 January 1789, was Speaker for only five months and his claim to fame rests on his subsequent career. He became Home Secretary on relinquishing the speakership and was eventually to head the ministry which finally abolished the slave trade. He was probably the youngest Speaker ever to occupy the Chair being only 29 at the time of his election as Speaker. Grenville was succeeded by Henry Addington, another Prime Minister-to-be, who was only 32 at the time. His was a contested election which introduced the custom whereby each candidate votes in favour of the other. Addington was Speaker for nearly twelve years and was unanimously re-elected to the Chair on three occasions, a testimony to his popularity and the satisfactory manner in which he discharged his duties.* It was during his tenure of office that a fixed salary was first voted for the Speaker, a total sum of 6000 pounds being agreed upon. On 12 February 1799 Addington spoke at great length in committee in favour of the union between Great Britain and Ireland and on 22 January 1801 he was formally re-elected to the Chair, becoming the first Speaker of the Parliament of the United Kingdom. Shortly afterwards he became Prime Minister, an office for which he lacked the necessary qualities, and in which his failure was in marked contrast to his comparative success as Speaker. Addington was succeeded on 10 February 1801 by Sir John Mitford who was Speaker for only a year and made little impact. He was the last Speaker to succeed to the bench on vacating the Chair.

The 19th Century

Throughout the 19th century the Chair of the House of Commons was occupied in the main by eminent men most of whom made a personal impact on the evolution of the office of Speaker. It was during this century that it emerged as the politically independent office we know today and that the high traditions set by Arthur Onslow were re-established on a permanent basis. But before this was achieved the speakership was to pass through a testing time.

* Apart from one unfortunate lapse when he failed to insist that his friend Pitt withdraw some unparliamentary language the latter had used in criticism of his opponent, Tierney.

The first two Speakers of this period, Charles Abbot and Charles Manners-Sutton, were far from being bad Speakers, but their experiences brought home forcibly the difficulties which were likely to occur if a Speaker remained politically active in a Parliament geared to the party system. Although impartial when in the Chair, both Abbot and Manners-Sutton were staunch party adherents, publicly committed on the controversial issues of the day. In an age of bitter party warfare theirs was a position not easy to sustain. In trying to effect a compromise between loyalty to the House and loyalty to a party, both were led into unfortunate situations, Abbot becoming the subject of a motion of censure and Manners-Sutton finding himself ousted from office after serving nearly eighteen years in the Chair.

Charles Abbot was elected Speaker on 10 February 1802 without a division, although a debate took place in which objections were voiced because he had previously held ministerial office. Similar objections had been raised at the time of the election of Sir John Mitford and Sheridan, the principal objector, also condemned the practice of looking to the legal profession whenever the Chair fell vacant. By this stage in the evolution of the speakership the candidate normally resigned any ministerial office he might have held prior to his nomination; but Sheridan and those supporting him were anxious to establish the principle that the Chair should be occupied by members who had not previously held office, thus promoting the independence of the Speaker from the ministry. It is interesting to note that even in the present century, the independence of the speakership having been fully established, the issue of a Speaker having previously held ministerial office has regularly given rise to discussion.

Abbot was re-elected Speaker on four successive occasions before resigning because of ill-health on 30 May 1817. The two highlights of his tenure of office were the motion of censure against him and his use of the casting vote in the matter of the impeachment of Lord Melville. The former arose as the result of a speech he made at the prorogation of the parliamentary session on 22 July 1813 in which he strongly attacked the movement to emancipate Roman Catholics. No protest had been made when he opposed in committee a bill to admit Roman Catholics to Parliament because he was expressing his views as a private member and this was in accordance with the conventions of the day. But as Speaker he was expected to speak on behalf of the House as a whole. In making a partisan speech in his capacity as Speaker, particularly on the most controversial issue of the time, he was in violation of convention. The motion against him was moved on 22 April 1814 and was framed with comparative mildness. An amendment couched in far more censorious terms was also moved but not pressed to a division. The original motion was defeated by 274 votes to 106, after which a resolution in vindication of the Speaker was accepted without a division.[23] The Speaker's critics had aired their grievance and had no wish to press it further. The debate went far towards detaching the speakership from direct involvement in controversial issues. Abbot, speaking during the debate in his own defence, was unable to produce a precedent in justification of the kind of partisan intervention he had made, and no Speaker was ever again to deliver a controversial speech at the

Bar of the House of Lords. In fact the Speaker's customary address at the end of a session was discontinued after 1854 when Parliament ceased to be prorogued by the sovereign in person.

The most dramatic occasion on which a Speaker has been called upon to use his casting vote occurred during Abbot's tenure of office. The Speaker had always been entitled to cast a deliberative vote, like any other member, in Committee of the Whole House, but when in the Chair he was (and is today) equipped only with a casting vote in the event of the numbers in a division being equal. The precedent was established in 1601.[24] In exercising his casting vote the Speaker has always been guided by special considerations. He does not use it to further his personal inclinations but where possible he votes in such a way as to keep the matter concerned open for further consideration. The principles governing this practice were enunciated by Speaker Addington on 12 May 1796.[25] It fell to Abbot to give his casting vote on the question leading to the impeachment of Lord Melville and he gave it for the 'Ayes'. Had he voted with the 'Noes' the report of the commission on which the charges against Melville were based would have been referred to a select committee of the House. His decision would therefore appear to have been in conflict with the principles enunciated by Addington as the effect of his vote was to deny Melville the benefit of a further enquiry. There is no reason to believe, however, that Abbot acted other than in accordance with his conscience as by all accounts his decision was taken only after agonising reflection.

Like Arthur Onslow before him, Abbot took a great interest in the administrative organization of the House of Commons. He was instrumental in the appointment of a select committee whose report led to the institution of the Private Bill Office, where information relating to the progress of private bills was made available for public inspection. This was a much-needed reform, implemented at a time when the output of private legislation was very great. It was on his initiative that the form of the votes and proceedings of the House of Commons was radically revised, their bulk being reduced and the entries shortened, and their delivery being expedited so that members received them at an early hour each day. Conscientious in his attention to the rules and practices of the House, he also made a major contribution to the 1818 edition of Hatsell's Precedents, a primary source in any study of English parliamentary law and custom. On his retirement as Speaker, Abbot was raised to the peerage with the rank of baron, the first Speaker to receive a peerage in recognition of his services in the office. He was voted a pension of 4000 pounds a year with a reversion of 3000 pounds to his male heir.

Charles Manners-Sutton was elected to the Chair on 2 June 1817 in a contested election by 312 votes to 152. He was six times re-elected and thus holds the record for the number of times any one man has been elected to the speakership. A strong Tory throughout his life, he was by all accounts an excellent Speaker who never allowed his political convictions to influence the impartiality of his conduct in the Chair. Like Abbot he allowed himself the latitude of expressing his views when speaking as a private member. He spoke three times in Committee of the Whole House subsequent to his appointment as Speaker, twice in opposition to bills for the relief of Roman Catholics and once against the admission of Protestant dissenters to the universities. It is noteworthy, however, that on two of the three occasions he prefaced his remarks with an apology for participating in the debate, an indication that the custom whereby the Speaker refrains completely from discussing partisan issues had already begun to mainfest itself.

Manners-Sutton was Speaker during a momentous period in the nation's political history and he witnessed from the Chair two reforms to which he had always been implacably opposed: the emancipation of Roman Catholics and the reform of the electoral system. He saw the first reform bill pass its second reading by 302 votes to 301 and must have wondered, as the tellers counted the members voting on either side, whether he would be called upon to use his casting vote on the most burning issue of the day. He witnessed the successful passage through the House of Commons of two further reform bills and on 7 June 1832 was present at the Bar of the House of Lords when the royal assent was signified to the bill which finally ushered in a new parliamentary era. Shortly afterwards he informed the House of his intention to retire, and the customary resolutions were passed and the same pension voted as was awarded to his predecessor. He nevertheless remained a member of the reformed House of Commons and the Whigs, finding themselves in the majority after the general election, and being apprehensive of the possible consequences of electing an inexperienced Speaker at the outset of a new and transformed Parliament, offered him their support if he would consent to serve another term of office. Manners-Sutton agreed and on 29 January 1833 he was elected Speaker for the seventh time. The Radicals objected to his re-election, however, on the ground that he had already retired and been voted a pension, and they put forward a candidate of their own. It was the first time Manners-Sutton had faced an opponent since he was first elected Speaker and he was re-elected by 241 votes to 31. It was during his final term of office that the Houses of Parliament were destroyed by fire. On hearing the news he hurried to Westminster and subsequently had a series of interviews with the King in order to discuss the matter of providing Parliament with a temporary meeting-place – interviews which were later made the basis of a groundless charge against him at the time of his removal from office. In the month following the fire Lord Melbourne's government was arbitrarily dismissed and Sir Robert Peel was called upon to form a new administration. It was at this point that the Whigs became suspicious of Manners-Sutton, whom they knew to be an influential Tory. That he had been in association with Wellington and Peel at this time was true and was candidly acknowledged by him. It was also known that the Tory leaders had met in his house in 1831 to plan their strategy against Earl Grey's government and its policy of parliamentary reform. But it was also asserted that he had actively conspired against the Melbourne government and had counselled the King to dissolve Parliament in order to further the interests of the Tory party. The Whigs therefore decided that they would oppose the re-election of Manners-Sutton as Speaker in the next Parliament.

But there was rather more at stake than the mere redressing of a grievance against the Speaker. The Whigs had been dismissed from office in spite of the fact that they commanded the confidence of the House of Commons, and they were determined to assert their long-cherished principle that no Government should be entitled to hold office without parliamentary consent. They were again returned with a majority at the ensuing general election and were determined to assert their predominance. The election of the Speaker provided them with a golden opportunity for doing so at the very outset of the new Parliament which met on 19 February 1835. Not all the Whigs were convinced of the wisdom of this course, but so strong was the feeling against Manners-Sutton in the rank and file of the party that Melbourne felt committed to opposing his re-election. The Whigs nominated James Abercromby, a reluctant candidate who yielded to Melbourne's urgent insistence to accept the nomination in the interests of Whig unity.

Sir Robert Peel, for his part, was determined to face the hostile House of Commons as Prime Minister and support the re-election of Manners-Sutton. Both sides mustered every available supporter and it was known that the election would be closely fought as not all the Whigs were prepared to abandon Manners-Sutton. The attack on Manners-Sutton was led by Lord John Russell and in doing so he made his debut as the Whig leader in the House of Commons. He accepted the late Speaker's assurance that he had not conspired against the Melbourne administration; but, he declared, the fact of having attended Privy Council meetings at all was inconsistent with the impartiality of the Speaker's office. Sir Robert Peel, in a spirited defence of Manners-Sutton's right to be re-elected, informed the House that the Speaker had declined to accept office under the Crown because, having served in the Chair for eighteen years, he felt that to take such a course would be to risk lowering its authority. He concluded by foreshadowing the principle he was later to enunciate on behalf of a Liberal Speaker: '. . . the office of Speaker was one which ought not to be made the subject of party feeling. The precincts of the Chair ought not to be converted into ground on which political battles might be fought.'[26] The division, which took place in an atmosphere of great tension and excitement, resulted in the rejection of Manners-Sutton by 316 votes to 306. He remained in the House of Commons but a short time following his ungenerous ejection from the Chair and was raised to the peerage with the rank of viscount.*

James Abercromby was the first Whig to occupy the Chair since Arthur Onslow and also the first Scotsman to become Speaker. A former cabinet minister, he was the last Speaker to maintain a close political connection with his party. Nevertheless, no acts of partiality were ever laid to his charge, and if he was ill at ease during his occupation of the Chair this was hardly surprising in view of the unfortunate circumstances which brought him to it. Some commentators suggest he was not an efficient Speaker[27] but Sir Denis Le Marchant, who became Clerk of the House in 1850 and whose testimony cannot lightly be disregarded, expressed the view that 'in ability, consti-

* Manners-Sutton was the last Speaker to take possession of his Chair at the end of each Parliament over which he presided and he must have accumulated seven all told. Thereafter this perquisite was abolished.

tutional knowledge, and even the practice of Parliament he was, undoubtedly, very superior to Mr. Manners-Sutton'.[28] Abercromby's most notable achievement during his speakership was his reform of the procedure relating to private bills and the consequent elimination of various undesirable practices connected with their promotion. He was unanimously re-elected for a second term of office in the first Parliament of Queen Victoria and retired somewhat abruptly on 6 May 1839 as the result, it is believed, of a dispute between himself and Lord John Russell. He was raised to the peerage with the rank of baron and voted the usual pension.

With the election of Charles Shaw-Lefevre to the Chair on 27 May 1839 the era of the modern speakership may be said to have been inaugurated. A Liberal like his predecessor, he was elected over his Conservative opponent, Henry Goulburn, by 317 votes to 299. He was re-elected on three subsequent occasions without opposition and it was during his tenure of the Chair that the principle of the continuity of the office was established on a basis which has since endured. The crucial test took place on the occasion of his election for the second time on 19 August 1841. At the general election of that year the Tories were returned in the majority and there were those among them who favoured deposing the Speaker from office in retaliation for the treatment meted out to Manners-Sutton by their opponents. Fortunately the wise counsel of Sir Robert Peel prevailed against taking such a course. Reiterating the arguments he had used in defence of Manners-Sutton, he pointed out that Shaw-Lefevre had been a good Speaker and that it would be improper to eject him purely for motives of revenge.[29] This magnanimous gesture went far towards setting the pattern for the modern speakership and since that time no Speaker has ever been rejected following a change of government.

To Shaw-Lefevre must go the personal credit for restoring the speakership to the same high standard of impartiality set by Onslow. By the time he came to the Chair the party system had assumed a form closer to that with which we are familiar today. The Reform Act of 1832 had transformed the entire political system, members becoming dependent for their election upon a direct appeal to the people. Once Parliament became responsive to a popular electorate, governments became obliged to seek the confidence of the House of Commons expressed through the support of a majority. The trend towards majority party government was greatly accelerated by the passing of the Act and had become an established constitutional principle by the time Shaw-Lefevre retired. The Speaker was thus able to hold aloof from adversary politics and assume the role of the independent arbiter in the manner of a judge. Where Onslow saw a need to give leadership in curbing the unscrupulous activities of politicians, Shaw-Lefevre was able to leave them to the judgment of the electorate and detach himself totally from political activity. Like Onslow he insisted on the proper observance of parliamentary forms but the exercise of his discipline was restricted to the realm of parliamentary practice. He was the first embodiment of the politically independent Speaker. He recognized in the speakership the very foundation of the parliamentary system and saw it as the highest seat of dignity to which any man could attain.

Important procedural reforms took place during Shaw-Lefevre's tenure of office and he played a significant part in bringing them about. The procedure of the House had undergone no essential changes for some two centuries prior to the Reform Act and it proved to be incompatible in many respects with the altered circumstances of parliamentary government. Under the impetus of reform there was a marked increased in the volume of government legislation and a greater demand by the government on parliamentary time. Shaw-Lefevre perceived the need, which was to be forcefully demonstrated later in the century, for procedures designed to limit debate and twice, in 1848 and 1854, he gave evidence to select committees on procedure in which he proposed time-saving reforms which were considered radical at the time. Many of the antiquated rules and forms were abolished and innovations were made which led to the expedition of business. But both committees shied away from Shaw-Lefevre's more far-reaching proposals and some years were to elapse before the House was persuaded to accept any radical revision of its rules of procedure.

Shaw-Lefevre retired on 21 March 1857 and was made a viscount. He was the last Speaker to receive a service of plate as a personal gift on taking office. As the result of a motion by the dedicated economist, Joseph Hume, this perquisite ceased to become the personal property of the office-holder but instead became attached to the office itself.

The next Speaker, John Evelyn Denison, was four times elected to the Chair and applied himself to maintaining the standards set by Shaw-Lefevre. Although less firm and forceful than Shaw-Lefevre, his personal dignity and high sense of duty ensured that he never lost the respect of the House. He and his two immediate successors were the first non-lawyers to be elected to the Chair since Sir Spencer Compton. They succeeded in demonstrating that it was not necessary to be a lawyer to be a good Speaker. Students of Parliament are in Denison's debt in that he left a diary which sheds an interesting light on contemporary parliamentary practice and the way in which one incumbent viewed his responsibilities in the office of Speaker.[30] He seems to have been called upon to use his casting vote more frequently than any other modern Speaker and he did so with a punctilious observance of the conventions relating to it. In every instance he offered the House a rational explanation, where possible voting in such a way as to keep the issue open for discussion; or if this was not possible, taking care that a change in the *status quo* was not effected by the use of the Speaker's casting vote.[31] His diary reveals his views on matters such as submitting questions to the Speaker, unparliamentary expressions, adjourning out of respect for a deceased member, and House of Lords encroachments on the financial privilege of the Commons. It also records his appreciation of and his debt to Thomas Erskine May who was Clerk Assistant when he first came to the Chair. On one occasion Denison intervened while the House stood adjourned to prevent a duel taking place between two members. His approach was in contrast to that of his predecessor Addington who, in a similar situation, not only failed to prevent a duel between Pitt and Tierney but actually rode out to witness it.

Shaw-Lefevre and Denison were the last Speakers to exercise their right to speak in Committee of the Whole House. The former spoke on 21 April 1856 on a non-controversial subject — the management of the British Museum. On 9 June 1870 Denison not only spoke in committee but used his vote to help defeat a budget proposal which he regarded as unjust — a measure which would have required farmers to take out a licence for a horse employed in the carting of materials for the repair of parish roads.[32] This appears to be the only occasion on which he departed from the strict course which had been charted by his predecessor and he does not seem to have been criticised for it. The participation of the Speaker in debates and divisions in Committee of the Whole House has since become completely obsolete.

Denison retired on 8 February 1872 and in taking his leave he paid a special tribute to Erskine May who had become Clerk of the House in the previous year. He was made a viscount but declined to accept a pension. In his obituary published in *The Times* on 8 March 1873 it was observed 'that he so exactly appreciated the feeling and disposition of the assembly over which he was called on to preside, the sources to which he could look for aid, and the exact limits and sphere of his authority'. This seems like a fair appreciation of a Speaker who discharged his functions with prudence rather than forcefulness, and whose conception of the office made him a natural successor to Shaw-Lefevre. Onslow had originated this conception and Shaw-Lefevre had restored it. Denison's achievement lay in its consolidation.

Denison's successor, Henry Bouverie William Brand, was unanimously elected Speaker on 9 February 1872 and served three terms of office. At the time of his first election some doubts were expressed as to his suitability because he had been Chief Liberal Whip but these were soon dispelled as he showed himself determined to continue in the same tradition as Shaw-Lefevre and Denison. It was during his occupancy of the Chair that the House of Commons faced one of its greatest crises, a crisis which transformed its procedures and ended that unrestricted freedom of debate which had been its greatest pride. It was precipitated by the Irish Nationalists who, under the leadership of Charles Stewart Parnell, embarked upon a campaign of systematic obstruction designed to bring Parliament to a standstill. They were dedicated with a ruthless singleness of purpose to the ending of the union of Ireland with Great Britain and they regarded parliamentary obstruction as a legitimate weapon. For them the House of Commons was the citadel of the enemy and their aim was to reduce it to impotence. Their tactics were mightily successful until the Speaker decided it had become his duty to intervene.

Matters came to a head following the general election of 1880 at which Parnell was returned at the head of a team sixty strong. With the rejection of Gladstone's Land Bill by the House of Lords the situation in Ireland deteriorated, and in January 1881 the Government sought the leave of the House to bring in a drastic Bill for the protection of person and property in Ireland—the so-called Coercion Bill. Parnell determined to fight this legislation with the weapon of systematic obstruction which he had evolved and perfected. To begin with he and his colleagues dragged out the debate on the Address over eleven nights. On 25 January Gladstone moved the suspension of the Standing Orders to give the Bill priority over all other business. The motion was carried after a sitting lasting twenty-two hours. The debate on the motion for leave to introduce the Bill itself began on Thursday, 27 January. No division had been taken when the House adjourned for the week-end, and when it resumed on Monday, the 31st, Gladstone grimly announced that the Government was determined to secure a first reading for the Bill before the House adjourned again. Thus, at 4 p.m. on 31 January 1881 there began the longest sitting which the House of Commons had ever known—a sitting which the Irishmen managed to protract for forty-one and a half hours and which was finally terminated by Speaker Brand's celebrated *coup d'état*.

On 1 February the Speaker saw clearly that Gladstone's strategy would not succeed and that Parnell and his supporters could keep the debate going indefinitely. He therefore sent for Gladstone and Sir Stafford Northcote, the Leader of the Opposition, and told them he proposed to close the debate on his own authority. On being assured of their support he arranged that the Deputy Speaker should take the Chair at midnight and that he, Brand, should relieve his colleague at 9 a.m. the following morning. The chamber was rapidly filling when Brand took over from the Deputy Speaker and motioned the member who held the floor to take his seat. He then addressed the House and declared that the usual rules had proved powerless to ensure orderly and effective debate. 'The dignity, the credit, and the authority of this House are seriously threatened, and it is necessary that they should be vindicated. . . . I am satisfied that I shall best carry out the will of the House and may rely on its support if I decline to call upon any more members to speak, and at once proceed to put the question from the Chair. . . . But I may add that it will be necessary either for the House itself to assume more effectual control over its debates or to entrust greater authority to the Chair.'[33]

Thus it was, on the initiative of the Chair, that closure was first imposed in the House of Commons (although it could be argued that the enforced adjournments of the Stuart period amounted to a form of closure). Having made his statement to the House the Speaker put the question on the amendment which the Irish members had moved to the government motion, after which, amid uproar, the amendment having been rejected, the main motion was agreed to. The Irishmen succeeded in further disrupting the proceedings until, on 3 February, 28 of them were suspended *en bloc* for disregarding the authority of the Chair while Gladstone was speaking on a motion for the adoption of a new standing order designed to counter obstruction. The standing order embodied in Gladstone's resolution provided for an urgency procedure so drastic that, in the words of Redlich, 'It proclaimed a parliamentary state of siege and introduced a dictatorship into the House of Commons.'[34] It provided for the suspension of the whole of the regular order of business during a time of parliamentary urgency and empowered the Speaker to substitute such rules as he should think fit. The declaration of a state of urgency rested with the House itself, and required a three to one majority in a House of at least 300 members on the motion of a Minister which would be subject neither to debate, amendment nor adjournment.

No sooner had Gladstone's resolution been adopted than a state of parliamentary urgency was declared by the House, and when it met on the following day, 4 February, the new urgency rule was in force. The Speaker expressed his sense of the grave responsibility which had been placed upon him, and announced the terms of the first rule which he had framed by virtue of his newly conferred emergency powers: 'That no motion for the adjournment of the House shall be made except by leave of the House, before the orders of the day or notices of motion have been entered upon.' He announced that further rules would be laid before the House within the course of the next few days. On 9 February sixteen further rules were tabled, the principal effects of which were to empower the Speaker to refuse dilatory motions, to refuse a division if unnecessarily claimed, and to direct a Member to discontinue his speech on the grounds of irrelevance or tedious repetition; and, most important of all, to provide for the application of the closure on the initiative of the Speaker, a three to one majority being required to carry it into effect.

From this day forward the closure became a permanent feature of the rules of the House of Commons. At the beginning of the session of 1882 Gladstone proposed a series of resolutions designed to implement permanent reforms in procedure, and at the end of the year the unusual course was taken of calling a special session of Parliament together for the purpose of considering the matter. The Government's proposals proved highly controversial, and the new rules, as finally passed in December, failed to prove entirely satisfactory. The matter of procedural reform was, in fact, to remain a vexed question for the remainder of the decade.[35] In 1887 the closure rule was revised, and the initiative in its application was transferred from the Speaker to the House itself, although the motion remained conditional on the approval of the Chair. Doubts were expressed, by Gladstone and others, as to the advisability of this course. It was feared that the Speaker in accepting the motion might be made to appear the tool of the Government, since it could be anticipated that the closure motion in most instances would be initiated by the majority. However, the proposal was carried, and the present closure rule is substantially similar to that of 1887.

Although these drastic procedural innovations were introduced under the pressure of a crisis, it is unlikely that procedural reform could have been long delayed even if the Irish Nationalists had never set foot in the House of Commons. Parliamentary business had greatly increased under the impact of electoral reform and it is notable that the modern standing orders, which arose originally from the necessity to counter obstruction, have become the basic machinery of procedure without which the House would never be able to cope with the great volume of business which is always before it. Shaw-Lefevre had anticipated the need for radical change many years before the advent of the Parnellites and when the crisis struck it was left to the Chair to supply the initiative. It was fortunate that it was occupied at the crucial moment by a Speaker who could measure up to such a responsibility.

Brand was less successful in his handling of the case of Charles Bradlaugh, an atheist who claimed the right to make affirmation instead of taking the oath following his election to Parliament. In a prolonged dispute with the House of Commons Bradlaugh was unseated and re-elected four times, even though he agreed to take the oath in the prescribed form, so strong was the feeling against him because of his heterodox opinions. At no point did the Speaker intervene to prevent the House from continuing to make a fool of itself. It was left to his successor to resolve the issue by calling on Bradlaugh to take his seat after he had been elected for the fifth time, and allowing no objection to be made after Bradlaugh had agreed to take the oath in the ordinary form.[36]

Like his two immediate predecessors Brand was created a viscount on retirement. Elevation to this grade of the peerage remained the customary expectation of a retiring Speaker until 1971 when Horace King became the first to be made a life peer which carries the lesser rank of baron.

The next Speaker was probably the strongest and most forceful personality ever to preside over the House of Commons. Arthur Wellesley Peel, the youngest son of Sir Robert Peel, was first elected to the Chair on 26 February 1884 and served four terms of office. He was unanimously elected on each occasion and his address to the House following his first election revealed the strength of the conventions which surrounded the Speaker's office at this advanced stage in its evolution. In the course of a powerful and eloquent speech he declared: 'I know how necessary it is for any man, who aspires to fill that great office, to lay aside all that is personal, all that is of party, all that savours of political predilection, and to subordinate everything to the great interests of the House at large.'[37]

Peel came to the Chair equipped with powers far more substantial than any of his predecessors had inherited, and at a time when the new rules of procedure were still in their experimental stage. These circumstances rendered the duties of the Speaker exceptionally arduous, and the intensity of party feeling added even greater weight to his responsibilities. The Irish Nationalists, while their opportunities for obstruction had been curtailed, were far from subdued, and the issue of Irish Home Rule was to provoke bitter dissension between the Liberals and the Conservatives. Peel was the first Speaker to invoke the closure rule which had been passed in 1882, and its unsatisfactory nature was revealed on the occasion of its first application. The initiative in applying the closure, it will be remembered, rested with the Speaker, but if more than forty Members voted against the motion, at least 200 were required to vote in its favour in order to carry it. On 24 February 1885 the closure was called into operation by the Speaker for the first time, in order to counter Irish obstruction, and although it was carried by 207 votes to 46 the requisite majority was only barely obtained. This division was hardly calculated to encourage the occupant of the Chair to make use of the closure rule. It was only once more invoked prior to its revision, in the early hours of Friday, 18 February 1887.* Later in the same year the initiative in applying the closure was transferred from the Speaker to the House, although the Speaker was left with the power to refuse the motion if he considered it an

---

* In actual fact it was twice applied, first on an amendment to the main question and immediately afterwards on the main question itself.

infringement of the rights of minorities or an abuse of the rules of the House.

The responsibilities of the Chair were further increased during Peel's speakership as the result of a further revision of the Standing Orders in 1888. The new rules effected a profound change in the debating habits of the House, for they limited the hours of sitting for the first time and provided for the automatic interruption of business at twelve midnight. Certain business was exempted from the operation of the automatic adjournment, in addition to which the rule could be suspended on the affirmed motion of a Minister of the Crown. The new rules, while tending to limit still further the opportunities of private members, went far towards expediting the despatch of business. During this period of radical procedural changes the Speaker's firm control and assured guidance of the proceedings of the House proved invaluable. He was called upon to resolve many a knotty problem and to establish some important precedents, and the fact that his rulings were seldom, if ever, seriously challenged bears testimony to his great prestige and authority. The House respected his strength with the result that he could always rely on its support. As he himself said on the occasion of his re-election in 1892: 'Without the support of the House a Speaker can do nothing; with that support there is little he cannot do.'[38]

It was fortunate that the Chair was occupied by a strong Speaker during this difficult period and various testimonies exist as to his impressive demeanour. He was criticised by some for being too severe. The traditional blind eye and deaf ear had no place in his equipment and an Irish member once complained of him that he was always 'on the pounce'. But he was always in control of the situation, whether subduing a brawl, administering a rebuke or simply dominating the House with his presence. The writer of his obituary in The Times observed that although in theory he was the servant of the House there were occasions when he appeared to be more like its master. In point of fact Peel was a great actor performing on an historic stage, inspired by a single-minded dedication to the Parliament which he revered.

The next Speaker, William Court Gully, first elected on 10 April 1895, could not help but be overshadowed by the image of his predecessor. He came to the Chair under adverse circumstances hardly calculated to bolster his authority. He faced the first contested election to take place since 1839 and his selection by the Liberal Party as their candidate placed a great strain on the principle of the continuity of the office which by that time had become well established. Gully, who was the sixth in an unbroken succession of Liberal Speakers, was elected at the tail-end of a Parliament and prior to a general election which the Conservatives confidently expected to win. They felt that a moribund Liberal Government was seizing a rather shabby opportunity of perpetuating the speakership as a prize for its own party, and they therefore decided to oppose Gully. He was elected by the narrow majority of eleven votes, whereupon the Conservatives reserved the right to unseat him should they find themselves in the majority after the election. They opposed him in his constituency in the general election of 1895 which they won. Gully held his seat in an election which otherwise went badly for the Liberals but the Conservatives relented and did not carry out their previous threat to supplant him. On the contrary, they selected their senior backbencher, who had proposed Gully's opponent in the previous Parliament, to propose his re-election to the Chair on 12 August 1895 and the continuity principle thus survived.

Gully was the first lawyer to be elected Speaker since Shaw-Lefevre, and his legalistic approach to the duties of the Chair was evident in his strict interpretation of the rules of procedure and the somewhat pedantic literalism on which he based his rulings. Peel, although he was far sterner and more masterful, had been flexible in his interpretation of the Standing Orders, with the result that debate was less restricted under his presidency than under Gully's. Gully, for example, virtually outlawed the supplementary question, and was in the habit of cutting short a Member who sought to ask one with unusual sharpness. Normally, however, he was mild of manner, and at the outset of his speakership he revealed a weakness in attempting to buttress his rulings with reasons and explanations, although this tendency in him diminished as he gathered experience. His particular virtue as a Speaker lay in his competence in dealing with procedural problems on the spur of the moment. 'It is on points of order suddenly sprung, demanding instant settlement, that the mettle of a Speaker is tried,' writes Henry Lucy. 'One does not remember a case within the last ten years that Mr. Gully's, thus assayed, has not rung true.'[39]

Gully was again re-elected on 3 December 1900. His speakership, like that of Peel, spanned a period of intense political strife during which the duties of the Chair continued to be difficult and burdensome. His most distressting experience occurred on 5 March 1901 when, having named twelve Irish members, he called the police into the Chamber to remove them bodily, all other attempts to force their withdrawal having failed.[40] The House felt the humiliation of this incident very acutely and Gully was strongly criticised for his action. The Irish members never forgave him, and were in the habit of calling derisively 'Send for the police!' whenever any excitement arose subsequently. His own confidence was severely shaken and he never fully recovered his prestige. Perhaps he might have resolved the dilemma by suspending the sitting of the House on his own initiative and thus anticipating the standing order which was introduced shortly afterwards empowering the Speaker to suspend a sitting of his own authority in circumstances of grave disorder. But it is easy to be wise after the event and it is a fortunate person who takes a happy decision in the stress of the moment.

Although Gully's speakership was not an unqualified success his impartiality was never in question and he did his best to maintain the standards of conduct which by that time were traditionally expected of the occupant of the Chair. The Speaker who presided over the House of Commons at the turn of the twentieth century was not the most impressive of the long line but it was an ordered inheritance and an unsullied trust which he handed on to his successor.

Notes to Chapter Two: The History of the Speakership

1. Enoch Powell, 'A Speaker before "The First"'; published in Parliamentary Affairs, Vol. XVIII, No. 1, Winter 1964/5, pp. 20–22.
2. See Arthur Irwin Dasent. The Speakers of the House of Commons, London, John Lane, the Bodley Head, 1911, p. 76.
3. Commons Journal, Vol. 1, p. 24.
4. Ibid., p. 37.
5. Sir J. E. Neale, *Elizabeth I and Her Parliaments*, vol. 1, p. 29, Jonathan Cape, 1953.
6. See Parliamentary History, Vol. 1, Cols. 951–3.
7. Hatsell's Precedents, 1818 edition, Vol. 2, p. 230.
8. Commons Journal, Vol. I, p. 617.
9. Ibid., Vol. II, p. 63.
10. Ibid., Vol. VII, p. 594.
11. See Grey's Debates, Vol. 2, pp. 186–8.
12. Ibid., Vol. V, pp. 1–17, pp. 122–144.
13. Commons Journal, Vol. IX, p. 643.
14. Ibid., Vol. XI, p. 272.
15. Ibid., Vol. XVI, 23 March, 1709, p. 382.
16. Hatsell's Precedents, 1818 Edition, Vol. 2, p. 237.
17. Commons Journal, Vol. 23, p. 148.
18. Hatsell's Precedents, op. cit., p. 232.
19. For details see O. C. Williams, The Clerical Organization of the House of Commons, 1661–1850, O.U.P., 1954.
20. The full text of the speech is to be found in the Commons Journal, Vol. 28, pp. 1108–1109.
21. Parliamentary History, Vol. XVI, pp. 807–11; Commons Journal, Vol. 32, pp. 707–8.
22. Parliamentary History, Vol. XIX, p. 213.
23. Commons Journal, 1813–14, pp. 203–4.
24. See Parliamentary History, Vol. 1, Cols. 951–3.
25. Commons Journal, Vol. 51, p. 764.
26. See Hansard's Parliamentary Debates, 3rd series, Vol. 26, Col. 52.
27. See for example Edward Porritt, The Unreformed House of Commons, Vol. 1, C.U.P., 1903, p. 480.
28. Quoted in Michael MacDonagh, *The Speaker of the House*, Methuen, 1914, p. 308.
29. For further elaboration see Sir Ivor Jennings, Parliament, 2nd Ed., C.U.P., 1957, p. 66.
30. John Evelyn Denison, *Notes from my Journal when Speaker of the House of Commons*, John Murray, 1899.
31. See for example Commons Journal, 1861, p. 282; and Ibid, p. 97.
32. Ibid., p. 257.
33. Commons Journal, Vol. 136, p. 50.
34. Josef Redlich, *The Procedure of the House of Commons*, Constable, 1908, Vol. 1, p. 164.
35. Ibid Vol. 1 for an exhaustive treatment of this subject.
36. See Hansard's Parliamentary Debates, 3rd series, Vol. 302, Cols. 21–29.
37. Ibid., Vol. 285, Col. 25.

38. Parliamentary Debates, Fourth Series, Vol. 7, Second Session, August 4, 1892, Col. 13.
39. Henry Lucy, *The Balfourian Parliament* 1900–1905, 1906, p. 398, London, Hodder & Stoughton, 1906.
40. Commons Hansard, 5th Series, Vol. 40. Cols. 217–219.

Part Two

The Speakership in the Parliaments of the Commonwealth

Chapter Three

The British Speakership in the Twentieth Century

As we have seen the pattern of the modern speakership was already well established by the turn of the present century. It evolved as Parliament itself evolved, developing naturally, almost accidentally, and is an illustration of the British genius for adapting ancient institutions to modern political conditions. The responsibilities of the modern speakership are considerable and the first task of this chapter is to summarize them and describe the essential characteristics of the office.

The Speaker is the principal officer of the House and the chairman of the House of Commons Commission which is the ultimate administrative authority. The Commission was established under the House of Commons (Administration) Act 1978 and replaced an earlier body set up under an Act of 1812 which the 1978 Act repealed. It includes, in addition to the Speaker, the Leader of the House and four other members of the House of Commons, one nominated by the Leader of the Opposition and the other three appointed by the House itself from among the non-ministerial members. The Commission is the sole employer of all House of Commons staff and determines their numbers, remuneration and other conditions of service which must, under the Act, be kept broadly in line with those of the Home Civil Service. The Commission is advised by a Board of Management consisting of the departmental heads of the House of Commons. The Board is responsible for the Co-ordination of staffing policy and the development of a unified service.

The departments of the House of Commons are presently those of the Clerk, the Serjeant-at-Arms, the Library, the Administration, the Official Report (Hansard) and the catering services (Refreshment Department). Under the previous administrative system the Speaker headed a department of his own which, although still referred to in the Act as the Department of the Speaker, has been largely disbanded.* The principal officers of the Speaker's office are the Speaker's Secretary, Speaker's Counsel, Speaker's Second Counsel and Speaker's Chaplain. The Speaker's Secretary is in charge of the office, deals with official correspondence and assists the Speaker in the

---

* The present administrative organization of the House of Commons is based on recommendations made by a Report to Mr. Speaker by Committee under Chairmanship of Mr. Arthur Bottomley, M.P., entitled House of Commons (Administration), H.C. 624, 7 August 1975.

discharge of his social responsibilities. The Speaker's Counsel is largely concerned with private business and is rarely called upon to give direct advice to the Speaker. He also assists the Select Committee on Statutory Instruments (which also sits with a similar committee of the House of Lords as a joint committee) in the scrutiny of delegated legislation. The Speaker's Second Counsel, first appointed in 1974, assists the Select Committee on European Secondary Legislation in its oversight of draft legislation and other documents which flow from the European Economic Community. The Speaker's Chaplain, whose office dates from 1659, reads prayers at the beginning of every sitting and, together with the Speaker's Secretary, takes part in the Speaker's daily procession.

Administrative continuity during an interval following a dissolution of Parliament is provided by the Ministerial and other Salaries Act 1972 and the Act of 1978 whereby the Speaker continues in office for the purposes of the Acts until a Speaker is chosen by the new Parliament.

The Speaker is the presiding officer of the House of Commons, the guardian of its privileges and its representative on all official occasions. He is elected for a constituency like every other member, reaching Parliament by the same route and representing the interests of his community in like manner. He is chosen by his fellow-members from among themselves and the first business of a new Parliament is always the election of the Speaker. Without a Speaker the House can transact no business, apart from the conduct of the election itself, and if a Speaker retires or dies in the course of a Parliament a successor must be chosen immediately. The election of the Speaker is attended with ceremony in accordance with the practice of centuries. At the opening of a new Parliament the Lord Chancellor instructs the Commons assembled at the Bar of the House of Lords to repair to their own chamber to choose their Speaker before Her Majesty arrives to declare the cause of summoning Parliament. When a Speaker is elected during the course of a Parliament the Prime Minister, Leader of the House or other senior minister announces that Her Majesty has been notified of the vacancy and gives leave to the House to proceed to the election of a new Speaker. Following the election, which is conducted according to a new procedure first used in 1974, the Speaker-elect presents himself at the Bar of the House of Lords for the royal approbation, signified on behalf of the Queen by the Lord Chancellor. At the outset of a new Parliament he also lays claim on behalf of the Commons to 'all their ancient and undoubted rights and privileges, especially to freedom of speech in debate, to freedom from arrest, and to free access to Her Majesty whenever occasion shall require, and that the most favourable construction shall be put upon all their proceedings.'

When only one candidate is proposed as Speaker his proposer is normally a senior government backbencher and his seconder a senior member of the official opposition. The Speaker is the choice of the House as a whole and the convention observed in the British House of Commons is that the candidate should never be proposed and seconded by ministerial or front-bench members. It is on record that William Pitt the younger, when Prime Minister, wished to be the proposer of his friend Henry Addington, but the Clerk, John

The Office of Speaker

Hatsell counselled against it. 'I think that the choice of Speaker should not be on the motion of the minister,' he said. 'Indeed, an invidious use might be made of it, to represent you as the friend of the minister, rather than the choice of the House.'[1] Under the new procedure for electing the Speaker, either the Chair is taken by the back-bench member with the longest unbroken period of service who is present in the House (for example, at the beginning of a new Parliament) or the retiring Speaker continues to occupy the Chair until his successor is elected. Previously, the Clerk of the House presided at the election of a Speaker, in accordance with historic tradition, but he was equipped with no powers to control and regulate the debate. The new procedure, which is laid down by standing order, equips the occupant of the Chair with the necessary power and authority.[2] The new procedure first came into operation on 6 March 1974 when Speaker Selwyn Lloyd was re-elected for a second term of office.[3] He was the first Speaker to preside over the election of his successor when Speaker George Thomas was elected on 3 February 1976.[4]

During the election of the Speaker certain traditions are observed in recognition of the fact that the House is without a spokesman until all the formalities have been completed. During the proceedings in the chamber the Mace rests in the brackets below the Table of the House unless the retiring Speaker is presiding over the election of his successor. It is lifted into the upper brackets when the Speaker-elect takes the Chair. However, the appointment has yet to receive the royal approbation, and in the procession to the Bar of the House of Lords the Serjeant-at-Arms carries the Mace in the crook of his left arm instead of on his shoulder, and the Speaker-elect is ungowned and wears a small bob-wig in place of his usual full-bottomed wig. The royal approbation having been signified, the Serjeant-at-Arms bears the Mace shoulder-high in the return procession and the Speaker before taking the Chair changes into his usual costume of gown and full-bottomed wig. Another tradition which persists is the token show of reluctance exhibited by the Speaker-elect when his proposer and seconder come to conduct him to the Chair. This custom has its origin in the genuine reluctance with which earlier Speakers submitted to the will of the House and it continued long after the office carried with it any danger to life and limb, sometimes degenerating into a ludicrous pantomime as the candidate resisted every inch of the way to the Chair. Speaker Onslow discontinued the practice in 1728 but the vestiges of the old tradition have never been completely eradicated.

Once elected the Speaker sheds his previous political affiliation and not only becomes totally impartial but is seen to be so. He not only resigns from his party but changes his life-style. He must restrict his club memberships and can no longer allow himself the informal social activities permitted to other members. He may not pursue friendships which would appear to favour certain members above others. To a great extent he isolates himself from the camaraderie of parliamentary life, at the same time remaining accessible to all his colleagues and ever a sympathetic listener to their problems, personal as well as parliamentary.

The Speaker presides over debates in the House but does not participate himself. He maintains order, enforces the rules as necessary, interprets the standing orders and the practice of the House, deals with points of order and gives rulings when called upon to do so. Rulings once given stand as precedents in the parliamentary case-law and may be given publicly from the Chair or privately in response to members seeking advice. Speaker Thomas instituted the practice of requiring that decisions given privately be recorded in the Votes and Proceedings. He is equipped with disciplinary powers by which he can call members to order, suspend a sitting in circumstances of grave disorder, order a member to resume his seat or withdraw from the chamber for the remainder of the day's sitting, or name a member to the House when a severer penalty is called for. He calls on members to speak in debate and his choice is not open to dispute. He has a particular duty to protect the rights of minorities, which no Speaker will ever fail to do, but in the exercise of his impartiality neither must he lose sight of the rights of the majority nor of any dissident elements or factions sumberged beneath the umbrella of a major party. He is equipped with powers which emphasize the judicial nature of his office such as his power to rule on the admissibility of bills, motions and amendments; to decide whether a question of privilege should have precedence over all other business; to interpret the *sub judice* convention; to select amendments; to determine whether an emergency adjournment motion meets the necessary criteria; to protect the privileges of the Commons from infringement by the House of Lords; to invoke the sanctions provided for dealing with disorderly conduct; and to pronounce the judgment of the House on those who violate its rights and immunities.

The Speaker's office is thus akin to that of a judge and lawyers have frequently, although not invariably, been selected to fill it. Of the 24 Speakers who by 1983 had held office since Arthur Onslow, all but nine have been lawyers.* Good judgment is certainly an essential element of a Speaker's equipment. He is, after all, interpreting the wishes of the House as well as its rules and practice. Only the House can change its rules and procedures although the Speaker, through his interpretation of them, can have a significant influence on their evolution. He is not expected, for example, to impose the letter of the law rigidly on every occasion. Much will depend on the circumstances of the moment, and the strength of the rules and conventions which have developed over the years lies in the fact that they can be administered with flexibility and prudence. The House, as one Speaker has written, 'would not welcome a Speaker who rigidly enforced on every single occasion every jot and tittle of the laws which he administers'.[5] Judgment is called for in the exercise of his power to call on members to speak, although under modern practice it is usually known in advance, depending on the bill or other matter to be debated, who the principal spokesmen for the government and opposition are going to be. The Speaker may also receive advice with regard to the members whom the whips would like to see called but this is in no way binding on him. On the contrary, he must always have an

---

* In this century Speakers Gully, Lowther, Morrison, Hylton-Foster and Lloyd were lawyers. Speakers Whitley, Fitzroy, Clifton-Brown, King and Thomas were non-lawyers, as is Speaker Weatherill.

eye to those members who may be out of favour with their parties and make sure that their rights are not ignored. He must take account of all shades of opinion, of geographical considerations, of members' constituency interests and of various other claims to recognition. He is expected to respect a custom, much resented by backbenchers, whereby privy councillors are accorded precedence in debate, a custom which was varied by Speaker Lloyd during his tenure of office with a view to effecting a compromise.[6] Members wishing to speak frequently write to the Speaker explaining their special reasons for wishing to participate in a debate, and while this does not guarantee they will be called it assists the Speaker in coming to fair decisions. Speaker Lloyd described this duty as 'one of the most worrying, time-consuming and frustrating aspects of my work'.[7]*

The Speaker does not vote in a division except to exercise a casting vote in the event of a tie. Should the occasion arise he is guided by special considerations which were referred to in the previous chapter. His vote is not an expression of his own preference for or against the measure. He votes in such a way as to keep the matter open for further discussion or, if this is not possible, in favour of the *status quo*. A former Speaker has cited examples of the application of these principles: 'If there were to be a tie in the division on the second reading (of a bill), the Speaker would vote "aye" to allow opportunity for further discussion.' At the report stage, after a bill has emerged from committee, 'If there is a tie on an amendment moved during that stage, the Speaker votes for the bill as it left the committee and against the amendment . . . . If there were to be a tie on the third reading, the final stage, the Speaker would vote "no" on the grounds that a change in the law requires a majority in the House, and should not be made on the Speaker's casting vote. The same would apply to a motion whether moved by the government or not.'[8] Only rarely is the Speaker called upon to use his casting vote but both Speaker Lloyd and Speaker Thomas found themselves in situations where they were obliged to do so.**

The office of Speaker is one of great prestige and dignity and an author writing at the turn of the century saw in it many of the attributes of royalty.[9] This exaltation is quite deliberate, designed to sustain the authority of even a weak incumbent, and a number of factors combine to lend emphasis to the honour and independence of the position. To begin with there are the outward symbols reflected in the robes he wears, the Chair in which he presides and the ceremony attending him including his daily procession to the

---

* On 10 November 1983 *The Times* published an article by a Liberal Member complaining that his party was being denied a fair share of debating time. The article provides an illustration of the difficulties facing the Speaker in satisfying the competing demands for parliamentary time in a House of 650 Members.

** See the explanation of Speaker Lloyd on 12 July 1974 (Commons Hansard, 5th. series, vol. 876, col. 1741). The casting vote was twice exercised the previous day by the Speaker and Deputy Speaker respectively in circumstances where, as it was subsequently revealed, the divisions had been incorrectly recorded and there had been no tied vote. See also statement of Speaker Thomas on 27 May 1976 (Commons Hansard, 5th. series, vol. 912, cols. 761–2.)

chamber preceded by the Serjeant-at-Arms bearing the Mace. Members bow to him on entering and leaving the chamber, or when encountering him within parliamentary precincts, and his isolation from the mainstream of political life enables them all to respect him as the impartial protector of their rights and privileges. His conduct may be criticised only on a substantive motion introduced for that specific purpose, and a reflection on his character or actions other than by this means could be judged as a breach of privilege or contempt. He has a house within the Palace of Westminster where he entertains officially. His salary is equal to that of a cabinet minister and in recognition of his political independence it is charged directly to the Consolidated Fund under permanent legislation instead of being annually voted by Parliament.[10] From 1689 to 1919 he ranked immediately after the peers as the First Commoner. Today he ranks sixth in the official order of precedence after the royal family and ahead of all other peers except those who hold offices which take precedence to his own.* On retirement he is normally elevated to the House of Lords, Speaker Whitley being the only retired Speaker to refuse a peerage during this century. Speaker King and Speaker Lloyd were both created life peers on retirement but Speaker Thomas was honoured with an hereditary viscountcy, thus reviving the earlier tradition. The Speaker is granted a pension when he retires under permanent legislation.[11] Prior to 1972 a retiring Speaker was awarded his pension by special Act of Parliament, and from 1832 to the retirement of Speaker Morrison in 1959 it was invariably 4000 pounds per annum. This precedent was broken in 1971 when Speaker King was awarded a pension of 5000 pounds.[12] The present legislation relates the size of the pension to salary increases.

The Speaker shares his duties in the Chair with three deputies. Before 1855 no provision existed for a deputy to take the Speaker's place in the event of his absence, and such was the degree of health enjoyed by Speakers prior to that date that between 1547 and 1853 only 29 absences are recorded, all of short duration. A select committee was appointed in 1853 to consider the problem and it recommended that the Chairman of Ways and Means as the officer already familiar with the duties of the Chair, should be empowered to discharge the functions of the Speaker during the latter's absence.[13] A standing order to this effect was adopted on 20 July 1855 and given statutory authority the same year with the passing of the Deputy Speaker Act, 1855. In 1902 provision was made for the appointment of a Deputy Chairman of Ways and Means and in 1971 for a Second Deputy Chairman of Ways and Means. Both may exercise all the powers of the Chairman of Ways and Means including his powers as Deputy Speaker.[14] Any one of these three officers may take the Chair as Deputy Speaker when requested to do so without any

---

* An order-in-council of 30 May 1919 established a revised order of precedence headed by the Royal Family, the Archbishop of Canterbury, the Lord Chancellor, the Archbishop of York, the Prime Minister, the Lord High Treasurer (now a defunct office), the Lord President of the Council, and the Speaker of the House of Commons. See London Gazette, 3 June 1919, p. 7059.

formal communication to the House, but they cannot exercise the full powers and authority of the Speaker unless certain formalities are observed.[15] The principal function of the Chairman of Ways and Means was formerly to preside over committees of the whole House, but with the abolition of the Committee of Supply and the Committee of Ways and Means and the reference of most bills to standing committees, the quantity of business transacted in committee of the whole is far less than in former years. Thus the main duties of the Chairman of Ways and Means and his deputies today involve taking the Chair as Deputy Speaker and sharing with the Speaker the responsibility of presiding over the House. In committee of the whole the Chairman does not take the Speaker's Chair but presides at the Table of the House alongside the Clerks, the Mace resting in the lower brackets instead of on the Table itself. Unlike the Speaker he does not wear robes, but he presides with the same impartiality and his authority is final. There is no appeal from his rulings to the Speaker and his conduct, like that of the Speaker, can only be called in question on a substantive motion. Although he is normally a member of the governing party, he does not participate in debate or divisions in the House and in committee of the whole he exercises only a casting vote.

The Continuity of the Speakership in the 20th Century

We have seen that the continuity of the speakership was a well-established convention by the turn of the twentieth century and that the political independence of the office is beyond dispute. Chance, however, has been a very important element in its evolution and the long-standing tradition of continuity is somewhat more vulnerable than is generally believed. There is no constitutional or legislative obstacle to prevent a Speaker from being replaced. The electors of his constituency are free to defeat him at the polls if they wish and the House is free to ignore the convention and elect any Speaker it chooses. There have been two crucial factors in the past 140 years which have protected the security of the Speaker's tenure of office. Firstly, no Speaker seeking re-election in his constituency has ever been defeated at the polls; secondly, no incoming majority following a change of government has ever attempted to violate the continuity principle.

It is sometimes assumed that a tradition exists whereby the Speaker is not opposed in his constituency during a general election. This is no doubt due to the fact that in the first ten general elections of this century no Speaker seeking re-election faced an opponent. The convention was broken in 1935 by the decision of the Labour Party to run a candidate in Speaker Fitzroy's constituency of Daventry. Since then there has been no occasion on which a Speaker seeking re-election has not faced one or more opponents, although they have not always been candidates officially sponsored by the major parties. Speaker Gully, who was obliged to fight for his seat in 1895, decided to address a public meeting, and although he made no reference to the political issues on which the election was being fought, he stated his views as to why a Speaker seeking re-election should not be opposed:

The first reason was that the English people were in the main lovers of fair play, and that it had struck them as being a somewhat unfair spectacle to see someone who, in the public interest, was disabled from protecting himself by the ordinary weapons of political warfare, exposed to an attack and unable to defend himself. A Speaker could not withdraw from the political arena. On the contrary, he must be a Member before he was a Speaker, but he was disarmed. It had occurred to our fathers and forefathers that it was unfair to put a man disarmed in the middle of a ring, and that the proper course was not to subject him to the conditions of a contest. That appeared to some people of the present day to be a quixotic piece of generosity. He hoped there would be some generosity left still in public life.[16]

The Labour Party's decision to oppose the Speaker in 1935 was deplored both in the press and by their opponents. The Conservatives and Liberals of Daventry unanimously adopted Fitzroy as their non-party candidate, and Stanley Baldwin, Ramsay MacDonald, David Lloyd George, Sir John Simon and Sir Herbert Samuel all signed a letter denouncing the Labour Party's violation of established custom. Fitzroy, in accepting the joint nomination, declared that the mere fact of opposing the Speaker weakened the authority of the Chair and his defeat would destroy it. Like Gully he addressed his electorate and warned them that the defeat of the Speaker at the polls would be 'the greatest blow to democratic government ever perpetrated.' In a statement issued in defence of the Labour Party, George Lansbury declared that there was an active Conservative Association in Daventry pursuing political propaganda on behalf of its party and the local Labour Party organization had therefore felt compelled to take up the challenge. He also made the interesting point that the Labour Party was opposed to the principle of the Speaker representing a constituency like any other member.[17]

In 1938 the Labour Party again announced its intention of contesting the Speaker's seat, and although the intervention of a world war upset the electoral schedule, the decision was implemented at the first post-war general election in 1945. On this occasion the Labour Party was making a determined bid for power, yet its opposition to Speaker Clifton-Brown at Hexham did not provoke the same heated indignation as its treatment of his predecessor ten years earlier. Perhaps it was so long since a general election had been held that the breach of convention passed unnoticed, or it may have been unable to compete for public attention with the many weightier issues of the day. However, Clifton-Brown was returned with the far from large majority of 4645. Had the Labour Party anticipated the extent of the success it was to enjoy at the polls a different decision might have been taken. But in 1945, as in 1935, it regarded itself as a struggling party which could not afford to miss any opportunity of gaining an extra seat.

There are also very real difficulties involved in keeping a constituency party organization together for the event of the Speaker's retirement. They have been stressed by Sir Ivor Jennings:

The Labour Party, in particular, relies for most of its electioneering on unpaid assistance rendered by enthusiastic supporters whose sole incentive is the hope of the ultimate election of their candidate. The highly complex organization which any well-organized divisional party has to evolve is kept in existence between elections, and the process of 'nursing' is continuous. The election contest itself, even if obviously doomed to failure, is interesting and exciting. The supporters are willing to work hard even if the chance of election be remote. If, however, there is no election, the difficulty of maintaining the organization is substantial. The honorary officers of the local parties are all the more discouraged if there is evidence that the political complexion of the constituency is changing. For these reasons the divisional Labour Party at Daventry, supported by the central Labour organization, decided to oppose Captain Fitzroy in 1935. They believed that, given an ordinary election, a Labour candidate would be returned. They believed also that, unless they could have an election, they could not keep an organization together ready to seize the seat when the Speaker resigned, whereas the local Conservative association, relying mainly on paid labour, could improvise the necessary organization . . . . The same considerations induced the Labour Party to oppose Colonel Clifton-Brown at Hexham in 1945.[18]

In 1950 the Labour Party refrained from opposing Clifton-Brown a second time, but an Independent, who had expressed the view that no candidate, not even the Speaker, should be allowed an unopposed return, decided to stand against him. He was a man who seemed to have a predilection for facing fearful odds for he had opposed Winston Churchill in 1945 for a similar reason. On this occasion the Speaker was returned with the overwhelming majority of 20,549. In 1955 Speaker Morrison was opposed at Cirencester and Tewkesbury by a member of the divisional Labour Party standing as an Independent without official backing.

At the general election of 1964 Speaker Hylton-Foster was opposed in his constituency by officially sponsored candidates of both the Labour and Liberal Parties. Speaker King was opposed by an independent in 1966 and in 1970 he faced two opponents, neither of them sponsored by the major parties. However, in the two general elections which took place in 1974 Speaker Lloyd faced Labour and Liberal opponents on both occasions. In 1979 Speaker Thomas was opposed by a Welsh Nationalist and a National Front candidate.

In 1938, the year in which the Labour Party had announced that it would again be contesting the Speaker's seat, the House of Commons appointed a Select Committee to investigate the problem. It consisted of sixteen Members, including Winston Churchill, David Lloyd George (the Chairman) and George Lansbury, and its terms of reference were 'to consider what steps, if any, should be taken to ensure that, having due regard to the constitutional rights of the electors, the Speaker during his continuance in office, shall not be required to take part in a contested parliamentary election'.

The committee considered a number of possibilities, including proposals to create a fictitious constituency for the Speaker, to make his a two-membered constituency, to transfer him immediately after election as Speaker to a constituency rendered safe for him, and to prohibit a contest in the Speaker's constituency by statute. All were rejected as being contrary to the spirit of the British Constitution and the committee recommended that no change should be made.

The committee recognized the existence of a conflict between the rights of the Speaker's electors and the Speaker's own political aloofness, but pointed out that it was the preservation of those very rights in the House of Commons which compels the Speaker to withdraw from all political combat.

The conclusions of the Committee were as follows:

> To attempt to deprive a constituency of the right to choose as its member one who is considered most representative of the popular will would be a serious infringement of democratic principles. To alter the status of the Speaker so that he ceased to be returned to the House of Commons by the same electoral methods as other members or as a representative of a parliamentary constituency, would be equally repugnant to the custom and tradition of the House. To advocate that a Speaker should modify, even in his own defence, the established attitude towards political controversy would be to reverse the whole trend of our parliamentary evolution. Such are Your Committee's conclusions. No scheme or proposal within their purview offers more than a partial solution, and each introduces new elements which, in your Committee's considered judgment, would be less acceptable than the ills they seek to cure.
>
> The fact cannot be disguised that the possibility of a contest cannot be excluded even when one of the candidates holds the office of Speaker. That such a state of affairs is undesirable is admitted by all who have considered the matter with care; but the only remedy lies not in attempts at suppression, criticism or evasion, but rather in the fuller education of the electorate towards the recognition and increased understanding of those vital democratic safeguards which it is the duty of the Speaker to defend. Development along these lines cannot be rapid but it can be most surely expedited by a firm maintenance of that code of principles which has slowly been built up during the last two centuries.[19]

This report seemed to dispose of the matter once and for all, but it is interesting to note that the idea of a special seat for the Speaker was revived some years later. On 24 April 1963 a group of private members sought leave to introduce a bill under the ten minutes' rule 'for the creation of a constituency to be known as St. Stephen's and represented by Mr. Speaker'. The motion was defeated quite narrowly by 76 votes to 68.[20] A motion in identical terms was introduced under the ten minutes' rule on 26 January 1982 and defeated by 252 votes to 15.[21]

The suggestion, sometimes heard, that the Speaker is not able to represent his constituents adequately because of the political restraints upon him does not seem to be well-founded. The select committee appointed in 1938 made the following comments on the matter:

> It has been argued by those who advocate some change in the existing system that the Speaker's non-political position after election further disfranchises his constituents, in that he cannot express their views in debate or by his vote in divisions, nor can he by political means seek to redress their grievances. Your Committee do not find themselves impressed by these arguments. In the British political system, whatever may be its merits or demerits, there is a strong party control over the action of members in the House and the sterilization of a single vote on whichever side it might have been delivered will have so small an influence on matters which are the subject of party divisions as to be entirely negligible. On the other hand, on non-controversial matters and particular grievances Your Committee feel assured that there are many members in any House who would most willingly place their services at the disposal of the Speaker and his constituents.
>
> In matters of individual interest or grievance the Speaker's constituents are in fact in a peculiarly favoured position. Though the Speaker himself can put down no questions, any matter affecting them which he feels justified in raising privately with a Department of State will, in the nature of human reactions, coming from such a source, receive the most careful consideration. Again, if the circumstances of a particular case require that a question should receive public expression it would be, and in fact is, willingly sponsored by other members. Apart from these considerations, it cannot be disputed that a great honour is conferred on the constituency whose member is chosen from among all others for those rare qualities which will enable him to fill the high office of presiding over the deliberations of the House of Commons and representing it as the first commoner in the land.
>
> There are many ways in which a member may, by actions within his constituency, advance the proper interests of his constituents of whatever party, while yet holding himself completely outside the field of political controversy; and the value of such services cannot fail to be enhanced by the status of their proponent. Your Committee are convinced that participation in such activities could in no way derogate from the authority and impartiality of the Speakership; and no man is in a better position to judge to what extent they might be carried than one who has been elected to this office.[22]

Those who have themselves held office as Speaker appear to agree with the views expressed by the committee.[23] Speaker Lloyd expressed the view to the author in a personal interview that he believed the Speaker could represent a constituency more effectively than a minister since the former is not bound by collective responsibility. He is therefore not inhibited in raising constituency problems even though he is obliged to raise them privately. He is also on record as defending the present system of electing the Speaker:

If this system is altered, a fundamental blow will be struck at the Speakership. If by some resolution of the House the Speaker becomes a notional Member for a fictitious constituency, it would gravely diminish his authority and standing. He would soon have only the status of an official of the House without a corresponding security of tenure.

In conducting the business of the House, moreover, the Speaker should be familiar with what ordinary people are thinking, by letters from those whose homes and backgrounds he knows, and by personal contacts with them.

There is a final point. The Commons can function only if certain of its Members accept self-denying ordinances. Government Whips hardly ever speak in the House; Parliamentary Private Secretaries do not speak on matters affecting the Departments of the Ministers whom they serve; members of the Chairmen's Panel, who have taken the chair of a Standing Committee during the Committee Stage of a Bill do not speak (or vote) during the Report Stage or Third Reading of that Bill; the Chairman and the two Deputy Chairmen of Ways and Means do not speak or vote. If the Speaker is to be given a special constituency, what about the Deputy Speaker, and these others? Should not they have special seats? Where would it end?[24]

A Speaker seeking re-election is to some extent handicapped since he cannot conduct a political campaign while his opponents are under no such restraints. However the record of electoral success which Speakers have enjoyed suggests a certain sophistication and an understanding of the Speaker's role on the part of their electorates. Gully won his seat in 1895 in an election which went very badly for the Liberals. Clifton-Brown's victory at Hexham in 1945 was against the national trend which produced a landslide for the Labour Party. On most other occasions the Speaker's majority has ranged from comfortable to overwhelming.

Consultation in the selection of the Speaker is an important element in promoting the continuity of the office since he is supposed to be the choice of the House as a whole, not the choice of the front benches or of the majority party. Failure to consult has on more than one occasion been the cause of friction, sometimes between government and opposition, sometimes between the backbenchers and the party leaderships. The choice of William Court Gully, it will be recalled, gave rise to a serious dispute between the government and the opposition of the day. His successor, James William Lowther, first elected on 8 June 1905, was accepted without objection even though, like Gully, he was proposed by a moribund government which was shortly to be swept out of power. The Liberals in according him a unanimous election were no doubt influenced by the fact that he was the first Conservative to be called to the Chair in 70 years and the recollection of their own experience in the case of Gully. The first discordant note during this century concerning the choice of Speaker was heard during the election of John Henry Whitley, the last Liberal to hold the office, on 27 April 1921. On that occasion two members, Mr. Ronald McNeill and Sir William Joynson-

Hicks, rose to complain that the rights of backbenchers had been violated because they had been insufficiently consulted on the nomination. Mr. McNeill drew attention to a press headline which read: 'The Prime Minister has offered the speakership to Mr. Whitley.' He went on to suggest that the statement 'not very unfairly represents what actually occurred'. He continued: '... the Government regarded their nomination of a candidate for the Chair as so completely tantamount to his election that there was no occasion even to pay the homage of decent pretence to the idea of any initiative in the matter residing beyond the narrow limits of the Treasury Bench'.[25] The next occasion on which a member was to complain of lack of consultation was on 9 March 1943 when Douglas Clifton Brown was first elected to the Chair. The aggrieved member, Captain Cunningham-Reid, alleged that the Speaker had in fact been chosen the previous week. 'It appeared in the press that the Conservative Party had decided that Colonel Clifton Brown should be the Speaker of this House.'[26] Cunningham-Reid's proved to be a lone voice, although there may have been some substance to his allegation since the coalition government of the day was said to favour another candidate.[27]

On the occasion of the election of Clifton-Brown's successor, William Shepherd Morrison, in 1951, the first contest for the speakership took place since Gully was opposed in 1895. It appeared that the consultative process broke down very badly and Lord Pannell has given an account of what took place. The Conservatives had just been re-elected to power and the former Speaker had retired with the dissolution of the previous Parliament. Morrison's name was advanced by Winston Churchill, and Clement Attlee and others in the Labour Party leadership, having no objection to his nomination, brought the matter to a meeting of the Parliamentary Labour Party as a fait accompli. At the meeting a back-bench revolt took place and the claims of Major James Milner, Chairman of Ways and Means in the previous Parliament, were pressed.[28] The minutes of the Parliamentary Labour Party for 31 October 1951 record as follows:

> The Chairman reported on the informal discussions which had taken place with government representatives regarding the election of a new Speaker, from which it appeared that the Conservatives proposed to move the election of Mr. W. S. Morrison, the Member for Cirencester and Tewkesbury. A considerable discussion took place, in which Mr. Charles Pannell, Mr. Sam Viant, Mr. Geoffrey Bing, Mr. Aneurin Bevan, Mr. Ivan O. Thomas, Mr. Shinwell, Mr. Paget, Major Milner, Mrs. Braddock, Mr. Richard Adams, Mr. Walter Edwards, Mr. Douglas Houghton and Mr. George Chetwynd took part, in the course of which it was argued that the party ought to put forward the name of Major J. Milner.
>
> On a vote, 108 to 89 voted that his name be put forward.
>
> Further discussion arose following this vote, in which Sir Hartley Shawcross, Mr. George Porter, Mr. Gordon Walker and Mr. George Brown took part, in the course of which it was suggested that an intimation should be given to the Conservatives that if Mr. W. S.

Morrison's name were brought forward, the party would find it necessary to put forward in opposition the name of Major Milner, but that if the Conservatives would withdraw Mr. W. S. Morrison and put forward Sir Charles McAndrew the party would acquiesce to this proposal.

The Chief Whip intervened at this point to give an account of the informal discussions with the Tories and explained that the Tories had in fact turned down both Major Milner and Sir Charles MacAndrew.

The discussion was continued by Mrs. Barbara Castle, Mr. J. Johnson, Mr. Fred Bellenger, and it was then agreed to take a vote on the motion that 'In the event of the proposition being put forward by the Tories to propose the election of Sir Charles MacAndrew the party would acquiesce'.

Vote 115 for – 107 against.

It was also agreed that the leader should approach the Prime Minister with this alternative proposal, but that if it were refused the party should nominate Major Milner, and Mr. Sam Viant and Mr. David Logan were asked to undertake this.

The result was a contested election, the Conservatives proposing Morrison and the Labour Party proposing Milner. The former was elected by 318 votes to 251, having had no idea he was going to be opposed until he arrived in the House on 31 October just before the election was to take place.

Morrison, like Clifton-Brown, retired at the end of a Parliament, which led to further difficulties in arranging consultations when his successor came to be elected in 1959. The Speaker had never been drawn from the ranks of the Labour Party. In the interests of the continuity of the office, they had magnanimously resisted the opportunity to claim the prize for themselves in 1945, a gesture which Speaker Clifton-Brown had described as an act of 'amazing political generosity'. Lord Pannell has related the story of how Clifton-Brown came to London with a pile of empty suitcases after the Labour Party victory expecting to pack up, and wept on being informed that he would be re-proposed as Speaker.[29] In 1959 it appears that the Conservatives, who had again been re-elected to office, would have been prepared to concede the speakership to Labour provided they chose the candidate. They put forward the name of Sir Frank Soskice and were not apparently prepared to consider any other candidate from the opposition benches. This was resented by the Labour Party and Soskice felt obliged to decline the offer, whereupon the Conservatives proposed one of their own members, Sir Harry-Hylton Foster. Although the opposition proposed no candidate of their own, strong protests were registered during the debate on Hylton-Foster's election on 20 October 1959. The new Speaker was nevertheless elected without a division, as, under the procedure which applied at that time, it was held to be out of order to divide on the nomination of the Speaker if there was only one candidate.

Sir Harry Hylton-Foster was re-elected in his constituency at the general election of 1964 which was won by a very narrow margin by the Labour

Party. He was unanimously re-elected Speaker although it has been suggested that, had Labour's majority been larger, the continuity convention might have been breached. Lord Pannell, in a letter written to the author prior to the election, surmised that this was a possibility. Other members, including a Conservative, had expressed dissatisfaction with Sir Harry's performance in the Chair, not on the grounds that he was partisan, but because he was too easily worn down by aggressive and persistent members who argued with him over his rulings. Sir Harold Wilson is on record as saying that Sir Harry had been assured prior to the election that a Labour Government would wish him to continue in office[30] but this does not accord with the recollection of Sir Harry Hylton-Foster's widow who granted the author an interview in 1973. At all events Sir Harry's second tenure of office was short-lived as he died suddenly on 2 September 1965 at a time when the House was not sitting. He was the second Speaker of the century to die while in office, the same fate having overtaken Speaker Fitzroy in 1943.

Speaker Hylton-Foster was succeeded by Dr. Horace King, the first Speaker to be drawn from the ranks of the Labour Party. He was elected on 26 October 1965, ironically at a time when the government with its wafer-thin majority could ill afford to lose one of its supporters. He was unanimously endorsed by all parties and twice re-elected before retiring from the Chair in 1971 and taking his seat in the House of Lords as the first ex-Speaker to be made a life peer. The election of his successor proved to be highly controversial and demonstrated once again that the leaderships of the two major parties had failed to heed the lessons of the past and had not held any meaningful consultations with their own back benches.*

The Conservatives, who had by that time been re-elected to office, approached the Labour Party leaders with the names of two candidates, Mr. Selwyn Lloyd and Mr. John Boyd-Carpenter, both former Conservative ministers. The Labour Party had no candidate of its own to propose and expressed their preference for Selwyn Lloyd, upon which the Leader of the House, Mr. William Whitelaw, informed the press that the two front benches had reached agreement on the choice of Speaker.[31] This *fait accompli* was not allowed to pass without protest. It provoked a serious back-bench reaction and the second contested election for the speakership of the century. It took place on 12 January 1971 and Selwyn Lloyd himself has left a record of the occasion. He had not anticipated the opposition which emerged once the press became aware of his candidature, neither had he been aware that his friend, Boyd-Carpenter, was also in the running. He was, however, prepared for trouble on the day of the election which he describes as 'a dramatic and traumatic day'. He also eschewed the traditional morning coat in favour of an ordinary suit as he did not want anyone to think that he was taking the result for granted.[32]

Selwyn Lloyd was proposed and seconded, in accordance with custom, by

---

* Although the chairman of the Conservative 1922 Committee had apparently raised the matter with Selwyn Lloyd both before and after the 1970 election which was won by the Conservatives. (See Selwyn Lloyd, Mr. Speaker, Sir, pp. 17–18.)

senior Conservative and Labour backbenchers, after which a debate ensued. The first to complain of the manner in which the candidate had been chosen was John Pardoe of the Liberal Party. He was followed by a Conservative, Robin Maxwell-Hyslop, who began by challenging the practice that no division can take place if only one candidate is nominated. Having cited precedents in support of this proposition, he went on to reiterate the protest of John Pardoe, asserting the right of the House to choose its own Speaker and rejecting the principle that the choice should be influenced by the party leaderships. At the end of his speech he dropped a bomb-shell by nominating a prominent Labour backbencher, Sir Geoffrey de Freitas, as a rival candidate, explaining that he was doing this to ensure a division would take place. Sir Geoffrey, surprised and embarrassed, rose to declare his support for Selwyn Lloyd who was elected in the ensuing division by 294 votes to 55, thus revealing a sizeable body of backbench discontent.[33]*

The protest was taken seriously and it led to an investigation of the procedure for electing the Speaker by the Select Committee on Procedure. Its report, tabled on 26 January 1972, was something of a milestone in the history of the speakership as it recommended changes in the traditional procedure which had been followed for centuries. The key recommendations, which were substantially adopted by the House on 26 January 1972,[34] were that a member of the House should preside over the proceedings instead of the Clerk of the House; that he should be equipped with certain powers under the standing orders; that a division on the motion to elect a Speaker should be permissible when only one candidate is nominated; and that the new procedure should be embodied in standing orders.[35]

The Committee rejected a proposal that the Speaker be elected by secret ballot but concluded 'that the criticisms levelled against the procedure in present use for election of a Speaker are largely justified'.[36]

It recognized that its proposal that the Clerk should no longer preside 'would result in the abandonment by the House of a procedure of some antiquity', but concluded 'that the House is placed in an unduly vulnerable position while the Clerk is presiding over its proceedings' by virtue of the fact that he has no powers under the Standing Orders.[37] The Committee therefore recommended 'that the retiring Speaker should, if possible, occupy the chair until his successor is elected' and 'that on all other occasions, including the re-election of a Speaker at the beginning of a new Parliament, the Member with the longest unbroken period of service who is present in the House on the back-benches should occupy the chair at the election of a Speaker'.[38]

Two new Speakers have been elected since the new procedure has been in force, but it would be unwise to predict that no problems relating to lack of consultation are likely to arise in the future. The election of Speaker Weatherill may be regarded as a triumph for the backbenchers because,

---

* The dissidents included the late Richard Crossman, a former Leader of the House, and it was estimated that between 150 and 200 of the members present abstained from voting.

although he was elected without a contest, attempts were made by the Prime Minister to promote other candidates. Two former cabinet ministers, Francis Pym and Humphrey Atkins, were approached but both declined to be nominated. It is to be hoped, however, that party leaders, present and future, will have learned a salutary lesson from the events described above, and that the party whips, who are responsible for maintaining good communication between the leadership and the back benches, will strive to ensure that thorough and effective consultation takes place. Since the re-election of Sir Harry Hylton-Foster in 1965 the continuity principle has been further reinforced, both Selwyn Lloyd and George Thomas having been re-elected to the Chair following a change of government.

The Select Committee on Procedure made reference to the problem which can arise when a Speaker retires at the end of a Parliament. Both Speaker Clifton-Brown and Speaker Morrison adopted this course, and in both cases difficulties arose over the selection of a successor.* It is much more difficult to arrange consultations following a dissolution of Parliament, a fact which led the select committee to recommend 'that whenever possible the Speaker should retire in the middle of a session, giving at least ten days' notice of his impending retirement. They recommend that in these circumstances the retiring Speaker should if possible occupy the Chair until his successor is elected.'[39] Another problem referred to by the committee was the situation which is created when a Speaker dies while in office. The standing orders make provision for his deputies to assume his functions in the event of his unavoidable absence but no such provision is made in the event of the Speaker's death because this would be a matter for legislation. It was in anticipation of such an eventuality that on 25 February 1953 a member moved for leave to introduce a bill under the ten minutes' rule 'to provide that in the event of the Speaker's death the Chairman of Ways and Means shall temporarily exercise the authority of the Speaker'. Leave was granted by 172 votes to 149 but the bill was not proceeded with.[40] The select committee recommended similar action[41] but at the time of writing no further legislative initiative has been taken.

Although service as Chairman of Ways and Means has never conferred any prescriptive right to the speakership, it is certainly a factor which has been taken into account. James William Lowther was the first of seven Speakers to be elevated from the lower Chair during the twentieth century, the others being Speakers Whitley, Fitzroy (who was promoted directly from the deputy chairmanship), Clifton-Brown, King, Thomas and Weatherill. Lowther's previous service as Chairman of Ways and Means was referred to as one of his qualifications when he was first elected.[42] It is notable also that when Speaker Morrison was elected in 1951 one of the arguments put forward on behalf of his opponent, Major Milner, was that he had experience as Chairman of Ways and Means. On the other hand, Anthony Eden, speaking on the occasion of the election of Speaker Clifton-Brown (the fourth Speaker in succession to be

* Speaker Thomas also retired at the end of a Parliament although he had let it be known that this was his intention.

promoted from the lower Chair) in 1943 emphasized that the Chairman of Ways and Means enjoyed no right of succession to the speakership.[43] The Select Committee on Procedure endorsed this principle in 1972 when it concluded: 'Your Committee are of opinion that there should be no automatic presumption that occupancy of the posts of Chairman or Deputy Chairman of Ways and Means constitutes a qualification for the office of Speaker.'[44]

Four of the Speakers of the twentieth century had previously held ministerial office and the choice of such a candidate sometimes gives rise to controversy. The first was Speaker Morrison who had served in various governments as Financial Secretary to the Treasury, Minister of Agriculture, Chancellor of the Duchy of Lancaster, Minister of Food and Postmaster General, and in 1943 he became the first Minister of Town and Country Planning. As a minister he had not been particularly conspicuous although he had the distinction of being included in the cast of 'Guilty Men' in the celebrated book of that title published in 1940.[45] Between 1945 and 1951 when the Conservative Party was in opposition he had not been very active in the House, but his previous ministerial career was nevertheless regarded by some as an objection to his appointment as Speaker. Morrison's successor, Sir Harry Hylton-Foster, had been Solicitor General immediately preceding his election as Speaker, and although he had never held any higher offices of state the opposition criticised his appointment on these grounds. The then Leader of the Opposition, Hugh Gaitskell, drew a distinction between a Speaker who had previously held ministerial office, like Morrison, and one who moved straight from the Treasury Bench to the Chair, echoing a view which had been expressed by Gladstone in 1871.[46] Curiously enough, the Labour Party leadership did not raise similar objections in relation to the choice of Selwyn Lloyd, even though he had held some of the highest offices of state including Foreign Secretary and Chancellor of the Exchequer. His ministerial career had also been highly controversial. He was Foreign Secretary at the time of the ill-fated Suez adventure in 1956 and as Chancellor of the Exchequer he was one of the victims of Harold Macmillan's notorious cabinet 'purge' of 1962. He subsequently became Leader of the House in Sir Alec Douglas-Home's government and gained popularity because of his co-operative spirit and concern for improving the conditions of members. He became increasingly detached from party conflict, served with distinction as chairman of the House of Commons (Services) Committee and gained a reputation as a good House of Commons man. Sir Harold Wilson, who twice in 1974 had occasion to congratulate him on his re-election as Speaker, acknowledged that he had changed his opinion as to the desirability of selecting a former minister as Speaker having seen how well Selwyn Lloyd conducted himself in that office.[47] Some backbenchers thought otherwise when he was first elected in 1971, the fact that he was a former minister being one of the grounds of protest voiced by those who opposed his nomination. The Select Committee on Procedure which in 1972 considered this factor among others did not find 'that the doubts of witnesses as to the fitness for the Chair of former Ministers have been realized. They agree, however, with the views expressed by Mr.

Gladstone and Mr. Gaitskell that the Speaker should not be elected direct from the Treasury Bench.'[48] Mr. Speaker Thomas came to the Chair as both a former Chairman of Ways and Means and a former Minister, having held several offices including that of Secretary of State for Wales. No objections were raised on either count when he was elected to the Chair.

The conventions on which the British speakership is founded have thus successfully withstood the pressures which have surfaced from time to time, and although they cannot be said to be invulnerable they have assuredly not been weakened in recent years. It is unlikely that the lower Chair will ever be ruled out as a training ground for future Speakers or that former ministers will ever be disqualified as candidates. It can be expected that Speakers seeking re-election will continue to be opposed in their constituencies, sometimes by officially sponsored party candidates, but if past experience is any guide it will not prove easy to unseat them. Candidates for the speakership are invariably senior members who have held their seats for many years. Should such a defeat occur, or should a new government ever have second thoughts about continuing a sitting Speaker in office, a further enquiry into the Speaker's status and method of his election might well result. The Select Committee on Procedure in 1972 emphasized the importance of consultation, and if their counsel is followed most of the problems which have arisen in the past are unlikely to surface in the future.

The Strains and Stresses of the Office

The great responsibilities carried by the Speaker impose great strains, principal among which appear to be the denial of private life and the adverse effect upon health. Speaker Lowther referred to the stresses of the office in his subsequent memoirs,[49] and there is no evidence to indicate they have in any way diminished since his day. Speaker King described them to the author as 'unimaginable' although Speaker Lloyd acknowledged that the appointment of a third deputy, coupled with the fact that the Speaker's deputies are now empowered to accept the closure in the House, had somewhat eased the burden. Speaker Hylton-Foster's widow expressed the view that the pressures of the office contributed to his early death and that the health of her father, Speaker Clifton-Brown, was visibly declining when he retired in 1951. There is no question that considerable sacrifices are required by any member who accepts appointment as Speaker.

Every incumbent since the turn of the century has made a personal impact on the development of the office. While all have consistently upheld its traditions they have nevertheless modified its character in certain respects. It was said of Speaker Lowther that he carried impartiality to a fine art by bringing wit and urbanity to bear on the discharge of his duties. His predecessors had tended to be grave and humourless, but Lowther was able to unbend without ever losing dignity. His tenure of office spanned a momentous era. It included the great constitutional crisis which culminated in the curtailing of the powers of the House of Lords by the Parliament Act of

1911 which imposed certain statutory duties on the Speaker, notably in relation to the certification of money bills.[50] It covered the First World War, the continuing conflict over Irish Home Rule and the most active period of the Suffragette movement. He was the first Speaker to chair a conference on electoral reform and was in the Chair when the first woman eventually took her seat in the House of Commons in 1918. He had a reputation for kindliness although this view was not entirely shared by all who served under his speakership.[51]

John Henry Whitley, who succeeded Lowther in 1921, was somewhat more self-effacing. Although not a forceful Speaker he was knowledgeable and fastidious in the application of his procedural responsibilities. Although his tenure of office was comparatively short he was re-elected no less than three times in consequence of three general elections in as many years. His speakership witnessed the partition of Ireland and the achievement of Home Rule for the South; the advent of the first Labour Government; the General Strike; and the final enfranchisement of women on the same terms as men. Lord Pannell tells a story illustrating the humanity of Whitley, who presided over the House at a time when distressing social conditions existed in the country.

> He was Speaker when there was a great new influx of Labour Members in 1922. In those days Mr. Speaker held levees. To attend was a command – only a Royal Command took precedence. Guests were expected to wear Court dress, uniforms, or at least full evening dress. The new Labour Members had come from factory, mine and mill and even the "unemployment" Exchange. One of them approached Speaker Whitley and asked to be excused. When asked "Why?", he replied, "Mr. Speaker, I stand in my only suit – this is my best suit." Mr. Speaker Whitley replied: "Then come in your best suit; no man can expect more than another man's best. I would be honoured to receive you – but you will come." Speakers' levees are a thing of the past. But the memory of Speaker Whitley's courtesy and humanity remains with old-timers.[52]

Whitley was succeeded by Edward Algernon Fitzroy on 25 June 1929. He was three times re-elected, dying in office on 3 March 1943, and was Speaker at the time of the financial crisis of 1931, the Abdication crisis of 1936, the Munich crisis of 1938, the outbreak of the Second World War in 1939 and the destruction of the House of Commons Chamber by German bombs in 1941. He was an authoritarian Speaker, probably because of his military background, and both Lord Hailsham and Lord Tranmire, who served under him, spoke of his methods to the author with approval. The former is on record as saying 'that the Speaker must be a little bit a man to be afraid of. You have got to be rather frightened of the Speaker in the House of Commons if you really want the House to be at its best. I have known Speakers who in the end go bad because they wanted to be loved too much. This is not at all possible. The Speaker is only loved when he is dead or retires. He has got to be a man whom we should be a little bit afraid of.'[53] No Speaker since Fitzroy has attempted to rule the House with quite such a rod of iron, and both Speaker King and Speaker Lloyd have expressed their view to the author that to do so in this day and age would be an inappropriate approach to the duties of the Chair.

Douglas Clifton-Brown, another soldier, succeeded Fitzroy on 9 March 1943 but was a very different Speaker from his predecessor — in fact he has been criticized as being too lax when dealing with an unruly House. He favoured a policy of flexibility, perhaps not altogether imprudently when one considers that it fell to him to preside over the first post-war House of Commons, a House whose composition had been considerably revolutionized by the electoral landslide of 1945. The Labour Party had never before won an overwhelming majority and many new members were returned to the House, eager for social reform but ignorant of parliamentary tradition and perhaps irreverently disposed towards it. An experienced hand was needed which would serve as a constant reminder of the dignity of Parliament. At the same time it was incumbent upon a Conservative Speaker to demonstrate his total impartiality to the supporters of the new regime, and to show himself as the protector of their rights no less than the rights of those in opposition.

It was Clifton-Brown who introduced the practice of explaining and justifying his rulings, no doubt with a view to instructing new members in the intricacies of parliamentary procedure. However, this opens the door to argument, and the tendency of members to argue with the Chair and thus expose it to the procedural tactics of insistent members can be traced to his speakership. His most trying period of office was probably during the short-lived Parliament of 1950–51, at the end of his speakership, when the Labour government struggled to carry on with the precarious majority of six. The bitter political rivalry between the evenly balanced parties led to long, arduous and often unruly sittings and frequent procedural disputes in which the Speaker was constantly being called upon to arbitrate. It was at this period that the firm hand of Fitzroy might probably have been seen to advantage.

William Shepherd Morrison restored some measure of discipline to the conduct of debate, although he continued his predecessor's practice of explaining his rulings. On one occasion the entire half-hour set aside for the daily adjournment debate at the end of the day (one of the opportunities greatly cherished by private members) was lost because various members persisted in challenging one of his decisions.[54] However, conscious as he was of having come to the Chair through a contested election, he determined to show his authority by dealing firmly with those who violated the rules of order, and found that those members who felt the weight of his discipline were among those who appreciated him best. Morrison possessed the physical attributes of an imposing Speaker and it has been said that Winston Churchill favoured him for the position because he looked the part!

Sir Harry Hylton-Foster very much wanted to be liked and sought to achieve this by being lenient. It is said that he found the responsibilities of the Chair very distressing and that he was in the habit of writing to members he was unable to call in debate in order to explain and apologize to them. Lord

Pannell has acknowledged that nobody tried harder to be a good Speaker, but his leniency gained him little popularity and was undoubtedly at the root of the criticisms levelled against him. He may well have felt that the speakership was not his metier as he had hoped to become Lord Chancellor, an office for which his distinguished legal career would have eminently fitted him. He had accepted the speakership out of a sense of duty when approached by Harold Macmillan but probably never felt completely at home in the role.

Horace Maybray King was undoubtedly the most unconventional of Speakers, being possessed of a great sense of fun which endeared him to many but was not approved of by all. He enjoyed entertaining children and playing the piano on social occasions, and he must have found the social isolation in which the Speaker is expected to exist most trying. He is on record as suggesting that it may have been carried too far.[55] The traditions of Westminster are deeply rooted, however, and when he proposed to take his meals occasionally in the Members' Dining Room at the table reserved for the Clerks he was dissuaded from doing so by a delegation of senior members. He was, nevertheless, a firm Speaker and knew how to exercise authority, particularly if the House became unruly. Neither did he shrink from imposing his disciplinary powers if he felt there was no other course.

Selwyn Lloyd restored the speakership to its more conventional pattern although most commentators consulted by the author regarded him as weaker than his predecessor in the exercise of his authority. He was far more flexible than Speaker King in his control of the question period and he has been criticised for his handling of two incidents: the assault by Bernadette Devlin on the Home Secretary on 31 January 1972 and the menacing of the Leader of the Liberal Party by a group of Labour members after the vote on the second reading of the European Communities Bill on 17 February 1972. In neither case did he impose any disciplinary sanction. On the other side of the coin he was very firm in adhering to decisions once he had taken them, and on one occasion ran into severe criticism for refusing to hear points of order. Explanations of his handling of these and other incidents occurring during his speakership are to be found in his book and may perhaps be seen to vindicate his actions.[56]

Different again was the personality of Speaker George Thomas, a man who combined warm humanity with natural dignity, and whose resonant Welsh-accented voice became familiar to those who listen to the radio broadcasts of House of Commons debates, first introduced in 1978. The second Speaker to be drawn from the ranks of the Labour Party, he brought a long experience of chairmanship to the Speaker's office and demonstrated at the very outset of his speakership that he was firmly in command. He re-established a tight control over the question period and made clear his disapproval of all tasteless language even if the expressions used were not strictly unparliamentary. He was not a Speaker who could be intimidated and he sternly resisted all attempts to influence him when crucial decisions had to be rendered. Yet, he probably enjoyed more personal popularity than any other Speaker of the century. He inspired the love as well as the respect of the House and this was evident in the tributes which were paid to him in the House on 12 May 1983, the day before Parliament was dissolved. Mrs. Margaret Thatcher, in the course of her speech on this occasion, described him as a legend in his lifetime.

In the maintenance of order the Speaker has certain sanctions available to him which are set out in Standing Orders 23-27 (1983 edition). Standing Order 23 empowers the Speaker to order a member who persists in irrelevance or tedious repetition to discontinue his speech, a rule which, needless to say, was never intended to be rigidly imposed. Its purpose is to counter obstruction and it was one of the disciplinary measures introduced in the 1880's to counter the obstructive tactics of the Irish Nationalists. Irrelevance and repetition are frequent ingredients of parliamentary debate and a Speaker who interpreted the rule too literally would be continually intervening and be none too popular.[57] Speaker King once commented on the manner in which the Chair should use its discretion in the exercise of this power:

> The scope of debate varies to some extent with the person. If some innocent person wanders out of order I hope that none of my colleagues will call him to order too soon. I hope they will remember the advice I received from a very old parliamentarian: If a Member gets out of order, let him say something of what he wants to say before you call him back to order. If someone, however, is deliberately using this means and is going out of order to frustrate the work of Parliament, if he is making a speech which is designed to obstruct, then I would say: Apply the rules of order strictly and tie him down to the last sentence and the last comma.[58]

Standing Order 24 empowers the Speaker to order a member whose conduct is grossly disorderly to withdraw from the House for the remainder of the day's sitting. The same order together with Standing Order 25 make provision for the severer sanction consequent upon the 'naming' of a member. In naming a member the Chair draws the attention of the House to his conduct and it is the House that imposes the penalty, namely suspension from the service of the House for five days in the case of a first offence, or as otherwise specified in Standing Order 25. The Standing Order places a clear obligation on the House to move for a member's suspension once he has been named, but although the motion is invariably carried it is usually taken to a division. Its rejection would amount to a severe rebuff to the Speaker's authority, although this does not discourage some members from demonstrating their loyalty to an offending colleague no matter how much he may be in the wrong. On 10 November 1937, for example, a Member who had refused to withdraw from the House when ordered to do so was named, but he proceeded to withdraw before the question on the motion for his suspension had been put. The Speaker was about to exercise leniency when the Member from beyond the Bar of the House addressed the Chair in the most intemperate language. The Speaker then put the question and the motion for the Member's suspension was carried. After the division had been taken a point of order was raised calling for an explanation as to why the motion for the Member's suspension was moved after he had left the House. The Speaker explained that he had been prepared to withdraw his naming of the Member until the Member had turned and offered insults to the Chair. One of the named Member's sympathizers pointed out, rather feebly, that the insults had been offered from beyond the Bar of the House, in reply to which the Speaker made it clear that this fact made no difference to the case. It is noteworthy that in spite of the fact that the Member's behaviour fully justified his suspension, no less than 104 Members voted against it.[59]

No Speaker will name a member unless he is driven to it. Speaker Lloyd never named a member throughout his tenure of office. Speaker King came to the Chair determined that he would never do so but found that he had no choice on one occasion. The incident, which took place on 23 May 1968[60] was the first in sixteen years to lead to the naming of a member, and Lord Maybray King informed the author that the occasion had been very distressing for him. Speaker Thomas was forced to invoke his disciplinary powers more frequently than his immediate predecessors. During the 1980–81 session he was obliged to name a member on three different occasions, two of which involved the same member who established a record by being named twice in one session. Since 1945 to the time of writing members have been named on 32 occasions in all. Perhaps disorderly behaviour has become more frequent in recent years because Speaker Thomas told the House on one occasion that he had been inundated with complaints from the public about the lack of decorum in the House.

If grave disorder arises in the House — that is to say, disorder of a general nature — the Speaker is empowered under Standing Order 27 to adjourn the House or suspend the sitting. This power was invoked for the first time on 22 May 1905 by Lowther when acting as Deputy Speaker and since then the Chair has regularly had occasion to resort to it. It is a particularly useful power as it allows the Speaker to suspend business for a short period to allow tempers to cool, without taking action against individual members. Furthermore, circumstances of grave disorder are sometimes engineered for publicity purposes and such tactics may be effectively frustrated by a temporary suspension of business.

No matter what precautions he may take to distance himself from controversy, the Speaker cannot avoid situations in which he is required to rule on highly sensitive issues. Of the many incidents which could be cited, three have been selected to illustrate the kind of problems which Speakers may be called upon to face and the manner in which the Speakers concerned dealt with them.

The first concerns the case of the reluctant peer, Mr. Anthony Wedgwood Benn, who, having been disqualified from membership of the House of Commons by reason of succession to a peerage, was readopted as the Labour Party candidate in his vacant constituency and re-elected by an impressive majority. On 5 May 1961 he arrived at the House to take his seat but was refused entry to the chamber by order of Speaker Hylton-Foster. On 8 May the Speaker read to the House a letter he had received from Wedgwood Benn requesting to be heard at the bar of the House. The Speaker ruled that this was a matter for the decision of the House as he was bound by a resolution of the previous 13 April confirming that Benn had ceased to be a member by virtue of his peerage.[61] He thus had the unenviable task of barring from the House a duly elected candidate for a constituency in order to uphold a constitutional anachronism. He may well have had misgivings as the House is seldom seen at its best when it comes into conflict with individuals. The matter was eventually resolved with the passage of the Peerage Act, 1963, which permitted peerages to be disclaimed. Wedgwood Benn was the first to take advantage of the Act and he eventually returned to the House of Commons.

The second case concerned Lord Lambton who, having disclaimed the peerages he inherited from his father on 23 February 1970, sought the right to continue to use his former courtesy title as a member of the House of Commons. Speaker King, who sought the advice of Garter King at Arms among others, decided he could not accede to the request. The reasoning behind the decision was to the effect that although courtesy titles have no status in law, the disclaimer of a peerage involves the renunciation 'of all right or interest to or in the peerage, and all titles, rights, offices, privileges and precedence attaching thereto'[62] and that courtesy titles are therefore included in the disclaimer. Prior to the general election of June 1970 Lambton was warned by the Speaker and the Clerk of the House that he risked disqualification from the House if he styled himself 'Lord Lambton' on his nomination papers. Lambton disregarded the advice and later informed the Speaker that he was contemplating legal action against him for threatening his election prospects.[63]

Lambton was re-elected, the words 'commonly called Lord Lambton' having appeared after his name on the ballot paper, and the question remained in abeyance until after the retirement of Speaker King who declined to entertain any further communication on the matter. With a new Speaker in the Chair, Lambton decided to renew his request, and Speaker Lloyd, having engaged in consultations of his own, took a different view of the matter. On 7 February 1972 he stated: 'In my view the practice of the House is that hon. Members should be called and described as they wish, and as they are known in their constituencies. I have therefore decided to accede to this request.' He added in answer to points of order that the question had been put to his predecessor 'in rather different terms' and that he was 'not pronouncing on courtesy titles'.[64]

Some members interviewed thought it remarkable that a Speaker should have reversed the ruling of his predecessor in the course of the same Parliament. One of them, Charles Pannell, immediately tabled a motion dissenting from the new ruling and another denying the right of Lord Lambton to be thus styled. On 9 March the question was referred to the Committee of Privileges which brought in a report declaring 'that to allow the honourable Member to be known in the House by the style which he claims would create an undesirable precedent.'[65] There the matter has since rested and been overtaken by completely unrelated events which resulted in Lambton's total withdrawal from public life.

In 1976 Speaker Thomas was faced with a highly technical question having far-reaching political implications. The then government had introduced a bill for the nationalization of the aircraft and shipbuilding industries, a highly controversial measure which had advanced beyond a bitterly fought committee stage when a point of order was raised to the effect that it was a hybrid bill. A hybrid bill is a public bill which affects private rights and is therefore subject to a special procedure. From the government's point of view the raising of the point of order threatened a major piece of legislation with serious delay and a consequent disruption of its parliamentary programme. On 25 May the Speaker ruled that the bill was not hybrid but on the following day, new information having been introduced, he reversed his decision.[66] The subsequent means adopted by the government to secure passage of the bill and the political acrimony thus engendered need not concern us here. The importance of the matter in the context of this study is that it illustrates the manner in which the Speaker must approach his duties. His decision was taken on procedural grounds alone, no other considerations being allowed to influence his ruling. He was no doubt involved in the most agonising deliberations and it is known, from a comment made by the Leader of the House in the course of debate, that ministerial representations on the subject were made to him.[67] We can suppose that they emphasized the effect on the industries and those employed in them which a delay in the legislation would have. But Speaker Thomas understood, as would all good Speakers, that such matters are the concern of government, not the concern of the Chair.

Even when the Speaker retires he can find himself at the centre of controversy and this has happened five times since 1895. On the first four occasions the representatives of the Labour movement in Parliament moved the reduction of the retiring Speaker's pension from £4000 to £1000 on the ground that such a pension was not justified in view of the depressed conditions of the working classes. The motion was first made by Keir Hardie on 23 April 1895 following the retirement of Speaker Peel. He drew attention to the fact that no system of pensions existed for the aged workers of the country, but on this occasion his was a lone voice and he could not even find a co-teller.[68] On 21 June 1905 he repeated his stand and moved an amendment to the financial resolution preceding the introduction of Mr. Speaker Gully's Retirement Bill, protesting that '£4000 was too much for one individual, and any sum was too much to pay to an official of that House so long as they could not find any sum, however small, to vote as pensions to aged workmen, of whom there were thousands'.[69] The amendment was lost by 245 to 17.[70] On 3 May 1921 a similar amendment was proposed to the financial resolution relating to the retirement of Speaker Lowther and was defeated by 248 to 31.[71] By the time Speaker Whitley came to retire the Labour Party had become the official Opposition and the regular protest against the Speaker's pension well established as a matter of party principle. On 27 June 1928 a similar amendment was moved to the financial resolution proposing Whitley's pension and on this occasion was lost by the much less substantial margin of 224 to 103.[72] In 1951 Speaker Clifton Brown was voted his pension without dissent, the social circumstances of the country having changed markedly after 23 years.

Speaker Morrison's pension was opposed for an entirely different reason. Shortly after his retirement as Speaker he was appointed Governor-General of Australia and his acceptance of this office was deplored by certain members of the Labour Party who held the view that a retiring Speaker should retire completely from public life. Speaker Morrison himself was unmoved by this argument. According to his widow he had no idea when he decided to retire as Speaker that he was going to be offered the governor generalship of Australia, although some of his critics believed that he had had advance knowledge. The then Australian Prime Minister, Robert Menzies, who was a personal friend of the family, deliberately waited until after the election of Morrison's successor before putting forward the proposition.[73]

The matter was first raised in the House on 12 November 1959 when the financial resolution was introduced, and again on the following 18 November when the second reading of Mr. Speaker Morrison's Retirement Bill was moved. The resolution was adopted without a division but in the second debate the dissenting members pressed their objections to the point of voting against the bill. A large minority opposed second reading which was carried by 300 to 155. There was a further short debate at the committee stage of the bill although no further divisions took place.[74]

The Speaker in the Chair

It is in the Chair that the Speaker fulfils his primary duties which are derived partly from custom and partly from the standing orders. The first major item of business on every sitting day except Friday is the question period and its regulation is one of the Chair's many crucial responsibilities. It occupies the greater part of the first hour of the parliamentary day and is subject to various conditions which are set out in standing order 8.[75] Notice is required of all questions and if an oral answer is desired it is distinguished by an asterisk, supplementary questions following the minister's answer being permitted at the discretion of the Speaker. Ministers take their turns to answer questions on specified days and questions are grouped accordingly, although the grouping is not a matter for which the Chair is responsible. The Speaker's control of the question period is exercised largely by convention and his key duty is the control of supplementary questions. At one time they were regarded as being out of order and when Speaker Gully occupied the Chair they were frowned on almost as a matter of principle.[76] Under his successor the attitude of the Chair relaxed considerably and today they are the essence of the question period, many an innocent-seeming main question being simply a peg for a barbed supplementary. Comparing the methods of four Speakers under whom he sat, Earl Winterton commented as follows:

> In the summer of 1928 Mr. Speaker Whitley retired and was succeeded by the Chairman of Committees, Mr. FitzRoy, who proved to be a very great Speaker. Soon after he was elected to the Chair, he stated one day that there were far too many supplementary questions, as this meant that

members with oral questions some way down on the list had little chance of getting them answered which was unfair to them. He announced that he would have to take steps to curtail the number of supplementary questions. His action raises an interesting point as to what should be the attitude of the Speaker towards undue delay over questions, through the insistence of members on asking supplementary questions. On more than one occasion Mr. Speaker Clifton Brown when his attention was called to the matter, said that the remedy was in the hands of the House, and apparently, the present Speaker takes the same view; but both Mr. Speaker Lowther and Mr. Speaker FitzRoy believed that they had a duty to ensure that a reasonable number of questions were answered each day, and both of them were more strict in preventing lengthy or unnecessary supplementaries than either of their successors have been. It would be improper and impertinent for me to say which school of opinion is right, but that there is a contrast between them is clear from looking at the average number of oral questions answered today compared with the number answered when Mr. Speaker Lowther or Mr. Speaker FitzRoy were in the Chair.[77]

Speaker King was said to regulate questions 'by the clock' and aimed to get through as many as possible. Speaker Lloyd, on the other hand, tended to allow a question to be pursued at some length through supplementaries if the House showed an interest in it. He took the view that question time is made too easy for ministers if supplementaries are curtailed too much. Although it has always been assumed that supplementary questions are a matter of tolerance and not of right, Speaker King, giving evidence before the Select Committee on Procedure on 11 February 1970, suggested that it was no longer possible to tell a member that the right did not exist. Speaker Clifton Brown initiated the practice of allowing as a matter of right the first supplementary to the member asking the original question,[78] and Speaker King suggested in his evidence that the situation had developed to the point where the opposite side of the House was claiming an automatic right to put an additional supplementary. He pointed out that the supplementary was 'very often far more important than the original question' and expressed the view that 'once the original question is asked, it becomes the possession of the House'.[79]

One of the cardinal rules relating to questions is that they must seek information only on matters falling within ministerial responsibility. However, the Speaker cannot compel a minister to answer a question, neither does he determine to which minister a question should be addressed. Erskine May lists numerous examples of questions which are inadmissible[80] and the Speaker must do his best to ensure that supplementary questions conform to these principles. Some questions attract more supplementaries than others and some could well launch a 'free-for-all' if the Chair were too flexible.* The

---

* On 23 April 1980 Speaker Thomas announced that he would refuse to call supplementary questions on questions asking a minister about his meetings or

Speaker constantly appeals to members and ministers to keep their questions and answers as short as possible and when he considers that a matter has been sufficiently aired he will cut short the barrage of supplementaries by calling the name of the member whose question is the next on the notice paper. At one time the question period was frequently interrupted by the raising of points of order, but the current practice is to hold over points of order until the end of questions to avoid cutting into the limited time available.[81] The Speaker may in his discretion receive a private notice question – that is to say a question which does not appear on the notice paper but of which he and the minister concerned have received notice – and which, if allowed, may be asked at the end of the question period. Apart from the weekly business question asked every Thursday normally by the Leader of the Opposition, a private notice question must be justified by urgency, the Speaker being the sole judge as to its admissibility.

There are certain items of routine business which, if they arise, would be taken immediately after prayers and before the question period. These items include formal communications by the Speaker to the House, as when he reads the contents of a letter from an external authority, or when he announces the death of a member. If any ministerial statements are to be made they immediately follow questions and may be regarded to some extent as an extension of the question period. Although they may not be debated, since no motion is before the House, it is an accepted practice that a minister may be questioned on a statement and the potentialities thus afforded can readily be imagined. The exchanges which ensue upon a ministerial statement are very often tantamount to a debate and their regulation calls for very careful judgment on the Speaker's part.

Standing order 10 provides a mechanism for the holding of emergency debates and a member wishing to launch such a debate would seek leave to do so following questions and ministerial statements. Any member, in the words of the standing order, 'may propose to move the adjournment of the House for the purpose of discussing a specific and important matter that should have urgent consideration'. The leave of the Speaker is required before the motion can be proceeded with and it is his duty to decide whether the request conforms to the conditions envisaged by the standing order. If he allows the motion it requires in addition the support of at least forty members which they signify by rising in their places. The procedure dates from the period of Irish Nationalist obstruction and was first embodied in a standing order on 27 November 1882. When first introduced it was a restriction on the rights of private members but today, given the government's control of the parliamentary timetable, it has become a means of protecting their rights. It is one of the areas of procedure where the Speaker's decision may affect the order of

---

Footnote continued from p. 89

appointments. Such questions were frequently used as a peg for asking a wide range of supplementaries and to circumvent some of the rules governing questions. See Commons Hansard, 5th. series, vol. 983, cols. 459–63.

business. The standing order provides that such a motion, if allowed, shall stand over until the commencement of public business on the following day unless the Speaker directs, in view of the urgency of the matter, that it be taken at 7 o'clock the same day.

Until the standing order was revised in 1967 it was interpreted with ever-increasing restrictiveness. Prior to the revision the motion was made for the purpose of discussing 'a definite matter of urgent public importance' and each word of this phrase acquired an ever-narrowing interpretation in the light of successive rulings of the Chair. A classic instance of the restrictiveness with which the criteria were applied was cited in a memorandum prepared for the Select Committee on Procedure by the Clerk of the House on 25 February 1966. A request for an emergency debate on the defence of Singapore shortly before its fall in 1942 was refused on the ground that the matter had been urgent for some time and was to be debated the following week.[82] The same memorandum gave a detailed description of the criteria which had customarily been applied by the Chair on the basis of the precedents which had been accumulated since the first introduction of the rule. The Select Committee on Procedure for which the memorandum was prepared addressed itself to the question and heard evidence from the then Speaker, Horace King. Speaker King stressed that the Speaker would require very precise guidelines before he would feel able to depart from the rulings of his predecessors. The committee agreed and came to the conclusion that the problem lay in the continued use of the formula, 'definite matter of urgent public importance', each word of which had come to acquire a particular significance in the light of past rulings. The committee recommended the adoption of the formula currently in use, 'specific and important matter that should have urgent consideration', not for any special significance contained in these words, but to relieve the Speaker from being bound by the precedents based on the previous formula. The committee further recommended that the new standing order should prohibit the Speaker from stating reasons for his decisions since explanations tend to add to the force of precedent. The committee's recommendations were adopted[83] and the new standing order has allowed the Speaker to exercise a wider discretion. Since it was adopted about four emergency debates have taken place during each session.

Among other items of business which, if they arise, are taken before the orders of the day are proceeded with are personal explanations and questions of privilege. Personal explanations may be made by a minister who has resigned or a private member whose conduct has been impugned. They may not be debated and must be strictly limited to the circumstances which are the subject of the explanation. The leave of the Speaker is required and he has ruled that a personal explanation may not be used as a means of attacking another member.[84] A member wishing to raise a question of privilege must give written notice to the Speaker at the earliest opportunity and the Speaker will decide whether the matter merits precedence over other business. If he so decides he will allow the member to raise the matter in the House before the commencement of public business on a subsequent day. This procedure, introduced in 1978, replaced the former practice whereby any member could raise a question of privilege prior to the orders of the day and the House and the Speaker were obliged to hear him out before the latter ruled as to whether or not the complaint should have precedence. This is another area of procedure in which the Speaker's discretion may affect the order of business. The new procedure saves the time of the House by allowing the Speaker to screen all questions of privilege before they can be raised on the floor of the House. It provides a means of eliminating trivial complaints and according precedence only to those of importance and substance. It places a heavy responsibility on the Speaker, since the right of a member to raise matters of privilege is fundamental, and Speaker Thomas has observed 'that the new system at Westminster could operate only where the office of Speaker has developed on Westminster lines'.[85]

It is important to emphasize that the Speaker is not the judge of whether a breach of privilege or contempt of Parliament has been committed. His function is limited to deciding whether or not the matter is sufficiently important to be given precedence over other business, and if he so decides it is normally referred to the Committee of Privileges, the House taking no further action until the committee has reported. If the Speaker declines to accord the matter precedence, it is open to the member concerned to proceed with his complaint by way of notice of motion, although it is unlikely that time would ever be found to debate it. In reaching a decision the Speaker has regard to the findings of the Committee of Privileges in previous cases, the right of fair comment which should be enjoyed by the press and public in a free country, and the availability of other remedies (e.g., through the courts if a member feels he has been libelled). The guiding principle is that privilege should be used as sparingly as possible, that its purpose is to protect the House, its members and its servants from obstruction, intimidation and undue interference in the fulfilment of their functions, and that it is not designed to place members of Parliament in a privileged category enjoying advantages which are not shared by other citizens.[86]

There are two other occasions when the Speaker's discretion determines the business to be discussed. These occur whenever the House adjourns for one of its regular holiday recesses and also every Thursday when he selects the subject to be discussed during the daily adjournment motion which occupies the final half-hour of each sitting. These are private members' occasions. Before each recess one whole day is devoted to the discussion of topics selected by private members, a motion for the adjournment of the House being the peg to which this series of debates is attached. The Speaker decides which of the topics proposed for debate shall be selected and the time to be allocated to each one. The half-hour debate on the daily adjournment motion is another private members' opportunity for which the competition is keen, and in 1955 a new system was introduced whereby members balloted for the right to choose the topic on three days a week and the topic was selected by the Speaker on two days a week. Since 1960 the Speaker has chosen the subject on Thursdays only and the ballot operates on the other four days of the week.[87]

A number of powers are vested in the Speaker which are designed to curtail debate and counter obstruction. Most of them were initiated in the 1880's and resulted from the obstructive tactics of the Irish Nationalists. Today they form a basic part of the machinery of modern procedure without which the House would never be able to complete its business. Prominent among these devices is the closure, first imposed on the initiative of Speaker Brand on 2 February 1881 as we have seen. Under modern practice any member may claim to move 'That the question be now put', although it is normally moved on behalf of the government by one of their whips. Under the rule[88] the question cannot be put if the Speaker believes that 'such motion is an abuse of the rules of the House, or an infringement of the rights of the minority' and his discretion in the matter is absolute. If he allows the motion the question is put without amendment or debate and is carried only if not less than 100 members vote in the majority supporting the motion. If a closure motion is carried the question which was under debate is put immediately and, with the assent of the Chair, any further question may be put which may be requisite to bring the matter before the House to a decision. The authority of the Speaker is thus an important safeguard in the operation of the closure procedure. As one author has commented, 'The mere knowledge that the power exists prevents the closure being demanded if there is any likelihood that the Chair would refuse it.'[89]

Where government bills are concerned the operation of closure has become fairly routine because, unless other arrangements are made through 'the usual channels', it is an accepted practice that debate on the second reading of a government bill should not occupy more than one sitting day. Different considerations apply where private members' bills are concerned because the acceptance of closure can make all the difference to the prospects of such a bill reaching the statute book. However, if the Chair were to accept a closure motion on a private member's bill it might prove difficult to muster the necessary 100 members required to vote with the majority because normally the attendance of members is relatively sparse when private members' business is before the House. Acceptance of a closure motion by the Chair in relation to government business is a virtual guarantee that it will be carried provided the whips do their job, so that the decision inevitably involves the Speaker in favouring one side against the other and he has not always managed to avoid criticism. At least twice during this century the Speaker has had a censure motion moved against him for having allowed a closure motion.[90] There have also been occasions when the Speaker's refusal to accept a closure motion has been disputed.[91] Disputes concerning the closure are relatively rare, however, and it is notable that in 1971 the power to accept a closure motion was extended to the Speaker's deputies, a reform which has gone far to relieve the personal pressure on the Speaker.

The Speaker is empowered to control dilatory motions – motions for the adjournment of the House or of the debate – when he considers them to be an abuse of the rules of the House.[92] Prior to the reforms of the 1880's they were frequently used for obstructive purposes but this is no longer possible under modern procedure. Also vested in the Chair is the power to refuse a division which is unnecessarily claimed,[93] a power which is rarely invoked because very few divisions are called 'frivolously or vexatiously' to use the words of the original standing order of 1888. Speaker Lloyd invoked the power on 1 July 1975 when the Liberal Party gave notice of its intention to call divisions on each of twenty amendments at the report stage of the government's Industry Bill, a proceeding which would have consumed many hours of parliamentary time. After one division had resulted in a vote of 222 to 13 the Speaker twice invoked the standing order, but following an intervention by the Government Chief Whip he agreed to a compromise whereby he allowed the Liberal Party two further divisions.[94]

Another important discretionary responsibility of the Speaker is his power to select amendments. While it is yet another method of curtailing debate, it is a power more consistent with the Speaker's impartial role than his control over the acceptance of closure motions. A decision with regard to closure is bound to favour one side against the other, while in the selection of amendments the Speaker is better able to take into account the feelings on all sides of the House and to give precedence to those amendments which represent the leading sections of opinion. The power was first introduced in limited form in 1909 and became a permanent power of the Chair in 1919. Under current practice[95] it is exercised in the House by the Speaker and, if the business of supply is under consideration, by the Deputy Speaker also. In Committee of the whole House it is exercised by the Chairman of Ways and Means and his deputies and in standing committees by the chairman. The responsibility is an onerous one although various principles exist for the guidance of the Chair. It is very unlikely, for example, that the Speaker would accept at the report stage of a bill an amendment which had been disposed of in committee, although exceptions are sometimes made if they raise principles of particular importance.[96] In determining the importance of amendments and the degree of support which they command the Speaker has unlimited freedom to consult, and he may call on a member to give an explanation of the purpose of an amendment. He will take account of amendments which raise new points while being on guard against those masquerading as new points while simply re-hashing points which have been disposed of. He will take account of what a member may wish to say and determine whether it would be possible for him to make his point while speaking to another amendment. By taking all such precautions the Chair has succeeded over the years in exercising this very crucial responsibility to the general satisfaction of the House, although there have been two occasions in committee of the whole House when motions of censure against the Chairman were debated because he declined to accept certain amendments.[97]

Important discretionary powers repose in the Chair in respect of anticipation and the raising of matters twice in the same session. Broadly speaking a question on which the House has come to a decision may not be raised again during the same session and a motion which anticipates a matter already standing on the order paper is out of order. But there are many considerations to take into account in the application of these rules and only general principles exist for the guidance of the Chair.[98] For example, a bill and a motion may raise a similar question but each has a form and purpose which is distinct from the other. Two bills may overlap each other in content but whether or not they are substantially the same for the purposes of the rule raises some complex considerations. The principle relating to anticipation is more straightforward as it is based on the effectiveness of the proceeding. For example a motion may not anticipate a bill because the latter leads to a more concrete result. Similarly a substantive motion is a more effective proceeding than a motion for the adjournment of the House or an amendment. At one time the mere fact that a matter stood upon the order paper was sufficient to prevent its being anticipated but the misuse of 'blocking' motions is now prevented by a rule which allows the Speaker to have regard to the probability of the matter being brought before the House within a reasonable time before deciding whether the rule against anticipation should apply.[99] The discretion of the Speaker is therefore wide and the flexibility with which the anticipation rule can be interpreted is well illustrated by the rulings of Speaker Clifton-Brown concerning the Bretton Woods Agreement on 12 and 13 December 1945.[100]

The Speaker is the arbiter of the *sub judice* convention, another area of onerous responsibility. It is an accepted principle that a matter awaiting judicial decision should not be referred to in debate or form the subject of a motion or a question to a minister if there is any danger of prejudicial effect. While simple to state, the principle is less easy to apply because of the many considerations which may affect its interpretation. It is important to emphasize that the convention was neither a rule nor a prohibition and prior to 1963 no attempt had been made to codify it. It was a voluntary restraint accepted by Parliament in the interests of justice and fair play, based on precedents dating back to 1844, its interpretation resting with the Chair. It has never applied to debates on bills because Parliament's right to legislate must not be limited. Speaker Clifton Brown gave a private ruling to this effect in 1949.[101] It does, however, apply to motions for leave to bring in bills under the 'ten minutes rule'[102] and this was specified in the resolution adopted by the House on 23 July 1963.[103]

The current practice is governed by the resolutions of the House of 23 July 1963 and 28 June 1972 which, while providing guidelines, leave the ultimate responsibility with the Speaker.[104] It is relatively straightforward to apply in criminal cases, less so in relation to civil cases and the proceedings of tribunals and statutory bodies other than courts of law. The Speaker must balance the right of Parliament to discuss any matter affecting the public interest with the need to protect individuals whose own interests stand to be affected by the judgments or findings of courts and other tribunals. The problem is compounded by the fact that the Speaker is seldom in full possession of the facts of the case; furthermore he is obliged to hear what a member has to say before he can intervene, at which point the damage might have been done.* A very unsatisfactory situation existed with regard to capital sentences prior to

---

* An interesting recent application of the convention occurred on 24 April 1978 and concerned the disclosure on the floor of the House of the name of a witness who had been allowed to give evidence in court anonymously. See Commons Hansard, 5th. series, vol. 948, cols. 1007–9.

the abolition of the death penalty for murder in 1965. A capital case was always *sub judice* until the sentence had been carried out because the possibility of a reprieve existed until the last moment. This unsatisfactory state of affairs was highlighted on 27 January 1953 when the Speaker disallowed an attempt to seek an emergency debate on the Home Secretary's refusal to recommend a reprieve for a man shortly to be executed;[105] and on 16 February 1961 when a motion of dissent was moved against the Speaker's ruling disallowing a question.[106]

Brief mention may be made of certain other aspects of the Speaker's functions in relation to procedure in order to round off the account. When motions relating to statutory instruments are being debated he is not obliged to put the question at the prescribed hour if he believes the time for debate has not been adequate. Instead he can bring about an adjournment of the debate by simply interrupting the business instead of putting the question.[107]

He will not allow a bill or motion to proceed if it is in any way irregular.[108] He allocates bills to Standing Committees[109] and certifies those relating exclusively to Scotland for reference to the Scottish Grand Committee.[110] He nominates the members of the Chairmen's Panel[111] and appoints the Chairmen of Standing Committees from the Chairmen's Panel.[112]

By way of summing up this section in general terms we can perhaps do no better than borrow the observations of the late Lord Morrison of Lambeth, one of the 20th century's most experienced parliamentarians, who wrote:

> New or unforseen situations arise and circumstances change, and it is here that the common sense and adaptability of our procedure manifest themselves. A *prima facie* case for a change in Standing Orders may arise, but it is highly probable that what is required is a new Speaker's ruling. If the Speaker were satisfied that something had to be done to assist the House to discharge its duties in the new circumstances, either he would be asked to give a new ruling or he would himself volunteer to do so. After careful consideration he would make a statement to the House indicating that he proposed to make modifications in parliamentary practice on the matter in question for the general convenience of the House. Some informal discussion might ensue which would or would not cause the Speaker to change his view. If it were clear that there was not fairly general agreement, Mr. Speaker would no doubt reconsider the matter and possibly consult with party leaders through the Whips, and then give a similar or a revised ruling. But on most occasions the Speaker is so successful in arriving at a common-sense conclusion and meeting the general wishes of the House that no great difficulty arises.[113]

Statutory and other duties of the Speaker

Among the statutory duties of the Speaker are his responsibilities relating to the certification of bills under the Parliament Acts, 1911 and 1949. The Acts reduced the powers of the House of Lords over public bills to one of delay, one month in the case of a money bill and two sessions or one year in the case of almost all other public bills. The 1911 Act also defines a money bill and the Speaker is required to certify as such all bills which fall within the definition of the Act. His certificate is conclusive and may not be questioned in a court of law. Should a bill from which the House of Lords withholds its consent be presented for the royal assent the Speaker would be required to certify that the provisions of the Act had been complied with. Conflict between the two Houses is very rare these days but it is evident that the Speaker's responsibilities under the Acts could be of crucial importance if a serious dispute were to arise.

Should any doubt arise as to which party should be recognized as the official opposition or who should be recognized as the Leader of the Opposition, the matter would be decided by the Speaker. This provision, originally enacted in 1937, is now contained in the Ministerial and other Salaries Act, 1975 (Section 2(2)). The only occasion on which a Speaker has been obliged to exercise this responsibility was in 1940 when, following the formation of a coalition government under Winston Churchill, the minuscule Independent Labour Party claimed that its leader was entitled to the salary and recognition due to the Leader of the Opposition. Speaker Fitzroy rejected the claim.

Under the Church of England Assembly (Powers) Act, 1919 (which was amended in 1969 by the Synodical Government Measure) the Speaker appoints the fifteen members of the House of Commons who, with fifteen peers appointed by the Lord Chancellor, comprise the Ecclesiastical Committee which considers measures framed by the General Synod of the Church of England.*

Other statutes which impose special duties on the Speaker include the Mental Health Act, 1959, which contains a statutory procedure for vacating the seat of a member of unsound mind (Section 137); the House of Commons (Redistribution of Seats) Act, 1949 (amended 1958 and 1979) under which the Speaker is *ex officio* chairman of the four permanent Boundary Commissions for England, Scotland, Wales and Northern Ireland); and the Recess Elections Act, 1975 which provides for the filling of seats vacated during a parliamentary recess. Under the Regency Act, 1937, the Speaker is one of a number of persons who, in the event of the Sovereign's incapacity, might be called upon to testify to the fact. Under the Consolidation of Enactments (Procedure) Act the Speaker together with the Lord Chancellor oversee routine alterations to legislation proposed to and approved by the Joint Committee on Consolidation Bills. They and the committee must be satisfied that the changes proposed are not sufficiently important to call for the enactment of separate legislation. Under the Statutory Instruments Act, 1946, the Speaker and the Lord Chancellor nominate the Statutory Instruments

---

* Church legislation is subject to parliamentary control by virtue of the union between church and state. It is initiated under a system of delegation, the Ecclesiastical Committee being the key element in the process of parliamentary supervision. A measure when adopted has the same effect as an Act of Parliament.

Reference Committee which considers such matters as the numbering, classification, printing and publication of statutory instruments. Under the Parliamentary Oaths Act, 1866, the Speaker must be present in the Chair while the members of the House of Commons take the oath or make affirmation at the beginning of a new Parliament. Under the National Debt (Conversion of Stock) Act, 1884, it is the duty of the Speaker to signify in writing to the Bank of England and for publication in the London Gazette any resolution of the House of Commons for the redemption of stock forming part of the National Debt. The British Museum Act, 1753, named the Speaker as one of the museum's principal trustees but under the British Museum Act, 1963, he is no longer a trustee *ex officio*.

The practice has arisen during the present century of referring questions of electoral reform to a conference of members of Parliament under the chairmanship of the Speaker. The first such conference was convened in 1916 under the chairmanship of Speaker Lowther, its terms of reference covering reform of the franchise, basis for redistribution of seats, reform of the system of registration of electors, methods of election and the manner in which the costs of elections should be borne. Its recommendations[114] led to the most sweeping electoral reforms since 1832 and the Representation of the People Act, 1918, was largely based on them. The most controversial recommendation, which was implemented although not unanimously agreed to by the conference, was the enfranchisement of women under certain conditions. In 1929 Lowther, by then Viscount Ullswater, was called out of retirement to preside over a second conference on electoral reform which was permitted to decide its own terms of reference. Proportional representation and the preferential vote were the principal matters considered but the conference failed to agree on any recommendations.[115]

The third electoral reform conference was convened in 1944 under the chairmanship of Speaker Clifton Brown, receiving its impetus, like the first, from the circumstances arising from a world war. Not all its recommendations were destined to find acceptance, although one which was adopted was the establishment of the four permanent Boundary Commissions under the chairmanship of the Speaker. The Representation of the People Act, 1948, established a single franchise based on residence and single-member constituencies, and abolished the business and university franchises which was contrary to the recommendation of the conference.[116] The next Speaker to preside over an electoral reform conference was Speaker King who announced its terms of reference to the House on 12 May 1965.[117] It issued its final report on 9 February 1968,[118] its most significant recommendation being that the voting age be reduced to 20. The voting age was in fact reduced to 18 by the Representation of the People Act, 1969.

On 16 March 1973 Speaker Lloyd announced to the House the terms of reference of another electoral reform conference.[119] Between July 1973 and February 1974 it issued four brief reports, the most significant recommendation being that the minimum age of candidates for parliamentary elections should be lowered from 21 to 18 years, thus bringing the minimum age for election into conformity with the voting age.[120] On 19 July 1977 Speaker

Thomas informed the House of Commons that he would be presiding over a conference which would consider the number of parliamentary constituencies there should be in Northern Ireland.[121] The conference reported on 13 February 1978[122] recommending that there should be not less than sixteen and not more than eighteen Northern Ireland constituencies and this recommendation was embodied in the House of Commons (Redistribution of Seats) Act, 1979.

In 1919 a conference was appointed under the Speaker's chairmanship on a matter other than electoral reform, namely the devolution of powers to subordinate legislatures within Great Britain. However, the conference failed to agree on satisfactory solutions and its report[123] was never debated in Parliament.

Notes to Chapter Three: The British Speakership in the Twentieth Century

1. Michael MacDonagh, *The Speaker of the House*, Methuen, 1914, p. 3.
2. Standing Order 124 in the 1983 edition of the Standing Orders of the House of Commons.
3. Commons Hansard, 5th Series, Vol. 870, Cols. 1–16.
4. Ibid., Vol. 904, Cols 1151–1170.
5. Horace King, The Impartiality of the Speaker, The Parliamentarian, Vol. XLVII, April 1966, p. 130.
6. See Selwyn Lloyd, *Mr. Speaker, Sir*, Jonathan Cape, 1976, pp. 79–80.
7. Ibid., p. 79.
8. Ibid., p. 94.
9. See Edward Lummis, *The Speaker's Chair*, Unwin, 1900, pp. 6–7.
10. See House of Commons (Speaker) Act, 1832, s. 1.
11. Parliamentary and other Pensions Act, 1972, Part II, as amended by the Parliamentary and other Pensions and Salaries Act, 1976, s. 5.
12. Mr. Speaker King's Retirement Act, 1971.
13. Report on the Office of the Speaker, H.C. 487, 1852–53.
14. Standing Order 125, 1983 edition.
15. Standing Order 126, 1983 edition.
16. The Times, 12 July, 1895.
17. Ibid., 27 June and 3 August, 1935.
18. Sir Ivor Jennings, *Parliament*, Cambridge University Press, 1957, p. 68.
19. See Report from the Select Committee on Parliamentary Elections, (Mr. Speaker's Seat), 1939, H.C. 98, Paras. 60–61, p. 24.
20. See Commons Hansard, 5th Series, Vol. 676, Cols. 229–34, also Cols. 425–6 where the result of the division which had been incorrectly recorded was corrected.
21. Ibid., 6th Series, Vol. 16, Cols. 751–756.
22. Report from the Select Committee on Parliamentary Elections, op. cit., paras. 37, 38, 39, p. 17.
23. See, for example, the election communications of Speaker Clifton Brown, Hexham, 1945; Speaker Morrison, Cirencester and Tewkesbury, 1955; Speaker Hylton-Foster, Cities of London and Westminster, 1964; Speaker

King, Southampton Itchen, 1966 and 1970; and those of Speaker Lloyd, Wirral, prior to both general elections of 1974.
24. See Selwyn Lloyd, op. cit., p. 141.
25. Commons Hansard, 5th Series, Vol. 141, Col. 310.
26. Ibid., Vol. 387, Col. 617.
27. See, for example, Earl Winterton, *Orders of the Day*, London, Cassell, 1953, p. 294.
28. See Charles Pannell's article in The Times, 4 March, 1972, p. 12.
29. Ibid.,
30. Harold Wilson, *A Personal Record: The Labour Government, 1964–70*, Little, Brown & Co., (American edition), 1971, p. 27.
31. See Alan Watkins, The Fix for the Speakership, New Statesman, 18 December, 1970, p. 823.
32. See Selwyn Lloyd, op. cit., Chapter 1.
33. See Commons Hansard, 5th Series, Vol. 809, cols. 8–24.
34. For full text of the resolution see Commons Hansard, 5th Series, Vol. 842, Cols. 1684–5.
35. For full text of the recommendations see First Report from the Select Committee on Procedure, 1971–72, H.C. 111, para. 28, p. xvi.
36. Ibid., para. 21, p. xiii.
37. Ibid., see also Sir Barnett Cocks' evidence to the Committee, pp. 32–36.
38. Ibid., para. 22, p. xiii.
39. Ibid., para. 22, p. xiii.
40. Commons Hansard, 5th Series, Vol. 511, Cols. 2095–2100 and Vol. 514, Col. 1717.
41. First Report from the Select Committee on Procedure, 1971–72, op. cit., para. 23, p. xiv, and para. 28. p. xvi.
42. See speech of his proposer, Sir M. Hicks Beach, Commons Hansard, 4th Series, Vol. 147, Cols. 1067–8.
43. Commons Hansard, 5th Series, Vol. 387, Col. 626.
44. First Report from the Select Committee on Procedure, Session 1971–72, op. cit., page xv, para. 26.
45. 'Cato', *Guilty Men*, London, Gollancz, 1940.
46. Commons Hansard, 5th Series, Vol. 612, Col. 9; and see Letters of Queen Victoria, second series, London, John Murray, 1926–28, Vol. 2, p. 164.
47. See Commons Hansard, 5th Series, Vol. 870, Col. 10 and Vol. 880, Col. 9.
48. See First Report from the Select Committee on Procedure, 1971–72, op. cit., para. 27, pp. xv–xvi.
49. Viscount Ullswater, *A Speaker's Commentaries*, Edward Arnold, 1925, Vol. 2, p. 30.
50. See Erskine May, *Parliamentary Practice*, 20th Ed., Butterworth, 1983, pp. 853–856.
51. See Selwyn Lloyd, op. cit., p. 58.
52. See text of Charles Pannell's broadcast, ' "Under Big Ben": Mr. Speaker', on the English service of the B.B.C. 30 May 1958.
53. Verbatim Report of the Proceedings of the Third Conference of Commonwealth Speakers and Presiding Officers, Monday 24th to Friday 28th September, 1973, pp. 36–37.
54. See Commons Hansard, 5th Series, Vol. 595, cols. 1607–1620.
55. See Horace King, *The Impartiality of the Speaker*, op. cit., p. 128.
56. See Selwyn Lloyd, op. cit., pp. 60–78.

57. See Speaker Lowther's comments on this matter in his memoirs: Viscount Ullswater, *A Speaker's Commentaries*, op. cit., Vol. 2, pp. 25—26.
58. Report of the Conference of Speakers and Presiding Officers of Commonwealth Parliaments, Canada, September 1969, p. 85.
59. See Commons Hansard, 5th Series, Vol. 328, Cols. 1770—3.
60. Ibid., Vol. 765, Cols. 893—5.
61. Ibid., Vol. 640, Col. 34. For the debates relative to this matter see Vol. 638, Cols. 499—642 and Vol. 640, Cols. 35—172.
62. Peerage Act, 1963, s. 3.
63. See Lord Lambton's evidence to the Committee of Privileges, Third Report, H.C. 324, 1971—72, p. 13.
64. Commons Hansard, 5th Series, Vol. 830, Cols. 975—978.
65. Third Report from the Committee of Privileges, H.C. 324, 1971—72, para. 11, p. vii.
66. See Commons Hansard, 5th Series, Vol. 912, Cols. 299—305 and 445.
67. Ibid., Col. 445, first sentence of the speech of Mr. Michael Foot.
68. Commons Hansard, 4th Series, Vol. 32, Cols. 1504—5.
69. Ibid., Vol. 147, Col. 1226.
70. Ibid., Col. 1228.
71. Ibid., 5th Series, Vol. 141, Cols. 895—904.
72. Ibid., Vol. 219, Cols. 535—554.
73. Interview with Lady Dunrossil, 22 October 1973.
74. Commons Hansard, 5th Series, Vol. 613, Cols. 610—620 and Cols. 1170—1214, and Vol. 614, Cols. 219—45.
75. Standing Orders of the House of Commons, Public Business, 1983 edition. For an exhaustive account of the origins and development of the question period see D. N. Chester and Nona Bowring, Questions in Parliament, Oxford, Clarendon Press, 1962.
76. See his ruling of 28 June 1901, Commons Hansard, 4th Series, Vol. 96, Col. 264.
77. Earl Winterton, *Orders of the Day*, op. cit., pp. 151—152.
78. See his ruling of 4 March 1947, Commons Hansard, 5th Series, Vol. 434, Cols. 239—40.
79. See Second Report from the Select Committee on Procedure, H.C. 198, 1969—1970, pp. 44—45.
80. See Erskine May, *Parliamentary Practice*, 20th edition, op. cit., 1983, pp. 337—344.
81. See, for example, the ruling of Speaker Lloyd on 27 January 1971, Commons Hansard, 5th Series, Vol. 810, Col. 524.
82. See Second Report from the Select Committee on Procedure, H.C. 282, 1966—67, p. 40.
83. Ibid., pp. v—ix.
84. See Commons Hansard, 5th Series, Vol. 164, Col. 1293.
85. See George Thomas, Parliamentary Privilege at Westminster, The Parliamentarian, Vol. LXI, No. 4, October 1980, pp. 212—214.
86. For further information and discussion of this question see Report from the Select Committee on Parliamentary Privilege, H.C. 34, 1966—67; and Third Report from the Committee of Privileges, H.C. 417, 1976—77.
87. For details of the rules which apply see Erskine May, 20th Edition, op. cit., pp. 371—372.
88. Standing Order 31, 1983 edition.

89. G. F. M. Campion, Methods of Closure in the Commons, Journal of the Society of Clerks-at-the-Table in Empire Parliaments for 1932, Vol. 1, p. 21.
90. See Commons Hansard, 5th Series, Vol. 184, Col. 1591 and Vol. 500, Col. 397.
91. Ibid., Vol. 595, Cols. 1607–20.
92. Standing Order 29, 1983 edition.
93. Standing Order 38, 1983 edition.
94. See Commons Hansard, 5th Series, Vol. 894, Cols. 1363–70, and Selwyn Lloyd, "*Mr. Speaker, Sir*", op. cit., pp. 96–98. See also the observations relative to the rule by Speaker Hylton–Foster on 25 April 1961, Commons Hansard, 5th Series, Vol. 639, Col. 371 and cols. 373–75.
95. Standing Order 34, 1983 edition.
96. See for example evidence of Speaker King to the Select Committee on Procedure, 17 March 1971: Second Report H.C. 538, 1970–71, p. 47.
97. See Commons Hansard, 5th Series, Vol. 489, Cols. 721–46 and Vol. 832, Cols. 268–69 and Cols. 432–548.
98. See Erskine May, 20th edition, op. cit., pp. 379–381.
99. Standing Order 13, 1983 edition.
100. See Commons Hansard, 5th Series, Vol. 417, Cols. 421–22 and 629–32.
101. See First Report from the Select Committee on Procedure, H.C. 156, 1962–63, para. 12, p. v.
102. Standing Order 15, 1983 edition.
103. See Commons Hansard, 5th Series, Vol. 681, Col. 1417.
104. See Erskine May, 20th edition, op. cit., pp. 429–430.
105. Commons Hansard, 5th Series, Vol. 510, Cols. 845–60.
106. Ibid., Vol. 634, Cols. 1773–1838.
107. See Standing Orders 3(1)(b) and 4(2), 1983 edition.
108. See Erskine May, 20th edition, op. cit., pp. 235–236 for examples of irregularities.
109. See Standing Order 63(2), 1983 edition.
110. See Standing Order 70(1), 1983 edition.
111. See Standing Order 127, 1983 edition.
112. See Standing Order 64(1) and (2), 1983 edition.
113. See Lord Morrison of Lambeth, Government and Parliament, Oxford University Press, 3rd edition, 1964, pp. 211–212.
114. See Cd. 8463.
115. See Cmd. 3636.
116. See Cmd. 6534.
117. Commons Hansard, 5th Series, Vol. 712, Cols. 520–23.
118. See Cmnd. 3550.
119. Commons Hansard, 5th Series, Vol. 860, Cols. 1412–14.
120. See Cmnd. 5363.
121. Commons Hansard, 5th Series, Vol. 935, part 2, Cols. 1379–80.
122. See Cmnd. 7110.
123. See Cmd. 692.

Chapter Four

The Speakership in Canada

Canada is a federal state which came into being on 1 July 1867 and today consists of ten provinces and two territories, each with its own legislature. The federal Parliament consists of the Queen represented by a locally appointed Governor-General, the Senate and the House of Commons. It is the only Commonwealth Parliament apart from that of Great Britain to have adopted the traditional English designation for its popularly elected House, an indication of Canadian fidelity to ancient parliamentary usages. The office of Speaker of the House of Commons is provided for in section 44 of the British North America Act and the formality which is observed at Westminster, whereby the Commons elect their Speaker at the command of the Sovereign, does not apply in Canada. Neither is the Speaker, once elected, required to submit himself for the royal approbation. Otherwise, the ceremonies attendant upon the election of the Canadian Speaker bear a close resemblance to those of Westminster.

On the day appointed for the opening of a new Parliament the Clerk reads to the members assembled in the House of Commons a letter advising that the Deputy Governor-General will proceed to the Senate Chamber to open the session. Shortly afterwards the Gentleman Usher of the Black Rod arrives at the door of the Commons Chamber and gives the customary three knocks. On being admitted he informs the Clerk, both in English and French, that the Deputy Governor-General desires the attendance of the Commons in the Senate Chamber. The members then proceed to the Senate headed by Black Rod, the Sergeant-at-Arms (without the Mace) and the Clerks-at-the-Table and as they stand at the Bar facing the Deputy Governor-General the Speaker of the Senate delivers the following message:

> I have it in command to let you know that His Excellency the Governor-General does not see fit to declare the causes of his summoning the present Parliament of Canada until the Speaker of the House of Commons shall have been chosen, according to law, but this afternoon, at the hour of—, His Excellency will declare the causes of calling Parliament.

Back in their own chamber, the Clerk presiding, the Commons proceed to elect their Speaker. It is interesting to note that in the Canadian House of

Commons the traditional Westminster practice whereby the Clerk presides continues to be observed although it is no longer observed in the British House of Commons. The Clerk sits at his normal place at the Table of the House, the Speaker's Chair remaining empty and the Mace resting in the lower brackets of the Table. To signify that the House is without a voice pending the election of the Speaker, the Clerk calls on the proposer and seconder by rising and pointing to them and they address the Clerk by name. In Canada the Speaker's nomination is invariably proposed by the Prime Minister and seconded either by another minister or the Leader of the Opposition. The British practice, whereby the proposer and seconder are always senior backbenchers in order to emphasize that the choice of Speaker belongs to the whole House and not exclusively to the front benches, has never been adopted in Canada although it has on various occasions been urged. As long ago as 1878 Sir John A. Macdonald, the first Prime Minister of Canada, advocated the adoption of the British practice[1] and similar suggestions have been made on subsequent occasions. It was one of the recommendations contained in a report on the speakership by Professor Denis Smith of Trent University which was commissioned by a parliamentary committee chaired by Speaker Alan Macnaughton in 1964–65.[2] Today it is fair to state that the proposing and seconding of the Speaker from the front benches is a firmly established practice.* The Leader of the Opposition frequently seconds the nomination as an expression of the official Opposition's confidence in the candidate. Since 1953 he has done so on seven occasions (in 1953, 1957, 1958, 1968, 1972, 1979 and 1980). In 1962, 1963, 1965 and 1974 the seconder was a cabinet minister. In 1974 the Leader of the Opposition, Mr. Robert Stanfield, explained his reason for declining the Prime Minister's invitation to second the Speaker's nomination. While it is accepted in Canada that the choice of the candidate is the prerogative of the government, the opposition is normally consulted over the nomination. On this occasion, according to Mr. Stanfield, no consultation took place and the first indication he had of the identity of the candidate was when he read it in the press.[3] However, the opposition did not carry its objection to the lengths of proposing an alternative candidate. A contest for the speakership has never taken place in Canada, but on two occasions, in 1878 and 1936, the government's nominee was opposed even though there were no alternative candidates proposed. On the former occasion attention was drawn to the fact that the British practice did not permit (at that time) of the taking of a vote unless more than one candidate was proposed.[4] A division took place nevertheless. On the latter occasion there was no recorded vote.

Having elected their Speaker the Commons reassemble at the appointed hour to await a further message from Black Rod. The Speaker reads a formal communication announcing that the Governor-General would be arriving in the Senate to declare the cause of summoning Parliament, after which Black Rod is again heard knocking at the door. He informs the Speaker that His

---

* Although a committee report tabled in the House on 3 December 1982 recommended that the Speaker should in the future be elected by secret ballot.

Excellency requires the attendance of the Commons in the Senate, and again the procession of members sets off, this time with their Speaker at their head, preceded by Black Rod and the Sergeant-at-Arms bearing the Mace. At the Bar of the Senate the Speaker mounts a low platform, doffs the tricorne hat which is worn in place of a wig, and addresses the following words to the Governor-General:

> May it please Your Excellency, the House of Commons have elected me their Speaker, though I am but little able to fulfil the important duties thus assigned to me.
>
> If in the performance of those duties I should at any time fall into error, I pray that the fault may be imputed to me, and not to the Commons, whose servant I am, and who, through me, the better to enable them to discharge their duty to their Queen and country, humbly claim all their undoubted rights and privileges, especially that they may have freedom of speech in their debates, access to Your Excellency's person at all seasonable times, and that their proceedings may receive from Your Excellency the most favourable construction.

The formula is similar to that in use at Westminster but it omits the claim to the privilege of freedom from arrest. The Speaker of the Senate, on behalf of the Governor-General, confirms His Excellency's confidence in the newly-elected Speaker of the House and the constitutional privileges of the Commons. The Governor-General then opens Parliament with the traditional speech from the throne which is a statement of government policies and legislative intentions prepared for him by the cabinet. Back in the Commons chamber the Speaker makes a formal report on the proceedings in the Senate. Before he refers to the speech from the throne the Prime Minister moves for leave to introduce a bill respecting the administration of oaths of office, a fictitious bill which is the Canadian equivalent of the Outlawries Bill. This custom asserts the traditional right of the Commons to decide on the order in which business shall be taken, not necessarily according priority to that of the Crown. The Speaker is not called upon to read the speech aloud in the House. This formality is dispensed with by unanimous consent of the House and the speech is simply printed in Hansard.

As Head of the House of Commons establishment the Speaker controls a staff of over 3000 and corresponds to the minister of a department although, as in Great Britain, the parliamentary establishment is independent of the public service. He is also, jointly with the Speaker of the Senate, administrative head of the Library of Parliament which employs about 230 people. The House of Commons Act provides for a Commission of Internal Economy which consists of the Speaker as chairman and four privy councillors. Although there is nothing in the Act to prevent the nomination of privy councillors who are not members of the government (provided they are members of the House of Commons) in practice they are always cabinet ministers. The Act also provides that the Speaker shall remain in office following a dissolution of Parliament to ensure administrative continuity until a Speaker is chosen by the new Parliament. The Commission approves the salary scales and conditions of service of the staff and meets from time to time to discuss the internal management of the House. It also approves the House of Commons estimates before they are forwarded by the Speaker to the President of the Treasury Board for inclusion in the annual estimates of expenditure for presentation to the House. An executive committee which consists of the Speaker as chairman, the Clerk of the House, the Sergeant-at-Arms and the Administrator is responsible for management policy and major decision-making. An administrative committee consisting of the three senior officers alone under the chairmanship of the Clerk of the House is responsible for day-to-day administration. The Speaker of the House shares with the Speaker of the Senate the chairmanship of the Joint Committee on the Library of Parliament and the Joint Committee on the Parliamentary Restaurant.

In Canada the Speaker ranks fifth in the order of precedence, those preceding him being the Governor-General, the Prime Minister, the Chief Justice and the Speaker of the Senate. Prior to 19 December 1968, when the existing Table of Precedence came into effect, the Speaker ranked relatively low, following all ambassadors and high commissioners, all cabinet ministers and other privy councillors, and the Lieutenant-Governors of provinces. This position was clearly not commensurate with the dignity of the office and was corrected after representations had been made to the Prime Minister. In the House the Speaker is addressed as 'Your Honour', apparently by custom rather than by any prescriptive right. His salary and allowances compare with those of a cabinet minister and like a cabinet minister he receives the same salary and emoluments of a member of Parliament over and above those which specifically attach to the office of Speaker. His powers and duties correspond broadly with those of his counterpart at Westminster but there are significant differences which will be noted in the course of this chapter. Like the latter he does not participate in any debate which takes place in the House, and is in fact expressly prohibited from doing so by standing order.[5] This prohibition has never applied to debates in committee of the Whole House and prior to the reorganization of the committee system of the House of Commons in 1969 he regularly piloted the House of Commons estimates through committee of supply. This was the single annual occasion when he would speak from the floor in his capacity as head of the House of Commons administration. It gave him the opportunity to give an account of his stewardship to his fellow members and answer any questions his colleagues might wish to raise in the manner of a minister in charge of a government department. Under the present system all estimates are referred to the various standing committees of the House and the Speaker answers to the Standing Committee on Management and Members' Services to which the parliamentary estimates now stand referred. A precedent was created in February 1981 when Speaker Jeanne Sauvé agreed to appear as a witness before the Public Accounts Committee to provide information on the reorganized administration of the House of Commons.

The last time a Speaker spoke in committee of the whole House on a matter other than the House of Commons estimates was on 7 April 1927 on a bill to amend the Post Office Act. The then Speaker, Rodolphe Lemieux, intervened in the debate by virtue of his experience as a former Postmaster-General. His action was sufficiently unprecedented to invite the following comments from the Leader of the Opposition:

> I rise to call the attention of the Committee to an incident which has just occurred and which I think should be noted. The presiding officer of this House has seen fit to address a few remarks to this Committee and I think we should take note of the innovation. I do not know that I draw attention to the fact by way of protest at all, because the remarks made by His Honour were very useful to the discussion and very elevating in their tendency, but the question is whether the Speaker of this House has the right to discuss any matters before the House. If His Honour has that right in this case, I do not see why he should not have the right to discuss any matter which comes before Parliament . . . I think we should take note of this proceeding, because in the future it may become a precedent and I think the Speaker in his own interest should be prevented from taking part in the debates of this House.[6]

The Continuity of the Speakership

The principle of the continuity of the Speaker's office has never become an established convention as in Great Britain although it has its advocates. The Speaker is elected for the duration of a Parliament and very often changes with each Parliament. It has been the practice to alternate an English-speaking Speaker with a French-speaking Speaker, although there have been a number of occasions when the same Speaker has been re-elected in a succeeding Parliament. The first Speaker of the Canadian House of Commons, James Cockburn, served in two successive Parliaments. Speaker Rhodes, who was first elected in 1917 in the final session of a Parliament, was re-elected in the following Parliament. Rodolphe Lemieux served in three consecutive Parliaments in the 1920's. Roland Michener, first elected in the short-lived Parliament opened in 1957, was re-elected in 1958 and would probably have been re-elected for a third term had he not lost his seat in 1962. Normally the Speaker remains a member of his party and if he seeks re-election at a general election he runs as his party's candidate, although he does not conduct a highly-charged political campaign. However, in 1968 a bold initiative was taken by Lucien Lamoureux, who had been elected Speaker in 1965. He made it known that he would not contest the 1968 election as the nominee of a political party and he secured an undertaking from the two major political parties, the Liberals and the Progressive Conservatives, that they would support him as an independent candidate seeking re-election as Speaker. Mr. Lamoureux easily won his seat and was re-elected to the Chair with all-party support. In 1972 he ran again as an independent but this time he was opposed by three other candidates including a Progressive Conservative. He retained his seat with a narrow majority and presided over his third Parliament before retiring in 1974. He was succeeded by James Jerome who became the first Speaker in Canadian history to be re-elected to the office following a change of government. In 1979 the Progressive Conservatives were returned to power although their number of seats fell short of an overall majority in the House of Commons. Mr. Jerome, a Liberal, was re-elected Speaker, a tribute to the high regard in which he was held as a result of his performance in the previous Parliament, although it is fair to comment that had the election result produced a clear majority for the new government a different decision might have been taken. The Progressive Conservative government was defeated on its budget only a few months after coming to power and another election took place in 1980. On this occasion Mr. Jerome was not a candidate. The Liberals were returned to power and Mrs. Jeanne Sauvé, the first woman to become Speaker of the Canadian House of Commons, was elected to the Chair.

It is difficult to anticipate the impact that the Lamoureux initiative and the Jerome precedent are likely to have on the future evolution of the Canadian speakership. Prior to the 1979 election Mr. Jerome entered into consultations with the political parties in order to determine their attitudes towards the continuity of the office. He found little enthusiasm for a repetition of the Lamoureux initiative among the opposition parties, mainly because they were unwilling to forego the opportunity of fielding a candidate in the Speaker's constituency and the possibility of winning an additional seat. Mr. Lamoureux himself, prior to his retirement in 1974, acknowledged that he had undergone a change of heart and had come to question the propriety of asking the electors in the Speaker's constituency to deprive themselves of a choice of candidates. Mr. Jerome took the view that such an arrangement is of no value unless it is supported by all opposition parties and he accordingly ran as a Liberal candidate in the 1979 election. He saw no inconsistency between the Speaker's participating in the normal electoral process while maintaining his traditional impartiality, a view which his own record would certainly confirm. While he addressed none of the political issues of the campaign he actively refuted the contention of the opposition candidates that the Speaker by virtue of his duties was unable adequately to represent a constituency.[7]

The issue of a 'permanent' speakership through the provision of a special seat for the Speaker has long had its advocates in Canada. The choice of adjective is open to question as those who propose this solution presumably have in mind the continuity principle which would ensure that the Speaker would not automatically change with the government. The House would obviously need to retain the ultimate right to choose and, if necessary, remove the Speaker. Proposing the election of Mr. Roland Michener on 14 October 1957, Mr. Diefenbaker referred to the principle of the continuity of the speakership in the following passage of his speech:

> The opinion has been expressed that we should have a permanent Speaker, but up to the present time the practice of Canada has not been to do so. Our practice, as constituted, is governed by the character and historic basis of our country. Under it, with few exceptions, the Speaker in one Parliament is of French origin, followed in the next Parliament by

one of English origin. Whatever our personal views may be as to having a permanent Speaker, only Parliament can make that decision and then only when there is generous unanimity in that regard.[8]

It appears that Mr. Diefenbaker, who became Prime Minister in 1957 after an election which failed to produce a majority for any party, had approached a member of a minor party, known at the time as the Co-operative Commonwealth Federation, to sound him out as to whether he would agree to his name being placed in nomination for the speakership. The member concerned, Mr. Stanley Knowles, was an acknowledged authority on parliamentary procedure and respected on all sides of the House. However, he declined Mr. Diefenbaker's offer because of the commitments he felt he owed to his party, although had there been any guarantee of continuity he might have felt compelled to accept.[9]

Prior to the election of 1962 a professor from Dalhousie University, James H. Aitchison, launched a one-man campaign urging all the political parties to take steps to establish the continuity of the Speaker's office. He proposed that the three parties then in opposition should refrain from contesting the Speaker's constituency and that he should run with all-party support as the Speaker seeking re-election. The proposal was not taken up and the cause of continuity suffered a severe setback with the defeat of Roland Michener, universally regarded as an ideal Speaker, in the ensuing election. The main obstacle to agreement between the parties on this issue has always been a general reluctance to forego the possibility of winning an additional seat, plus the demoralizing effect on a constituency party organization of not having a campaign to prepare for and fight. A widely canvassed solution to this problem has been the creation of a special seat for the Speaker and a plan for its implementation was devised by Professor Aitchison and published in the Ottawa Citizen of 19 April 1963. It was also one of the recommendations of the report submitted by Professor Denis Smith in 1965 (see above). Neither suggestion was acted upon but on 29 October 1971 a brief debate took place on a private member's bill incorporating a similar proposal. The bill provided that to be eligible for election as Speaker in the first instance, the candidate must have been elected to the House of Commons in the normal way. A Speaker who had completed two sessions in office could, if the House so wished, be designated by resolution as the member for Parliament Hill. Such action would increase by one the number of seats in the House of Commons. The seat formerly held by the Speaker would be declared vacant and a by-election held. The Speaker himself would retain all the rights and privileges of a member of the House. He would be eligible for re-election to the Chair in the following Parliament without having to contest a seat in the general election.[10]

The bill was sponsored by Stanley Knowles whose party, the New Democratic Party, had declined to participate in the electoral pact which had enabled Lucien Lamoureux to be elected as an independent in 1968. The party explained at the time that it was not motivated by any desire to oppose Mr. Lamoureux but by the fact that it supported the principle of creating a special seat for the Speaker. There is evidence that the Leader of the Opposition, Mr. Robert Stanfield, was also sympathetic to the idea. Seconding the nomination of Mr. Lamoureux on 12 September 1968 he asked 'that early consideration be given to alternative methods of removing the election of the Speaker from partisan considerations.'[11] Nearly three years later he issued a prepared statement warning that the Progressive Conservatives could not be expected to refrain from nominating a candidate in the Speaker's constituency a second time. 'I have urged upon the Prime Minister the creation of an additional seat in the House of Commons specifically for the Speaker who has been chosen by the House. This proposal has been rejected and no alternative proposal has come from the government.'[12]

The creation of a special seat for the Speaker is a controversial proposition which is unlikely to command universal support if it is ever revived in Canada. Speaking in the debate on Stanley Knowles' bill, a former Speaker, Marcel Lambert, stated the widely held point of view that the Speaker derives his authority and the respect of members essentially from the fact that he is one of them. The argument that a Speaker cannot adequately represent a constituency has little to commend it and has been frequently refuted by members who have themselves held office as Speaker. The premise that membership of a political party is incompatible with the impartial discharge of the duties of the Speaker is also very doubtful, particularly in Canada where the impartiality of the Chair has seldom been called into question. Speakers do not attend party meetings or actively campaign for their parties, which can become a handicap at the time of a general election. Relative to this problem a former Speaker, René Beaudoin, made the following observations:

> In Canada Speakers have refrained from taking part in any political activity outside the House, even their own constituencies. Ever since I was appointed Deputy Chairman of Committees, and Deputy Speaker and Speaker, from 1949 to the present, I have abstained from attending any political meetings except during the General Election which took place in 1953. Prior to 1949, I used to call a meeting at least once a year of all my organizers, in order to review with them the political situation both cosmetic and external. No such meeting has been held in my constituency since 1949. It is difficult for my constituents to realize that as Presiding Officer I must abstain from exercising some of the activities in which a member usually engages. While I remain idle politically, prospective opponents do not necessarily have to follow my example.[13]

The speakership of the Canadian House of Commons is not normally regarded as a stepping stone to political office, although there have been a few occasions on which a Speaker has been appointed to the cabinet following service in the Chair. The last time this occurred was in 1963 when Speaker Lambert was appointed Minister of Veterans' Affairs. The appointment was widely criticised, although it was made following a dissolution of Parliament and in the circumstances of a cabinet crisis. There are other high offices to which Speakers have been appointed following their tenure of the Chair. Speaker Alan Macnaughton, who succeeded Speaker Lambert, was subsequently appointed a senator. Lucien Lamoureux was appointed an ambassador and James Jerome became a judge of the Federal Court. The highest appointment of all was attained by Roland Michener who was Governor-General from 1967 to 1973. Some occupants of the Chair have served as cabinet ministers prior to being appointed Speaker, the most recent being Jeanne Sauvé who held various ministerial appointments between 1972 and 1979. As in Great Britain, service as a Deputy Speaker confers no prescriptive right to the speakership itself. Lucien Lamoureux was the last Speaker who had had prior service in the lower chair. Nearly all Canadian Speakers have been lawyers, Jeanne Sauvé being the first non-lawyer to be elected to the Chair of the House of Commons in many years.

In spite of the attachment which the Speaker normally retains to his political party, the Canadian speakership can boast a tradition of impartiality which has developed and become refined over the years. This has occurred even though Speakers have always been dependent for future preferment on the government of the day. There is evidence that in the early years of the Canadian Parliament the speakership was sometimes used as a consolation prize for a member who had been disappointed in his hopes of cabinet office. The government regarded the Speaker as one of their own and little was done to boost his authority or encourage practices which would assist him in gaining the confidence of the opposition. It says much for successive occupants of the Chair that they rarely fell foul of the opposition parties to any serious extent and only once has a Canadian Speaker been the object of a motion of censure. This occasion was undoubtedly the low point in the history of the Canadian speakership and its victim was, ironically, the first Speaker whose nomination had been seconded by the Leader of the Opposition at his election to the Chair in 1953. The Speaker concerned, René Beaudoin, had been highly regarded until the occurrence of the sequence of events which led to his downfall. These events, dealt with below, would seem to confirm a view expressed by Professor Aitchison in a letter to the Toronto Globe and Mail on 9 April 1962 in which he wrote: 'The Canadian practices concerning the speakership are almost wholly bad. The degree of impartiality achieved by Canadian Speakers has been achieved in spite of them, not because of them.' Since this letter was written the speakership has gained impressively in authority and prestige, largely because of the calibre of the occupants of the Chair since that time and a certain change of attitude on the part of governments with regard to the office. In the matter of preferment, for example, it is interesting to note that it was a Liberal government which appointed Roland Michener, a Progressive Conservative Speaker, Governor-General, and a Progressive Conservative government which appointed the Liberal James Jerome a judge of the federal court. Perhaps the day will dawn when the Canadian speakership may yet become an end in itself, the culmination of a highly distinguished career in public life as in Britain.

Speaker Beaudoin and the Pipeline Debate

The ordeal of René Beaudoin took place in 1956 and arose from the bitter controversy aroused by the so-called Pipeline Bill of that year's session. It was a controversy which led to the first use of closure in the Canadian House of Commons in 24 years and because of the circumstances in which it was invoked a measure of odium has attached to the closure ever since that time. Although it has been invoked on a number of occasions since, governments were for many years hesitant to resort to it because of its associations with the Pipeline Bill. It is also interesting to note that Canadian closure procedure, unlike that of Westminster, does not involve the discretion of the Chair. It is moved by a minister, notice of intention to do so having been given at the previous sitting, and decided without amendment or debate. It is less draconian in its operation than the British closure since, if carried, debate may be continued on the question before the House until 1 a.m. the following morning, speeches being limited to twenty minutes.[14] It is undoubtedly fortunate, given the many other pressures on the Speaker, that he was at least spared the responsibility of deciding whether or not the closure motion should be allowed. As it was, he was embroiled in a series of complex procedural disputes which culminated in the only motion of censure against the Speaker which the Canadian House of Commons has ever known. In the course of these unfortunate proceedings the Speaker was dragged into the thick of the party conflict. Twenty-five rulings from the Chair were challenged during eighteen days of acrimonious and sometimes disorderly debate. Allegations of partisanship were made against him, and so far did the relationship between the Speaker and the Opposition deteriorate that in some quarters of the House lack of respect for the Chair was openly manifested, and defiance and resentment were freely expressed.

In 1951 Trans-Canada Pipe Lines Ltd., a company controlled by American interests, proposed to build a trans-Canadian pipeline to convey natural gas from Alberta to Quebec. Difficulties arose regarding the Northern Ontario section of the line, where the nature of the territory was such as to make the cost of constructing and operating this part of the line beyond the capacity of private finance. In 1956, therefore, the Canadian Government proposed the constitution of a Crown Corporation to finance the building of the Northern Ontario section of the line, the Corporation to be empowered to borrow money up to a limit of 130 million dollars and to lease its section of the line, when completed, to Trans-Canada Pipe Lines, Ltd., with an option to purchase. Two of the parties in the House, the Conservatives who formed the official Opposition, and the Co-operative Commonwealth Federation, objected to the proposal on the ground that it would make public funds available to assist foreign interests to establish effective control over one of Canada's major natural resources. The first debate on the issue took place on 15 March when the House went into committee to consider a government resolution that the Crown Corporation should be constituted. On 8 May the Government entered into an agreement with the Trans-Canada Company whereby the latter undertook to construct the Alberta-Saskatchewan-Manitoba section of the line in 1956 provided certain loans had been authorized by Parliament by 7 June. The effect of this agreement was to necessitate the conferring of wider powers upon the proposed Crown Corporation in respect of the granting of loans, and, more significantly, to place a deadline on the passage of the Bill constituting the Corporation.

On 9 May the Government gave notice of a new resolution embodying the terms of the first and making provision also for the additional powers required by the Corporation to enable it to implement the agreement with the Trans-Canada Company. The Leader of the Opposition, Mr. Drew, submitted that it was irregular for two motions dealing with the same subject matter to be before the House at the same time, but on 10 May the Speaker ruled that this was not irregular provided that when the House had arrived at a decision on one of them the other was not proceeded with. The ruling was challenged and sustained on a division. On 14 May a similar objection was raised on the motion that the House go into committee on the resolution and a further lengthy argument took place on a question of order. The Speaker again ruled in favour of proceeding with the resolution, and his ruling was again challenged and sustained on a division. The dispute was raised again in Committee of the Whole House, as a result of which the Government gave notice of the application of the closure on the ground 'that some hon. Members prefer to obstruct this motion rather than debate it'. This move, of course, heightened the conflict further, and as one confused sitting followed another the mood of the House became angrier and the procedural wrangles more complex. The closure was adopted for the first time on 15 May, and when the question was put for leave to introduce a Bill based on the resolution a point of order was raised claiming that the closure applied only to the proceedings on the resolution, and that since the normal hour of adjournment had passed the Bill could not be introduced in that sitting. The Speaker ruled that a Bill based on a financial resolution was customarily introduced as soon as the resolution had been agreed to, and his ruling was confirmed by the House on a division. On 17 May, Mr. Knowles rose to a point of order when the order for the second reading of the Bill was called, claiming that the Bill infringed the principle of parliamentary control over finance in that the agreement to which it referred was not before the House. The Speaker ruled against the submission, and again his ruling was challenged and confirmed on a division. Assisted by the application of the closure, the Bill was given a second reading on 22 May. On 28 May, after four stormy days had been spent in committee on the Bill, the Leader of the Opposition sought leave to move the adjournment of the House on a definite matter of urgent public importance, namely, 'the subordination by the Government of the office of Chairman of the committee of the whole to serve the partisan interests of the Government'. He endeavoured, somewhat unconvincingly, to justify the abnormal use of this procedure on the ground that the motion as framed did not constitute a censure upon the Chairman. This contention was rejected by the Speaker who refused to allow the motion.

The application of the closure to the Committee stage of the Bill sparked off further procedural disputes and led to an extremely confused situation. On 31 May the Speaker was recalled to the Chair after a ruling by the Chairman had been challenged in committee, but before the Speaker could put the question, Mr. Gordon Churchill rose to a point of order, the substance of which was that a ruling of the Chairman should be subject to review by the Speaker before the House is called on to give a decision on it. A debate on this point of order was interrupted by the dinner recess. When the House resumed Mr. Alistair Stewart moved the adjournment of the House, after which, the motion being negatived, the Speaker ruled that a Chairman's ruling is not subject to review by the Speaker. This ruling was challenged, whereupon the Speaker stated that in his opinion an appeal to the House was irregular in this case since it concerned a ruling given in Committee of the Whole House, and the Speaker's duty in respect of it consisted only of receiving the Chairman's report of the matter and submitting it to the House. Having stated this authoritative opinion, the Speaker unfortunately proceeded to compromise his position by adding: 'However, I am sure we will advance much better if I allow the appeal, but I repeat that I do not want this to be taken as a precedent.' The appeal was made and the House confirmed the ruling. Another motion to adjourn the House was then negatived on a division, but before the Speaker could put the question for which he was recalled to the Chair in the first place, Mr. Colin Cameron raised a question of privilege arising out of certain letters published in the Ottawa Journal which related to the proceedings of the House in the course of the pipeline debate. Having drawn attention to the letters he moved 'that these statements in the newspaper are derogatory of the dignity of Parliament and deserving of the censure of this House'. This motion was debated until the automatic interruption of business at 10 p.m., when the House adjourned without having come to any decision on the Chairman's ruling.[15]

Before the debate on the privilege motion could be resumed on the following day, the Speaker rose at the outset of business to make the following statement:

> I have read carefully the articles complained of and I have come to the conclusion that because of the unprecedented circumstances surrounding this pipeline debate and because of the remarks that were made in this House by Members themselves, it was and it is impossible, if we are to consider freedom of the press as we should, to take these two articles as being breaches of our privileges. It is my opinion that if it had not been for some of the insinuations or attacks directed perhaps to one another or the Chair or to the occupants of the Chair, these articles may not have been written. I think we should settle our problems among ourselves and that those who outside of this House, either in editorial comment or by letters to the editor, write what I consider to be—and this is the case of these two articles—comments which do not go beyond the bounds of unfairness, I think they should be allowed. Therefore, I rule the motion . . . . out of order.[16]

The Speaker refused to permit debate on this ruling which was sustained by the House on appeal. Immediately afterwards, Mr. Knowles moved the adjournment of the House, but the Speaker, having recapitulated the sequence of events of the previous day, expressed the opinion that he had made a serious mistake in not putting the question on the Chairman's ruling immediately on taking the Chair. He continued:

> I want to say this to hon. Members—it has been said very often – the rules of this House are devised in order to protect the minorities; yes, they are. But I will add the counterpart to that. I will say – and the authorities support me in this – that the rules of this House are devised to protect minorities against the oppression of the majority and the majority against obstruction by the minority.
>
> Now, the House is the master of its own rules and it is my right to submit a matter to the House. I intend at the moment to submit to the House that, in my view, the House should revert to the position where it was yesterday when I was brought back to the Chair to receive the Chairman's report at 5.15. I submit to the House that the intervening proceedings should not be superseded, and it is up to the House to decide as to the situation which I take at the moment.

The effect of the Speaker's submission was to disallow the adjournment motion. The Leader of the Opposition then proceeded to move a motion of no confidence in the Speaker, but was reminded by the latter that such a motion required forty-eight hours' notice. Mr. Knowles rose next to a point of order, claiming that as the Speaker had ruled his motion to adjourn the House out of order, he, Knowles, was entitled to appeal against the ruling. The Speaker acknowledged the validity of Mr. Knowles' point of order and indicated by his reply that he had shifted from his previous position. 'I will agree with him that his motion was made before I had indicated my position, and I will allow his appeal and submit it to the House.' After further exchanges the Speaker agreed to put the question on the motion itself, which was negatived. After an unsuccessful attempt by Mr. Cameron to revive his question of privilege, the Speaker rose to make a statement at the commencement of government business. He reminded the House that it had come to no decision on the Chairman's ruling from the previous day, and that the first order of the day ('House again in committee of the whole') might therefore be regarded as irregular. But, he pointed out, the proceedings of the previous day had been entirely unprecedented. He continued:

> Therefore I had to deal with the problem last evening before I left, and the matter which was before the House was, as provided in the rules, an appeal . . . of a ruling made by the Chairman in committee, and that report must be submitted to the House and the committee must resume the consideration of its business at once. Therefore I gave instructions to the Clerk to put the order on the order paper and it is in relation to that instruction, for which I take responsibility, that I suggest the action I outlined a moment ago to the House. It is absolutely unprovided for; it is unprecedented; and the matter I outlined a moment ago is one which I thought I had the right to submit to the House at the time I did.

After some angry exchanges had taken place the Speaker concluded his statement with the following words:

> What I intended to submit to the House is that in neglecting to submit at once to the House yesterday the report of the Chairman of the committee on an appeal from his ruling . . . I made a serious mistake and the House should not suffer any prejudice or detriment on my account, and that the House, which is master of its own proceedings, should be placed in exactly the same position as it was when I resumed the Chair yesterday to submit the Chairman's ruling to the House.

He then called upon the House to take a vote on his proposed course of action, upon which an angry scene ensued. Several Members attempted to address the Chair, and the bitterly reproachful words of Mr. Fleming reflected the general acrimony:

> Mr. Speaker, it should be placed on the record that when an hon. Member rose on a question of privilege you sat down and refused to hear him and the Liberals instigated such an outburst of disorder that no one could be heard. That ought to be on the record. This is the lowest moment in Canadian parliamentary history; the lowest moment. There has never been anything like it.

The course of action proposed by the Speaker was carried by 142 votes to nil, the Conservatives and the Co-operative Commonwealth Federation having abstained from voting because they took the view that no question was properly before the House. The House then recessed for lunch, after which the Speaker proceeded immediately to put the question on the Chairman's ruling of the previous day, refusing to hear any further submission on the matter from the opposition parties. The ruling was confirmed and the committee resumed.[17]

On 4 June the Leader of the Opposition moved a motion of censure against the Speaker in the following terms:

> In view of the unprecedented action of Mr. Speaker in (a) improperly reversing his own decision without notice and without giving any opportunity for discussion; (b) repeatedly refusing to allow Members to address the House on occasions when the rules provide that they have the right to be heard; (c) subordinating the rights of the House to the will of the Government, this House resolves that it no longer has any confidence in its presiding officer.

In his speech the Leader of the Opposition reviewed the events which had led to the motion of censure, and concluded:

> A partisan vote on the motion now before us will not relieve the unhappy situation in which we now find ourselves. Never before has this

House been faced with so serious a situation. Never before were Members of this House conscious as they now are that something good, decent, precious and valuable has been destroyed. There is only one way this situation can be relieved. I appeal with all the earnestness I possess to the Prime Minister as head of the Government to follow the only course which will restore the dignity, honour and traditions of Parliament. That course is to dissolve this House and let the people elect a new Parliament more in harmony with our traditions and concepts of government. To let this motion go to a vote that divides the House denies the very basis upon which the Speaker occupies the Chair.

It has long been our tradition that the Speaker is the unanimous choice of the House. Let there be no uncertainty about the fact that the Speaker is not the choice of most of the Members on this side of the House at this time.

The Leader of the Co-operative Commonwealth Federation, Mr. Coldwell, spoke in support of the motion. A spokesman for the other minority party, Social Credit, then spoke in support of the Speaker, observing in the course of his speech:

The Speaker of this House is the unfortunate victim of circumstances that were not of his making. I think that this is something we must keep in mind at all times. He was not responsible for the situation that developed in this House during the past few days. I think most of us will agree, and the Leader of the Opposition has already stated it, that he had earned a fine reputation for impartiality and for fairness. I would say that he invariably leaned over backwards in order to meet the requests of the Opposition, and it was probably that very action that got him into trouble in this debate. It is a very fine way to act in normal times but you cannot act that way in times of lawlessness because those who are committing those acts will take advantage of that type of leniency.

The Prime Minister spoke next, repudiating the arguments of the Leader of the Opposition and upholding the Speaker's conduct with the aid of various citations and quotations from a newspaper editorial. He concluded by moving the adjournment of the debate which was carried on a division. The question was then raised as to whether it was proper for the Speaker to continue to preside while the question of his conduct remained undecided. The Prime Minister replied that it was the Speaker's duty, in terms of law and the practice of the House, to continue to occupy the Chair even though the proceedings involved a question of his personal conduct. On 5 June, the closure having again been called into operation, the Pipeline Bill passed through its final stages in the House of Commons. The debate on the motion of censure was continued on the 6th, 7th and 8th of June, when it was negatived by 109 votes to 35.[18]

The matter unfortunately did not end there. On 29 June the Leader of the Opposition drew the attention of the House, as a matter of privilege, to the publication in the press of parts of a letter written by the Speaker impugning the conduct of certain Members of the House during the course of the pipeline debate. The Speaker explained that the comments complained of were an expression of personal opinion contained in a private letter which was never intended for publication, and he gave an account of the circumstances in which the extracts came to be published. The explanation did not, however, alter the view of the Leader of the Opposition who observed:

> Whether the Speaker is a permanent Speaker, as at Westminster, or a Speaker chosen by a motion of all the Members, as is done here, the Speaker, if there is to be any dignity in the proceedings of the House, must command the confidence of the Members that the decisions he makes will be impartial decisions within the reasonable bounds of human frailty. Whether it was intended that this letter be published or not is in itself unimportant. We now know that the Speaker, whose impartiality we are expected to respect, holds the opinion that arguments that were made here falsified the facts or, to use the alternative expression the Speaker has used, distorted the facts for political ends.[19]

On 2 July, the next sitting day, the Speaker placed his resignation before the House, to take effect at the pleasure of the House. 'Throughout my term of office, I assure you,' he said, 'I have never acted, nor have I ever been motivated, by any other interests but the best interests of the House itself. Never was I motivated by any partisan feelings; and my conscience is perfectly clear. Had it not been as clear as it is, I do not think I could have gone through all the difficulties that came my way in the past month.' He was, however, persuaded by the Prime Minister to withdraw his resignation, and he continued in office until the end of the Parliament. Speaking on 9 July the Prime Minister, Mr. St. Laurent said:

> I share, and I am sure most hon. Members share, the regret of the Speaker that any part of his personal letter was published. I cannot, however, share the view that because the Speaker had expressed in private the views he did express in that letter, he could no longer continue to be an impartial and competent Speaker. It does not seem to me that the publication by someone else of an extract from a private letter would justify me, or the majority in this House, in taking any formal action in consequence of what has taken place. During the debate on the motion relating to his conduct and subsequently Mr. Speaker has discharged his duties in this House with dignity and impartiality.
>
> My confidence in Mr. Speaker is unshaken, and I know of no other Member better qualified than he is to preside over our deliberations; I believe that confidence is shared by an overwhelming majority of Members, a majority by no means confined to the supporters of the Government.

> Now, as the one responsible for the leadership in this House, I have expressed that view to Mr. Speaker and I have found that he was willing to subordinate his personal feelings to his duty to Parliament and the country, and to continue in the office in which he has served with great distinction.[20]

An objective study of the sequence of events suggests that the Speaker allowed himself to become an instrument of the government's parliamentary strategy. With the advantage of hindsight, it is clear that many of his decisions and actions were ill-advised and that he allowed himself to be unduly influenced by government pressure. It is unlikely that he was consciously partisan, but the distressing circumstances in which he was placed were such that his only hope of emerging with his reputation untarnished would have required him to place at risk the government's entire pipeline policy. The government regarded this policy as essential to the national interest and used the force of this argument to bring pressure to bear on the Speaker. The Speaker should no doubt have resisted this pressure, pointing out that his job was to ensure correct procedures were observed, that the government and not he was responsible for the national interest, and that if the government had mismanaged its parliamentary strategy it should not look to the Speaker to rescue it. In cool retrospect this is an easy judgment to make. Under the strain and stress of the moment the dilemma of a Speaker lacking the security and confidence which come with total political independence is also easy to appreciate. Another lesson to be learned from the pipeline debate is that the right to challenge a ruling from the Chair other than by substantive motion (a rule which has since been changed) and a virtually unrestricted freedom to debate points of order are not in the best interests of the parliamentary institution.

The Speaker and Procedure

Until comparatively recently any member had the right to appeal from a ruling of the Chair simply by standing in his place immediately after the ruling had been given and announcing his intention to do so. The Speaker would then enquire of the House whether his ruling be sustained and if five or more members rose in opposition the House would be summoned as if for a division. The members having been called in, the Speaker repeated his ruling, announced that an appeal had been entered and again asked whether the ruling be sustained, at which point a division would normally take place. If the rule had any advantage at all, it was that it created the possibility of challenging a ruling without having to resort to a motion of censure. In practice the rule had little to recommend it. In an essay written prior to the abolition of the rule, Professor Aitchison made the following observations:

> The case for the abolition of appeals is overwhelming even in the absence of a permanent Speakership. Appeals are almost always made by Opposition Members and are almost always lost. When the ruling is a

good one, an appeal adds nothing to the prestige of the Speaker; when the ruling is bad, a bad ruling is confirmed by a vote of the House. The use that I have suggested Opposition Members have latterly discovered for appeals is an illegitimate one and should be denied them. Appeals are ineffective as a means of obstruction, for the Canadian closure, once invoked, is inexorable. There has, however, been a persistent belief among Opposition Members that the appeal procedure affords them some protection. Since there is always a possibility that the Government will avail itself of it, the procedure, on the contrary, is a positive danger to Opposition Members. It has also been frequently asserted in the Canadian House that the abolition of appeals would be inconsistent with the position of the Speaker as a servant of the House and the fact that the House is master of its own procedure. But there are no appeals in the British House where the Speaker is equally the servant of the House and the House the master of its procedure. The Speaker best serves the House if his rulings cannot be reversed, and the House best serves its own interest by controlling its procedure through the deliberate amendment of the rules when necessary, and not through the determination by majority vote of the application of the rules to particular cases.[21]

It is very difficult to challenge the validity of these arguments, the more so since the use of the right of appeal for purely political motives had become an accepted practice in the Canadian House of Commons. An incident which occurred on 31 January 1963 provides an illustration of the kind of unfortunate situation which can arise in consequence. A request by Mr. Lester Pearson, then Leader of the Opposition, for leave to move the adjournment of the House for the purpose of discussing a definite matter of urgent public importance was refused by Speaker Lambert on the ground that it did not comply with the requirements of the relevant Standing Order. Mr. Pearson then announced his desire to appeal against the ruling, but the Speaker ruled that such a decision admitted of no appeal, citing a specific precedent in support of his contention. Thereupon, another Member appealed against the ruling that there could be no appeal. In the ensuing division the three Opposition parties combined against the governing party to defeat the Speaker's second ruling by 122 votes to 104. The first ruling was then put to the House and defeated on a voice vote. Speaker Lambert thus became the first Speaker in thirty-seven years to have his rulings overridden by the House. It was nowhere suggested that his decisions were not entirely in accord with established procedure and precedent; in fact, it was generally conceded that they were consistent with previous practice. The validity of the rulings themselves was not the issue in question, for it was openly acknowledged by Opposition Members that their vote had been intended as an attack on the Government rather than on the decisions of the Chair.[22]*

* The last time a Speaker's ruling was overturned on appeal was on 24 February 1965, shortly before the rule was changed. Speaker Alan Macnaughton had ruled that no *prima facie* case had been established concerning a question of privilege and his ruling was reversed by the House.

One of the recommendations of the report by Professor Denis Smith (referred to above) was that the rule permitting appeals should be abolished, and it was in fact abolished on a provisional basis in 1965 and permanently in 1968.[23] The House stopped short, however, of removing the right of appeal against the rulings of the Chairman in committee of the whole House, such appeals now being decided by the Speaker.[24] This rule when invoked places the Speaker in the most invidious position of having to pronounce upon the judgment of his colleague. On 26 January 1967 Speaker Lamoureux reversed a ruling of the Chairman concerning the admissibility of an amendment to a bill, but in doing so he took the opportunity to question the propriety of a rule which required him to substitute his own judgment for that of the Chairman.[25] If the right to appeal against Chairman's rulings is to be retained it would probably be better to leave the decision in the hands of the House, as before.

The report by Denis Smith made a number of recommendations the majority of which were not implemented. The general thrust of the report was to secure for the Speaker the level of political independence enjoyed by his counterpart in Great Britain. Some progress has been made, however, in the direction urged by the report, including the advancement of the Speaker in the order of precedence and the equating of the Speaker's salary with that of a cabinet minister. The administrative reorganization of the House of Commons has also gone some way towards clarifying the Speaker's jurisdiction over Parliament Hill and other buildings allocated to the use of the House of Commons, another area where Professor Smith saw a need for improvement.

It is fair to say that the Canadian speakership enjoys the dignity and prestige which should properly attach to the presiding officer of a democratically elected assembly although the strength of his authority may fall short of that of a Speaker whose political detachment is total. It is questionable, for example, whether, if called upon to use his casting vote at the third reading of an important government bill, a Canadian Speaker would observe the British precedent of voting with the nays. Speaker Jerome, although he was never faced with such a decision, has speculated on what a Canadian Speaker might do in such circumstances:

> In exercising the casting vote the Speaker is guided by certain precedents. He is not expected to give weight to his own personal inclination but rather to use his casting vote in such a way as to keep the matter before the House open for further consideration wherever possible. I have always been fascinated by the obvious corollary of the proposition, namely that if a measure is before the House for a final vote at third reading, with no opportunity for further amendment or discussion, and the votes for and against are equal, the Speaker should use his casting vote to reject the measure. The principle here is that the Speaker should not by his casting vote sanction a change in the law but should opt for the *status quo*. On the other hand it has been argued that the Speaker should not by his casting vote make himself responsible for the rejection of a government measure.[26]

The Speaker is empowered by the standing orders to select or combine amendments or clauses to be proposed at the report stage of a bill.[27] Although this would appear to confer on the Speaker the formidable power over the selection of amendments which is vested in his British counterpart, no Canadian Speaker has ever interpreted the rule in this way. He has used the discretion permitted by the standing order to combine similar amendments rather than assume the power to select and thereby reject certain amendments as sanctioned by the British practice. A Canadian Speaker would probably require a clear direction from the House before he would venture to follow British precedent in the interpretation of this power.

A further illustration of the delicate tightrope on which a Canadian Speaker can find himself balanced is to be found in the circumstances attendant upon the controversial constitutional debate which took place in 1981. The debate in question had been taking place for a number of weeks when the government introduced a motion to limit the number of days devoted to its continuation and extend the hours of sitting on those days. This provoked the opposition into organizing a strategy of systematic obstruction through the raising of points of order and questions of privilege which for six days prevented the House from proceeding with its normal business. It was a situation which could not have arisen in the British House of Commons where the Speaker can decline to entertain a question of privilege before it is even raised on the floor of the House and where the Chair would never allow extensive debates to take place on either points of order or questions of privilege. Speaker Jeanne Sauvé was faced with an unprecedented situation which she handled with great skill. It would have been contrary to the customs of the Canadian House to have taken too hard a line with the members continually claiming to raise points of order and privilege. To have done so would have invited a motion of censure against the Chair since the tactics were those of the entire official opposition. On the other hand the Speaker, as she recognized, had a duty to control deliberate obstruction through a reasonable interpretation of the rules of procedure. While never losing her patience she dealt sharply with members who continually returned to matters on which she had already ruled, and on 2 April 1981 she invited members who had given notice of questions or privilege relating to the constitutional issue to withdraw them voluntarily. She also announced that thenceforward members raising questions of privilege would be cut off after five minutes if they had not made their point within that time.[28] The deadlock was finally resolved by agreement between the government and the opposition parties with concessions made on both sides, a constructive result to which the Speaker's handling of a difficult situation undoubtedly contributed. Her patience, firmness and resistance to pressure preserved the integrity of Parliament in circumstances where it could easily have been menaced. She successfully avoided the pitfall in which Speaker Beaudoin had found himself ensnared, forcing the parties to resolve the political dilemma by themselves and refusing to place at risk the independence of the Chair.

In March 1982, Speaker Sauvé was once again faced with a problem of unprecedented difficulty and probably the severest test that any Speaker had experienced since the ordeal of Speaker Beaudoin. The crisis was precipitated on 2 March when the Speaker ruled that a major bill incorporating a number of important principles was in order and did not have to be divided. Her ruling was in accordance with previous precedents relating to so-called omnibus bills, although her two immediate predecessors had both expressed concern at the practice of incorporating a number of different principles into a single piece of legislation. The Opposition, after considerable argument had taken place, reacted to the ruling by moving the adjournment of the House, a motion which is not debatable.[29] There is, however, a convention whereby the division bells may ring indefinitely in cases where a vote was not anticipated. This convention is based on courtesy, it being accepted that the House will not be called upon to vote until the whips on both sides have satisfied themselves that all their members are assembled. In this instance, however, the Official Opposition decided to use this practice as the basic plank of their strategy for obstructing the bill. Having called for a division, they announced that they would not attend the House to vote until the Government agreed to divide the bill. They allowed the division bells to ring continuously, day and night, for 16 days before agreeing to return to the House after receiving from the Government what they regarded as an acceptable offer to negotiate.

During this period the Speaker declined to intervene, taking the view that the political parties had brought about the crisis and it was therefore up to them to resolve it. The House eventually assembled on 17 March and voted on the adjournment motion. On the following day Speaker Sauvé made a statement explaining the attitude she had taken during the crisis. She pointed out that she had no precedents to guide her and that she found herself faced with a conflict between her duty to be impartial and her responsibility for ensuring that the House functioned as it should. She underlined the need for procedural reform and for guidelines which would assist the Chair in areas where the rules and practice were not specific. She concluded by saying:

> It is my hope that such a situation will never again occur in this House. However, should it occur again, the Chair, unless it is provided with firm guidelines, would need to consider its course of action with very great care under the new circumstances. I trust that in the overriding interests of this honourable institution, the House will take steps to make known its will as to how the Chair should act before any such situation occurs again.[30]

A number of commentators expressed the view that it was the responsibility of the Chair to end the paralysis of the House. But had the Speaker intervened it would almost certainly have been seen as a move against the Official Opposition and there is little doubt she would have faced a motion of censure.*

---

* Since this incident took place, the Chair has instituted the practice of interrupting the bells at the moment of automatic adjournment. On May 9, 1983, in the case of a

The above examples of Canadian practice illustrate certain contrasts between the authority of the Canadian Speaker and that of his British counterpart. However, on the other side of the coin, there is an important area of financial procedure which does not seem to have involved the Chair in Great Britain, but where Canadian Speakers have regularly been called upon to render highly controversial decisions. This involves the use of token votes and other items in the estimates of expenditure for the purpose of launching programmes and financing projects which would normally require specific legislation. Canadian parliamentarians have consistently complained about the use of supply items for legislative purposes, the central question being whether the government can obtain by means of a supply item in an appropriation bill a financial authority which it does not have under existing legislation. On 22 March 1977 the official opposition used an allotted day to debate a non-confidence motion condemning the government for its use of 'dollar items'.[31] In Great Britain this is a problem to which the Public Accounts Committee has repeatedly drawn attention but it does not appear that the Speaker has ever been called upon to give a ruling on the issue. Whether the authority given by the Appropriation Act is an adequate substitute for authorization by a specific bill does not seem to have been resolved in Britain, and Erskine May points out that 'there is, so far as this question is concerned, no legal restraint on the discretion of the Crown in presenting an estimate, or on that of Parliament in authorizing the expenditure provided by such an estimate by the Appropriation Act.'[32]

In Canada one can point to clear precedents as a result of successive interventions of the Chair. Before the procedural reforms of 1968 all estimates were debated on the floor of the House in committee of supply. Objections were frequently raised to the government's use of 'dollar items' but they were tolerated because unlimited time was allowed to the consideration of supply and there were better opportunities for scrutiny. The first major ruling from the Chair on this issue was handed down by Speaker Lamoureux on 10 March 1971. He declared that because of the changes in supply procedure three items which were legislative in intent were not before the House in proper form.[33] Another major ruling was given on 22 March 1977 by Speaker Jerome who took the opportunity to comment on the difficulties of the Chair in resolving such questions. He set aside two items but took a more lenient view of a number of others to which objection had been taken because of what he regarded as the inadequacy of the procedure for the guidance of the Chair.[34] A recent ruling on the issue was given by Speaker Sauvé on 12 June 1981. Its effect was to strike out ten items as being not properly before the House, one of which even went so far as to confer a power to make regulations on the executive.[35] It was a ruling which did not please the government but it was amply supported by precedent. The Canadian practice imposes a very

---

Footnote continued from p. 123

substantive motion, the bells continued to ring at 9:00 a.m. the following morning. On May 17, 1983, a motion for the adjournment of the House, being a dilatory motion, was declared to have lapsed at the moment of automatic adjournment.

invidious responsibility on the Speaker and raises the question of whether such a function should properly belong to the Chair. At least one Speaker has expressed reservations, as we have seen, and it could be argued that government abuses of this kind should more appropriately be attacked by political methods such as censure motions and exposure by committee investigation.

As in the British House, difficulties have occasionally been encountered by Speakers in the interpretation of the *sub judice* convention. Its operation with regard to criminal cases has always been fairly straightforward, but where civil cases are concerned its application has always been very flexible and no settled practice has developed. It has sometimes been invoked in respect to the proceedings of tribunals which are designated courts of record but has never been deemed to apply to royal commissions. In February 1976 a case arose in which a member who had been served with a civil writ for libel sought to question a minister on a matter relevant to the action. Speaker Jerome, having expressed some doubts about allowing the question, subsequently ruled that it was admissible because the action had not been set down for trial.[36] This incident was one of the considerations which led to the appointment of a Special Committee under the chairmanship of the Speaker on the Rights and Immunities of Members whose first and only report was devoted to the operation of the *sub judice* convention. The committee found that the basic parliamentary immunity of freedom of speech was to some extent limited by the *sub judice* convention and expressed the view that the justification for it had not been established beyond all doubt. It did not, however, propose its total abolition but recommended 'that any modification of the practice should be in the direction of greater flexibility rather than stricter application'. The committee recognized that in the last resort there could be no substitute for the discretion of the Chair in the application of the rule but felt that the responsibility for exercising restraint should be shared by all members of the House. 'It is the view of your Committee that the responsibility of the Chair during the question period should be minimal as regards the *sub judice* convention, and that the responsibility should rest principally upon the Member who asks the question and the minister to whom it is addressed.' The committee recommended that the Speaker should invoke the rule only in exceptional cases and that in cases of doubt a presumption should exist in favour of allowing debate rather than applying the convention.[37] The House and the Chair have since been guided by the findings of this report.

In the matter of parliamentary privilege the Speaker, like his British counterpart, has the responsibility of determining whether or not the matter raised should be given precedence over other business. Canadian practice with relation to privilege questions, while to some extent relying on the British practice, has nevertheless evolved differently. Matters of alleged privilege are regularly raised by members, although most of them do not conform to the criteria which define a genuine question of privilege. The principal intention of members is to place the matter on the record and this is their main concern even when they have a valid question of privilege. The Chair, for its part, will allow the matter to be aired and sometimes take it under advisement before

The Office of Speaker

rendering a decision. Usually the ruling will be such as to avoid leading to a debate on a formal motion or the referral of the question to the Standing Committee on Privileges and Elections. This is because the Canadian House of Commons, in recent decades at least, has been less sensitive than the British House of the need to protect its privileges from encroachment. It has, for example, shown a consistently tolerant attitude to exaggerated press comment, and has enjoyed a relative freedom from the kind of cases based on a technical interpretation of privilege which some years ago led to embarrassing situations in the British House of Commons and a serious reappraisal of the whole question by a select committee of that House in 1967. One result of that reappraisal in the British House is that questions of privilege must now be cleared with the Speaker before they can even be raised on the floor of the House. In Canada the Speaker cannot prevent the matter being raised in the House provided he receives written notice at least one hour beforehand. Once the matter has been aired, however, his discretion in dealing with it is very wide and flexible. Some examples will illustrate the manner in which questions of privilege are dealt with in Canada.

Abundant evidence is to be found in the debates of the Canadian House of Commons of its concern for the freedom of the press. On 24 October 1966, for example, a cabinet minister, Mr. George McIlraith, warned against 'interfering with the right of members of the press freely to report the proceedings in this House as they see them.'[38]

A few years later a case arose which constitutes a truly remarkable example of parliamentary tolerance. On 9 June, 1969 a member drew attention by way of a question of privilege to a newspaper report on the proceedings of a parliamentary committee. The report included the following paragraphs:

> Throughout their hearings on the seal hunt, the committee has functioned like a hanging jury in a kangaroo court. As usually happens in such cases, and as is evident in the report, they got the verdict they wanted. . . . To accomplish their purpose the committee members proceeded with vigour. They maligned and insulted opponents of the seal hunt; they accepted unquestioningly the testimony of witnesses whom they liked, and rejected the testimony which did not accord with their prejudices.[39]

The Speaker declined on procedural grounds to accord the member's question of privilege priority over other business, and in the course of his ruling, he made the following observations:

> I indicated this afternoon that when one considers the matter of parliamentary privilege in relation to newspaper comments, two conflicting interests must be taken into account. The first is the privilege of honourable Members to exercise their duties free from undue interference. The second is the freedom of the press in relation to its reporting of parliamentary activities. On this point I should like to refer to a ruling of Mr. Speaker Macnaughton reported at page 4434 of

Hansard of June 18, 1964. This ruling reads, in part, as follows: 'It seems to me that if this editorial referred in general terms to Members of Parliament none of us, I suppose would be so thin-skinned that we could not accept some rather healthy criticism. . . .' At the same time I would suggest that the language used is very strong and might well be considered to constitute contempt of Parliament. Against this there has to be weighed the requirements of a free press reporting and commenting objectively on parliamentary activities.[40]

In Canada no clear statement exists as to whether or not it is a breach of privilege to disclose confidential committee proceedings, and the Canadian practice in this matter contrasts markedly with the very serious view taken by the British House of such disclosures. There is even a ruling on the record, although it is couched in rather uncertain terms, to the effect that reference by a member in the course of debate in the House to what takes place at a committee meeting held in camera is not a breach of privilege.[41] It is worth noting by way of contrast that in 1968 a British member was reprimanded in his place by the Speaker by order of the House for having revealed confidential evidence received by a committee of which he was a member to a journalist;[42] and that in 1976 The Economist newspaper was censured by the Committee of Privileges for having published the confidential report of a select committee.[43] Two comparable cases have arisen in the Canadian House in recent years. On 21 October 1975 the Commons chairman of a joint committee raised as a matter of privilege the publication in the press of extracts from the committee's confidential draft report. He maintained that its premature publication had reduced the ability of the committee to deal with its task and misled the public into believing that the draft represented the committee's final recommendations. The Speaker, delivering his ruling on the following day, declined to give the matter precedence over the business of the day, observing *inter alia*:

> The difficulty about the motion before us is not that it fails to deal with what appears to be a well accepted question of privilege in general terms but, rather, that it fails to be sufficiently specific. I refer to the absence from the motion of any allegation of misconduct which is specifically complained of in terms of a breach of the privileges of the House. Has there been an action by the publishers of the newspapers involved, or by the radio or television station, which constitutes a breach? The motion does not say. Has there been an action by a member of the House of Commons or by a member of the other place? The motion does not suggest it. Has there been an action by a staff member, perhaps, here or in the other place? Again, the motion does not suggest it. In other words, it seems to me that what the motion seeks is not an investigation of a *prima facie* case of privilege but, rather, an investigation to determine whether a *prima facie* question of privilege exists or whether a substantive motion would be in order.[44]

The second case arose on 6 May 1977 when a member complained that the confidential proceedings of a committee had been published in the press, the implication being that the document concerned was stolen by a journalist. The Speaker reserved his ruling until 23 June when he acknowledged that the case contained all the elements of a *prima faice* matter of privilege. However, he went on to say:

> It concerns me, however, that the motion appears to attack the press for publishing a confidential document but does not attack ourselves as members of the House for our own attitude in respect of our own confidential documents. Since it misses that point it misses something I think most important with respect to the privileges of the House.[45]

He proposed that the question of premature publication of parliamentary documents be referred to the Special Committee on Rights and Immunities of Members which was holding regular meetings at that time under his chairmanship. The session was prorogued before the committee could consider the matter and it was not reconstituted.

As a final illustration of the flexibility with which Canadian Speakers deal with matters of privilege, a case which arose on 12 May 1978 is of particular interest. Using a procedure which enables members to place a protest on the record without any ensuing debate, a member strongly criticized the proceedings of a court which had tried and convicted a man under the Official Secrets Act. On 29 May a judge of the court issued a three-page rebuke to the member in the course of which he stated: 'In the name of judicial independence, we cannot tolerate the remarks of (the member) who was wondering whether the law had not been well understood or had been wrongfully applied by the judges.' In raising the question of privilege in the House on 1 June the member concerned asserted that such language constituted a threat or an attempt to intimidate him. Ruling on the matter on 8 June the Speaker placed great stress on the right of members to criticize the institutions of the country including the courts. He acknowledged that the judge had probably gone too far in his remarks but suggested that they were also open to the more generous interpretation that he was merely seeking to defend his court. He also made an interesting distinction between words which contained a direct threat and those which only implied a threat, suggesting that it would be risky 'to extend the precedents from those cases in which a threat by language was clearly stated into that area where it was not clearly stated but implied.' He added: 'I do want to stress again that this kind of intervention by a judge in public was an extraordinary intervention, and I do not think the judge would have to do much more than he did to offend the privileges of the House.'[46]

The ruling thus contained a clear rebuke against the judge but was at the same time consistent with Canadian practice in that it did not allow the matter to be taken any further. Successive Canadian Speakers have bolstered with their decisions a practice which is both wise and tolerant, one which enables members to register their protests without undue flaunting of parliamentary privilege and which avoids inflating such matters out of proportion to their importance.

As in many other jurisdictions the Speaker plays a crucial role in the control of the question period. In the Canadian House of Commons every parliamentary day begins with an oral question period of about 45 minutes duration. Questions are asked without notice and all cabinet ministers, including the Prime Minister, may be called upon to answer questions on any day. Until 1964 oral questions were not recognized by the standing orders. They evolved as a matter of custom but for many years they have formed the substance of the question period and are normally the highlight of the parliamentary day. In theory oral questions must deal with matters of urgency but if this rule were strictly applied the essence of the question period would be destroyed. The oral question period is a period of confrontation between opposition and government, in which the former tries to expose the weaknesses of the latter, and each seeks to score political advantage. Members genuinely seeking information are more likely to give notice of written questions which are answered as and when the government chooses to do so. Despite the nature of the oral question period the Speaker must do his best to ensure that it does not become an uncontrolled free-for-all and certain rules apply and are enforced through the discretion of the Chair.[47] Speaker Jerome has commented that the question period provides 'the most fascinating challenge to any Speaker'. Having no advance notice of the questions there is a limit to the measure of control which can be exercised and some of an inadmissible nature must inevitably elude his vigilance. The guidelines relating to inadmissible questions are numerous and to apply the multifarious criteria in every instance would tax the capacity of the most experienced occupant of the Chair. Speaker Macnaughton once stated that in many cases the restrictions were inoperable even in respect of written questions. 'I suggest that if each and every one of these restrictions were applied in every case very few questions would ever reach the order paper.'[48]

The Speaker is empowered by standing order 44(5) to order a question to be set down for written answer if in his opinion it is not urgent and he normally adopts this course when a question is asked which calls for a lengthy answer. Since 1964 a member who is dissatisfied with the answer to a question or who has been told by the Speaker that his question is not urgent may give notice that he intends to raise the matter at the adjournment of the House on Monday, Tuesday or Thursday. This variation of the British procedure on the daily adjournment motion permits of up to three matters to be raised during the thirty minutes provided under standing order 45(1). The Speaker determines the order in which matters shall be raised but, unlike the British Speaker, is not equipped with any powers to select the subject for discussion.

Under Canadian practice the question period is regarded principally as opposition time and while some government members can hope to be recognized their opportunities to participate in the question period are far more limited than those of members of the opposition parties. By convention the Leader of the Opposition usually asks the first question, usually directed to the Prime Minister, and several supplementary questions are likely to ensue before it is disposed of. The leaders of any other opposition parties represented in the House are then given their turn, after which the remaining time is apportioned by the Speaker as fairly as possible. Some questions will be asked by shadow ministers, who are likely to be pursuing a party line; others will be asked by backbenchers pursuing regional or local interests or motivated by personal views on the matter concerned. Regard must be had for seniority without causing too much frustration among more recently-elected members, and special interests must be taken into account without allowing them a disproportionate amount of time. The Chair receives advice from the whips without necessarily being bound by it and a record is kept of members who have been recognized at each question period to enable the Speaker to distribute the opportunities fairly over the longer term. On 5 November 1974 Speaker Jerome ruled that parliamentary secretaries (the Canadian equivalent to parliamentary private secretaries in Great Britain) should not expect to enjoy the privilege of questioning ministers. He indicated that he was prepared to listen to further representations on the matter but he made it clear that parliamentary secretaries could not expect to be recognized during the question period while he was in the Chair.[49] His position was not entirely consistent with previous practice, as none of his predecessors had ever denied that parliamentary secretaries had the right to ask questions, but it stands as the most recent pronouncement of the Chair on the matter. As in the British House, points of order and questions of privilege are not entertained until after the oral question period, unless the Speaker considers the matter to be extremely grave.[50]

The Speaker has disciplinary powers which are similar to those of his British counterpart. He can name a member for disregarding the authority of the Chair, upon which a motion for the member's suspension is normally moved and carried by the House. Suspension is normally for the remainder of the day's sitting, a much less severe penalty than is imposed at Westminster following the naming of a member. The power to order a member to withdraw for the remainder of the sitting is possessed by the British Speaker in his own right, but the Canadian standing orders do not confer this power on the Chair, neither do they spell out in any detail the procedure consequent on the naming of a member. As in the British House, the Speaker will go to the utmost lengths to avoid naming a member and when forced into it, it is often because the member concerned is seeking the attendant publicity. The power to suspend a sitting in circumstances of grave disorder is not specified in the standing orders but could probably be invoked under standing order 1 which permits the House to follow British practice in unprovided cases. On occasions when uproar has broken out in the House the Speaker has usually stood his ground until it has subsided. Under the Speaker of the House of Commons Act 1970 the Deputy Speaker is vested with the full powers of the Speaker when the unavoidable absence of the latter has been formally notified to the House. When presiding as Chairman of a committee of the whole House the Deputy Speaker is not empowered to name a member but can make a report to the Speaker. Standing order 57(5) makes provision for the appointment of two deputies to the chairman of Committees who are vested with his full powers including his powers as Deputy Speaker during the Speaker's unavoidable absence. Unlike their British counterparts the Speaker's deputies wear traditional parliamentary costume when presiding. Deputy Speakers do not normally participate in the debates of the House but they have not all felt obliged to abstain from voting or attending party meetings. The practice has varied with the incumbents.

During the 1960's the procedures of the House of Commons underwent radical changes affecting, among other things, financial procedure, the committee system, the legislative process and the rights of the opposition through the provision of allotted days on which opposition motions take precedence. The groundwork for these changes, which were adopted on a permanent basis at the end of 1968, was laid by a Special Committee on Procedure and Organization which was appointed in 1964 under the chairmanship of Speaker Macnaughton. The committee, on which five parties were represented, included a former Speaker, Marcel Lambert, and the Deputy Speaker, Lucien Lamoureux, who later became Speaker. The committee also initiated important changes in the administrative organization of the House. The input of these occupants of the Chair towards the implementation of the procedural and administrative reforms was of great significance, particularly that of the chairman who patiently guided the committee towards a consensus on a wide range of controversial issues. As Speaker he felt he could only associate himself with recommendations which the committee was prepared to accept unanimously. Lucien Lamoureux, when he became Speaker, felt that the Speaker should be less directly involved in the process of procedural reform. He would not have accepted the chairmanship of a procedure committee, and was even reluctant to appear as a witness before such a committee although he was prepared to discuss matters informally with committee members. He believed that procedural questions were a matter for the committee and the House to decide without his intervention and it was his habit, when dealing with certain points of order in the House, to suggest that the matter raised should be considered by the committee (which was established as a standing committee after 1968).

His successor, Speaker Jerome, took a different attitude towards the matter of procedural reform and expressed himself willing to appear as a witness, offer his views and involve himself directly in any process directed towards the improvement of the practices of the House. He is on record as stating:

> . . . I believe the Speaker can assist the House by involving himself in the continuing process of procedural reform. For example I have made it clear that I am always at the disposal of the Standing Committee on Procedure and Organization should it wish to call me as a witness. I believe the Speaker's evidence in such matters can be of the utmost importance. It is he who comes into regular contact with procedural problems. He knows the varying moods of the House and the difficulties with which he has to contend. It is he who has to render decisions and resolve procedural impasses when they arise. Who is better placed than

The Office of Speaker

the Speaker to propose solutions to problems of which he has day-to-day experience?'[51]

He continued with suggestions which would greatly extend the Speaker's powers and impose duties which perhaps some occupants of the Chair would be reluctant to accept:

Another area where the Speaker can play his part if he has the backing of the House is in the regulation of debate. Again I have made it clear that given the support of the House and the assurance that I am acting within its mandate, I would willingly accept responsibilities which would assist in the process of allocating time to debate. These powers would be discretionary, and would come into operation only after the parties had themselves taken their own responsibility in organizing the programme of business. The powers I have in mind include a discretionary power to extend the debate, subject to a maximum number of hours laid down by Standing Order, in cases where a Bill had been made subject to an allocation of time order. Such rulings could be controverted but no Speaker can escape the need to make controversial decisions. There already exist numerous areas in which he is called upon to use his discretion and they are all potential areas of controversy. He exposes himself to criticism in his regulation of the Question Period, in deciding whether or not to allow an emergency adjournment debate, in ruling whether or not discussion should be allowed on a matter *sub judice*, in grouping amendments for the purpose of debate and voting at the report stage of a Bill. What matters is that all such decisions are made, and are seen to be made, objectively and impartially.'[52]

Whatever should be the extent and limits of the Speaker's involvement in procedural reform, there is no question that the decisions he is called upon to render must affect the evolution of procedure. On 20 January 1970 Speaker Lamoureux ruled that any member may move concurrence in a committee report whether or not he is a member of the committee.[53] This was not a ruling which pleased the government as it led to a debate on a report which the government was not anxious to have debated. On 18 June 1973 another important ruling was handed down by Speaker Lamoureux which crucially influenced the procedure for dealing with estimates and the use of allotted days established under the new rules adopted some five years previously. The government had argued that under the new procedure whereby the estimates were referred to standing committees for consideration, those committees were competent to recommend the adoption, reduction or rejection of the estimates referred to them but not to make substantive reports. The basis of the argument was that the standing committees had inherited the powers of the former committee of supply and that the latter had never made substantive reports to the House. The Speaker upheld the government's argument, saying:

The fundamental question to be considered is whether the House or the standing committee is to remain paramount. Will the committees direct the House by virtue of their reports or will the House direct the Committees by means of orders of reference?

If a standing committee is permitted to make reports of a substantive nature when considering the estimates of a department, it would follow that no limit could be placed on the number of reports from a committee. Surely the House would be hard pressed to consider all of such reports on motions during the daily routine of business.

It has been suggested that the powers and scope of committees should be and have been enlarged under the recently adopted procedure, but surely it cannot be contended that the committees have powers which exceed those of the House.[54]

Prior to this ruling other standing committees considering estimates had submitted substantive reports although no motion for concurring in these reports had previously been made. The effect of the Speaker's ruling ran counter to the intention of the committee which had made the original recommendations for the reform of the procedure. They had seen the new procedure as providing opportunities for the standing committees to make critical reports which would have provided the subjects for debate on allotted days. The ruling, while soundly based in terms of the standing orders as drafted, introduced a significant modification into the operation of the procedure and underlines the importance of Speakers' rulings as an element in the evolution of parliamentary practice.

Under existing supply procedure not more than six motions which express or imply no confidence in the government may be made by the opposition within their twenty-five allotted days, two such motions falling within each of the three periods during the session into which the allotted days are divided. The fact that the term 'no-confidence motions' is employed in the relevant standing orders (standing orders 62(9) and 62(10)) creates a risk that the Speaker may one day be called upon to rule whether a motion constitutes one of no confidence or not. The view has been expressed that such a term does not belong in the standing orders because it is not the speaker's function to determine such matters; it is the prerogative of the government to decide whether or not it will treat an issue as one of confidence. No Speaker has yet been faced with this dilemma, although Speaker Lamoureux dealt peripherally with the question when he was called upon to rule on the admissibility of a non-confidence motion on 6 March 1973. The government claimed that the motion in question was out of order because it conflicted with a decision already taken by the House approving the general budgetary policy of the government. The Speaker, while acknowledging the force of the government's argument, allowed the motion, pointing out that the standing orders allowed the opposition very wide scope in proposing motions on allotted days. In the course of his remarks he said:

> This is an opposition day, when a non-confidence motion can be introduced on a subject to be chosen by the mover. In my view the Speaker should not intervene to prevent debate, or a vote, unless the motion is clearly and undoubtedly irregular. When the procedural aspect is open to reasonable argument, I suggest it is the duty of the Chair to accept the motion and allow the House to make the decision on the question of confidence.[55]

As with any dynamic parliamentary institution, the practice of the Canadian House of Commons is in a continuing state of evolution and the examples cited above of decisions of the Chair in crucial areas of procedure illustrate the role played by the Speaker in this process. Sometimes, however, the Speaker is called upon to discharge the duties of the office under very frustrating conditions. During the long and acrimonious session of 1980–83 the Chair probably experienced its most trying period since the ordeal of Speaker Beaudoin. Procedural tactics were employed which sometimes had the effect of paralysing the House and challenging the authority of the Chair. At times the inter-party hostility generated by the proceedings gave the impression that the Chair itself was under attack. In such circumstances, it is difficult for the Speaker to contribute much to the improvement of the practices of the House.

Since 18 October 1977 the proceedings of the House of Commons have been broadcast live by radio and television. Continuous coverage is provided on a special television channel and the tapes are available to the media to use such extracts as they see fit. Speaker Jerome, who held office at the time broadcasting was instituted, has stated that most of the problems which were anticipated did not materialize. Those which have arisen have been mainly concerned with the method of visual coverage of the proceedings. The rule is that the camera must remain on the member who has the floor. The camera must not editorialise by focusing on empty seats or on a member who happens to be asleep. This can detract from the drama of certain occasions as Speaker Jerome has explained:

> During my tenure in the Chair, members crossed the floor on at least two occasions. Once the whole Social Credit caucus left the Chamber. They did it in a very orderly fashion. They were seated down on the right. They all came forward, following their leader. They bowed to the Chair and left in a very polite fashion. This occurred while a former minister was on his feet questioning the Prime Minister.
> ... here was a very significant event. Should the camera possibly cut from the questioner or cut from the Prime Minister to this event? Should it do that for someone crossing the floor? ...
> We have stuck very rigidly with the rule that the camera stays on those tight shots of persons who have the floor.[56]

Live broadcasting of debates has now been taking place for over six years and has not produced any appreciable change in the debating habits of members. One effect of the televising of debates has been to focus attention on the Speaker who is seen by the viewing public to be a figure of considerable authority, in many respects the 'star' of the show. He is seen regulating debate, maintaining order, rendering decisions, remonstrating with members, imposing the discipline of the Chair whenever necessary, a discipline to which all members including the Prime Minister are subject. Television has been a major force in bringing public attention to the importance of the Speaker's role and functions and thus to a better understanding of how the parliamentary system works.

Speaker Jerome informed the author that the introduction of broadcasting did not affect the discharge of his duties except that he took account of a member's desire to get on the air at a particular time. The advent of television may lead to certain changes in the practices of the House in the future but at the time of writing no significant trend in that direction has been apparent. In some respects this is surprising. For example, some government backbenchers had earlier indicated that once Parliament was on the air for all to see they could not continue to accept the convention which accorded the opposition parties the lion's share of the time during the question period. Their constituents, they reasoned, would expect to see them on their feet questioning ministers along with their opposition colleagues. However, up until now there has been no change in the convention and there has been no government back-bench revolt in protest. The Speaker could not, of course, alter the practice without a clear direction from the House. Former Speaker Jerome believed that government members derive greater advantage from the exposure they receive on the local television stations in their constituencies, particularly if they can bring in a minister to be interviewed. This is why, in his view, their misgivings have been largely allayed.

Addressing delegates to the Sixth Conference of Speakers and Presiding Officers of Commonwealth Parliaments in Ottawa on 23 April 1981 Speaker Jeanne Sauvé dealt with the responsibilities and problems which face the occupants of the Chair in the Commonwealth and in the course of her presentation she made the following observations:

> Our role is said to be twofold: Not only are we arbiters, but we are also interpreters of regulations. We are not disciplinarians, but, in a way, judges inspired by fundamental principles and guided by a proven jurisprudence. The latter is not, however, immutable. Is it in fact up to us to change it, or to let it fall into abeyance if we feel it no longer corresponds to present-day situations? Our approach must be realistic and pragmatic. We act in a human environment, in an evolving conjuncture where people are constantly called upon to make increasingly complex decisions. Most of us have also been elected. We are therefore in a position to understand that the practice of procedure is just as a question of psychology or politics – and a Speaker can be 'political' without being partisan – as it is of legal behaviour. In fact, we must take into account both the letter and the spirit of laws and regulations, and stress, if need be, the most natural rule – that of common sense.

The above words summarize very adequately the Canadian conception of the Speaker's role and the practical philosophy which has motivated Canadian Speakers in recent decades.

The Speakership in the Canadian Provinces

While a detailed study of the speakership in Canada's provincial legislatures is not possible within the compass of this work, it is important to stress that there are thirteen legislative jurisdictions in Canada, each with its own practices and traditions. Some of them have legislatures which pre-date the founding of the Canadian Confederation in 1867 and each preserves certain customs which underline their separate identity. For example, in the three maritime provinces, Nova Scotia, New Brunswick and Prince Edward Island, this is reflected in the costume of the Speaker where custom decrees the wearing of a top hat. The President of the Quebec National Assembly wears no special costume. In the other provinces, Ontario, Manitoba, Saskatchewan, Alberta, British Columbia and Newfoundland, the Speaker's costume resembles that of the Speaker of the House of Commons. In addition to the ten provinces there are two centrally administered territories, the Yukon and the North-West Territories, each having its own fully elected legislature presided over by a Speaker. However, the office of Speaker in the territories is of relatively recent origin and insufficient time has elapsed to permit of identifiable traditions having developed.

Provincial Speakers always actively campaign for their seats as the candidates of their political parties and are usually appointed from the ranks of the governing party. There have only been two exceptions to this practice in recent years, both of which were brought about by the electoral fortunes of the parties in the provinces concerned. In Ontario between 1977 and 1981, when the governing party lacked an overall majority in the Legislative Assembly, the Speaker, Mr. Jack Stokes, was a member of an opposition party. He served two terms of office, but when the Progressive Conservative government regained a majority in the election of 1981 he was replaced by a member the governing party. His successor, Mr. John Turner, was nominated by the Premier and seconded by the Leader of the Opposition, although the leader of Mr. Stokes's own party, the New Democratic Party, complained that he had not been consulted on the choice of Speaker. The Premier paid a warm tribute to Mr. Stokes and credited him with having strengthened the office. It appears, nevertheless, that his appointment was simply a matter of political convenience and that the politicians of Ontario have no interest in promoting the continuity and political independence of the speakership. In 1979 the Progressive Conservative government of New Brunswick, holding a very narrow majority in the legislature, offered the speakership to Mr. Robert McCready, a member of the Liberal opposition, who had held the office on a previous occasion when his own party was in power. He accepted but incurred the wrath of his own party in doing so, as it was felt he should have consulted his party colleagues before agreeing to help the government out of a tight spot. He remained Speaker until 1981 and afterwards sat as an independent.

The prospects of moving towards a Westminster-style speakership in the Canadian provinces are therefore not very promising. The office of Speaker is frequently used as a consolation prize or a stepping-stone to cabinet office. It is quite common for provincial Speakers to move directly from the Chair to the cabinet and over the past ten years such shifts have taken place in at least six provinces – Manitoba, New Brunswick, Nova Scotia, Newfoundland, Quebec, and, most recently, British Columbia. A former Speaker from British Columbia, Mr. Gordon Dowding, writing in the Vancouver Sun on 28 February 1978, deplored the method of choosing the Speaker in his own province, pointing out that he was reliant on the government for his election, his departmental funding and his political future. It is interesting to note, however, that when he was elected to the Chair in 1972 he was not nominated by the Premier, as is usual, but was proposed and seconded by backbenchers from opposite sides of the House in accordance with Westminster practice.

The political attachments of the Speakers of the provincial legislatures do not make their jobs any easier, although most of them strive to be impartial in the Chair and refrain from attending their party caucuses while in office. They are, however, vulnerable when obliged to give controversial rulings and motions of censure against the Chair are not uncommon. Speaker John Brockelbank of Saskatchewan faced motions of censure on three recent occasions in 1980 and 1981, although only one of them was debated and taken to a division.* On 24 November 1981 a motion of censure against Speaker Gerard Amerongen of Alberta alleging that he had refused to allow a member to explain a point of privilege, was debated and rejected by 51 to 4. On November 16, 1981 a motion of censure against Speaker John Turner of Ontario, initiated by the New Democratic Party, was debated and rejected by 86 to 17, the Liberal opposition voting with the government. It is notable that his predecessor, Mr. Jack Stokes, having had some experience of the problems of being Speaker, broke ranks with his party and spoke in support of the Speaker.

In some jurisdictions a move has been discernible to promote the prestige and authority of the Speaker. At one time the standing orders of most provincial legislatures provided for the right to appeal from Speakers' rulings without notice from the floor of the House. Several have followed Ottawa's lead in abolishing this practice. The first to do so was the Quebec National Assembly which abolished it in 1969. Alberta, Saskatchewan and Nova Scotia have since followed suit. In a number of jurisdictions the Speaker has been directly involved in the process of procedural reform. Reforms implemented in Quebec, Saskatchewan, Manitoba, New Brunswick and Nova Scotia were

---

* See Debates of the Legislative Assembly of Saskatchewan, 24 April 1980, 29 April 1980 and 26 March 1981. On 29 April 1980 a debate took place which resulted in the defeat of the motion by 29 to 11. It is interesting to note that the motion proposed on 26 March 1981 called for a royal commission to study the concept of an independent permanent Speaker.

all based on recommendations of committees appointed under the Speaker's chairmanship.[57] In Alberta the Speaker was closely involved in the complete re-writing of the standing orders in 1975. Speaker Amerongen, who has held the office ever since 1972 when his party was first elected to power, has from the beginning applied himself to the strengthening of the speakership in his jurisdiction. It is widely believed that he could long ago have had cabinet office had he wanted it. He has preferred to devote his energies to promoting the effectiveness of the Chair and has been consistently conscious of his duty to protect minorities in a legislature where governments have long been accustomed to winning overwhelming majorities. The recent motion of censure against him is all the more regrettable in view of the absence of partisanship on which he has always prided himself. An interesting innovation introduced by Speaker Amerongen has been to allow questions addressed to members other than ministers in cases where the member concerned has been appointed to a departmental board or committee to which a certain executive authority has been delegated.

In British Columbia the Legislative Procedure and Practice Inquiry Act, enacted in 1972 and since re-titled the Legislative Procedure Review Act, authorized the Speaker to conduct a continuing study of the rules of the Legislature. The Act has given rise to various initiatives on the part of the Speaker, one of which led to the institution of a question period in the Legislative Assembly in 1973. Previously British Columbia was the only province where no provision existed for the questioning of ministers in the Legislature. The Act has enabled the four Speakers who have held office since 1972 to assert a measure of leadership in procedural and administrative matters, although their efforts have not so far led to a clear definition of their administrative authority or to procedural reforms of a particularly radical nature. However an important initiative was taken when Speaker Dean Smith commissioned a study of parliamentary practice in British Columbia by the Deputy Clerk of the Legislative Assembly. It was published in 1981, having been completed under the authority of Speaker Smith's successor, Speaker Harvey Shroeder.[58] In the same year the latter Speaker commissioned a study of the administrative authority and status of the Speaker, which was published in 1982. Among the recommendations, which at the time of writing have yet to be considered by the Legislative Assembly, were the establishment of a Board of Internal Economy under the Speaker's chairmanship and the provision of autonomous financial services for the Legislature; the improvement of the Speaker's remuneration and his place in the order of precedence; the abolition of appeals from Speaker's rulings; the proposing and seconding of the Speaker's nomination by backbenchers; and the continuation of the administrative authority of the Speaker under statute following a dissolution of the Legislature.[59]

In the area of administration some Speakers have more clearly defined powers than others. The President of the Quebec National Assembly has complete authority within the parliamentary building and a large well-paid staff to assist him. He is also chairman of the Committee on the National Assembly, which includes the Vice-Presidents, house leaders and whips of the various parties, and plays a crucial role in the procedure and organization of the Assembly. In Nova Scotia the Speaker has become responsible under the new rules for the administration of Province House (the parliamentary building) and its staff. In Ontario the Speaker's administrative authority is less extensive, but the Legislative Assembly Act confers on him the power to require of any ministry or agency of the Crown any service or commodity for or on behalf of the Assembly that the Speaker considers necessary.

Generally speaking the prestige and authority which attaches to the Speaker's office at Ottawa, and to an even greater extent at Westminster, are not reflected at the provincial level. In no provincial jurisdiction does the Speaker's rank or salary equate with those of cabinet ministers. In most of them his salary is less than that of the Leader of the Opposition and in only one (Newfoundland) is he paid more. In all provinces the prerogative of nominating the Speaker is recognized as belonging to the governing party but in most jurisdictions his election has on occasion been contested. In British Columbia three of the five most recent incumbents of the Chair faced opponents and the acrimony of the debates which took place on the election of Speaker revealed a scant respect for the office on the part of some members. In 1970 Speaker Murray, who had already served two terms of office, was opposed by the official opposition who alleged he had shown partisanship towards one of their number during his previous incumbency. Ironically this is believed to have been the first occasion when the Premier of the province had actually consulted the Opposition on the nomination of the Speaker. In 1972 Speaker Dowding was elected by acclamation when the opposing candidate declined to accept the nomination. In 1976 Speaker Smith was opposed on the ground that while still Speaker-designate he had subordinated his authority to the government in the matter of hiring staff.[60] In the annals of the history of the speakership the Legislature of British Columbia has at least one claim to fame in that it was the first legislative chamber in the Commonwealth to elect a woman to preside over it. Mrs. Nancy Hodges was Speaker of the Legislative Assembly from 1950 to 1952.*

The Speakers of the provincial and territorial assemblies, together with the Speaker of the House of Commons, comprise the Canadian Regional Council of the Commonwealth Parliamentary Association. They meet once every year in Ottawa in the spring and each takes his turn in hosting the Canadian Regional Conference in the summer. Each province and territory is entitled to send one delegate to the international C.P.A. Conference which is also held annually, and it is frequently the Speaker who is chosen to represent his branch on these occasions.

---

* Two other women have presided over provincial legislatures: Thelma Forbes and Marion Reid elected respectively in Manitoba in 1963 and Prince Edward Island in 1982.

Notes to Chapter Four: The Speakership in Canada

1. See Canada, House of Commons Debates, 1878, Vol. 1, p. 2.
2. See Denis Smith, The Speakership of the Canadian House of Commons: some proposals. A paper prepared for the Special Committee on Procedure and Organization, April 1965. Appended to the Votes and Proceedings, 2 June 1965.
3. See Canada, House of Commons Debates, 1974, Vol. 1, p. 2.
4. Ibid., 1878, Vol. 1, p. 11.
5. Standing Order 13 of the Canadian House of Commons (1982 edition) reads: 'Mr. Speaker shall not take part in any debate before the House. In case of an equality of voices, Mr. Speaker gives a casting vote, and any reasons stated by him are entered in the Journal.'
6. See Canada, House of Commons Debates, 1926–7, Vol. 2, p. 2036.
7. See James Jerome, The Speakership in Canada, The Parliamentarian, April 1978, Vol. LIX, No. 2, pp. 82–84.
8. Canada, House of Commons Debates, 1957–58 Session, Vol. 1, p. 2.
9. See Mr. Diefenbaker's answer to a question on the subject, Canada, House of Commons Debates, 1957–58 Session, Vol. 1, p. 31.
10. Canada, House of Commons Debates, 1971, Vol. IX, pp. 9186–9192.
11. Ibid., 1968, Vol. 1, pp. 1–3.
12. Statement published in the Ottawa Journal, 29 June, 1971.
13. Address by René Beaudoin to the Empire Club of Canada, 25 October, 1956.
14. Standing Order 37 reads: 'Immediately before the order of the day for resuming an adjourned debate is called, or if the House be in committee of the whole, any Minister of the Crown who, standing in his place, shall have given notice at a previous sitting of his intention so to do, may move that the debate shall not be further adjourned, or that the further consideration of any resolution or resolutions, clause or clauses, section or sections, preamble or preambles, title or titles, shall be the first business of the committee, and shall not further be postponed; and in either case such question shall be decided without debate or amendment; and if the same shall be resolved in the affirmative, no Member shall thereafter speak more than once, or longer than twenty minutes in any such adjourned debate; or, in committee, on any such resolution, clause, section, preamble or title; and if such adjourned debate or postponed consideration shall not have been resumed or concluded before one o'clock in the morning, no Member shall rise to speak after that hour, but all such questions as must be decided in order to conclude such adjourned debate or postponed consideration, shall be decided forthwith.'
15. See House of Commons Debates, 1956 Session. Vol. 5, pp. 4517–34.
16. Ibid., 1956, Vol. 5, p. 4537.
17. Ibid., 1956, Vol. 5, pp. 4539–44, 4551–6.
18. Ibid., 1956, Vol. 5, pp. 4643–61.
19. Ibid., 1956, Vol. 6, p. 5511.
20. Ibid., 1956, p. 5763.
21. James H. Aitchison, The Speakership in the Canadian House of Commons. Contained in Canadian Issues: essays in honour of Henry F. Angus, edited by Robert M. Clark, University of Toronto Press, 1961.
22. Canada, House of Commons Debates, Session 1962–63, Vol. III pp. 3292–3300; and Session 1964–65, Vol. XI, pp. 11669–11673.
23. Canada, Standing Orders of the House of Commons, 1982 edition, Standing Order 15(1).

24. Ibid., Standing Order 59(4).
25. Canada, House of Commons Debates, 1967, Vol. XII, pp. 12269–70.
26. James Jerome, The Speakership in Canada, op. cit. p. 78.
27. Standing Order 79(10), 1982 edition.
28. Canada, House of Commons Debates, 1981, pp. 8892–94.
29. Ibid., 1982, pp. 15532–15539.
30. Ibid., 1982, pp. 15555–15557.
31. Ibid., 1977, Vol. IV, pp. 4210–4243.
32. Erskine May, 20th edition, op. cit., p. 791.
33. Canada, House of Commons Debates, 1971, Vol. IV, pp. 4125–27.
34. Ibid., 1977, Vol. IV, pp. 4220–22.
35. Ibid., 1981, pp. 10546–47.
36. Ibid., 1976, p. 10844.
37. Canada, House of Commons Journals, Vol. CXXII, 1976–77, pp. 720–729.
38. Canada, House of Commons Debates, 1966–67, Vol. IX, p. 9000.
39. Ibid., 1968–69, Vol. IX, p. 9855.
40. Ibid., 1968–69, Vol. IX, pp. 9899–9900 for full text of ruling.
41. Ibid., 1955, Vol. V, p. 4790.
42. Great Britain. House of Commons Debates, 5th Series, Vol. 769, Cols. 665–6.
43. Great Britain. House of Commons, First Report of the Committee of Privileges, Session 1975–76, H.C. 22.
44. Canada. House of Commons Debates, 1974–76, Vol. VIII, pp. 8451–8453 for full text of ruling.
45. Ibid., 1976–77, Vol. VII, pp. 7043–7047 for full text of ruling.
46. Ibid., 1978, Vol. VI, pp. 6183–5 for full text of ruling.
47. For details see Beauchesne's Rules and Forms of the House of Commons of Canada, Carswell, Toronto, 5th edition, 1978, pp. 129–134.
48. Canada. House of Commons Debates, 1965, Vol. XII, p. 12935.
49. Ibid., 1974, Vol. I, pp. 1059–1064.
50. Beauchesne, op. cit., p. 134.
51. James Jerome, The Speakership in Canada, op. cit., p. 80.
52. Ibid.
53. Canada, House of Commons Debates, 1970, Vol. III, pp. 2575–76.
54. Ibid., 1973, Vol. V, p. 4827.
55. Ibid., 1973, Vol. II, pp. 1944–45 for full text of ruling.
56. James Jerome, Televising The House of Commons: A Retrospective, Canadian Parliamentary Review, Winter 1981–82, pp. 8–9.
57. At least two articles have been written on procedural reform in their own jurisdictions by Canadian provincial Speakers: see Jean–Noel Lavoie, New Standing Orders for the National Assembly of Quebec, The Parliamentarian, Vol. LIV, No. 4, October 1973, pp. 266–274; and Arthur Donahoe, Procedural Change in the Nova Scotia House of Assembly, Canadian Parliamentary Review, Vol. 4, No. 2, Summer 1981, pp. 8–10.
58. See E. George MacMinn, Parliamentary Practice in British Columbia, Victoria, B.C., 1981. The reader's attention is also directed to the thesis by Clarence Reser, The Speakership in British Columbia, 1970–1979, submitted to the University of Victoria in 1981. This is probably the only detailed study available of a Canadian provincial speakership.
59. See E. George MacMinn, Legislative Procedure Review Act: The Speaker and the Legislative Assembly of British Columbia, Victoria, B.C., 1982.
60. See Clarence Reser, pp. 68–74.

Postscript

After this book had gone to press the appointment of Speaker Jeanne Sauve as Canada's first woman Governor-General was announced, to take effect in January 1984. During her speakership she presided over an important reorganization of the administration of the House of Commons, involving the appointment of an Administrator who took over many of the functions relating to staff, finance and services to members which had previously fallen under the responsibility of the Clerk of the House.

Chapter Five

The Speakership in Australia

The Commonwealth of Australia is a federation of six States and one Territory. It was formed in 1900 of the former colonies of New South Wales, Victoria, Queensland, South Australia, Western Australia and Tasmania. The Northern Territory, which has a fully elected Legislative Assembly presided over by a Speaker, is moving towards statehood. The federal Parliament is bicameral as are the State Parliaments with the exception of that of Queensland. A feature of the Australian parliamentary system is that the upper as well as the lower Houses are elected bodies. In the Commonwealth order of precedence the President of the Senate and the Speaker of the House of Representatives follow the Governor-General, the State Governors, the Prime Minister and a State Premier within his own state. Precedence between the two presiding officers is determined by length of service, the President of the Senate taking precedence if both have been in office for an equal period of time. Both presiding officers may wear the traditional black silk gown and full-bottomed wig with lace ruffles and jabot and a white bow tie, a costume which is not varied for special occasions. However, when the Labour Party is in office this costume is normally dispensed with in deference to the party's distaste for ceremonial insignia and the presiding officers simply wear a dark suit for all occasions.

The complete political detachment which is such an important feature of the speakership at Westminster is not a characteristic of the office in Australia. At a general election he contests his seat on a party basis like any other Member, and as the appointment of the Speaker is regarded as the privilege of the party in power, there is little likelihood of his being re-elected in the event of a change of government. Experience has shown that it is not impossible for a political partisan to discharge the duties of Speaker with fairness and impartiality; but it has also shown that in these circumstances it is not always feasible to elevate the Speaker's office to the same high plane of dignity which it occupies at Westminster. When the Speaker is known to favour the governing party and is permitted to campaign on its behalf it is not so easy for him to win and retain the confidence of the opposition which, in turn, may be less inclined to accord him that unqualified respect which should be due to the Chair on all occasions. In a paper advocating the adoption of the Westminster convention relating to the Speaker, an Australian Speaker has commented:

In the Australian House of Representatives there has always been an inherent lack of confidence in the impartiality of the Chair. While not always justified this suspicion has resulted in members showing a lack of respect for the Chair, engaging in behaviour which detracts from the orderly proceedings of the House and in a consequent lowering of the standing of Parliament in the eyes of the community.[1]

The same author points out in another article:

A Speaker in Australia has to survive three elections, viz.: (a) at the hands of the people; (b) at the hands of the party; and (c) at the hands of the House. So the prospective Speaker needs the name of the party and its support behind him to gain preselection as a political candidate, to gain party nomination in caucus as the candidate for Speaker and to gain majority parliamentary support.[2]

The office of Speaker is provided for in section 35 of the Australian constitution which reads:

The House of Representatives shall, before proceeding to the despatch of any other business, choose a Member to be the Speaker of the House and as often as the office of Speaker becomes vacant, the House shall again choose a Member to be the Speaker.

The Speaker shall cease to hold his office if he ceases to be a Member. He may be removed from office by vote of the House, or he may resign his office or his seat by writing addressed to the Governor-General.

Standing Order 12 of the Australian House of Representatives makes detailed provision for the election of Speaker. The election is the first business of a new Parliament. It takes place as soon as all the Members present have been sworn in and no prior instruction from the Governor-General is required. When the first Commonwealth Parliament met in 1901 the Speaker of the House of Representatives* presented himself following his election for the approval of the Governor-General and also made the formal claim for privileges. These practices were dropped when the second Parliament met in 1904, and the current usage, prescribed in the Standing Order, requires the Speaker merely to present himself to the Governor-General and to report the fact subsequently to the House. His appointment does not require confirmation and no claim is made in respect of privileges. However, section 49 of the Australian Constitution provides that the powers, privileges and immunities of the House of Representatives, its Members and Committees, shall, until declared otherwise by Parliament, be those of the House of Commons at the establishment of the Commonwealth.

As was once the tradition at Westminster, the Clerk of the House presides over the proceedings during the election of the Speaker. Only Members of the

---

* And the President of the Senate also.

Right: Rt. Hon. George Thomas MP, now Viscount Tonypandy, Speaker of the House of Commons, Westminster, 1976–83.

Below: The Speakers procession at Westminster with Speaker Weatherill.

Left: The presentation of the Speaker to Queen Elizabeth in 1584.

Below: The Speaker admonishing a prisoner kneeling at the Bar in the reign of James I.

Right: Disraeli holding the floor as Chancellor of the Exchequer in 1867, with Speaker Denison in the Chair.

Below right: Cromwell dismissing the Long Parliament.

Left: The Speaker's Chair, Westminster.

Below: The Honourable Jeanne Sauve, the first woman to be elected Speaker of the Canadian House of Commons.

Above: Speaker Harrison of the New Zealand House of Representatives.

Above right: Speaker Forrest of the House of Representatives of Jamaica.

Right: Speaker Jenkins of the Australian House of Representatives. When the Labour Party is in office, the Speaker wears no robes.

Left: Speaker Jakhar of Lok Sabha, India. Indian Speakers wear no special robes of office.

Below far left: Y. B. Datuk Mohamed Zahir Haji Ismaili, Speaker of Dewan Rakjut, Malaysia.

Below left: The Hon. Tomasi R. Vakatora, MP, Speaker of the House of Representatives in Fiji.

Right: Speaker Nabulyato of the National Assembly of Zambia, one of the longest-serving Speakers in the Commonwealth.

Below: Speaker Kolane of the National Assembly of Lesotho, a Speaker who was formerly a Clerk-at-the-Table.

Group photograph taken on the occasion of the Sixth Conference of Speakers and Presiding Officers of Commonwealth Parliaments held in Canada, April 1981.

House are eligible for election, and a candidate, who must be proposed and seconded, is required to inform the House whether he is prepared to accept nomination. When the Clerk is satisfied that no nominations remain outstanding he declares that the time for proposals has expired. If only one candidate is nominated no debate on the motion is permitted, and the Clerk declares him elected without putting the question, whereupon his proposer and seconder conduct him to the Chair. When an election is contested debate may ensue as soon as the Clerk has announced that the time for proposals has expired. If a debate arises no Member may speak for more than five minutes, and it is open to a Minister at any time during the debate to rise and move the closure,* in which case the Clerk is bound to put the question on the closure motion. In the event of an equality of votes the question is decided in the negative. Should the closure be carried, or alternatively on the cessation of the debate, a secret ballot is held to determine the successful candidate. Should more than two candidates be nominated an overall majority is required by one of them in order to secure election. If no candidate secures an overall majority of the votes on the first ballot the candidate with the least number of votes is eliminated and a fresh ballot takes place, the process continuing if necessary until one of the candidates receives the requisite majority. A candidate may withdraw his name from the election after the result of the first ballot or any subsequent ballot has been declared. The Standing Order also makes provision for the unlikely contingency of an inconclusive ballot.

The role played by the Clerk of the House when presiding over the election of the Speaker is of particular interest. Under Australian practice he is possessed of certain powers, unlike the Clerk of the British House of Commons who had no powers at all under the standing orders in the days when he too presided over the Speaker's election. The Australian Clerk is obliged, if a member has exhausted his time, to draw his attention to the fact. It is considered that, in addition to putting the question on a closure motion, he would be obliged to accept any motion for some purpose relevant to the election of the Speaker. He could call for the withdrawal of an offensive expression and suspend the sitting in the event of grave disorder. It is doubtful that he has the power to name a member. There was one occasion when he used a casting vote and another when he ruled on the admissibility of a motion. Many questions relating to the authority of the Clerk while presiding over the election of the Speaker nevertheless remain undetermined.[3]

Following the election the Speaker thanks the House for the honour conferred on him and as he takes the Chair the Mace is placed on the upper brackets on the Table. He receives the congratulations of the Prime Minister, Leader of the Opposition and other members, after which the House is suspended until the time fixed for his reception by the Governor-General. At the appointed hour the Speaker accompanied by other members proceeds to the Parliamentary Library where he is received and congratulated by the Governor-General.

---

* In Australia the closure is moved in the same form as in the British House of Commons, namely, 'That the Question be now put'.

The first business of a new session, following the election of the Speaker in the case of a new Parliament, is the reading of the speech from the throne by the Governor-General. Traditional British practice is followed. The Usher of the Black Rod arrives at the chamber of the House of Representatives, knocks at the door, and on being admitted delivers the summons to the House to attend His Excellency in the Senate chamber for the purpose of hearing his speech. Preceded by the Serjeant-at-Arms bearing the Mace, the Speaker heads the procession of members to the Senate where he is invited by the Governor-General to be seated at the Table of the Senate. At the door of the Senate Chamber the Mace is left in the care of an attendant as it is not now taken into the presence of the Governor-General.* On other occasions, as when a new Speaker is received by the Governor-General, the Mace is covered by a green velvet cloth. Having heard the speech from the throne, the House returns to its own Chamber, but before the Speaker reports on the proceedings in the Senate, it is customary for the Prime Minister to announce his Cabinet and for the Leader of the Opposition and the leader of any other minority party to make announcements with respect to the leadership of their own groups. A first reading is then given to a formal bill, again in accordance with Westminster tradition, the practice being provided for by standing order.[4]

Australian Speakers are usually chosen from among the more experienced members of the House but a legal background has never been regarded as a necessary qualification for the position. Of the 20 Speakers who have held office since the first meeting of the Australian Parliament in 1901, only three have been lawyers, namely Speakers Groom, Nairn and Snedden. Most Speakers are chosen from the back benches but occasionally a former minister will be appointed, and at least one went on to become a minister subsequent to his term of office as Speaker. Sir Billy Snedden, Speaker of the House of Representatives from 1976 to 1983, previously served as Attorney-General, Leader of the House and Leader of the Opposition. He is on record as stating that he found his ministerial and leadership experience infinitely more important in the position than back bench experience.[5] Five Speakers, including the present incumbent, Dr. Harry Jenkins, have previously served as Chairman of Committees.

The Chairman of Committees is also the Deputy Speaker and under the Parliamentary Presiding Officers Act 1965 he is empowered to discharge most of the functions of the Speaker in the event of the latter's death, absence or incapacity. He is deemed to be Speaker until a new Speaker is elected or the absent or incapacitated Speaker returns to duty. His powers do not extend to the exercise of the Speaker's constitutional functions, namely the issuing of writs to fill vacancies and the receipt of resignations from members. In the absence of the Speaker these powers would be exercised by the Governor-General. In terms of the constitution and standing order 14 the Chairman of Committees takes the Chair as Acting Speaker when the Speaker's absence is formally notified to the House by the Clerk. In his capacity as Acting Speaker, as distinct from Deputy Speaker, the Chairman of Committees assumes all the

---

* The practice of taking the Mace into the Senate was discontinued in 1957.

Speaker's functions without restriction. He may take the Chair as Deputy Speaker whenever requested to do so by the Speaker. Under standing orders 18 and 19 the Speaker must nominate no less than four members and may nominate any additional number of members to act as Deputy Chairmen of Committees and may call on any one of them to take the Chair as Deputy Speaker. It is the practice to appoint Deputy Chairmen from both the government and opposition sides of the House and on one occasion as many as 13 were appointed.[6]

The Australian speakership has developed an element of continuity as a result of the tendency to re-elect the same Speaker in a new Parliament which produces no change of government. Between 1950 and 1972, a period during which the same government remained in power, there were only three Speakers. The first, Mr. Archie Cameron, served four terms and died in office. The second, Sir John McLeay, also served four terms and holds the record as the longest-serving Speaker of the House of Representatives, his tenure spanning ten years. The third, Sir William Aston, served two terms and was defeated in the general election of 1972.

The first Speaker of the Australian House of Representatives, Sir Frederick Holder, was elected unanimously. He collapsed in the Chair on 23 July 1909 at a time of bitter party strife and died within a few hours. Both the parties nominated a candidate to succeed him, and the Liberals, being in the majority, carried their man. In the following year the Labour Party was returned to power and installed its own candidate in the Chair. Ever since that time the Australian speakership has been regarded as a political appointment. But although it is now recognized in Australia that the Government enjoys the right to nominate the Speaker, the opposition does not necessarily accord the Government-sponsored candidate an uncontested election. The opposition very often nominates a candidate of its own in order to secure the right to debate the matter in terms of Standing Order 12, and if it has any strong objection to the government candidate it will most certainly oppose his nomination. When a debate on the election of the Speaker does take place it is usually frank and uninhibited. If the opposition has any objections to the government candidate it will express them, and is unlikely to be precluded by any considerations of etiquette from saying exactly what it thinks. If any Members are of the opinion that a candidate for the speakership lacks the necessary qualifications for the office they will say so, and in no uncertain terms. The late Mr. Archie Cameron was the object of some scathing denunciations on the part of the opposition. Mr. Cameron, a colourful political figure and a rugged partisan, was not opposed when he was first elected to the Chair on 22 February 1950. He assured the House at the time that during his tenure of office he would not take part in debate or attend party meetings. The tenor of the speeches of congratulation on that occasion reflected the spirit of Australian political life and were, by House of Commons standards, faintly outrageous!

The then Prime Minister, Sir Robert Menzies, concluded his remarks by saying:

The only other thing that I should like to say to you, Sir, is that those of us who belong to that growing group of Members who have been suspended from the service of the House take great comfort from the fact that you know what it feels like, and, therefore, we anticipate with great confidence that you will do your disciplining gently.[7]

Mr. Rosevear, Mr. Cameron's predecessor in office, in the course of his congratulatory remarks said:

> I have to admit that you, Sir, had a great advantage over any other aspirant on the Government side of the Chamber for the office of Mr. Speaker, because I do not think that any Member of the Opposition in the last Parliament raised so many points of order as you did, and was so consistently incorrect as you were.[8]

When Mr. Cameron was proposed for re-election on 12 June 1951 the Opposition was no longer prepared to accept him without a protest. He had given great dissatisfaction to the opposition during his first term of office, and was accused among other things of having cast personal reflections on its Members and having used his position 'to air public vendettas against highly placed persons, and private ones against Members of the Opposition'. But the principal complaint against him was his interpretation of a standing order which at that time read:

> The Speaker or the Chairman shall order a Member whose conduct is grossly disorderly to withdraw immediately from the House during the remainder of that day's sitting; and the Serjeant-at-Arms shall act on such orders as he may receive from the Chair in pursuance of this Standing Order. Any Member ordered to withdraw from the House pursuant to this Standing Order shall not return during the same sitting except by permission of the Speaker or Chairman.'*

---

* The House as a whole, irrespective of party, was never happy about Speaker Cameron's use of this Standing Order, and the present Standing Order 306 now reads:

> When the conduct of a Member is of such a grossly disorderly nature that the procedure provided in Standing Order 301 would be inadequate to ensure the urgent protection of the dignity of the House, the Speaker or the Chairman shall order the Member to withdraw immediately from the Chamber and the Serjeant-at-Arms shall act on such orders as he receives from the Chair in pursuance of this Standing Order. When the Member has withdrawn he shall forthwith be named by the Speaker or the Chiarman as the case may be, and the proceedings shall then be as provided in Standing Orders 301 and 302 except that the question for the suspension of the Member shall be put by the Speaker without a motion being necessary.
>
> If the question for the suspension of the Member is resolved in the negative he may forthwith return to the Chamber.

The opposition alleged that he had been deliberately partisan in his use of this Standing Order. Said Mr. Calwell:

> It was promulgated for the purpose of authorizing the removal of any Member who might be under the influence of liquor. But it was used during the Nineteenth Parliament for the removal of honourable Members who, for the moment, happened to have cause for dissatisfaction with Mr. Speaker!

He went on to refer to the occasion when Mr. Cameron had himself been ordered to withdraw from the House:

> He was removed from this Chamber for the duration of one sitting on the motion of his own Prime Minister. A man with a conviction of that sort recorded against him is not worthy to be Speaker of this House.[9]

Mr. Cameron, completely unmoved by the accusations levelled against him, gave scant comfort to the opposition by assuring the House that he would continue to administer the Standing Orders in exactly the same way as in the past.

On 4 August 1954 Mr. Cameron was again the government nominee for the speakership, but the opposition, unfortunately, had not grown to like him any better. His use of the standing order quoted above was still the Opposition's principal grievance, one of whose spokesmen accused him of having perverted and twisted its purpose, and declared that there could be few men worse qualified for the office of Speaker than Mr. Cameron. The latter, acknowledging the congratulations of the Prime Minister and Leader of the Opposition after his re-election, remarked that he was conscious of his shortcomings and that doubtless he would proceed in the same old fashion. He was re-elected for a fourth term of office on 15 February 1956, again in the face of strong opposition from the Labour Party. On this occasion his record was described by Mr. Calwell as one of disgraceful partiality. He complained that 'under his administration many Members on this side of the House have been expelled from the Chamber for trivial reasons, having been named unfairly and unjustly, and that not one Government Member . . . has been dealt with at all. . . . As a matter of fact, the Speaker, on occasions, has seemed, at any rate, to organize interruption from the Government benches when Labour men are speaking.' Speaking for the Government, Sir Eric Harrison counter-attacked with recriminations against the Labour Party. 'I well remember,' he said, 'a Speaker who, in the Chair, represented, not the House, but the Labour Party. That Speaker, who, I think, was the instigator of a certain line of procedure in this House that was referred to as Rafferty's rules, established a new standard of chair work in this place. In due time he was replaced by a Deputy Speaker. That Deputy Speaker distinguished himself in such a fashion that we on the Opposition side at that time had to submit against him a motion which, I think, contained every form of stricture that could be found in the English language.'[10]

No Speaker at Westminster could survive the kind of criticism which was levelled against Mr. Cameron during his tenure of office, and it is inconceivable that debate of the nature indicated above would ever take place in the House of Commons in relation to the election of a Speaker. Sir Billy Snedden has commented that the occasion of electing the Speaker 'is the only time when the character of a member can be attacked without a substantive motion directed to that purpose'.[11] Speaker Cameron was a particularly controversial Speaker even by Australian standards. Within a month of taking office he made a personal attack on the then Governor-General from the Chair, and during his tenure of office he gave a number of dubious rulings of a partisan nature. He was Speaker when in 1955 the House dealt with the case of the 'Bankstown Observer', which resulted in two journalists being adjudged guilty of a breach of privilege and sentenced by the House following a division to three months imprisonment. Professor L. F. Crisp has expressed the view that what was seen by many as a violation of natural justice was the joint responsibility of the Speaker and the Prime Minister.[12]

Perhaps the most partisan action ever perpetrated by any Australian presiding officers occurred on 21 June 1943 when both the Speaker and Chairman of Committees resigned following the introduction of a motion of 'no confidence' in the government by the Leader of the Opposition. They had agreed in 1941 to continue in office following a change of government to facilitate the working of an evenly divided House. Their action demonstrated that party considerations were of greater importance to them than respect for the traditional values of the Chair.[13]

Some Australian Speakers have, nevertheless, succeeded in winning the appreciation of their opponents. Sir John McLeay, although he faced a rival candidate when he was first elected Speaker on 29 August 1956, was re-elected three times without opposition. Congratulating him on the occasion of his first re-election on 17 February 1959, the Leader of the Opposition said:

> During your previous term of office, the Opposition was greatly impressed by your efficiency in the Chair and above all by the spirit of fairness and tolerance that you showed during all the debates. I mentioned that fact at the close of the last Parliament. Having regard to your fairness and your other qualities, the Opposition believes that the House has been fortunate to retain your services as Speaker.[14]

On 21 April 1983 the opposition accorded a signal tribute to Dr. Harry Jenkins by allowing him an uncontested election on being nominated Speaker for the first time. Congratulating him on his election his predecessor, Sir Billy Snedden, announced that he himself intended to retire from the House in keeping with his conviction that the Westminster practice relating to the Speakership was the proper one.

Most authorities consulted by the author believed there was little likelihood that the Westminster-style tradition regarding the speakership would ever develop in Australia. A former Speaker, Mr. Gordon Scholes, who held office for a brief and stormy period in 1975, pointed out that the standing orders would require radical alteration in order to make them compatible with an independent speakership. They are very restrictive, very favourable to the government and allow little discretion to the Speaker. Strict time limits are imposed on speeches and debates, and a number of other rules and practices, including the guillotine and the closure, are available to the government to counter opposition obstruction. The Speaker has no power to refuse a motion for the closure. In terms of Standing Order 93 any Member, either in the House or in committee, is entitled to rise at any time and move without notice 'that the question be now put'. If such a motion is moved the Chair is bound to put the question, which must be decided without amendment or debate, at once, and if carried the question which was before the House when the closure was moved must be put forthwith. Standing Order 94 provides that a motion may be made that a Member who is speaking 'be not further heard', in which event the question must immediately be put from the Chair and decided without amendment or debate. The Speaker may not refuse a dilatory motion for the adjournment of the House or of the debate, neither is he empowered to prevent a division if called for by more than one member, nor to exercise any discretion in relation to the selection of amendments. Although he calls on the members wishing to participate in debate the speaking order is determined by the whips. The Chair therefore has no sanction at its disposal should it wish to withhold the floor from a member who has offended in some way. As Sir Billy Snedden has pointed out:

> The Australian system requires of its Speaker impartiality yet continued a system which obstructs it.
>
> A Speaker must remain politically active if he is to hope for re-election in his constituency. Sir Billy himself wrote a regular newspaper column and accepted numerous speaking engagements.
>
> Because the system gives no guarantee of continuance there is no independence except in the character of the person and his own sense of security. If he has to incur the ire of his own party in his rulings then a Speaker with material security will feel better about doing so.[15]

A rule which would need to be changed as a part of any programme designed to promote the authority of the Speaker is that which permits motions of dissent from Speaker's rulings. Standing Order 100 reads:

> If any objection is taken to any ruling of the Speaker, such objection must be taken at once, and a motion of dissent, to be submitted in writing, moved, which, if seconded, shall be proposed to the House, and debate shall thereon proceed forthwith.

This provision for challenging the decisions of the Chair, as we have seen in the case of Canada where there was once a comparable rule, does not tend to bolster the authority of the Speaker's rulings, and in view of the political nature of the Speaker's appointment arguments relating to his decisions inevitably tend to be conducted along party lines. The Speaker's party usually feels obliged to support him in his decisions, and in these circumstances a contested ruling would not necessarily be regarded as a binding precedent by a future Speaker of a contrary political persuasion. An incident which occurred in the House of Representatives on 2 December 1953, however, demonstrated that the Speaker cannot necessarily rely on the support of his own party when he rules in favour of the opposition. On this occasion Speaker Cameron ruled that a statement which had been made by the Prime Minister accusing an opposition member of having Communists as his friends and supporters was unparliamentary. A government spokesman moved that this ruling be dissented from, and after debate the motion was carried by 56 votes to 40. In terms of parliamentary ethics this use of a party majority to reverse a decision of the Speaker was somewhat questionable. The governing party would have been better advised to have accepted the ruling with a good grace in the interests of sustaining the authority of the Chair.

On 27 February 1975 there occurred an even worse example of a government failing to support the authority of its own Speaker. The incident arose out of a personal explanation given by the Minister of Immigration and an intervention by an opposition member who asked:

> Mr. Speaker, is the minister entitled under the privilege of Parliament to tell a monstrous lie?

When ordered to withdraw by the Chair the opposition member substituted the word 'untruth' for 'monstrous lie'. The minister rose to protest and the Speaker called him to order. The minister retorted 'Look, I don't give a damn what you say' and refused to apologize when called upon to do so by the Speaker. The Speaker thereupon named the minister, and as no member of the government rose to move for their colleague's suspension, the motion was moved by a member of the opposition. In the resulting division the motion for the minister's suspension was defeated by 59 votes to 55. The Speaker, Mr. James Cope, immediately interpreted this result as an expression of non-confidence in himself and tendered his resignation to the Governor-General the same day.[16] This is the only occasion on which the government majority has failed to support the Speaker after a member has been named.

On leaving the Chair Mr. Cope asked the Chairman of Committees, Mr. Scholes, to take the Chair as Deputy Speaker and he was subsequently elected Speaker. Mr. Scholes was chosen by his caucus as candidate for the speakership by a majority of eight and was apparently not the choice of the then Prime Minister, Mr. Gough Whitlam. This was no doubt because he had abstained from voting on the motion for the suspension of the minister, feeling that the government had let the Speaker down in failing to support him. Mr. Scholes took office in very difficult circumstances and presided over a very disorderly House. He was Speaker at the time of the constitutional crisis which resulted in the dismissal of the Prime Minister by the Governor-General. 11 November 1975 was a momentous day in the House of Representatives. The

Prime Minister, Mr. Gough Whitlam, had been dismissed and the Leader of the Opposition, Mr. Malcolm Fraser, commissioned to form a caretaker government. On that day the House, in which Mr. Whitlam's party still held a majority, adopted a resolution expressing want of confidence in the new Prime Minister and requesting the Speaker to advise the Governor-General to recall Mr. Whitlam to office. The Speaker suspended the sitting and sought an appointment with the Governor-General, but the latter dissolved both Houses of Parliament before a meeting could take place. On 12 November the Speaker wrote to the Queen condemning the Governor-General's action and requesting her to restore Mr. Whitlam to office. On 17 November the Queen replied through her private secretary that it would be improper for her to intervene in a matter clearly within the jurisdiction of the Governor-General. The subsequent general election settled the issue by returning Mr. Fraser to power with a substantial majority.[17]

Australian Speakers have regularly spoken and voted in committee of the whole House. One Speaker, Mr. Rosevear, even spoke in the House in the debate on the second reading of the Parliamentary Allowances Bill in 1947. Speaker McLeay, at a time when the government had a bare majority of one, consistently used his vote in committee to preserve the government's majority. On 10 September 1929 an incident took place which indicates the kind of reaction to be expected should any Australian Speaker attempt to raise the office above partisanship. The then Speaker, Sir Littleton Groom, abstained from voting during a crucial division in committee, citing British precedent in justification of his decision. His action brought about the fall of the government and its subsequent electoral defeat, the Speaker himself being one of the electoral casualties. His party never forgave him for his action and he never again held any office.[18]

The Speaker has no deliberative vote in the House itself but has a casting vote in the event of an equality of votes. This provision is contained in section 40 of the constitution, and standing order 210 provides that any reasons stated by the Speaker for his casting vote shall be entered in the votes and proceedings. Pettifer indicates that the decisions of successive Speakers in giving a casting vote have not always been consistent but that certain principles have emerged which conform to the guidelines established at Westminster. The illustrations given include two cases where the Speaker's casting vote was used to defeat a closure motion.[19] It is inconceivable, however, that any Australian Speaker would ever use his casting vote against the government in a crucial division. It is interesting to note the comments of Speaker McLeay at an informal meeting of Commonwealth Speakers held in Canada in 1966. He said that, 'A Speaker who used his casting vote to overthrow the government would be regarded as certifiable,' adding that 'he would be expected to use it to preserve the right of the government to stay in office.'[20]

As in most other jurisdictions one of the Speaker's responsibilities is the control of the question period. Australian practice resembles that of Canada in that it provides for two kinds of question: those of which notice is given and which are answered in writing and those which are asked without notice and which occupy the first 45 minutes or so of most sitting days.[21] The duration of the question period is entirely within the discretion of the Prime Minister who can, in fact, even decide that no question period will take place on a particular day. The Speaker has no discretion in the matter at all. The criteria relating to the asking of questions resemble those which apply at Westminster[22] but they tend to be relaxed in respect of questions asked without notice. It is difficult for the Speaker to apply these criteria rigidly when he has no indication of the questions to be asked. Unlike the Canadian practice, where the question period is regarded largely as an opposition prerogative, the Speaker allocates the questioning opportunities evenly between government and opposition, except that first priority is given to the Leader and Deputy Leader of the Opposition. The question period is the one occasion when the Speaker may choose 'to see' or 'not to see' a member and at least one example has been recorded of a Speaker declining to call a member during question period for the purpose of imposing a sanction.[23] Supplementary questions are permitted at the discretion of the Chair. Standing Order 152 provides that a question without notice may be put to the Speaker relating to any matter of administration for which he is responsible. In 1977 the Speaker was asked whether his writing articles for the press on contentious political issues was not incompatible with his role as Speaker. The Speaker replied to the effect that since the Westminster convention regarding the speakership did not apply in Australia, he was obliged to be an active politician and could not therefore withdraw totally from the political scene.[24]

In many respects the duties of the Australian Speaker correspond to those of his Westminster counterpart, although he does not possess the wide range of discretionary powers of the latter. He is responsible for determining whether a complaint of privilege should take precedence over other business.[25] Privilege cases when well-founded are taken very seriously in Australia and, in contrast with the Canadian practice, are likely to be pursued by the House. The Speaker determines whether a proposal to discuss a definite matter of public importance is in order, and since this procedure is one of the few opportunities available to the opposition to initiate a discussion, he tends to be flexible in his interpretation of the criteria. A proposal for an urgency debate must be supported by at least eight members and the discussion is unlikely to last more than two hours, as it is open to any member to move at any time 'That the business of the day be called upon', such motion being decided without amendment or debate. If more than one matter is proposed for discussion on the same day the Speaker decides which should have priority.[26] The Speaker's discretion under this standing order may not be challenged by a motion of dissent. Proposals for debating a definite matter of public importance are made almost every day and the majority are allowed. The debates are invariably vehicles for criticising the government but they do not lead to a vote as there is no motion before the House.[27]

As in other jurisdictions the Speaker is the interpreter of the *sub judice* convention. The guide-lines established by the British House of Commons are to a large extent followed, but there has been a variation in the interpretations applied to certain cases by successive Speakers. Speaking at a conference in 1969 on the Australian practice over the previous twenty years, Speaker Aston indicated that out of 28 recorded cases 22 related to matters before a royal commission or an industrial tribunal. The convention had been interpreted as applying to the proceedings of such bodies.[28] Speaking at a subsequent conference in 1981 Speaker Snedden stated that he had declined to follow the precedents referred to by his predecessor. 'I believe that a general prohibition of discussion of matters before a royal commission restricts the House unduly,' he said, adding that too restrictive an application of the convention to a body such as the Conciliation and Arbitration Commission would deprive Parliament 'of the right to speak on major elements of the economic management of the country'.[29] Speaker Snedden's interpretation accords more with the practice followed in the Canadian House of Commons.

Except in moving dissent from a ruling, the Speaker's conduct can only be criticised by a substantive motion moved for that purpose, with the notable exception of the occasion of the election of the Speaker. Pettifer lists seven occasions on which motions of censure have been moved against the Speaker or Deputy Speaker.[30] None has ever been carried, the House having divided in each case on strict party lines. Quite apart from motions of censure, one finds in the robust uninhibited debates of the House of Representatives many comments critical of the Speaker, the members concerned being frequently called upon to withdraw their remarks. This is hardly surprising in a Parliament where the Speaker remains an active politician. He is assumed to be partisan no matter how he may conduct himself in the Chair. The Speaker, for his part, tends to be severe with members who reflect upon their opponents or use language he considers unparliamentary. A random scrutiny of the debates will almost certainly reveal interventions by the Speaker calling on members to withdraw unqualifiedly or threatening to take disciplinary action.* Speaker Snedden has taken the view 'that what is unparliamentary when alleged against one member and is required to be withdrawn will be treated likewise in relation to a group'. This is contrary to Westminster practice, but Speaker Snedden has argued that accusations made against a group can lead to every member of that group rising in individual protest, thus subtracting from the dignity of the House.[31] Australian Speakers do not hesitate to pour withering scorn on offending members when they see fit. A story is told of how Speaker Cameron dealt with a member whom he was continually calling to order for failing to make obeisance to the Chair on entering and leaving the chamber. One day the member made a great show of bowing to the Chair and asking, 'How low should I get?' Speaker Cameron is said to have retorted: 'How should I know how low the honourable member can get?'[32]

The Speaker is the administrative head of the House of Representatives and

---

* However, on 18 February 1982 Speaker Snedden, having 'named' a member for calling the Prime Minister a liar, declined to put the question on the motion for the member's suspension. He explained that in his judgment the interest of the House would be better served by proceeding no further with the matter. See The Parliamentarian, vol. LXIII, no. 3, July 1982, pp. 183–184.

exercises a joint control with the President of the Senate over the parliamentary buildings as a whole. The Library of Parliament, the parliamentary reporting staff and the catering and other amenities also fall under the joint jurisdiction of the two presiding officers. The chairmanships of the Library Committee and the Joint House Committee are shared by the Speaker and the President of the Senate, each taking the chairmanship of one committee and the deputy chairmanship of the other. The Speaker has a number of statutory duties including those under the constitution already referred to. Under the Parliamentary Presiding Officers Act, 1965, for the purpose of maintaining administrative continuity, he remains Speaker following his resignation or a dissolution of Parliament until a new Speaker is chosen. In terms of the Public Service Act he has control, either separately or jointly with the President of the Senate, over the staff of the parliamentary departments. Separately or jointly the two presiding officers make recommendations to the Governor-General on appointments, promotions and the application of public service regulations. They also determine leave entitlements and the classification of officers and offices. Under the Parliamentary Proceedings Broadcasting Act, 1946, the Speaker is a member of the Joint Committee on the Broadcasting of Parliamentary Proceedings and has been elected chairman of the committee in all Parliaments except for the initial election in 1946, when radio broadcasting of parliamentary proceedings was first introduced.[33] By resolution of the House adopted in successive Parliaments the Speaker has been for some twenty years joint chairman of the Joint Standing Committee on the New Parliament House. Under Standing Order 25 he is a member of the Standing Orders Committee and is always elected its chairman. The Speaker is also directly concerned in the activities of international parliamentary associations. He is joint president with the President of the Senate of the Australian Branch of the Commonwealth Parliamentary Association and the Australian Group of the Inter-Parliamentary Union. The Australian presiding officers have regularly attended the conferences of Speakers and Presiding Officers of Commonwealth Parliaments since their inauguration in 1969 and the fifth such conference was held in Australia in 1978.

Australian Speakers cannot be described as typical parliamentary presiding officers if the Westminster tradition is to be taken as a yardstick. They do, however, reflect the robustness of Australian political life. They serve in a tough arena in which there is no place for those who bruise easily. But underlying the apparent ruthlessness of the Australian adversary system there is nevertheless a parliamentary camaraderie which offers occasional glimpses of generosity and good humour between opponents. This spirit was well embodied in a statement made to the House by Speaker Snedden on 18 September 1980 just before the dissolution of Parliament. He paid particular tribute to those members who had made life uncomfortable for him and spoke of the need for parliamentary reform if full advantage were to be taken of the accumulated talents of members on all sides of the House. He also reiterated his commitment to the principle of an independent speakership, saying:

It is necessary that every member in this House has total and absolute confidence that the Speaker will be impartial.[34]

The Australian speakership would seem to be some way removed from this ideal, not because successive Speakers have not done their best to be impartial, but because of the political system and the procedural structure of the House.

The practices relating to the Speakership in the Australian State assemblies are very similar to those which apply in the House of Representatives. State Speakers are active politicians who campaign for their seats and attend their party caucuses. The nomination of the Speaker is normally regarded as the prerogative of the party in power and a change of government is likely to result in a change of Speaker. This was not always so, however. The Australian parliamentary tradition pre-dates the establishment of the Australian Federation and all six States had their own Parliaments before the federal Parliament came into being. Five of them achieved responsible government between 1855 and 1859, Western Australia acquiring it in 1890. In the 19th century the Australian Parliaments adhered more closely to Westminster practices than they do today, and the Speaker sometimes retained his position despite a change of government.

Today the Speaker is seldom able to stand aloof from party politics although situations can arise to force a departure from the usual political conventions. This can happen when the parties in the assembly are closely balanced, for it is not uncommon in these relatively small Parliaments for an electoral result to produce a near stalemate.

The governing party in the Victoria Legislative Assembly has more than once supported the nomination for the Chair of a candidate drawn from the ranks of the opposition, and has even, on occasions, permitted a free vote of the House when the Speaker's election has been contested. Minority party candidates have also been elected to the Chair in the New South Wales Assembly, on one occasion in circumstances productive of considerable rancour. In 1911, when the governing Labour Party lost its majority as a result of two pending by-elections, a Liberal, Henry Willis, consented to take office on the understanding that if the government lost the by-elections it would advise the dissolution of Parliament. His public-spirited gesture was not, unfortunately, applauded by his own party.

In at least one State, Tasmania, the desirability of a permanent Speaker has received consideration. Until 1959 the Tasmania House of Assembly consisted of only thirty Members, elected by proportional representation, with the result that the parties were invariably very closely balanced. To overcome the deadlock which would be produced in the event of a general election resulting in a tie, an unusual constitutional amendment was passed in the last hours before the dissolution of Parliament in 1954. It provided that when the parties in the House were numerically equal the party receiving the higher aggregate of votes throughout the State should form the government and the other party should have the right to nominate the Speaker; but should the opposition decline to exercise this right the governing party would nominate the Speaker and an additional Member would be elected to the

Assembly as if a vacancy had occurred. The first Speaker to be elected in terms of this provision was Mr. H. W. Strutt, the nominee of the opposition, who was unanimously called to the Chair in 1955. Strangely enough, a deadlock had resulted for the first time in the history of the State from the very first general election following the passing of the constitutional amendment. Another deadlock resulted in 1956, when the procedure was repeated, but in 1958 a further constitutional amendment was passed increasing the size of the House of Assembly to thirty-five, and this rather novel provision relating to the election of the Speaker was repealed at the same time.[35]

In Tasmania, where the Labour Party has been in power for most of the past 50 years, the government's nominee for Speaker is normally accepted by the opposition. The Speaker is the choice of the Labour Party caucus and is very much a party man. However, a recent Speaker, Mr. Glen Davies, won the support of the opposition for his fairness and his acute feeling for the spirit of Parliament. This Speaker, following his first term of office, was not re-nominated by his caucus, but subsequently regained the speakership at the insistence of the opposition.

In South Australia in the 1960's an independent member, Mr. T. C. Stott, was on two occasions elected Speaker because the governing and opposition parties were equal in numbers. In 1979 the government's nominee for Speaker was defeated by the combined vote of the other parties in the House. The Liberal Party caucus selected Mr. Russack as their candidate but the Country Party nominated Dr. Eastick, also a Liberal. The latter was elected by a bare margin. Interestingly enough a similar situation occurred in the Legislative Council, where the government's nominee for President was also defeated by a candidate supported by the combined opposition.

The process of electing the Speaker in the State Assemblies is similar to that in the House of Representatives, the procedure being spelled out in detail in the standing orders. Labour Party Speakers are usually elected by their caucuses before they are proposed to the House. It is not abnormal for a Speaker to participate in debate and vote in divisions, and in the New South Wales Legislative Assembly it has been known for the Speaker to cast a deliberative vote in the House as well as in committee. In 1949 an Independent Member of the Tasmanian Assembly, Mr. W. G. Wedd, consented to take the Chair on the express understanding that he would be permitted to speak and vote in Committees of the Whole House and remain active on behalf of his constituents. In South Australia in 1962 the Speaker's right to speak and vote in committee of the Whole House was challenged, but the Chairman of Committees upheld his right to do so. Although six previous South Australian Speakers had availed themselves of the same right, the ruling was appealed and this led to a rather bizarre situation. Following the appeal from the Chairman's ruling, the Speaker took the Chair and upheld by his casting vote the ruling given in his own favour.[36]

The use of the Speaker's casting vote in the Australian State Assemblies has led to unusual situations on more than one occasion. The first Speaker of the New South Wales Assembly, Sir Daniel Cooper, used his casting vote against the government within three months of taking office. He had been elected by a majority of one with the combined support of the anti-government factions and his action brought the government down. Speaker Kingston of South Australia twice used his casting vote against the government on a censure motion and brought it down on both occasions. Stating the reason for his action in 1871 he declared that when the votes are equal on a confidence motion the government does not command a majority and it is therefore the duty of the Speaker to vote against the government. This was somewhat dubious reasoning, and clearly inconsistent with the principle that the Speaker should not by his casting vote alter the *status quo*. More recently the independent Speaker, Mr. Stott, used his casting vote to bring about the resignation of the government on the first day of a new Parliament meeting in 1968. Later in the same year and again in 1969 he used his casting vote to sustain the government in office. In 1970 he brought about the demise of the same government by using his deliberative vote in committee of the Whole House against the government on an amendment to a bill which the latter chose to treat as an issue of confidence.[37] More frequently the Speaker's vote has been used on behalf of the government and governments are sometimes openly dependent on it. In 1868 the Speaker of the Queensland Assembly used his casting vote no less than four times in a single day to save the government from defeat. In most situations, and barring unusual circumstances such as those referred to above which arose some years ago in South Australia, the Speaker can normally be relied upon to support the government with his vote. There may be situations where the Speaker will make a concession to the opposition provided the security of the government is not threatened. For example, the author was informed that the New South Wales Speaker has been known to use his casting vote against the government on a motion for an allocation of time order.

Inherited as they were from the British House of Commons, the procedures of the Australian State Assemblies together with those of the federal Parliament are basically similar although there are variations to be noted. The standing orders of most of the State assemblies incorporate a procedure for dissenting from Speaker's rulings. In Tasmania such an objection must be taken at once and in writing and a motion of dissent moved and seconded. An immediate debate takes place which the Speaker is entitled to terminate after 60 minutes, speeches being limited to ten minutes.[38] In Queensland notice is required of a motion of dissent from a Speaker's ruling and it must be considered within three days of the ruling being given, otherwise it lapses. As in Tasmania the Speaker may terminate the debate after 60 minutes and speeches are limited to ten minutes.[39] New South Wales has a similar rule to that of Queensland, except that the Speaker may terminate the debate after 30 minutes.[40] In Western Australia the relevant standing order simply states:

> If any objection is taken to the ruling or decision of the Speaker, such objection must be taken at once.[41]

Although not specified in the standing order, a debate may ensue when such objection is taken and the issue must be decided immediately. In South

Australia an objection is taken immediately. It must be stated in writing and a motion made and seconded. Only two speeches are allowed each of ten minutes duration, one in favour of the motion and one against. The Speaker is entitled to make a statement in defence of his ruling before the question is put.[42] One effect of the procedure which allows members to appeal from Speaker's rulings is to weaken the force of precedent. Rulings invariably take political considerations into account and one Australian Clerk informed the author that he normally advised his presiding officer not to feel necessarily bound by previous rulings. A Speaker would be unlikely to interpret an adverse vote following an appeal as an expression of want of confidence in himself.

All the State assemblies have a closure rule with the exception of the House of Assembly of Tasmania, where no provision exists either for closure or for allocation of time.* New South Wales, South Australia and Western Australia have a rule similar to that of the House of Representatives, the Speaker having no discretion with regard to the acceptance of a closure motion. Victoria has a rule comparable to that of the British House of Commons, the Chair being empowered to refuse the motion if it appears to be 'an abuse of the rules and forms of the House, an infringement of the rights of the minority, or is moved for the purpose of obstructing business'.[43] In Victoria the Chair is also empowered on similar grounds to decline to accept a motion that a member 'be not further heard'.[44] In Queensland the Chair has a certain discretion with regard to a closure motion, the question being put if the Speaker or Chairman 'is of opinion that the question has been sufficiently debated'.[45] In most Australian jurisdictions a closure motion is put in the form 'That the question be now put'. In Western Australia, however, the formula employed is 'That the House do now divide'.[46]

In Tasmania the Speaker is empowered to refuse a division which, in his opinion, 'is frivolously or vexatiously claimed', a power possessed by the Speaker of the British House of Commons.[47] The disciplinary powers of the Chair are similar in all Australian jurisdictions and follow the traditional pattern with regard to controlling disorder, preventing irrelevance and tedious repetition in debates, and naming a member for disregarding the authority of the Chair. Certain variations are evident with regard to the extent and the application of these powers. For example, the Queensland Speaker or Chairman of Committees may order a member to withdraw for the remainder of the day's sitting without first naming him to the House.[48] The Speaker and Chairman in New South Wales have a similar power in cases where a member has been called to order more than three times in the course of one sitting for a gross breach of the rules.[49] All State jurisdictions provide for an emergency adjournment procedure although the standing orders are not always specific as to the extent of the Speaker's discretion in allowing such a motion. Only in New South Wales and Western Australia is reference made

---

* However, the standing orders of the House of Assembly incorporate a procedure for the previous question, which if moved is debatable. See Standing Orders 114–120, House of Assembly of Tasmania, 1981.

in the standing order to a discretionary power on the part of the Speaker.[50] As in the House of Representatives, the rules of the State assemblies tend to be restrictive from the opposition's point of view and the provision for holding urgency debates is one of the few areas of Australian procedure in which the opposition can hope for a certain latitude. A Queensland member informed the author that in the Legislative Assembly of his State an emergency debate is unlikely to take place unless the government agrees to it. One must assume, therefore, that the Speaker's discretion is a crucial factor in allowing a debate, although the standing order gives the impression that such a debate cannot be prevented provided one hour's notice of the subject to be debated has been given to the Speaker in writing and five members rise in their places to support the motion.[51]

It is the general practice throughout Australian jurisdictions that the Speaker is not obliged to be a member of any select committee although he is a member and usually the chairman of certain standing committees, notably those dealing with the Standing Orders, the Library and other parliamentary services. In the bicameral Parliaments some or all of these committees are joint committees, the Speaker sharing with the President of the Legislative Council the responsibility for joint services and the administration of the parliamentary buildings. As in the case of the federal Parliament the precedence between the two presiding officers is determined by length of service. In some jurisdictions the Speaker's membership of certain standing committees is specified by standing order.

Australian Speakers are usually chosen from among the more experienced members of the House — an important consideration in view of the difficult situations with which they sometimes have to contend. The proceedings in some of the State assemblies can be very disorderly at times and in some jurisdictions the conduct of the Speaker is frequently assailed. Some Speakers are more openly partisan than others, but with the best will in the world it is difficult to maintain an appearance of impartiality while remaining closely involved in the hurly-burly of politics. In some State Parliaments the Speaker can expect to be criticised by the government if he affords too much latitude to the opposition. The Legislative Assembly of Queensland is one which is very tightly controlled by the government and its practices provide the opposition with little scope. The Australian parliamentary system nevertheless works in accordance with the political traditions which have developed over more than a century. The parties which win elections control the system and this normally includes the speakership. At the State level, just as at the federal level, there appears to be no great pressure in favour of adopting the Westminster conventions relating to the speakership.

Notes to Chapter Five: *The Speakership in Australia*

1. Sir Billy Snedden, The Westminster Convention and the Speaker, The Parliamentarian, Vol. LX, No. 3, July 1979, p. 130.
2. Sir Billy Snedden, The Speaker of the Australian House of Representatives, The Parliamentarian, Vol. LIX, No. 4, October 1978, pp. 205–206.

3. See J. A. Pettifer, editor, House of Representatives Practice, Australian Government Publishing Service, Canberra, 1981, pp. 200–201.
4. Standing Order 7 of the House of Representatives reads: 'Before the Governor-General's Speech is reported some formal business shall be transacted.'
5. Sir Billy Snedden, The Speaker of the Australian House of Representatives, op. cit., p. 207.
6. See Pettifer, op. cit., pp. 232–234.
7. Parliamentary Debates of the Commonwealth of Australia, Vol. 206, p. 19.
8. Ibid., p. 20.
9. Ibid., Vol. 213, p. 25.
10. Ibid., Vol. H. of R. 9, pp. 9 and 10.
11. Sir Billy Snedden, The Speaker of the Australian House of Representatives, op. cit., p. 206.
12. For specific illustrations of Speaker Cameron's rulings see L. F. Crisp, Australian National Government, Longmans, 4th edition, 1978, pp. 280–281.
13. Ibid., pp. 282–283.
14. Vol. H of R. 22, p. 8.
15. Sir Billy Snedden, The Speaker of the Australian House of Representatives, op. cit., p. 208.
16. See House of Representatives Debates, 27 February 1975, pp. 824–829. Accounts of this incident are also to be found in Pettifer, op. cit., page 228 and The Parliamentarian, Vol. LVI, No. 2, April 1975, p. 140.
17. This series of events is documented in detail in Pettifer, op. cit., pp. 50–68.
18. Ibid., p. 221.
19. Ibid., pp. 218–221.
20. Report of a Conference of Commonwealth Speakers held at Ottawa on 29th and 30th September 1966, pp. 34–35.
21. See Standing Orders 142–153 of the House of Representatives. Questions without notice were not recognized in the Standing Orders until 1950 although the practice was inaugurated when the Federal Parliament was first established. See Pettifer, op. cit., pp. 479–482 for an historical account.
22. Ibid., pp. 488–497.
23. Ibid., p. 487.
24. See The Parliamentarian, Vol. LVIII, No. 2, April 1977, pp. 133–134.
25. Standing Order 96.
26. Standing Order 107.
27. See Pettifer, op. cit., pp. 503–512.
28. See Report of the Conference of Speakers and Presiding Officers of Commonwealth Parliaments, Canada, September 8th to 12th, 1969, pp. 56–57.
29. See Report of the Sixth Conference of Commonwealth Speakers and Presiding Officers, Ottawa, April 23rd, 24th and 25th, 1981, pp. 98–99.
30. See Pettifer, op. cit., pp. 226–227.
31. See Speaker Snedden's comments at the Sixth Conference of Commonwealth Speakers and Presiding Officers, op. cit., p. 61.
32. Fourth Conference of Commonwealth Speakers and Presiding Officers, 7 to 10 September 1976, Houses of Parliament, London, p. 31.
33. Other statutory duties are detailed in Pettifer, op. cit., pp. 204–206.
34. Debates of the House of Representatives, 18 September 1980, pp. 1577–1578.
35. A most useful article on the Australian speakerships by Geoffrey Bolton was published in Parliamentary Affairs, Vol. 15, No. 3, for Summer 1962.

36. See G. D. Combe, The Speaker's Vote topples Governments, The Table, Vol. XXXIX for 1970, p. 83.
37. Ibid., pp. 82–84.
38. Standing Order 187, House of Assembly of Tasmania, 1981.
39. Standing Order 117, Legislative Assembly of Queensland, 1977.
40. Standing Order 161, Legislative Assembly of New South Wales, 1972.
41. Standing Order 143, Legislative Assembly of Western Australia, 1977.
42. Standing Order 164, House of Assembly of South Australia, 1972.
43. Standing Order 70(a), Legislative Assembly of Victoria, 1975.
44. Standing Order 91, Legislative Assembly of Victoria, 1975.
45. Standing Order 142, Legislative Assembly of Queensland, 1977.
46. Standing Order 160, Legislative Assembly of Western Australia, 1977.
47. Standing Order 202, House of Assembly of Tasmania, 1981.
48. Standing Order 123A, Legislative Assembly of Queensland, 1977.
49. Standing Order 392, Legislative Assembly of New South Wales, 1972.
50. See Standing Order 49(c), Legislative Assembly of New South Wales, 1972, and Standing Order 48, Legislative Assembly of Western Australia, 1977.
51. Standing Order 137, Legislative Assembly of Queensland, 1977.

Chapter Six

The Speakership in New Zealand

Responsible government in New Zealand dates from 1856 and the parliamentary traditions of that country closely reflect those of Great Britain. This is particularly apparent in the customs relating to the speakership. The New Zealand Parliament is unicameral, the Upper House having been abolished on 1 January 1951. This constitutional development did not, however, involve any radical change in the ceremony connected with the Speaker's election. It was never the practice for the Speaker to present himself to the Governor-General at the Bar of the Legislative Council, but to proceed instead to Government House, a practice which is still followed. Parliament is opened by commission, the Chief Justice and two other judges acting as commissioners. They arrive at the House of Representatives on the opening day and take their places at the head of the Table. The Chief Justice then addresses the House in the following words:

> Members of the House of Representatives, We have it in command from His Excellency the Governor-General to inform you that on —— His Excellency the Governor-General will declare to you in person the cause of his calling this meeting of Parliament together. But since it is necessary that a Speaker of the House of Representatives be first chosen, His Excellency requests that you, Members of the House of Representatives, do now proceed to make choice of a fit and proper person to fill that high and important office, and that having chosen him, you present him . . . at the Government House at Wellington, for His Excellency's approval.

The commissioners having withdrawn, the Clerk of the House reads the commission authorizing him to administer the oath or affirmation of allegiance to Members, and proceeds to administer it to those Members present. The House then proceeds to elect its Speaker.

As in Australia, detailed directions for the election of the Speaker are provided by the standing orders.[1] The Clerk of the House presides, and in the event of a debate taking place the Australian practice of enforcing a five minute time limit on speeches is observed. If an election is contested the House votes in the same manner as on any other question, but if any division relating to the election of the Speaker results in an equality of votes, the question is decided by means of a secret ballot. Where more than two candidates are proposed an absolute majority must be received by one of them in order to secure election, as in Australia. In accordance with the ancient practice of Westminster, the Speaker, on being elected, is required to present himself for the approbation of the Governor-General and to make the formal claim for privileges.* The privileges specifically mentioned in the petition are freedom of speech in debate, free access to the Governor-General whenever occasion may require it and the placing of the most favourable construction on all the proceedings of the House. The claim for freedom from arrest is omitted as in Canada. This ceremony takes place at Government House, whence the Speaker, accompanied by his fellow-Members, proceeds immediately following his election. The Speaker addresses the Governor-General in the following words:

> May it please Your Excellency, In obedience to Your Excellency's commands, the House of Representatives, in the exercise of their undoubted rights and privileges, have proceeded to the election of a Speaker, and, as the subject of their choice, I now submit myself for Your Excellency's approbation.

The Governor-General replies:

> Mr. Speaker, it is with much pleasure that, on behalf of the Queen, I approve and confirm the choice which the House of Representatives have made in your person.
> I congratulate you on your election to this distinguished position, marking as it does the appreciation of the House of Representatives of your impartiality and ability.

The Speaker then says:

> Thanking Your Excellency for your approbation of the choice made by the House of Representatives of me to be their Speaker, I have now, on behalf of the House of Representatives of New Zealand, to lay claim to all their privileges, and especially to freedom of speech in debate, and to free access to your Excellency whenever the occasion may require it, and that the most favourable construction may be put on all their proceedings.

To which the Governor-General replies:·

> I, on behalf of the Queen, confirm all the rights and privileges of the House of Representatives to the same extent as they have been granted

---

* On 13 March 1970 Her Majesty the Queen opened the New Zealand Parliament in person and Speaker Jack, re-elected for his second term of office, became the first New Zealand Speaker to seek the approbation of his election from the Queen herself.

hitherto. I also assure you that the House of Representatives will always have ready access to me, and that I will at all times place the most favourable construction upon their proceedings.

On this occasion the Speaker wears no wig unless he is a barrister, in which case he wears a barrister's wig. His normal attire comprises a full-bottomed wig and Q. C.'s gown worn over evening dress and a bib with a lace frill.

The Governor-General declares the cause of summoning the Parliament in the Chamber formerly occupied by the Legislative Council. A message is sent to the House desiring the attendance of Members in the Council Chamber, whence they proceed headed by the Serjeant-at-Arms with the Mace, the Speaker and the Clerks-at-the-Table. Instead of remaining at the Bar they enter the Chamber itself. The Speaker, the Serjeant and the Clerks take a central position in the Chamber and the Members take seats behind them. The Mace is not left outside the door, neither is it covered in the presence of the Governor-General. Having heard the speech from the throne the Speaker returns with the Members and officials to the House of Representatives where he reports on the proceedings which took place at Government House as well as on those which have just taken place in the Council Chamber. Before the Speaker refers to the Speech from the throne a first reading is given to the Expiring Laws Continuance Bill, after which the speech is laid on the Table of the House. It is not read out aloud but is printed in Hansard.

Although the continuity of the speakership following a change of government is not a principle which has been adopted in New Zealand, the strong partisanship which has characterised some of the incumbents of the office in Australia has been much less evident among New Zealand Speakers. As in Australia, the Speaker is nominated by the party in power and normally changes with the government. His proposer and seconder are usually the government whips. An element of continuity in the office has developed as a result of the tendency of governments when re-elected to continue the same Speaker in office. Once elected to the Chair the Speaker conducts himself in a completely impartial manner and is usually well-accepted by the opposition. He does not normally attend party meetings except during parliamentary recesses, although he has been known to attend important caucuses such as those explaining the budget. Although he is obliged to fight for his seat at a general election he conducts a low key campaign and does not indulge in highly partisan politics. The office in New Zealand has evolved in such a way that, although it has never happened, it is not inconceivable that a Speaker might one day be continued in office following a change of government, particularly in circumstances where an incoming government did not have an overall majority in the House. This could well occur since the House of Representatives consists of only 92 members. The parties in the past have frequently been evenly balanced, and the emergence of the Social Credit Party as a force to be reckoned with has led in recent years to three parties being represented in the House.

The opposition recognizes the right of the government to nominate the Speaker and usually allows him an uncontested election in the House.

However, this convention was breached in 1976 when Sir Roy Jack who had previously served as Speaker from 1967 to 1971, was again proposed for the Chair. The debate on this occasion was unusually acrimonious. The objections of the Labour Party opposition appear to have been based on Sir Roy's behaviour as a member of the opposition during the previous three years when the Labour Party had been in office. The Leader of the Opposition referred to an occasion when Sir Roy had been 'expelled from this Chamber for open defiance of the Chair on the last sitting day of the last Parliament'. The opposition may also have been influenced by the fact that Sir Roy had held cabinet office for a very short period in 1972. No alternative candidate was proposed, however, and the opposition, while not supporting Sir Roy's nomination, did not force a division on his election.[2]

Because of the small size of the New Zealand Parliament the withdrawal of the Speaker from active politics could create an acute problem for the governing party. When the parties are evenly balanced his vote in committee can be vital. During the 1958—61 Parliament, when the Labour Party held 41 seats to the National Party's 39, the Speaker, Mr. R. M. Macfarlane, regularly voted in committee and attended his party's caucuses. In 1970, at a time when the National Party held 44 seats to the Labour Party's 40, the Speaker voted in committee on numerous occasions to ensure the government's majority. In spite of the Speaker's party commitments, the conduct of the Chair has seldom been assailed. It is perhaps significant that the New Zealand House of Representatives observes the British practice in relation to Speaker's rulings. They may not be disputed or debated and may be challenged only by way of a substantive motion which would constitute one of censure. Such motions are rare, the most recent examples dating from 1966, 1970 and 1976. On the last-mentioned occasion, following a ruling by the Speaker that a *prima facie* case of privilege had been established involving a member of the opposition, the Leader of the Opposition gave notice of a motion expressing 'deep regret that by his actions Mr. Speaker no longer enjoys the confidence and respect of Her Majesty's Opposition.' The motion was not debated but it was an unfortunate blemish on the good relations which normally exist between the opposition and the Chair.

Speakers' rulings constitute binding precedents which are printed in book form and annotated from session to session. Adherence to the Westminister practice governing decisions of the Chair has been an important factor in sustaining the authority of the Speaker in New Zealand. It may also account in some measure for the relationship of trust and cordiality which has developed over the years between the opposition and the Chair and which has never been seriously damaged despite the unfortunate experiences of Sir Roy Jack.

The procedure of the New Zealand House of Representatives does not diverge radically from that of the House of Commons, and Standing Order 2 provides that in any case not envisaged by the Standing Orders 'Mr. Speaker shall decide, taking for his guide the rules, forms and usages of the House of Commons of the Parliament of the United Kingdom of Great Britain and Northern Ireland in force for the time being, so far as the same can be applied to the proceedings of this House'. As at Westminster, the Speaker is empowered to reject a motion for the closure if it appears to him to be an abuse of the rules of the House or an infringement of the rights of the minority.[3] He is not, however, empowered to select amendments. He decides whether a motion to adjourn the House for the purpose of discussing a definite matter of urgent public importance conforms to the terms of the relevant Standing Order[4] and he is additionally empowered, where more than one such motion is submitted on the same day, to decide which shall receive priority as being the most urgent and important.[5] The Standing Order expressly prohibits the discussion of more than one such motion on the same day. If the Speaker agrees that the matter proposed to be discussed is one contemplated by the standing order, he is required to read the statement to the House, and he is sometimes heard to complain about the length of the statements he is obliged to read. On 16 June 1981, Speaker Harrison requested members to make their submissions more concisely.

> When lengthy argument in support of the case is included in the statement, the effect is to put the statement of the case into my mouth. It is inappropriate for the Speaker to have to state the case, whether or not the matter is accepted. If it is accepted, the mover of the motion has what amounts to a second opportunity to have the case stated. If, on the other hand, the matter is rejected, then it has been stated in the words read by the Speaker, and there is no opportunity for reply. I accordingly make a plea to members preparing statements under these Standing Orders to confine themselves to a succinct statement of the matter proposed to be discussed.[6]

As in other jurisdictions the control of the question period falls within the discretion of the Speaker, but he sometimes seeks the guidance of the House as to how the question period should be conducted. As at Westminster, notice is required of questions for both oral and written answer, and like his British counterpart the New Zealand Speaker regularly expresses his concern because of slow progress during the oral question period. The greater the number of supplementary questions which are allowed, the fewer the number of main questions likely to be reached, and the Speaker has sometimes sought the guidance of the House as to which should be given priority.[7] In the final analysis, of course, the matter must reside within the Speaker's discretion as only he can interpret the will of the House. The Speaker's discretionary powers also extend to the asking of questions without notice. Standing Order 85 provides: 'Any Member desiring to ask a Question without notice on the ground of urgency in the public interest shall furnish to Mr. Speaker a copy of such proposed question marked "Urgent Question", and shall also furnish a copy to the Minister to whom it is intended to address such Question. After Questions for oral answer have been dealt with, Mr. Speaker (if he considers that the proposed Question is one which in the public interest should be answered immediately), shall state its nature to the House, whereupon such Member may forthwith ask such Question . . . ', and the Minister may answer or request that it be placed on the Order Paper for oral answer. A further discretionary power is conferred on the Speaker in terms of Standing Order 86(4) which reads: 'Questions shall not repeat the substance of questions already answered, disallowed, or to which an answer has been refused, unless in the opinion of Mr. Speaker it is reasonable that the Question be asked again.'

As in other jurisdictions, the raising of questions of privilege is another area of practice which poses problems for the Chair. As at Westminster, a member wishing to raise a question of privilege must first submit it to the Speaker before he may raise it in the House. This practice was recently introduced following a period during which members were frequently raising matters which, although trivial, were technically valid on *prima facie* grounds. Under the new procedure the Speaker will try to persuade a member not to insist on pursuing a minor point.[8] It appears, however, that he does not, like the Speaker at Westminster, have the power to disallow the raising of the question in the House except by way of notice of motion. Speaker Harrison explained to the author that when a complaint is made by one member against another, he, the Speaker, will invite the member against whom the complaint is made to make a statement designed to remove any misunderstanding. The member concerned would not, of course, be obliged to comply and the new procedure does not seem to have eliminated the difficulties completely.

The New Zealand Speaker is equipped with a casting vote and if called upon to use it he would most likely be guided by the conventions applicable at Westminster. Speaking on this matter at a conference in 1978, Speaker Harrison commented:

> I come back to the conventions of Westminster which say that his casting vote should be cast in certain ways to maintain the status quo, if necessary. It is certainly not for him to be responsible for the change in the lives of people that could be brought about by a proposed change in the law.[9]

However, the practice in New Zealand departs more radically from that of Westminster than this statement would suggest. It is most unlikely that a New Zealand Speaker would ever use his casting vote in a manner which might result in the defeat of the government on an issue of confidence. His deliberative vote in committee of the whole has frequently been used to sustain the government and it is hardly conceivable that a different approach would be taken in the House itself in cases where the survival of the government may hang on his vote.

In 1982, Speaker Harrison made a considered statement in the House on the use of the casting vote in the course of which he underlined the variations from Westminster practice. He indicated among other things that he would reserve his right to vote against the *status quo* on an issue of conscience and he summed up his guiding principles in the following words:

> In the pursuit of those principles I would vote in favour of a Bill's being introduced, being referred to a select committee, and read a second time.

To avoid changing the law, I would vote against the third reading unless the Government decided to make the vote an issue of confidence. On the third reading of Bills involving a matter of conscience I would vote as my conscience led me in each case. On the third reading of appropriation and supply Bills, and on other motions of confidence that affect the tenure of office of the Government or Parliament, I would vote to sustain the Government.[10]

The Speaker is possessed of the disciplinary powers normally vested in the Chair in those Parliaments which observe Westminster practices. He may order a member to withdraw for the remainder of the sitting or, if he feels more serious disciplinary measures are called for, he can name a member to the House. Perhaps the measure of the New Zealand Speaker's authority may be judged from the fact that he has been known to impose mild sanctions on his own initiative even though the rules and practice do not fully support his power to do so. In recent years Speaker Harrison has introduced an innovation whereby he will order a member who continually interrupts while a point of order is being made to withdraw from the chamber until the point has been stated. He first applied this sanction against a minister and has placed a description of the occasion on record:

> How do we cope with the problem of the persistent interjector? Do I suspend him for the rest of that sitting day simply for interjecting? Do I ask that he be named? I believe those remedies are somewhat too drastic and dramatic and are unlikely to be used. I had warned the House many times that I would take some sort of action and last November when I was hearing a point of order it occurred to me that I should invite the interjector to leave the Chamber as a sort of temporary suspension while the point of order was being discussed. The first time this happened was when a Minister interjected in a very loud voice. I turned to him and said: "Order! Would the Minister mind leaving the Chamber for a minute or two while we speak to a point of order?" The Minister for Internal Affairs withdrew from the Chamber. I might say that he had a surprised look on his face as he gathered up his papers and walked out. Unfortunately he had been out of the Chamber when I had been delivering the homily. Somewhat to my relief he complied. Within a few minutes of that we were still discussing a fairly tricky point of order when there was a loud interjection from a former Minister, a member of the present Opposition. I said: 'I ask the honourable Member to leave the Chamber briefly while this point of order is being discussed.' The honourable Member for Manukau withdrew from the Chamber. He came back a minute or two later to pick up his papers because he had left rather precipitately. I have found this procedure very useful indeed.
>
> One of my friends in the Cabinet afterwards said: 'If you had done that to me I would not have gone.' I asked why and he said: 'There is nothing in the Standing Orders that would require me to go.' I said: 'If you had defied the Chair perhaps I would have had you out for the rest

of the day. You could take your pick.' Since then we have had one or two modifications to this procedure. Recently we were discussing a point of order and a Member from the backbenches shouted out something which, while it may not have been an unparliamentary comment, was quite unhelpful. So I invited him to leave the Chamber. As he was stomping out the Government Whip caught him and said: "Come and sit down here. If you are quiet you will probably be able to stay." I did not see that he had stopped but I learned this later. On another occasion I issued an invitation to withdraw with the proviso that I was prepared to allow the Member to stay provided he was silent. If the Member fails to agree with that injunction I have no option to or hesitation in suspending him for the rest of the day. This is a useful device which I have found works well in New Zealand. I have no doubt that New Zealand Members of Parliament are no more angelic than Members of other Parliaments. This procedure is something between the requirements for a Member to resume his seat or to withdraw and apologise, which are inappropriate on these occasions, and the summary suspension for the rest of the day's sitting or the naming for a 24-hour period. I leave the suggestion for what it is worth.[11]

A special power is invested in the New Zealand Speaker in relation to the protection of the Maori language.* He is authorized in terms of Standing Order 97, should he deem it expedient, to order that speeches addressed to the House by the Governor-General, Bills or clauses of Bills specially affecting Maoris, and papers of special interest to the Maori race be translated and printed in the Maori language for the information of the Maori people. The Standing Orders also provide that petitions may be submitted in the Maori language and that reports of the Petitions Committee on petitions from persons of the Maori race may, if the Speaker so directs, be translated and printed in the Maori language.[12]

Certain duties are imposed on the New Zealand Speaker by statute. In terms of the Civil List Act, 1950, all salary payments to Members, other than Ministers, are made during the session under a certificate issued by him; during a parliamentary recess such certificates are issued by the Clerk of the House. The same Act provides that the Speaker, for the purpose of drawing his salary, shall be deemed to hold office following a dissolution of Parliament until a new Speaker is elected at the first meeting of the next Parliament. Under the Electoral Act, 1956, the Speaker is required to notify vacancies in the House of Representatives for publication in the Gazette and to issue his warrant to the

---

* In practice the Maori language in Parliament is dead. It has been ruled that Maori members can address the House in Maori if an interpreter is available. Today all speak English fluently and the Speaker has ruled that if they can speak English they should address the House in a language that can be understood by the other Members. Today there is no provision for an interpreter. There are few Maoris who cannot read and understand English and the provisions for translation are completely obsolete. Indeed there are Maoris who cannot understand Maori.

Clerk of the Writs for the filling of any such vacancy. The Act contains the rather strange provision that the Governor-General shall deputise for the Speaker in the event of the latter's absence from the country or in the event of the Speaker's office being vacant. In terms of the Redemption of the Public Debt Act, 1925, the Speaker is required to sit as a member of the Public Debt Commission.

Administratively, the Speaker's position is somewhat unusual. His control over the staff and parliamentary buildings is only partial. There is a minister, normally the Prime Minister, in charge of the Legislative Vote. The Speaker is not empowered to authorize expenditure against the Legislative Vote, although he may, and frequently does, recommend certain expenditures for the approval of the government. The Clerk of the House, as the permanent head of the Legislative Department, is responsible to the minister for all expenditure relating to the parliamentary establishment, excluding the payment of members' salaries. Any expenditure which is not covered by the Clerk's authority requires the approval of the minister. The officers of the House are appointed by the government on the Speaker's recommendation, and their salary scales and conditions of service are determined by the government. The Clerk of the House and his staff are not members of the public service but the Librarian is seconded from the National Library which itself comes under the Department of Education. In all matters related to their parliamentary duties, expenditure excepted, the Clerk and his colleagues are responsible to the Speaker. The control and administration of the parliamentary grounds and buildings are vested in the Speaker both in and out of session, except for those parts which house ministers and their suites and which are expressly excluded from his jurisdiction.[13] This division of authority limits the Speaker's administrative powers quite severely and has been known to create unfortunate situations. For example, in 1976 Speaker Jack refused permission to the Parliamentary Labour Party to hold a political rally in the parliamentary grounds, explaining that while the grounds were open for the enjoyment of the public they were not to be made available for party political meetings. He was severely criticised for his decision by the Leader of the Opposition, who implied that it had been influenced by government pressure. The Speaker responded with a public statement in which he declared that the decision was his own and the government had not been informed of the opposition's request to hold a rally.[14]

The Speaker is the chairman of the Library Committee and has the overall responsibility for the reporting organization and the production of Hansard. He is also normally a member of the House Committee which is concerned with members' facilities. He is chairman of the Standing Orders Committee and can be expected to take initiatives in proposing procedural changes. Speaker Harrison at the time of his first election on 10 May 1978 underlined his concern with regard to the rules and practice of the House. He said:

> There has been much criticism about procedures and practices, and there have been various calls for a revision of our Standing Orders. While I must concede that there are some rules I would like to amend—such as

those governing the lodging of notices of motion—by and large I consider that it is their general application that is in need of change. In 1961 Sir Ronald Algie, in much the same position as I am now, referred to this question of the public standing of Parliament. He observed that people enjoy a fight, but considered that in Parliament the people wanted it to be a battle of ideas, of wit and argument, not an irrelevant slanging match bedevilled with personalities.[15]

Professor Keith Jackson in an article entitled 'Parliamentary Reform in New Zealand' referred to an opinion expressed by a former member 'that it is not the Standing Orders which are at fault, rather they are abused and the major problems centre about the weakness of the office of Speaker of the House in New Zealand'. The member concerned averred 'that reappraisal of the role of the Speaker is "the first and best move to beat mounting criticism of the condition of Parliament" '. The same article referred also to a view expressed by the Social Credit Party that a judge should be appointed Speaker.[16] Assessing these views against the record of the speakership in New Zealand, these judgments appear rather harsh. It does not have a record of partisanship. The role of the Speaker has always been viewed in a very traditional light: so much so that Speaker Harrison, when first elected in 1978, put up a strong show of resistance when his proposer and seconder came to escort him to the Chair. He had to be forcibly dragged from his seat and even made a pretence of trying to dodge into the front row of the opposition benches.[17] Although this was a light-hearted diversion it was nevertheless an observance of an ancient custom.

The tradition of the New Zealand speakership is one of fidelity to the conventions of the office. Its prestige has been recognized in recent years by advancing the Speaker from eighth to third place in the official order of precedence, following the Governor-General and Prime Minister. Speaking on the occasion of his election to the Chair on 20 June 1961, Mr. R. M. Algie noted that he was the fifteenth in the line of succession of Speakers since parliamentary government was first established in New Zealand. 'It is, of course,' he said, 'one thing to be fifteenth in the line of succession here, but to me it is a little more to feel that I am one of a great number of Speakers who have formed part of an institution which has endured almost without a break for 600 years in the land which we still love to call Home.' He went on to say:

> Since I have been in this House, I have listened with pleasure to a very great number of extremely able debaters and I have noted that the best of them are brief, terse, concise, relevant, and constructive. I have noted also that in their best moments they have been supremely polite, courteous, and free from personalities. That is the standard, honourable members, that we would like to attain and which the public would like us to reach.[18]

This was the true voice of the dedicated Speaker and provides a fitting commentary on the principles by which New Zealand Speakers have been guided.

Notes to Chapter Six:
The Speakership in New Zealand

1. Standing Orders 5—13, House of Representatives of New Zealand, 1979.
2. For an account of this incident see The Parliamentarian, Vol. LVII, No. 4, October 1976, p. 269. See also New Zealand Parliamentary Debates, 22 June 1976, Vol. 403, pp. 2—6.
3. Standing Order 201.
4. Standing Order 88.
5. Standing Order 91.
6. New Zealand Parliamentary Debates, Vol. 437, p. 432.
7. See for example New Zealand Parliamentary Debates, 10 and 18 June, 1981, pp. 263—265 and 534—535.
8. See C. P. Littlejohn, New Privilege Rules in New Zealand, The Table, Vol. XLIX for 1981, pp. 42—45.
9. Report of the Fifth Conference, Speakers and Presiding Officers, Commonwealth Parliaments, 28 August—1 September, 1978, Canberra, pp. 29—30.
10. The full statement is to be found in New Zealand Parliamentary Debates, 1982, pages 4917—4919 and in The Table, Volume LI for 1983, pages 150—152.
11. Ibid., pp. 172—173.
12. Standing Orders 396 and 414.
13. Standing Order 436.
14. See The Parliamentarian, Vol. LVIII, No. 2, April 1977, pp. 119—120.
15. New Zealand Parliamentary Debates, Vol. 417, p. 2.
16. Keith Jackson, Parliamentary Reform in New Zealand, The Parliamentarian,
17. Vol. LX, No. 4, October 1979, p. 213.
18. See The Parliamentarian, Vol. LIX, No. 3, July 1978, p. 186.
    New Zealand Parliamentary Debates, 1st Session, 33rd Parliament, 1961, pp. 3 and 4.

Chapter Seven

The Speakership in India

The speakership in India dates from 1921. In that year an Englishman, Mr. (afterwards Sir) Frederick Whyte, a former Member of the House of Commons, was appointed by the then Governor-General as the first President of the Central Legislative Assembly. He was succeeded four years later by an elected presiding officer, Mr. Vithalbhai Patel, who defeated by a majority of two a rival candidate with government backing. Whyte and Patel between them laid the foundations of the Indian speakership and set a tradition which, notwithstanding the radical changes which have taken place since 1947, has not been without its influence in the shaping of the office since the achievement of Indian independence. During his four years of office Whyte concentrated on setting and maintaining a standard of complete impartiality and guiding the proceedings of the Assembly in accordance with the practice of the House of Commons. He was also influential in establishing the ground rules of financial procedure, including the creation of a Public Accounts Committee. As an appointed officer he could hardly have done more. Patel was able to go further. Since he had been elected by the Assembly in opposition to a government nominee he was able to claim that he was responsible to the Assembly and to no other authority. He asserted the complete independence of the Chair from the influence of the executive, and although he frequently came into conflict with the government in the process, his principle was conceded before his tenure of office came to an end in 1930. He made some impressive gains during his occupancy of the Chair. Shortly after his first election he asserted the right of the Chair to exercise its discretion in the allowance and disallowance of motions by ruling out of order a government resolution on a Bill relating to public security on the ground that it would be impossible to debate the motion without referring to a case which was *sub judice*. He vindicated the right of the President to immunity from criticism in respect of his rulings other than by substantive motion at a time when official Members were openly deprecating certain of his decisions. He successfully asserted the authority of the President of the Assembly over the maintenance of order and security within the precincts of Parliament. And he demanded that the staff of the Legislative Department should be brought under the direct control of the President, a reform which was implemented in 1928, one year after his re-election to the Chair with the unanimous support of both officials and elected Members.

Patel's first act on being elected to the Chair was to sever his ties with the party to which he had belonged. Explaining his action to the House, he stressed that as President he was no longer a party man and requested the leader of his former party to absolve him from all party obligations. In March 1926 when that party walked out of the Assembly in a body, President Patel declined to join them. At the ensuing general election he stood as an independent candidate and was returned unopposed. In 1930, following a call by the Indian National Congress to boycott the legislatures, Patel declined to resign his office as demanded by Congress on the basis of the principle which he observed throughout his tenure of office: that the President could not allow his conduct to be influenced by any political party or by his own personal sympathies. Of the four Presidents who succeeded Patel during the pre-independence period, only one followed his example in severing his political ties, although the others all declared that they would discharge their duties in a strictly impartial manner.[1]

The next milestone in the history of the Chair in India was in 1946 when the country was on the threshold of independence. Mr. G. V. Mavalankar was elected as the last President of the Central Legislative Assembly by 66 votes to 63 in opposition to a nominated Member who had been sponsored by the government. In 1947 the style of Speaker was first assumed, and Mr. Mavalankar was re-elected to the Chair in the Constituent Assembly (Legislative) which on 20 January 1950 became the Provisional Parliament of the Indian Union until 1952 when the two Houses of the new Parliament were constituted in terms of the republican Constitution. On 15 May 1952 Mr. Mavalankar was elected the first Speaker of the House of the People (Lok Sabha), an office he retained until his death on 27 February 1956. Mavalankar's speakership thus spanned the entire crucial period of India's transition from dependence to nationhood. It is not surprising that the Indian speakership should bear the impress of his forceful personality, for it was he who undertook the groundwork of moulding the institution to the requirements of an independent India.

Mavalankar did not, however, resign from the Congress Party. He took the view that the removal of the Speaker from his party associations should be accompanied by a convention whereby he should not have to face a contest in his constituency. In the absence of such a convention he felt it would be asking too much of the Speaker to sever his political connection totally. He maintained also that political experience was an important asset in a Speaker and that this could only be gained through active membership of a political party. He stressed, however, that a Speaker should not attend party meetings or participate publicly in the discussion of controversial issues.[2]

Mavalankar's successor, Speaker Ayyangar, did not resign from the Congress Party, on whose ticket he was elected, but he did resign from the Congress Parliamentary Party. Speaker Hukam Singh, who held office from 1962 to 1967, took a more equivocal position. In an article published in 1967 he wrote:

The Speaker has to seek election every five years. To get himself elected, he must have the support of his party. It is in the interest of the majority party that the Speaker commands the confidence and respect of the minority. But this is seldom realized and the ruling party on certain occasions expects some favours. If the Speaker agrees, then he must be charged with partiality. If he refuses, then next time there will be pressure in his party that he must be replaced. The Speaker cannot sever his connexions absolutely from the party, if he has to seek its patronage again. And as long as he maintains his association, or even simple membership of the party, there always remains a suspicion in the minds of the Opposition that the presiding officer is partisan. Thus the Speaker would be unable to retain the confidence of the minority, however much he might try to be impartial. That is generally the case in many nascent democracies.[3]

However, on being elected to the Chair he assured the House 'that as long as I occupy the Chair you would not get the impression that I belong to any party or to any group at all.' For some members this was an insufficient assurance, because on 24 August 1966, following his rejection of a complaint of privilege directed against a minister, an opposition member called on him to resign his membership of the Congress Party. On the following day the Speaker denied that he was a member of the party, stating 'that the position is that as soon as I was elected I said that thenceforward I shall not be a member of any political party. I had said that. Since then I have not paid a single pie even as a primary member as my subscription.'[4] It appears, nevertheless, that Speaker Hukam Singh never formally resigned from his party.

The first Speaker of the post-independence period to do so was Dr. N. Sanjiva Reddy, who held office from 1967 to 1969. Responding at the time of his election to a request from an opposition member that he should sever his political connections, he announced his resignation from the party to which he had belonged for 34 years. His decision has been described as 'an act of great courage and vision' on the part of a man who had been an active politician of very high standing. In an address to the Presiding Officers' Conference held in October 1967 he explained that changed circumstances had altered the role and position of the Speaker of the House.

It is no use taking the same position as was taken by either Speaker Ayyangar or Mavalankar when there was absolutely no opposition and it was all an one-party affair mostly and there was no need to satisfy the Opposition or to keep up a balance. I feel that the circumstances have changed so radically today and the Speaker sitting in the Chair today will have to create that confidence not only in the party which has put him up as the Speaker, but in the whole House.[5]

However, on 26 March 1977 Dr. Reddy was again elected Speaker following a change of government, he himself having been returned as a member of the Janata Party. He was unanimously called to the Chair but relinquished the office after only two months in order to become President of the Republic.

Speaker Dhillon, who succeeded Speaker Reddy in 1969, remained a member of his party but resigned from its executive committee and the Congress Parliamentary Party, as he had done previously on his election as Speaker of the Legislative Assembly of Punjab. Speaker Hegde, who succeeded Speaker Reddy on 21 July 1977, was a former judge who came to the Chair without previous parliamentary experience. By his own account, the question of resigning from the party on whose ticket he was elected did not arise. 'My judicial background and record on the bench have made any announcement of formal severance of political affiliation unnecessary, even as a symbolic act of averment of neutrality.'[6] Speaker Hegde was not a candidate at the ensuing general election and his successor, Speaker Jakhar, who was elected on a Congress Party ticket, has observed the usual conventions of the speakership without formally severing the connection with his party. He was unanimously elected Speaker on 22 January 1980.

Some commentators believe that greater efforts should have been made to achieve the total detachment of the Speaker from his political affiliation. Mavalankar, Ayyangar and Hukam Singh all expressed their support for the principle, provided it were coupled with a convention whereby the Speaker's seat would not be contested, but they took no active steps to promote it. Ayyangar acknowledged that it was 'the opposition that suffers by throwing the Speaker into the hands of the majority party.'[7] For example, it has not apparently been the custom to consult the opposition parties over the choice of Speaker and this has led to a sense of grievance among the minorities. It has been argued that since the duty of the Speaker is to protect minorities they should at least have some input into the selection of the member who will preside over them.[8] Walk-outs and demonstrations are a common feature of the proceedings of Lok Sabha and it has been suggested that such tactics on the part of minority parties might be less general if they had complete confidence in the Speaker.[9] Such confidence is unlikely to develop while the Speaker remains dependent on government patronage. Despite the example of Mavalankar, whose renown rests exclusively on his tenure of office as Speaker, the speakership has not become established as an ultimate ambition of a career in public life. Speaker Ayyangar became a State Governor. Speaker Dhillon moved directly from the Chair to the cabinet, and was subsequently appointed High Commissioner to Canada. Speaker Reddy, as we have seen, became President of the Republic, an appointment not inconsistent, perhaps, with the concept of a politically independent speakership. Had Mavalankar taken advantage of his great prestige to sever his party connection, as Reddy was to do later, without any corresponding guarantee of an uncontested election in his constituency, the Indian speakership might have evolved differently. As it is, the Speaker can expect to face opponents in his constituency at a general election and must conduct an electoral campaign on a party ticket. It is not unknown for a Speaker to go down to defeat, as happened to Speaker Dhillon in 1976. If re-elected to the House, he has a good chance of being unanimously re-elected to the Chair, as were Speakers

Ayyangar and Dhillon in 1957 and 1971 respectively. There is no guarantee of this, however.

The Indian Constitution makes detailed provision for the functioning of Parliament, and the relevant sections owe much to Mavalankar's influence. Those relating to privilege and financial procedure were based directly on his recommendations, and it was at his instance that the independent parliamentary establishment for which Patel had successfully fought is now enshrined in the Constitution. In terms of Article 98 each House of Parliament has a separate secretarial staff whose recruitment and conditions of service are regulated by Parliament itself. Provision is made for the creation of posts common to both Houses. The office of Speaker is provided for in the Constitution, which also prescribes certain of his duties. Article 93 provides that 'The House of the People shall, as soon as may be, choose two Members of the House to be respectively Speaker and Deputy Speaker thereof . . .'. Article 94 stipulates that these officers may hold office only for so long as they remain Members of the House, with the proviso that the Speaker shall continue in office following a dissolution of Parliament until immediately before the first meeting of the new House of the People. This Article also provides that the Speaker may resign his office by writing addressed to the Deputy Speaker, and vice versa, and that either officer is removable by a resolution passed by a majority of all the Members of the House of which fourteen days' notice has been given. Article 95 provides that in the event of both offices being vacant the President of the Republic may appoint a Member of the House to discharge the functions of Speaker, and that during the absence of both officers from any sitting of the House, 'such person as may be determined by the rules of procedure of the House or, if no such person is present, such other person as may be determined by the House, shall act as Speaker'. A Panel of Chairmen of not more than six Members is nominated by the Speaker in terms of Standing Order 9,* and in the absence of both the Speaker and Deputy Speaker one of them would normally be requested by one or the other officer to act as Speaker. If it so happened that none of the Panel of Chairmen was available during the absence of both presiding officers, the House, presumably, would proceed to elect another Member to take the Chair in terms of the constitutional provision for this eventuality. The salaries and allowances of both the Speaker and the Deputy Speaker are charged directly on the Consolidated Fund under Article 112(3)(b) of the Constitution.

Article 100(1) provides that the Speaker shall be equipped with a casting vote but no deliberative vote. Article 100(4) requires the Speaker to adjourn the House or to suspend its meeting in the event of the absence of a quorum, which in terms of the preceding clause is fixed at one-tenth of the total number of Members of the House. Article 110 defines a Money Bill and provides that should a question arise as to whether a Bill is a Money Bill or not 'the decision of the Speaker of the House of the People thereon shall be final'. In terms of the

---

* The Standing Order references in this Chapter are taken from the Rules of Procedure and Conduct of Business in the House of the People, 6th edition, 1977.

same Article the Speaker is required to certify every Money Bill when it is transmitted to the Council of States (the Upper House) and when it is presented to the President for his assent.[10] Article 108 makes provision for the holding of joint sittings of the two Houses of Parliament and Article 118 empowers the President, after consultation with the Chairman of the Council of States and the Speaker of the House of the People, to make rules as to the procedure with respect to joint sittings of, and communications between, the two Houses. It also provides that the Speaker shall preside at a joint sitting, or in his absence such person as may be determined by the rules of procedure referred to above. Article 120(1) empowers the Speaker, in his discretion, to permit any Member of the House who is unable to express himself in Hindi or in English to address the House in his mother tongue.

In India the importance of emphasizing the prestige and authority of the Speaker has been recognized from the outset of the country's independence. Speaking on 8 March 1948 on the occasion of the unveiling of a portrait of Vithalbhai Patel, Pandit Nehru observed:

> The Speaker represents the House. He represents the dignity of the House, the freedom of the House and because the House represents the nation, in a particular way, the Speaker becomes the symbol of the nation's freedom and liberty. Therefore, it is right that that should be an honoured position, a free position and should be occupied always by men of outstanding ability and impartiality.

In the order of precedence the Speaker ranks equally with the Chief Justice at sixth place.* He wears no special costume on any occasion, and it is interesting to note that one of Mr. Mavalankar's first acts on taking office in 1946 was to discard the wig which had hitherto been worn by the presiding officer. Before entering the House at the commencement of a sitting he is announced by the Marshal. On hearing the announcement Members of the House rise, and on reaching the Chair the Speaker bows to the House before taking his seat. The Marshal, who is the equivalent of a Serjeant-at-Arms, wears a prescribed uniform but carries no Mace. Other than the simple ritual described above, there is no ceremonial associated with the speakership in India.

The procedure for the election of the Speaker is laid down in Standing Order 7. The date of the election is determined by the President, and the Secretary (Clerk of the House) is required to send every Member notice of the date. Written nominations, duly proposed and seconded, may be accepted by the Secretary at any time before noon on the day preceding the election, and must be accompanied by a statement from the nominee to the effect that he is willing to serve if elected. The motions are put to the House in the order of their receipt, no debate being permitted, and once a motion has been carried, no further motions are put, the Member proposed in the successful motion

---

* Those who precede him are the President, Vice-President, Prime Minister, Governors of States within their respective states and ex-Presidents.

being declared elected. The Standing Order stipulates that no Member may propose or second a motion proposing his own name, or propose or second more than one motion.

The duties of the Indian Speaker correspond in large measure with those of the Speaker of the House of Commons, although in some respects, as will be seen below, his powers exceed those of his Westminster counterpart. He is the representative of the House in its relations with the President, the Council of States (Rajya Sabha) and all external authorities. In his capacity as presiding officer he regulates the proceedings of the House and is equipped with disciplinary powers comparable with those of the Speaker of the House of Commons. His rulings may not be questioned save by substantive motion, and they constitute precedents which are collected for future guidance. Sometimes they are embodied into the written rules of procedure. From time to time the Speaker issues directions in amplification or elucidation of the rules and practice of the House in order to ensure the proper conduct of business. Debate is not permitted on a point of order, although it is provided that 'the Speaker may, if he thinks fit, hear Members before giving his decision'.[11] A Member wishing to bring to the attention of the House a matter which is not a point of order may do so, given the consent of the Speaker, on giving notice to the Secretary in writing of the matter he wishes to raise and his reasons for wishing to raise it.[12]

The Standing Orders of the House of the People confer wide discretionary powers on the Speaker. He determines the order in which Members shall sit in the House,[13] and in this respect it is interesting to note that in India the Speaker is empowered to recognize parties and groups in the House. In terms of the Standing Orders relating to the sittings of the House,[14] the Speaker, having regard to the state of business, may determine the days on which the House shall sit and vary the normal times of commencement and termination of sittings. In consultation with the Leader of the House he determines the order of business, which may not be varied unless he is satisfied that sufficient grounds exist for doing so.[15] He is empowered, in various circumstances, to allot time for debates and to impose time limits on speeches. These powers are exercisable in relation to the debate on the Motion of Thanks in reply to the President's Address at the beginning of a Budget session;[16] to financial debates, including those on the Budget and the Appropriation and Finance Bills;[17] to a debate on a motion to adjourn the House on a definite matter of urgent public importance,[18] and on a motion to discuss a matter of general public interest;[19] to a debate on a motion of no confidence in the Government;[20] and to any debate in relation to any matter when the Speaker, after taking the sense of the House, decides it has become unduly protracted.[21]

Various powers are conferred on the Speaker in relation to questions to Ministers. Standing Order 41(2) lists the conditions of admissibility of questions, and its interpretation is vested in the Speaker in terms of Standing Order 43(1) which reads: 'The Speaker shall decide whether a question or a part thereof is or is not admissible under these rules and may disallow any question or part thereof when in his opinion it is an abuse of the right of questioning or is calculated to obstruct or prejudicially affect the procedure of the House or is in contravention of these rules.' He may also vary the Question Hour, normally the first hour of every sitting day;[22] waive the rules relating to notice of questions,[23] and permit a question to be asked at short notice if it relates to a matter of public importance and he is of the opinion that it is of an urgent character;[24] decide that a written answer would be more appropriate than an oral answer;[25] permit a question, on the representation of a Minister, to be answered after the Question Hour has expired;[26] at the request of a Member, direct that a question be answered notwithstanding the absence of the Member in whose name it stands;[27] and, when all questions for oral answer have been called, if time permits, call again any question which has not been asked by reason of the absence of the Member in whose name it stands, and permit a Member to ask a question standing in the name of another Member, if so authorized by him.[28]

The Speaker also decides on the admissibility of resolutions and amendments. He has a general discretion with regard to the admissibility of resolutions in terms of Standing Order 174, which is couched in similar terms to Standing Order 43(1) relating to the admissibility of questions (see above). In terms of Standing Order 198(2) he decides whether a motion expressing lack of confidence in the Government is in order.* Standing Order 211 empowers the Speaker to rule on the admissibility of a 'cut' motion (i.e., a motion to reduce an expenditure proposal). Standing Order 341 provides that the Speaker may refuse a dilatory motion (i.e., a motion for the adjournment of a debate or the recirculation or re-committal of a Bill) if he considers it to be an abuse of the rules of the House. In addition, his consent is required to a motion to adjourn the House for the purpose of discussing a definite matter of urgent public importance,[29] to a motion for discussing a matter of general public interest,[30] and to any motion for adjourning the debate on a Bill.[31] The Speaker is empowered to select amendments in relation to Bills and motions,[32] and he may refuse to propose an amendment which is, in his opinion, frivolous or meaningless.[33]

In terms of Standing Order 172 petitions may be submitted only with the Speaker's consent. Similarly, a Member requires the consent of the Speaker in order to raise a matter of privilege.** The Speaker, on being requested to do so, may order the publication of a Bill in the Gazette, in which case it becomes unnecessary to move for leave to introduce the Bill in the House.[34] He may, if he thinks fit, postpone the consideration of a clause of a Bill.[35] In respect of the Appropriation Bill he may, in his discretion, modify the normal procedure relating to Bills,[36] and in order to avoid repetition in the course of the debate on the Bill he may require Members to give advance intimation of the points

---

* In the House of the People a motion of no confidence in the Government may be admitted only if the leave of the House is signified by not less than fifty Members rising in their places.

** Standing Order 222. In addition to the Speaker's consent, a Member seeking to raise a matter of privilege also requires the leave of the House. If objection is taken, at least 25 Members must rise in their places in order to signify that the leave of the House is granted.

they wish to raise.[37] The permission of the Speaker is required by a Minister wishing to make a statement on resignation[38] and a Member wishing to make a personal explanation.[39] Standing Order 55 makes provision for half an hour discussions on matters arising from the answers to questions provided they are of sufficient public importance, the decision as to whether a matter conforms to the requirements of the Standing Order resting with the Speaker. Where a motion embodies two or more separate propositions the Speaker may separate them and propose them to the House as separate questions.[40] Closure procedure is similar to that of the House of Commons. The closure motion takes the form 'That the question be now put', and it may be refused by the Speaker if it appears to him that it is an abuse of the rules or an infringement of the right of reasonable debate.[41]

Standing Order 95 empowers the Speaker after a Bill has been passed by the House to correct patent errors and incorporate consequential amendments. He is required to authenticate with his signature two copies of every Bill which is passed by both Houses.[42] He may, in his discretion, order any word or words to be expunged from the record of the proceedings of the House if he deems such word or words to be defamatory, indecent, unparliamentary or undignified.[43] He controls the admission of strangers and may, whenever he thinks fit, order their withdrawal from any part of the House.[44] Standing Order 248 provides for the holding of secret sittings at the request of the Leader of the House, and Standing Orders 249 and 250 vest in the Speaker a complete discretion with regard to the manner of reporting the proceedings and the procedure to be adopted on such occasions. Standing Order 26 confers certain powers on the Speaker in relation to Private Members' business, namely, the allotment of time, the determination of its order of precedence and the arrangement of ballots.

The Speaker is in supreme control of all parliamentary committees, some of which are appointed by the House and some by himself.* He appoints their chairmen, directs them on matters relating to their work and procedure and co-ordinates their activities where necessary. He consults regularly with the chairmen of committees, who turn to him for guidance in settling their problems, and he keeps in close touch with the proceedings of all committees. Certain powers relating to committees are reserved to the Speaker; for example, they cannot meet outside the precincts of Parliament without his permission, and they cannot summon officials of State Governments to give evidence before them without his previous sanction. Appeals by committee members from chairmen's decisions are decided by the Speaker, and where a dispute arises with regard to the production of a document before a committee the matter is referred to the Speaker for settlement and his decision is final. Some committees are specifically provided for in the Standing Orders, including the Business Advisory Committee, the Committee on Private Members' Bills and Resolutions, the Committee on Petitions, the Committee

---

* Indian parliamentary procedure makes no provision for the Committee of the Whole House. There are no Committees of Supply or Ways and Means, and Bills are referred to *ad hoc* Select Committees.

on Public Accounts, the Committee on Estimates, the Committee of Privileges, the Committee on Subordinate Legislation, the Committee on Government Assurances and the Rules Committee. The Business Advisory Committee and the Rules Committee, among others, work directly under the Speaker's chairmanship.

The authority of the Indian Speaker is thus wider than that of any other Speaker in the Commonwealth. Most Assemblies insist on maintaining a wide measure of control over their procedure and practice, but in India the House of the People has been content to entrust the shaping of its rules to its presiding officer. As a result the Standing Orders have largely been evolved by the Speaker himself, assisted by his Secretariat, and the various changes which they have undergone from time to time have been due almost entirely to their initiative. The Constitution empowered the Speaker to make such modifications and adaptations to the rules of procedure of the Provisional Parliament as were necessary to suit them to the needs of the House of the People until such time as the House framed its own rules. In effect the Speaker continued to exercise this temporary power after 1952 when the Indian Parliament was inaugurated.* A Rules Committee was first established under the Speaker's chairmanship in 1948, and was formally embodied in the Standing Orders as a permanent committee in 1952. Its proposals have almost invariably been agreed to, and when Members outside the Committee have been invited to submit their suggestions the response has tended to be slight. Whether or not this indicates a general lack of interest by Indian Members of Parliament in matters of procedure, it certainly suggests that most of them repose an absolute confidence in the Chair. This lack of insistence on the part of the House to exercise its constitutional right to control its own procedure has made for a considerable flexibility of the rules, with the result that changes, sometimes of a far-reaching nature, have been effected smoothly and easily. Although the relationship of the Government to the legislature is different today from what it was in the pre-independence period Mr. Mavalankar, in his shaping of the Standing Orders, was at pains to preserve the independence of the House from the executive in the tradition established by Vithalbhai Patel. The wide discretion which is reserved to the Speaker in so many matters bears testimony to this. The structure of the committee system is such as to strengthen the independence of Parliament, and in particular the reservation to the Speaker of the power to appoint the chairmen of committees, and the exclusion of Ministers from membership of the Public Accounts and Estimates Committees. The establishment of a Committee on Government Assurances was an important innovation, its functions being to scrutinize the assurances, promises and undertakings given by Ministers in the House from time to time, and to report on the extent to which they have been implemented.[45] Among other innovations which have been incorporated into the Indian rules of procedure are two which have the effect of widening

---

* In 1954 a Member contended, in a petition to the President, that the Speaker had exceeded his authority in continuing to exercise his transitional power for so long a period.

the opportunities of Private Members. The provision for half an hour discussions on matters arising out of the answers to questions enables a Member, with the permission of the Speaker, to draw the attention of the House to a matter of public importance, provided he does so without seeking to revise the policy of the Government. This device may be compared with the daily half-hour debate which takes place in the House of Commons on the motion 'That the House do now adjourn', and which is the traditional opportunity for the Private Member in Britain to raise any matter he cares to raise. In 1953 provision was also made for discussion of matters of urgent public importance other than by the adoption of the emergency procedure of moving the adjournment of the House for the purpose. In terms of Standing Orders 193 and 196 any Member, provided he is supported by at least two other Members, may give notice that he wishes to raise a discussion on a matter of urgent public importance, specifying the nature of the matter he wishes to raise. The Speaker decides whether the matter is sufficiently urgent and important to be admitted, and if his decision is favourable he may allot two sittings in a week on which such matters may be discussed and allow not more than one hour for each discussion. Both this practice and that relating to the half an hour discussions involve a radical departure from the procedural tradition of the House of Commons in that debate may take place although there is no formal motion before the House, and no vote or decision is taken at the conclusion of the discussion.

The Speaker is entitled to address the House at any time on any matter before the House with a view to assisting Members in their deliberations,[46] and it was not unusual during Mavalankar's speakership for the Chair to intervene in the course of a debate in order to elucidate the point or argument which a Member was developing. In India the function of the Speaker in relation to the scope of a debate goes beyond the mere checking of irrelevance and tedious repetition. Mavalankar was a stern interpreter of the rules he had done so much to shape, but in his decisions and control of the proceedings he displayed a judgment as shrewd as it was strict. Only rarely did he allow a motion to adjourn the House for the purpose of discussing a definite matter of urgent public importance. Prior to independence the presiding officers of the Central Legislative Assembly were inclined to be lenient in their interpretation of the emergency adjournment rule. The changed attitude of the Chair was explained in a ruling given by Speaker Mavalankar on 21 March 1950. He pointed out that before India became independent the popularly elected Members of the Assembly were in perpetual opposition to the Government, and as the opportunities for discussing matters of public importance were few, presiding officers had felt justified in relaxing the rule in order to widen the scope for discussion and afford more time for the expression of popular views. 'The Government then was not responsible to the legislature, nor were they amenable to its control. There was, therefore, good ground for the presiding officers to relax the strict House of Commons practice and allow opportunities for discussion of all-important questions on adjournment motions.' But the position had changed since 15 August 1947. 'The Ministry is fully responsible to this House and Members have now ample opportunities of discussing various matters.' Therefore, it was no longer possible 'to look upon an adjournment motion as a normal device for raising discussion on any important matter'. Mavalankar's attitude when matters of privilege were raised was, wisely, a cautious one. He discouraged any impulsive assertions of privilege on the part of Members, preferring to discuss matters of privilege privately before admitting them for discussion in the House. The Speaker may, on his own initiative, refer any matter concerning privilege to the Committee of Privileges.

The Speaker's authority over the staff of the House, its precincts and its security arrangements is absolute. All visitors are subject to his discipline, and a breach of order may be punished by means of exclusion from the precincts of Parliament, or, in more serious cases, dealt with as a contempt or breach of privilege. The Speaker is responsible for the protection of the rights of Members, and for ensuring that all reasonable amenities are provided for them. He does not mix socially with his fellow-Members but is accessible to all of them for consultation by previous appointment. Should a Member be arrested on a criminal charge, or sentenced to a term of imprisonment, or detained under an executive order, the fact must be immediately intimated to the Speaker in terms of Standing Order 229. No arrest may be made within the precincts of Parliament except with the Speaker's permission.

Apart from his formidable powers under the rules, the Speaker has residuary powers by virtue of his authority to issue directions from time to time for the regulation of matters not specifically provided for in the rules. For example, while he may not be able to compel a minister to answer a question, a direction by the Speaker has laid down 'that answers to questions given in the House shall be complete and, as far as possible, each part of a question shall be answered separately. The Speaker may direct a Minister to give a complete answer, where, on his attention being drawn to an answer, he finds that it does not fulfill the said conditions.'[47] It is now a settled practice that the Chair does not pronounce on the constitutionality of legislative proposals, but it is the right of the Speaker to interpret the constitution, as well as the rules, so far as matters in or relating to the House are concerned.*[48] Speaker's rulings admit of no argument and may be questioned only by way of a substantive motion. Sometimes they can be of a very far-reaching nature, as, for example, the ruling of Speaker Jakhar of 28 August 1981 upholding the government's right to intercept and censor the mail of members of Parliament. The Speaker said that the law empowered the government to intercept citizens' mail in the interests of public safety and the privileges of Parliament did not place a member on a footing different from that of an ordinary citizen.[49]

Writing in 1967, Speaker Hukam Singh referred to a growing tendency among opposition members to defy the Chair and create unruly scenes. He attributed this to frustration on the part of a numerically weak opposition faced with a strongly entrenched government which appeared to be

---

* On 19 February 1982 Speaker Jakhar ruled, by virtue of this power, that the appointment of a member of Rajya Sabha, the upper House, as Minister of Finance was not unconstitutional.

irremovable. He saw this as a threat to democracy and spoke of the difficulties of the Speaker's task in dealing with such circumstances.[50] Speaker Bhagat, who occupied the Chair for a brief period in 1976 in succession to Speaker Dhillon, also referred to the problem of disorderly conduct when speaking at the Fourth Conference of Commonwealth Speakers and Presiding Officers in London in 1976. He indicated that the Speaker places great reliance on the Business Advisory Committee, of which he is chairman, to assist him in the strict application of the rules. Government and opposition leaders are represented on the committee which agrees as to how the programme of business should be organized and time allocated to the various items. They also devise rules and practices for the enforcement of the agreements reached and this had led to more orderly debate. In view of the multiplicity of parties and the assortment of independent members represented in Lok Sabha, it is not possible to offer a place on the Business Advisory Committee to every splinter group and individual interest. The Speaker selects as members of the committee those whom he considers to be broadly representative of the House as a whole and will attempt, in his role as a moderator, to safeguard the interests of the other minorities himself. When Mavalankar was Speaker he would use his personal discretion to a great extent in the resolution of conflicts. No subsequent Speaker has approached Mavalankar's strength in the area of personal decision-making, and his successors have seen themselves more as mediators when chairing the Business Advisory Committee. They have preferred to urge and persuade the parties to reach agreement among themselves on the organization of business rather than impose solutions of their own. Speaker Dhillon informed the author that the committee was not in the habit of voting on issues and that the Speaker reserved the right of decision if no consensus emerged. If undue obstruction of business occurred in the House he would also call meetings of party leaders in an attempt to resolve deadlocks.

Speaker Bhagat, at the conference referred to above, spoke of a phenomenon in Lok Sabha known as 'zero hour', whereby members attempt to raise all sorts of matters which are not on the order paper after the question period and before the main business of the day is entered upon. In order to curb this abuse he called a meeting of the Business Advisory Committee and said, in his own words:

> This is the forum in which the entire House is represented. . . . I will not allow any zero hour. Zero hour is outside the rules, there is no provision of zero hours in our rules of business. Therefore, any matter which has not been brought before me . . . is not allowed. Any hon. Members bringing any matters are to come to me and, if I allow it, it can be raised after the question hour, but I will not permit any business which has not received my consent. I have been very firm and have enforced it and occasionally, sometimes in a week, there are one or two matters for five minutes or seven minutes and I allow some Members. But zero hour has disappeared and one element of bringing disorder to the House has been successfully eliminated.[51]

Speaker Hegde, writing in 1978, also made reference to 'zero hour' and the need for the Speaker to take a firm stand.[52] It is of interest to note that he was Speaker during the only Parliament in which the combined opposition parties had managed to unseat the Congress Party government, but this apparently brought little change in the manner in which the House conducted itself.

The Speaker normally refrains from airing his views in public on controversial issues, although he has been known to express himself on matters of broad public concern. However, it is a firmly established convention that he never participates in the debates of the House. When he finds it necessary to raise a constituency matter he does so by means of private communication with the government. Although motions of censure against the Speaker are rare, when they have occurred they have tended to arise from the fact that his severance from his political affiliation is not usually total. Chawla and Bhalla have written:

> While, outside the House, Mr. Speaker Mavalankar was making ceaseless efforts to build up a convention that the Speaker should be above party-politics, there seems to have grown some misunderstanding about his role inside the House which climaxed into a resolution for his removal being moved and debated in the House on December 18, 1954. . . .
>
> The resolution was defeated by an overwhelming majority, but a perusal of the speeches made on the occasion shows that certain members had not taken kindly to the statement made by Mr. Speaker Mavalankar on the day of his election to the Chair in which he had said that he would not leave the Congress Party.[53]

In 1966 Speaker Hukam Singh also faced a motion for his removal in which various accusations of partisanship were alleged against him. The motion was not debated as its supporters fell short of the minimum number required for the moving of such a motion.[54]

The procedure for moving a motion against the Speaker or Deputy Speaker is provided for by Standing Orders 200 to 203. Such a motion requires the leave of the House, signified by at least fifty Members rising in their places. Speeches may not exceed fifteen minutes except with the permission of the Chair. The Constitution provides, when such a motion is moved, that the Speaker or Deputy Speaker, as the case may be, shall not occupy the Chair while the motion is under discussion.

The tradition of impartiality set by the Speaker of the House of the People has not invariably been followed by the Speakers of the State Assemblies. Some of them have remained heavily committed to their parties, and there have been instances, not only of open partisanship on the part of the Chair, but of deliberate government pressures designed to prevent the Speaker from being impartial. However, the institution of the Speakers' Conference has gone far towards developing a sense of community of interest among Indian Speakers. The Speakers' Conference was first called in 1921, and it has continued to meet under the chairmanship of the presiding officer of the central legislature at irregular intervals ever since. It was instituted primarily to encourage the uniform development of parliamentary procedure throughout India, and since independence it has retained its original purpose. It provides a valuable forum of discussion for the Speakers of the Indian Assemblies, where experiences can be exchanged and procedural problems thoroughly analysed. The experience of the House of the People, as is to be expected, is the principal source of guidance, and it is the Speaker of the House who is expected to give the lead to the Conference. His function, nevertheless, is purely an advisory one, and there is no question of his directing that a certain line of procedure should be followed.

The Conference has long been concerned with the question of the Speaker's party affiliation and as long ago as 1951 expressed the opinion that the Speaker's seat should not be contested and that he should take no active part in politics. A resolution to the same effect was adopted by the Conference in 1953, and Speaker Mavalankar took up the matter with Jawaharlal Nehru in his capacity as president of the Congress Party. The party's favourable response was reported by Mavalankar to the next meeting of the Conference in 1954, although no further action was taken. In 1967 Speaker Reddy declared to the Conference that Speakers had an obligation to resign from their parties after their election to the Chair, even without a guarantee of electoral protection. His own example was not emulated by his State colleagues, but in the following year the Conference issued a report outlining a procedure to be adopted if the independence of the speakership were to be attained.[55] In spite of what appears to be widespread support for the principle, the realities of Indian state politics are such that the requisite conditions for the emergence of an independent speakership cannot be said to exist at the state level.

In many states, because of unstable majorities and shifting party alignments, the Speakers have very difficult assemblies to control and cannot avoid being drawn into political controversies. For these reasons it is considered important that the Speaker should be a reliable party man and he is normally the choice of the majority party leadership. Sometimes the speakership is used as a consolation prize for a member who was hoping for cabinet office, and as a result it has tended to become a stepping stone to higher political preferment. In these circumstances it is difficult for a State Speaker to take an impartial stand on crucial issues or to become a genuine protector of minority interests.

Constitutional provisions relating to the Speaker and Deputy Speaker of Lok Sabha and their counterparts in the State Legislative Assemblies are identical, and the rules of the State Assemblies are modelled on those of Lok Sabha. One commentator has drawn attention to the interesting point that Indian Speakers, in contrast with the British Speaker whose political independence has long been established, have some of their rights protected even against the House itself. Article 179 of the constitution provides that fourteen days notice shall be required of any resolution for the removal from office of a Speaker or Deputy Speaker of a State Assembly, a similar provision to that contained in Article 94 in respect of the Speaker and Deputy Speaker of Lok Sabha.[56] Motions for the removal of the Speaker are not unusual in the

State Assemblies, a symptom, no doubt, of the close political alignment which exists between the Chair and the executive. The Speaker's response has usually been, either to refuse to admit the motion, or to invoke a power conferred on him by standing order which enables him to adjourn the House for a fixed or indefinite period. The use of this power has led to some complex constitutional situations. In 1967 it was invoked by the Speaker of the West Bengal Assembly in an effort to save a government which appeared to have lost its majority. In 1968 the Speaker of the Punjab Assembly adjourned the House for two months after a motion for his removal had been moved against him. In 1972 the Speaker of the Assembly of Tamil Nadu adjourned the House following the introduction of a motion of no confidence against him, and after advising the government to seek a fresh mandate from the people. Following his departure from the chamber the Deputy Speaker, who had been conducting a parallel sitting of the House in defiance of the Speaker, occupied the Chair and the resolution for the Speaker's removal from office was carried. In 1973 the Speaker of the Manipur Assembly adjourned the House *sine die* while a motion for his removal was pending. In all these cases the Speakers concerned subsequently found themselves out of office; in three cases as the result of the imposition of presidential rule in their states, and in the case of Tamil Nadu following a court ruling that the Speaker had been constitutionally removed from office. These extraordinary situations were clearly inconsistent with the proper exercise of the powers of the Chair. As one commentator has observed:

> The crucial question that might be asked in this context, therefore, is whether the Speaker has unlimited and unfettered right to adjourn the House and prevent it from functioning for whatever period he likes and on whatever grounds he may deem fit in the exercise of his discretion. The question of the Speaker's powers is not a question of politics. It is a question basically whether the Speaker is the guardian of the privileges and the rights of the House and its Spokesman or whether he has any rights independent of the House. An answer to this question undoubtedly, depends on a correct understanding of the precise role and functioning of the Speaker and his relationship with the House in a parliamentary democracy.[57]

It is not unknown in the Indian State Assemblies for the entire opposition to be suspended from the service of the House. This happened in Gujarat in February 1981 following a riotous scene which led the Speaker on the following day to name individually all those members of the opposition who had been present at the time. They left the chamber in a body, held a parallel assembly and elected their own Speaker, before returning to the House four days later following their period of suspension.

As in Lok Sabha, the Speakers of the State Assemblies chair a Business Advisory Committee which does its best to organize the programme of business by consultation and agreement. The Speaker selects the members with a view to making the committee as representative as possible. In Gujarat, for example, where the committee consists of eight government and three oposition members, the Speaker leaves it to the various opposition parties to select three members who will collectively represent them.

Most commentators on Indian parliamentary affairs express concern at the disorderly scenes which seem to have become a regular feature of some of the State Assemblies and which also erupt from time to time in Lok Sabha. The arduous job of the Speaker is rendered even more difficult in such circumstances, but India's parliamentary institutions have nevertheless survived these onslaughts. The traditions of the Indian speakership rest on firm foundations, thanks to the early influence of Patel and Mavalankar and adherence to the principles established by them on the part of their successors. The example of the speakership of Lok Sabha may be said to have exercised a salutary influence on the State speakerships in spite of the unfortunate lapses which have occurred. The Conference of Presiding Officers has provided a forum in which the Speaker of Lok Sabha has been able to give a lead and promote the goals for which he and his colleagues continue to strive.

Notes to Chapter Seven: The Speakership in India.

1. See M. C. Chawla and K. S. Bhalla, Speakers and Party Membership, Constitutional and Parliamentary Studies, 1968, pp. 41–45.
2. See Maya Dube, The Speaker in India, S. Chand, New Delhi, 1971, pp. 61–63.
3. Sardar Hukam Singh, The Speaker in India, The Parliamentarian, Vol. XLVIII, No. 1, January 1967, p. 10.
4. See Chawla and Bhalla, op. cit., pp. 49–52; and Dube, op. cit., pp. 64–67.
5. See Dube, op. cit., p. 71.
6. K. S. Hegde, The Speakership in India, The Parliamentarian, Vol. LIX, No. 1, January 1978, p. 11.
7. See Dalip Singh, Depoliticizing the Indian Speaker, Journal of Constitutional and Parliamentary Studies, January–March, 1971, p. 112.
8. See Dube, op. cit., pp. 318–319.
9. Ibid., pp. 327–331.
10. For a consideration of some of the problems involved in the exercise of this important duty, see J. N. Singh Yadav, The Speaker and the Money Bills, Journal of Parliamentary Information, Vol. 22, No. 3, July–September, 1976, pp. 382–395.
11. Standing Order 376(4).
12. Standing Order 377.
13. Standing Order 4.
14. Standing Orders 11 to 15.
15. Standing Order 25.
16. Standing Orders 16, 20 and 21.
17. Standing Orders 207(1) and (3), 208(1), 218(1) and (3), 219(2) and (4).
18. Standing Orders 62 and 63.
19. Standing Orders 194(2) and 196.
20. Standing Orders 198(3) and (5).
21. Standing Order 363.
22. Standing Order 32.

23. Standing Orders 33 and 35.
24. Standing Order 54(1).
25. Standing Order 44.
26. Standing Order 46.
27. Standing Order 67(3).
28. Standing Order 49.
29. Standing Order 56.
30. Standing Orders 184 and 187.
31. Standing Order 109.
32. Standing Orders 83 and 346.
33. Standing Order 347.
34. Standing Order 64.
35. Standing Order 89.
36. Standing Order 218(1).
37. Standing Order 218(5).
38. Standing Order 199(1).
39. Standing Order 357.
40. Standing Order 181.
41. Standing Order 362(1).
42. Standing Order 128.
43. Standing Order 380.
44. Standing Orders 386 and 387.
45. Standing Order 323.
46. Standing Order 360.
47. Hegde, op. cit., p. 10.
48. M. N. Kaul and S. L. Shakdher, Practice and Procedure of Parliament (with particular reference to Lok Sabha), Metropolitan Book Co., Delhi, 1968.
49. See The Parliamentarian, Vol. LXIII, No. 1, January 1982, p. 39.
50. See Sardar Hukam Singh, op. cit., p. 10.
51. Fourth Conference of Commonwealth Speakers and Presiding Officers, 7–10 September 1976, Houses of Parliament, London, p. 24.
52. See Hegde, op. cit., p. 12.
53. Chawla and Bhalla, op. cit., p. 47.
54. Ibid., p. 52.
55. See Des Raj Mahajan, Evolution of Speaker's Office, Journal of Constitutional and Parliamentary Studies, October–December 1968, pp. 34–35.
56. See Subhash Kashyap, The Role of the Speaker – Some Random Thoughts, Journal of Constitutional and Parliamentary Studies, October–December 1968, p. 63.
57. S. L. Shakdher, Powers and Functions of Speakers, Journal of Parliamentary Information, October 1973, p. 920. Detailed discussion of these cases is to be found in this article and in J. N. Singh Yadav, Term and Vacancy in the Speaker's Office, Journal of Constitutional and Parliamentary Studies, July–September 1980, pp. 222–251.

Chapter Eight

The Speakership in the African Parliaments of the Commonwealth

We now come to a region of the Commonwealth where it is necessary to consider the office of Speaker in a very different parliamentary context. Although the British parliamentary system has been exported to various parts of the world, it has undergone significant adaptations and modifications, and this is nowhere more evident than in the countries of Africa. As an African author has pointed out, authority in a new nation is normally personified in the leader who is likely to be a dominant personality. If Parliament is to remain an effective institution of government, the leader must ensure that its power does not become totally subordinated to his own, that it does not degenerate into an assembly for his own glorification. Similarly, in a country where only one party can legally operate, Parliament, if its independence is not protected, is in danger of becoming a rubber stamp with the sole function of endorsing party decisions.[1]

Several of the African states of the Commonwealth are one-party states, either *de facto* or *de jure*. Zambia, Malawi, Tanzania and Sierra Leone have constitutions establishing them as one-party states. Kenya, which had long been a one-party state in practice, became one officially in June, 1982. Lesotho and Swaziland have Parliaments which are not directly elected. The former has an entirely nominated Parliament, to which opposition as well as government members are appointed, the opposition even being represented in the cabinet. This system was introduced in 1973 following a popular election, held in 1970, the result of which was declared to be null and void. In Swaziland in 1973 all political parties were dissolved and prohibited on the ground that they engendered hostility among the people and were incompatible with the national way of life. The Parliament of Swaziland Order of 1978 provided for a bicameral Parliament partially elected by an electoral college and partially nominated by the King. Zimbabwe, Uganda, Botswana, The Gambia, Nigeria and Mauritius, at the time of writing, all have popularly elected Parliaments in which two or more parties are represented, but there are many differences between them in other respects. Zimbabwe has a constitution in which twenty seats in the 100-member House of Assembly are for the time being reserved for white members, but the party in power has been openly advocating the establishment of a one-party state. Uganda has only recently emerged from the yoke of a brutal dictatorship and it remains to be seen how their new parliamentary system will evolve. Botswana has been a stable democracy since it became independent in 1966, an unusual feature of its constitution (which it shares with Kenya) being that the President of the Republic is himself a member of the National Assembly. When participating in the debates of the House he is thus subject to the authority of the Chair and could presumably be called to order, if the occasion arose, like any other member. The Gambia, which recently entered into a confederation with neighbouring Senegal, following an attempted *coup d'état*, has retained its membership of the Commonwealth and its own Parliament which includes, at the time of writing, a three-man opposition. Nigeria, following many years of military rule, adopted a federal constitution and a system of government based on the separation of powers, similar in principle to that of the United States. Ghana, where parliamentary government was restored for a brief period, also adopted a separation of powers system prior to reverting once again to military rule in December 1981. The election which took place in Mauritius in 1982 swept the former government out of power with the loss of all its seats but in 1983 the former Prime Minister returned to power at the head of a new coalition.

The degree of parliamentary freedom which exists in these countries varies in relation to the political circumstances, and the influence of the Chair is a crucial factor in its determination. Humphrey Slade, a former Speaker of the National Assembly of Kenya, once made the following comments in respect of that country's National Assembly (Powers and Privileges) Act, which provides that no legal action shall be taken against any member in respect of anything he may say in the House or its committees:

> I could wish that this provision had been written into the Constitution of Kenya, but, however that may be, I warn hon. Members that the day upon which, by your own Act, you remove that protection and expose yourselves to prosecution for what you say in this House, that will be the day when, by suicide, our National Assembly ceases to be the supreme instrument of the State of Kenya.[2]

This statement contrasts significantly with the comments of Mr. Narendra Patel, Speaker of the National Assembly of Uganda prior to the Idi Amin take-over, delivered at a conference of Commonwealth Speakers and Presiding Officers in India in 1970. Speaker Patel virtually acknowledged that Parliament and the Chair were powerless in the face of executive action. He stated that a number of members of Parliament were at the time in detention, and that some members were searched when they entered the Parliament building. Although he disapproved he did not intervene as he felt he was not sufficiently well-informed on the security situation. In the course of his speech he made the following telling remarks:

> Talking about privileges, it is very well to talk about privileges. But, where the security of the State is concerned, what we have to decide is what is paramount—whether the parliamentary privileges are paramount or whether it is the security of the State which is paramount, because, if the security of the State is endangered, the whole par-

liamentary institution is endangered and if we do not have Parliament, there would not be any parliamentary privileges. We shall have to consider these matters seriously whether we should try to preserve parliamentary privileges at the cost of the security of the State.[3]

There is a sad irony in recalling these remarks in view of what happened in Uganda shortly afterwards. Speaker Patel was a member of the Asian community who were among the first to suffer oppression under the regime of Idi Amin.

In any country where the law permits of preventive detention without trial the value of parliamentary privilege is bound to be regarded as doubtful. The author referred to above, in his book *Parliamentary Practice in Kenya*, has commented in relation to this problem:

> When therefore there is the invidious necessity for the law to allow preventive detention without trial, the situation becomes more dangerous; because it is hardly possible to provide statutory protection against such detention in respect of parliamentary utterances, on account of the inevitable right of Government to refuse to publish reasons for the detention of any person.[4]

He also refers to a case which arose in 1967 concerning a Kenya representative in the Central Legislative Assembly of the former East Africa Common Services Commission. This member was detained in circumstances which gave rise to suspicion that his detention was due to comments he had made in that assembly.

> The problem was resolved not by legislation, but by the release of the representative concerned, and by Government giving a firm undertaking to the House that no member would be subjected to detention for anything said there; while the House on the other hand, accepted that, in the event of any member being detained, other members would have to be content with an assurance that such detention was not on account of anything said in the House, and could make no further inquiry as to the cause. This incidentally provides a good example of immunity being established by way of insistence and recognition, as opposed to legislation; as well as showing how jealous and vigilant members must be for the preservation of their privileges and immunities.[5]

In another case which arose in Kenya some years later the Deputy Speaker himself was detained under the preventive detention legislation. This occurred during a period of crisis in 1975 when the government was taking strong action against dissidents. The Deputy Speaker had ruled in favour of a member who had made a critical observation concerning the government party. When another member called upon the Chair to order that the remark should be either withdrawn or substantiated, the Deputy Speaker ruled that it was not necessary to substantiate a matter which was obvious. The same

Deputy Speaker served on a select committee appointed to investigate the assassination of a member who was a well-known critic of the government. The authorities failed to co-operate in the investigation and the committee reported that it was unable to produce any findings because it could not obtain the necessary evidence. The only reason given for the Deputy Speaker's detention was that it was in the interests of national security, but it was suspected by many that his ruling and his participation in the select committee had a bearing on his arrest. President Daniel arap Moi has since given assurances that the government would not use its powers of preventive detention in order to curb freedom of speech in Parliament.

It is not intended, in referring to the above cases, to suggest that the Kenya National Assembly is the only jurisdiction in which the Chair is faced with inhibiting factors. In most African Parliaments, as indeed in many Parliaments elsewhere, the Speaker is heavily dependent on government preferment. In most one-party states he is chosen by the party before being elected by the House. In Malawi he is directly appointed by the President and is removable by the President. In such circumstances the Chair is unlikely to enjoy complete freedom of action. It is not unknown in some jurisdictions for the police to demand the files of members of Parliament and in such cases it appears that the Speaker often does not have the authority to intervene, or if he has authority he might be hesitant to use it. In Zambia in 1970 the Speaker of the National Assembly halted police officers who were attempting to serve restriction orders on opposition members of the National Assembly, although he declined to entertain the matter as a question of privilege subsequently. In the course of a ruling he made the following observation:

> I warn Hon. Members that the more they talk about their privileges the more weakened and exposed their dignity becomes in the public eye. Thus the less said the better about privileges which are merely conventional.[6]

Speakers, like everybody else involved in public affairs, have to be realists. During crisis conditions, such as those which arose in Kenya in 1975, the Chair has to be very careful not to aggravate a dangerous situation and its actions are likely to be influenced by wider considerations which go beyond the rules and practice of the House.

Opening a seminar for Clerks and parliamentary officials of the Eastern, Central and Southern African Region of the Commonwealth in Lusaka on 18 May 1982, the Prime Minister of Zambia, Mr. Nalumino Mundia, referred to the importance of evolutionary change in parliamentary procedure. He emphasized that not all Westminster practices were suitable for adoption in African Parliaments and suggested that the Clerks-at-the-Table had a responsibility 'to see which colonial parliamentary procedures inherited from Westminster can be discarded and replaced by new innovations which would be appropriate to our conditions and benefit your people. This means that you should start deliberate moves to change some archaic parliamentary procedures which you find to be obstacles on accelerating your people's political, economic and cultural changes.' Mr. Mundia was echoing a view which has frequently been expressed at parliamentary conferences.

The fact remains that the customs and procedures of most Commonwealth African Parliaments, superficially at least, continue to be modelled to a great extent on the practices of Westminster. Nearly all the Speakers are traditionally robed in wig and gown, one exception being the Speaker of the National Assembly of Tanzania who wears the robes of a chief. The standing orders of the various assemblies owe a great deal to Westminster practices. Standing Order 1 of the Legislative Assembly of Mauritius provides that in cases of doubt the House shall have recourse to the relevant practice of the British House of Commons. Some of the other assemblies also make provision for unprovided cases without tying themselves so closely to Westminster. Standing Order 1 of the Kenya National Assembly empowers the Speaker to decide all matters not expressly provided for. Standing Order 5 of the Malawi Parliament makes similar provision. Standing Order 162 of the National Assembly of Zambia provides that the Speaker shall decide, 'taking into account the customs and usages of the Assembly since its inception and the relevant practice in Commonwealth Parliaments.'

The powers of the Speaker within the various jurisdictions are very similar and reflect those of the British Speaker. Their disciplinary powers enable them to call a member to order for using unparliamentary language, to check irrelevance and tedious repetition, to order a member to withdraw for the remainder of the day's sitting, to 'name' a member, and to suspend or adjourn a sitting in case of grave disorder. An interesting refinement in the standing orders of the National Assembly of Kenya provides that a member may invite the Speaker to name a member, The Speakers have similar powers to those of their British counterpart in relation to the control of the question period,* the acceptance of a motion for an emergency debate, and the discretion to accord precedence to a matter of privilege. Most of the assemblies have a closure rule similar to the British, empowering the Speaker to decline to accept closure if he deems it to be an abuse of the rules of the House or an infringement of the rights of the minority. In a number of jurisdictions, including Kenya, Zambia, Zimbabwe and Mauritius, the Speaker may refuse to entertain a dilatory motion.

In Mauritius, Lesotho and Zimbabwe the Speaker is empowered to decide that a division has been unnecessarily claimed. In Tanzania and Malawi a motion to suspend the standing orders in whole or in part requires the leave of the Speaker. In Lesotho the Speaker's consent is required if the motion is made without notice. In Zimbabwe the Speaker may in his discretion suspend business or vary the time laid down for the interruption or suspension of business. In most jurisdictions the leave of the Speaker is required by a member wishing to make a personal explanation and the power to order the removal of strangers is vested in the Speaker in most of the assemblies under consideration. It also seems to be a general practice in African Parliaments that

---

* Except in the House of Representatives of Nigeria where there is no question period.

a Speaker's ruling may not be challenged except by way of a substantive motion. Most African Speakers are equipped with a casting vote in the event of the numbers in a division being equal, but not a deliberative vote. This provision is often incorporated in the constitution itself. Exceptions to the general practice include Zimbabwe and The Gambia, where the Speaker has neither a casting nor a deliberative vote, and Mauritius where the Speaker has both. The conventions which govern the use of the casting vote in Great Britain do not necessarily apply in the Parliaments of Africa. In many cases the Speaker would be expected to use his casting vote in support of the government.

In most of the Parliaments under consideration there is one major departure from Westminster practice to be noted, namely that the Speaker does not have to be a member of the assembly. Provision for the Speaker is to be found in the constitutions of all the countries concerned. In Kenya, Tanzania, Uganda, Botswana, Malawi, Lesotho, Swaziland and Sierra Leone it is provided that the Speaker may be either a member or a non-member. In those Parliaments where the option exists the Speaker is usually a non-member, that of Malawi being an exception. Except in the case of Lesotho, where no qualifications are specified, a non-member must be qualified to be a member in order to be eligible. In one-party states this usually means that a candidate for the speakership must be a party member, although in Sierra Leone, where a tradition has developed of appointing ex-judges to the office, this is not a requirement. The constitutions of Tanzania, Uganda, Malawi and Botswana provide that if a member is chosen as Speaker he shall cease to be Speaker if he ceases to be a member otherwise than by a dissolution of Parliament. The Kenya constitution provides that if a non-member is chosen as Speaker he becomes a member *ex officio*. In Zambia, Zimbabwe and The Gambia the Speaker may not be a member of the assembly and if elected from among the membership he is required to vacate his seat. The Zambia constitution specifies that the Speaker must have the qualifications of a member which effectively means that he must be a member of the party. In Zimbabwe eligible candidates are restricted to those who are or have been members of the House of Assembly or the Senate. In Nigeria and Mauritius the Speaker is elected from among the members themselves, although in the case of Mauritius special provision was made for the Speaker who held office at the time of the achievement of independence. In the constitutions of most of these countries it is specified that ministers, deputy ministers, and, in some cases, parliamentary secretaries may not hold office as Speaker. In Sierra Leone members of the armed forces are also excluded, and it is provided that if a public officer or judge is elected Speaker he must retire from his previous office.

In Kenya, Tanzania, Lesotho and Mauritius the election of the Speaker, if contested, is conducted by secret ballot. In Kenya a two-thirds majority is required for the election of the Speaker and in Mauritius a clear majority over all other candidates. In Lesotho the number of candidates is limited to three. In Sierra Leone a two-thirds majority is required to elect the Speaker, unless three resolutions fail to produce such a majority in which case a simple majority suffices. In most other jurisdictions a simple majority is required for the election of the Speaker, except in Malawi where he is appointed by the President. In all the countries being considered, except Kenya and Malawi, the Speaker may be removed by a two-thirds majority vote of the assembly. In Kenya a majority of 75% is required and in Malawi he is removable by the President. In 1971 a Malawi Speaker was removed by presidential intervention. In his book 'Parliamentary Practice in Kenya', H. B. Ndoria Gicheru points out that a motion of no confidence in the Chair should not be confused with a motion of dissent in respect of a ruling. Although decisions of the Chair may not be challenged during debate, 'That does not, nevertheless, prevent a member who thinks the decision wrong from discussing the matter on a substantive motion after due notice, and such a proceeding need accuse the Chair of nothing more than human fallibility.'[7] This distinction is probably made in most of the jurisdictions under consideration, and if a motion dissenting from a ruling were to be adopted the Speaker would probably not feel under an obligation to resign in consequence. No motion of dissent from a Speaker's ruling has been moved in the Kenya National Assembly since 1963. In the Zambia National Assembly no such motion has ever been moved.

Kenya's first Speaker was appointed in 1948 when the country was still a colony and its Legislative Council, although the unofficial members formed the majority, included only four African members. A former judge, Sir W. K. Horne, held the office from 1948 to 1955 and was succeeded by Sir Ferdinand Cavendish-Bentinck who served until 1960. Mr. Humphrey Slade, the first elected member to become Speaker, followed Cavendish-Bentinck and he remained in office until 1969, bridging the transitional period during which Kenya attained full independence in 1963. Although he had been an opponent of majority rule prior to independence, it was President Kenyatta himself who insisted that he remain Speaker after independence was achieved. The writer of his obituary published in The Times on 18 August 1983 observed that as Speaker 'he did a great deal to integrate the political viewpoints of black and white and, in his later association with Kenyatta, to influence the comparatively smooth transition of the country from Crown colony to independent republic.' In a personal tribute to him, H. B. Ndoria Gicheru referred to his efforts on behalf of the arrested parliamentarians alluded to above and commented: 'Through his tolerant, liberal and philosophic temperament and approach, Mr. Slade gave the office of the Speaker a lustre and majesty which will be long remembered.' In 1969 he was succeeded by Speaker Mati, the first African Speaker, who has remained in office ever since. Both Speaker Slade and Speaker Mati can be credited with having done their best to promote the stability of Kenya's parliamentary system during the post-independence period. Both faced testing challenges in balancing the rights of individual members with the political realities which have threatened that stability and the descipline imposed by the Chair has sometimes tended to be strict. For example, the misuse of points of order is treated as disorderly[8] and in May 1968 Speaker Slade, having warned a member several times, ordered him out of the chamber for abusing the right to raise points of order. More recently, in May 1981, Speaker Mati took similar action against a member who constantly interrupted a minister who was answering a question by raising spurious points of order. It is also a rule in Kenya that public discussion by members outside the House of matters before the House is not allowed and the Chair is expected to enforce this rule strictly.

Speaker Mati has placed on record some of his concerns in respect of the Speaker's role as the protector of the rights of members. He has underlined the different approach which the Speaker must take according to whether he presides over a multi-party or a one-party Parliament. In the former case the Speaker must protect the rights of minorities whose policies may vary drastically from those of the governing party. In the latter case 'the Speaker is mainly protecting the rights of Members as individuals or as representatives of given areas or as holders of certain views which may not amount to a different policy from the policy of the governing party'.[9] Kenya being a one-party state, Speaker Mati indicated that he saw no reason to refrain from attending meetings of the party Parliamentary Group, although he is excluded from holding any office within the party. 'I listen to what is said there but I do not speak at such meetings. I do not take part at all. But I sit there as an observer and I think in a way it helps me to know exactly what the ruling party, the party that forms the Government, is thinking. . . . I am still a member of the party and, of course, I observe the policies of the party. But where there is another party it would be undesirable for the Speaker to involve himself in matters like parliamentary group meetings.'[10]

Speaker Mati emphasized that the Speaker must be the genuine spokesman of the Parliament as a whole and, like his predecessor, spoke of the importance of the National Assembly Powers and Privileges Act. Under the Act the Speaker is the chairman of the Committee of Privileges, and Speaker Mati expressed some reservations as to whether this is a proper role for the Speaker. If the committee were to bring in a report critical of a member's behaviour, or perhaps recommending punitive action against a member, the Speaker's duty as chairman of the committee might be seen to be in conflict with his duty to be impartial.[11] At a subsequent conference Speaker Mati indicated his methods of controlling the question period in such a way as to protect the rights, not only of members, but also of their constituents.

> The situation arises where a member asks a question about his constituent whom he believes has been mistreated. The question is how is this kind of question likely to affect the person concerned? In our case I always insist that I should have at least some idea whether any other method has been used before the matter is brought to the House, and whether the person concerned has been consulted or has approached the member himself. I say this because I believe it would be dangerous to accept questions of this nature without some scrutiny. Sometimes questions are asked which end up being very damaging to the person for whom help is intended.[12]

He also described his method of handling questions asked by members about other members' constituencies. Even though such a question might be in order, Speaker Mati insists that some consultation should take place between the members concerned in order to avoid unnecessary rancour.[13]

Zambia is a country with a well-established parliamentary system and its National Assembly, although a one-party Parliament, is one in which the Speaker asserts a considerable measure of independence in his sphere of responsibility. It is often the case that the personality of the incumbent has a significant influence on the evolution of an office, and this would appear to be so in respect of the speakership in Zambia. Zambia's constitutional development has to some extent paralleled that of Kenya, particularly where the evolution of the speakership is concerned. As in Kenya, the first Speaker was appointed in 1948 to preside over the Legislative Council of what was then the protectorate of Northern Rhodesia. He was a farmer, Mr. T. S. Page, and he was succeeded by another appointed Speaker, Mr. Thomas Williams, prior to Zambia's attainment of independence in 1964. In December of that year Mr. W. P. Nyirenda became the first Speaker to be elected by the National Assembly, and also the first African Speaker, of the newly independent country. He was subsequently appointed to the cabinet and was succeeded in 1969 by Speaker Nabulyato who has remained in office ever since. He is the senior speaker in the Commonwealth in terms of unbroken length of service, Speaker Mati of Kenya, who was also elected Speaker in 1969, being a close runner-up. In addition Speaker Nabulyato is the only Speaker to have attended all the conferences of Commonwealth Speakers and Presiding Officers since their inception in 1969. The independence of the speakership in Zambia owes much to his assertiveness in promoting it, and to the prestige he enjoys as one of Zambia's most respected parliamentarians.

Zambia being a one-party state, the Speaker is likely to have a background of service to the party but he ceases to be a political activist on becoming Speaker. Once elected by the members of the National Assembly, he submits himself for the formal approval of the President, although it is unlikely that the President would reject the choice of the members. He attends party meetings and conferences, although he does not normally participate in the discussions, but he never attends parliamentary party caucus meetings. He detaches himself from the regional factions and other interests within the party and maintains an attitude of neutrality when conflicts arise between the front and back benches. In the words of Speaker Nabulyato himself, the impartiality of a Speaker in a one-party system 'is judged by the extent to which he avoids being identified with the Executive or any particular interest group within or outside the House. It is only an impartial Speaker who can successfully keep at bay the conflicts of responsibility to the House, the party, and other loyalties.'[14]

There is no lack of evidence of the application of this principle. For example, the Speaker maintained a neutral stance on a recent occasion when a member accused the government of building torture chambers. The Prime Minister and others raised points of order by way of protest, and the Speaker ruled consistently that it was up to the government to refute such allegations. When the points of order continued he declared that the Chair was not to be intimidated. Several days later he upheld certain rulings given by committee chairmen and stated that the rulings of the Chair, whether in the House or in committee, may not be questioned. On another occasion, when a member alleged by way of a point of order that a ministerial statement contained false information, the Speaker requested the minister to make another statement. As an example of a most unusual use of a point of order, reference may be made to an occasion when a member drew attention by way of a point of order to the fact that a sick member was present in the House. The Speaker responded by ordering the Minister of Health to escort the said member to hospital!

In Zambia the Speaker not infrequently interprets his powers in such a way as to rule on matters which might not be seen as falling within the jurisdiction of the Chair in other Parliaments. When first elected to the Chair, before Zambia became a one-party state, Speaker Nabulyato declined to recognize the leader of the 23-member opposition party as Leader of the Opposition on the ground that 27 members were required in order to constitute a quorum of the House. The Speaker argued that if the government resigned or were defeated on a motion of censure the opposition could form neither a quorum nor a government.[15] Subsequently two members of the opposition party crossed the floor and joined the governing party. When this occurred the opposition party leader, Mr. Harry Nkumbula, claimed that the seats of the two members were automatically vacated under a constitutional amendment of 1966 which required by-elections to take place in cases where a member resigned from the party on whose ticket he was elected. The Speaker declined to act on the formal notice given by Mr. Nkumbula on the ground that the latter had not been recognized as the leader of a political party. Mr. Nkumbula took his case to court and received a favourable verdict, which led the Speaker to make a lengthy statement to the House pointing to what he saw as a constitutional anomaly giving the Chief Justice and the Speaker conflicting powers and subjecting Parliament to the jurisdiction of the courts.[16]

Having had experience of presiding over both a multi-party and a one-party Parliament, Speaker Nabulyato has placed the following observations on the record:

> My job is much easier now than it used to be under a multi-party Parliament. If any problem arises the Chief Whip of the party will take care of it, and I will just remain doing my administrative job. When something becomes a parliamentary issue, I am more respected than I used to be. In the past Members of the Opposition parties used to suspect that because I came from the ruling party I was not impartial. They thought that I was doing them in from time to time. Members of the Government also used to think that I was giving the Opposition parties too easy a time. I was almost like a football being tossed here and there. In the multi-party Parliament I was once or twice threatened with being taken to court as Speaker for what I had ruled in the House.[17]

In Zambia the Speaker has important duties relating to committees, and is himself chairman of a number.[18] He is chairman of the Standing Orders Committee, a very important committee having wide-ranging functions. It determines the size and nominates the members of select committees, considers the amendment of the standing orders, judges matters of privilege, examines petitions, makes recommendations concerning salaries and benefits of members and staff, and considers any other matter the Speaker may refer to it. He is chairman of the Library Committee and of the House Comitee which considers all matters connected with the comfort and convenience of members. He chairs a committee called the Committee on Parliamentary Procedure, Customs and Traditions whose function is to 'assist Mr. Speaker with matters pertaining to the variations to parliamentary procedure, customs and traditions and to consider any matters connected therewith'. He appoints the chairman and members of the Committee on Delegated Legislation, the Committee on Parastatal Bodies and the Committee on Government Assurances. The first-named committee reports to the House through the Speaker and scrutinizes delegated legislation in accordance with criteria specified by standing order. In appointing its chairman the Speaker is required to give preference to members having legal background and experience. The Committee on Parastatal Bodies considers the reports, accounts and administrative efficiency of public corporations and exercises such other functions as the Speaker may allot to it. The Committee on Government Assurances fulfils comparable functions to those of a similarly-named committee of Lok Sabha of India. It scrutinizes and reports on the implementation of government undertakings and examines the annual reports of government ministries. It also exercises such other functions as the Speaker may allot to it. The Speaker appoints all the members, other than the Chairman, of the Committee on Absence of Members from Sittings of the House and Sessional Committees, which considers applications for leave of absence and recommends disciplinary action in cases of absence without permission. The chairman of the committee is the Chief Whip. The Speaker is required to convene a meeting of any select committee nominated by the Standing Orders Committee within three days. He determines the rates and conditions governing the payment of expenses to witnesses. He is empowered to appoint a sub-committee of any sessional committee to investigate a specific matter. A sessional committee requires the authority of the Speaker in order to meet beyond the precincts of Parliament. This compares with a power vested in the Speaker of Zimbabwe whereby no committee, even though empowered to travel beyond the precincts of Parliament, may do so without the approval of the Speaker.[19]

The Speaker of the Parliament of Malawi, which, like Zambia, is a one-party state, is more of a political conformist that his counterpart in Zambia. Appointed by the President, he comes to the Chair as a strong party supporter who is very active within the party. Most questions that come before the House have already been approved by the party and the government and, according to Speaker Khonje of Malawi, members are as anxious as the executive to support such measures. 'The Speaker must, therefore, espouse party policy and, therefore, government policy, or else he is not elected.'[20] While Speaker Khonje has acknowledged the right of members to criticise the executive, and the duty of the Chair to protect that right, the issue of impartiality in its strictest sense does not apply as the Speaker must share with all other members the built-in bias towards the one party and the one set of policies which underlie the system of government. It appears that the Speaker in Malawi has a duty to expedite the business of Parliament as best he can. In the words of Speaker Khonje:

> It is the responsibility of the Speaker to liaise with the Leader of the House and the Chief Whip to make sure that Government business is transacted on time and quickly. It is, therefore, the responsibility of the Speaker to make sure that the minimum of time is wasted in the conduct of transactions in the chamber.[21]

Although the constitution provides that the Speaker may be a member or a non-member, the practice in Malawi has been that the Speaker represents a constituency and must fight for his seat like other members. Speaker Khonje has expressed the view that this is logical in view of the Speaker's strong party obligations.[22]

Zimbabwe is the most recent of the Commonwealth African countries to have attained independence; or more precisely to have emerged as a sovereign state recognized by the international community on the basis of a legal constitution. Zimbabwe became an independent Commonwealth country in 1980 following a long period of crisis and civil war. Its road to nationhood was a difficult one because of historical circumstances which had conferred on the colony of Southern Rhodesia, as Zimbabwe was previously known, an advanced constitutional status which had effectively placed the government of the colony under the control of the white minority. In 1923 Southern Rhodesia became a self-governing colony with a Legislative Assembly of thirty members and an electoral system which ensured white political domination. This constitution remained unchanged until 1961 when the Legislative Assembly was enlarged and the electoral system expanded to provide for African representation. Prior to the election of 1962 no black member had ever sat in the Legislative Assembly, and although the constitution of 1961 placed fifteen out of 65 seats in the control of African voters it continued to ensure that the control of government would be in white hands.

Between 1953 and 1963 Southern Rhodesia had been associated with Northern Rhodesia (now Zambia) and Nyasaland (now Malawi) in a federation, the government of which was also white controlled. With the collapse of the federation, resulting from black nationalist pressure, Zambia and Malawi became independent. Southern Rhodesia's white government also demanded independence from the British government, and when this was not forthcoming declared independence unilaterally and illegally on 11 November 1965. The struggle which took place over the ensuing fifteen years belongs to the broader course of Zimbabwean history, but its resolution resulted in the present constitution which came into force on 18 April 1980 and provides, *inter alia*, for a bicameral parliament consisting of a Senate and House of Assembly, the white community electing one-fifth of the members of the latter House on a separate electoral roll.

The 1923 and 1961 constitutions of Southern Rhodesia provided that the Speaker could be a member or a non-member of the assembly. He was usually elected from among the membership in the first instance but if re-elected Speaker in the succeeding Parliament it was usually as a non-member. The republican constitution introduced by the Smith government in 1969 provided that the Speaker could not be a member of the assembly and if elected from among the membership would be obliged to vacate his seat. A similar provision was included in the 1980 constitution of Zimbabwe. Mr. A. R. W. Stumbles, Speaker at the time of the unilateral declaration of independence, elected to resign his seat immediately after being elected to the Chair in 1964. His speakership is of particular interest as it was he who was called upon to rule as to whether or not the Legislative Assembly was legally constituted following the declaration. The Governor of Southern Rhodesia had immediately dismissed from office the Prime Minister, Ian Smith, and his government, and the British government had issued an order-in-council prohibiting the assembly from transacting business. When the assembly met it was contended by an opposition member that the assertion of independence had no legal validity and was, in fact, an act of rebellion. Stumbles ruled that any member who felt that the provisions of the British order-in-council were binding upon him should dissociate himself completely from the transaction of the assembly's business and he refused to entertain any further points of order on the matter.[23] He thus associated himself with the act of rebellion and subsequently ruled out of order the use of the term 'illegal regime'. Previous Rhodesian Speakers had succeeded in maintaining the tradition of the impartiality of the Chair. They had respected the conventions of the speakership and done their best to follow the practices of Westminster, although they had tended to be too restrictive in their interpretation of the rules of debate and their conception of what constituted unparliamentary language. Stumbles was the first Rhodesian Speaker who had been called upon to make such a dramatic decision and, as no doubt most of us would have done in like circumstances, he opted to keep his job.

As in most other African countries, the speakership in the new state of Zimbabwe is closely associated with the governing party, the present Speaker, Mr. Didymus Mutasa, being its secretary-general. He is therefore very senior in the party hierarchy and has openly advocated the establishment of a one-party state in his country. He is nevertheless dedicated to the parliamentary system, strictly impartial as a presiding officer, and magnanimous towards his former political enemies. At a recent parliamentary seminar held in Zimbabwe he made a point of acknowledging the parliamentary expertise of three former Prime Ministers who were present, one of whom was Ian Smith.

Among the Commonwealth's longest-serving Speakers is Chief Adam Sapi Mkwawa, Speaker of the National Assembly of Tanzania, who, except for a break in 1974–75 has held office since 1962. He is very senior in his party's hierarchy, being a trustee of the party and the chairman of the Electoral Commission. He attends the meetings of the National Executive Committee of the party which selects the candidates for each constituency.

In the House the Speaker plays a crucial role in the process of procedural reform and is chairman of the Standing Orders Committee which reviews the standing orders and makes recommendations for change whenever necessary. The proposals considered are frequently initiated by the Speaker himself, and a scheme of reform designed to increase the powers of committees was under consideration in 1982. Recommendations made by the Standing Orders Committee are considered in a committee of the Whole House which is chaired by the Leader of the House, the Speaker being free to participate in the debate. Any changes approved must be adopted by the House itself.

The Speaker appoints all committee members and is chairman of the steering committee which consists of the chairmen of all other committees. The organization of business in the House is determined by the Leader of the House in consultation with the Speaker, and any change in the order of business would require the Speaker's approval, unless authorized by a resolution of the House. The Speaker may terminate a debate if he decides it is becoming too repetitious. He can refuse a motion to extend a debate, although he seldom does so. Neither does he often refuse a request for an emergency debate.

The Speaker has some unusual powers relating to questions, not all of which are set out in the standing orders. Standing Orders 28, 29 and 30 of the Tanzania National Assembly elaborate in some detail the conditions relating to the questioning of ministers and other members, many of the Speaker's powers being specified. However, it appears that he is also empowered in certain circumstances to order that a question be answered. It is customary to require that the answer to a question be prepared within four days, and the Speaker can order that the answer be read out in the House.

In Uganda, where parliamentary government has only recently been restored, the National Assembly and the Chair face a great challenge in protecting the strength and integrity of the country's representative institutions. The threat posed to Parliament by an overbearing executive should never be far from their thoughts in the light of their own country's recent history and the experience in certain other countries both inside and outside the Commonwealth. The present Speaker, Mr. Francis Butagira, does not see his office as resembling that of a judge. He regards it as a political office with its roots in popular support and feels that the Speaker should retain his political associations. While conceding that the Speaker should avoid controversial debates and attacks on other political parties, he believes the Speaker should be free to participate in party conventions and address party meetings. He does not see these activities as being inconsistent with the need to maintain impartiality while in the Chair.[24]

In Mauritius the Speaker is a party member who has to fight for his seat under the complicating factor of an electoral system whereby each constituency returns three members. Thus, even if there were a disposition among the parties to allow the Speaker an uncontested election it would be difficult to do so in these circumstances. This problem was not faced by Sir Harilal Vaghjee, the Speaker at the time Mauritius became independent, because of an unusual constitutional provision which confirmed him in the position for as long as he chose to remain in office, subject always to the right of the House to remove him by a two-thirds majority vote. Speaker Vaghjee was already Speaker of the Legislative Assembly prior to the attainment of independence in 1968 and was so highly regarded that special arrangements were made to continue him in office. Section 10 of the constitution provided that the Speaker in office at the time of its coming into force would be deemed to be a member of the assembly and to have been elected Speaker. In all he remained Speaker for 19 years and died in office in 1979. He was a member of the majority party but never attended party meetings and conducted himself for all practical purposes as a politically independent Speaker. This practice was followed by his successor, Speaker Jeewoolall, who underlined the problems posed by the electoral system when addressing a conference held in Ottawa in 1981.[25] Following the rout of the government in 1982, a young lawyer, Alan Ganoo, was elected Speaker at the age of 26. He was defeated in 1983 and succeeded by another 26 year-old lawyer, Mr. Ajay Daby, who had previously been Deputy Speaker. In Mauritius the Speaker has important committee duties, being chairman of the Committee of Privileges, the Standing Orders Committee and the Selection Committee. The members of the last-named committee are appointed by the Speaker from all the parties represented in the House and it has the function of appointing the members of the select committees.

Botswana is one of Africa's few multi-party democracies and the Speaker is a member of no party. Although the constitution provides that the Speaker may be elected from inside or outside the National Assembly, the three men who have so far occupied the Chair have all been non-members and they have all been white. The Speaker once elected becomes a member *ex officio*. The first two Speakers were missionaries who came to the Chair without any previous parliamentary experience, a reflection perhaps of the high regard felt by the people of Botswana for the contribution made by missionary activity to the welfare and development of their country. The first, Dr. Alfred Merriweather, was appointed to preside over the Legislative Council prior to the attainment of independence. He was re-elected Speaker of the Legislative Assembly which was constituted after the pre-independence elections in 1965, and remained Speaker of the National Assembly when the country became independent on 30 September 1966. He was succeeded in 1968 by the Rev. Albert Lock who retired in 1979. The Speaker at the time of writing is Mr. J. G. Haskins.

One of the responsibilities of the Speaker in Botswana is to determine who should draw the special allowance payable to the Leader of the Opposition and this has sometimes created difficulties for the Chair. Speaker Lock referred to this problem at a conference held in Australia in 1978.

> It is a very invidious position to be in, because when there is such a balance amongst the Opposition parties and they will not coalesce in any way to allow one to choose the Member who represents the majority of those Opposition seats one is not able to declare who is the Leader of the Opposition. This has been unfortunate in that it has hindered the development of across-the-floor business arrangements.[26]

In the course of the same speech Speaker Lock declared: 'We are a total democracy — as totally a democracy as the Mother of Parliaments', and this has enabled the Speaker to adopt a completely neutral position. The oppostion parties were consulted at the time of Lock's appointment. Even so, he was several times the object of a motion of censure by some members of the opposition, with such frequency at one period that the House, without consulting him, changed the standing orders to require a minimum number of members to support such a motion in order for it to be moved. At the same time he was criticised, on one occasion by the Leader of the House, for being over-indulgent with the very members who were seeking his downfall! It would thus seem reasonable to conclude that, whatever mistakes he may have made, they did not arise from lack of impartiality.

The Speaker of the National Assembly of Lesotho is also independent of party, although he presides over a very different kind of assembly as it is not directly elected. This was not always the case. In the early years of Lesotho's independence the assembly was directly elected and the opposition was strongly represented. The country did not adapt easily to the parliamentary system, however, and the difficulties were such that Lesotho's first Speaker, Mr. W. P. Stanford, spoke at a conference held in Canada in 1969 of the difficulties posed by the obstructive tactics of oppositions in newer Parliaments and the problem of balancing the rights of minorities with the requirements of government business.[27] Although opposition parties are represented in the present nominated Parliament it appears that the problems which preoccupied Speaker Stanford have largely disappeared. Speaker Stanford was a white man who was originally appointed by the colonial government to preside over the legislature prior to the attainment of independence. He was elected Speaker by the National Assembly when the country became independent and remained in office until parliamentary government was suspended in 1970. Lesotho's first African Speaker, Mr. J. T. Kolane, was elected by the National Assembly set up under the constitution of 1973. A former Clerk-at-the-Table who had served in the colonial Legislative Council and as Clerk of the Senate subsequent to independence, Speaker Kolane is not a politician and has brought to the Chair an experience somewhat different from that which usually forms the background of a Speaker.

The appointment of a former Clerk as Speaker is not a unique precedent in the Commonwealth although such occurrences have been few. Speaker Kolane keeps in close touch with the British House of Commons and, no doubt because of his background as a Clerk, consults regularly with the experts at Westminster on questions of parliamentary practice and procedure. Unlike the Speaker in Botswana, the Speaker in Lesotho does not become a member of the assembly if he is elected from outside the House.[28]

Turning now to West Africa, another of the Commonwealth's most senior Speakers was until recently to be found in the tiny state of The Gambia, recently federated with neighbouring Senegal. The Gambia's first Speaker, himself a Gambian, was appointed by the colonial government in 1954 to preside over the then Legislative Council. In 1960 the House of

Representatives was constituted and in 1962, three years prior to the attainment of full independence, the first Speaker to be elected by the House took office. He was Sir Alieu Jack and he remained Speaker until 1972. From 1972 to 1977 he served as a minister but he was again elected Speaker after the general election of 1977 and he remained in office until 1983. He left the Chair in circumstances which were rather obscure. It was suggested in a local newspaper that he resigned under government pressure, having been involved in an attempt to damage the reputation of the Minister of Justice. He was succeeded by Mr. Momodou B. N'Jie who was elected unanimously, his seconder being a member of the opposition. It is expected that, like Speaker Jack before him, he will also become Speaker of the Confederal Parliament of Senegambia.

Speaker Jack was a strong defender of the principle that the Speaker should not be an elected member of the House. In an article published in 1978 he expressed the view that if the Speaker sits for a constituency it cannot be properly represented and that the impartiality which is such an essential quality in a Speaker is more likely to be found in a person elected from outside the House.[29] There are many who would dispute these arguments and at a conference held in 1969 Speaker Jack went so far as to say that he would welcome a vote on the issue.[30] During the same debate Speaker Lock of Botswana, himself a Speaker without a constituency, said he was glad that the conference did not have to vote on the issue and commented:

One of the things which have been said about 'half-Speakers' is that we become civil servants. I can assure this honourable Assembly that I do not feel like a civil servant, but I can see dangers that we could be treated just as chairmen, and the Speaker is surely something more than the Chairman over a meeting of Parliament. In the short time I have been holding the office I have sensed a little of this danger in the position and it is something which has to be resisted . . . [31]

In making these observations Speaker Lock, perhaps without realizing it, was underlining one of the principal arguments against the election of the Speaker from outside the House, namely that his strength and prestige derive from his reaching the House by the same route as every other member.

In The Gambia the Speaker is likely to be a member of the party which forms the government. Unlike the Speaker in Botswana he will probably be a person who has been actively engaged in the political life of the country. Once elected Speaker he loses direct political contact with an electorate, in regard to which Speaker Jack has commented:

. . . the office of Speaker compares in this regard with the office of the Prime Minister, and, as such, to compensate for the loss of personal political contact with the electorate, I consider it justifiable for the Speaker to maintain very good relations with the Government of the day—of course, without being hostile to the Opposition.[32]

In The Gambia it is the Speaker who determines the order paper for the day, a power which confers a very significant responsibility on the Chair. As Speaker Jack has himself observed, 'being in a position to stipulate what actually gets debated, the Speaker's position *vis-à-vis* the control of debate becomes even more delicate. He must ascertain that all sides of the House are afforded the opportunity to have their subjects of interest put on the floor of the House for debate and, in the process, ensure that individual members on the opposition side, and in many cases on the government back benches, are given time, not always adequate, to air their views.'[33]

Sierra Leone, like many other African countries, embarked upon independence with a Westminster-style parliamentary system and afterwards became a one-party state. It is interesting to contrast the comments of two presiding officers in speaking of the role of the Speaker in the two situations. Mr. Justice Luke, speaking at a conference in 1969 when he was Speaker of the House of Representatives, prior to Sierra Leone becoming a one-party state, acknowledged the difficulties he had encountered in presiding over a divided House in which government and opposition were little disposed to co-operate and recognize each other's point of view. He felt the task of promoting the necessary tolerance and goodwill was not an impossible one provided the Speaker could convince the House of his total impartiality. 'As a Speaker, it is only the interest of the community and of the people that should be paramount in his mind.' He also said that the people were committed to parliamentary democracy and opposed to the one-party state which an earlier Prime Minister, Sir Albert Margai, had attempted to impose.[34] However, a one-party state was subsequently established in 1978, following a referendum, under the presidency of Sir Albert Margai's opponent, Dr. Siaka Stevens, and at a conference held in Australia in 1978 the Deputy Speaker of Parliament, Mr. Conteh, contended that the role and functions of the Speaker were the same in a one-party state as in a multi-party state.

> In a one-party Parliament there is no real reason for the Speaker to divorce himself from politics, since the need to allay the suspicions of an institutionalised opposition does not arise. He is very much liberated, not only in conducting the proceedings of Parliament but also in working in various areas of national development. In the same way as members of the one party maintain their integrity by opposing the majority party view, the Speaker can preserve his fairness to the House collectively. It would be cynical to take the view that politics will necessarily pollute the Speaker. Psychologically, the involvement of the Speaker in the politics of a one-party state will help promote the concept of national cohesion which is a major objective in the one-party system.[35]

Nigeria, after a long period of military rule, adopted a new federal constitution in 1979 based on the United States congressional system. The National Assembly, as the legislature is styled, consists of the Senate and the House of Representatives, the President of the Senate and the Speaker of the

House being elected members of their respective Houses and active politicians. To stand for election to either House a candidate must be a member of a political party and the presiding officers are likely to be drawn from the party having the greatest number of members in the House. Speaking at a conference held in 1981 the Speaker of the House of Representatives, Mr. Ezeoke, said:

> I attend all the functions of my political party. I am a member of the central working committee, a member of the central executive, a legal adviser to the state branch of my party. Therefore, I am fully involved in party activities.
>
> This does not mean that the principle of impartiality which I think is inherent in the parliamentary system of government is not observed in our various legislatures. We try as much as possible to be impartial and to conduct the House in the most impartial manner. However, when you are a member of a political party, particularly where the political party is based on an ideology, it is very difficult for a Speaker to operate without bearing in mind the ideology of the political party which brought him to that position . . . .[36]

The Speaker of the Nigerian House of Representatives is a political leader whose role can to some extent be compared with that of the Speaker of the United States House of Representatives. Together with the majority leader he directs the business of the House. He appoints the chairmen of all committees in consultation with the party leaders and is the chairman of the Committee of Selection which controls the membership of committees. When parliamentary delegations are composed it is the Speaker who sets the proportionate number of members for each party although he does not select the members themselves. Although the system of government is based on the separation of powers, which assumes the complete independence of the legislature from the executive, most of the business considered by the legislature is government-sponsored. Committees do not have as much power as congressional committees in their control of legislation, and the Speaker is expected to expedite the passage of government bills and to put pressure on a chairman whose committee is holding up a bill. He has no formal powers to terminate a debate in the House but he can seek a consensus among the members with a view to suggesting that enough time has been spent on a measure and that it is time to put the question.

Ghana, after a long period of military rule, also had a new constitution based on the separation of powers, under which the Speaker was a non-member of Parliament and independent of party. Unfortunately a further *coup d'état* overturned this constitution at the end of 1981 before it had had a proper chance to function. An American-style system of government is one which can only be expected to operate successfully in a country where political and economic conditions are relatively stable. Its operation can even tax the ingenuity of a sophisticated and highly-developed society such as that of the United States. The foundations of democracy are very fragile in some of the countries with which this chapter has been dealing, which no doubt accounts for the failure of Ghana's most recent constitutional experiment. The experience in Nigeria will be followed with great interest and hope by all her friends in the Commonwealth and elsewhere.

In a number of African Parliaments, including those of Kenya, Tanzania, Malawi, Mauritius and Lesotho, the Speaker sometimes takes the Chair when the House is in committee of the whole. While provision is normally made for a Chairman of Committees who doubles as Deputy Speaker, the standing orders of some jurisdictions allow the Speaker to preside in committee of the whole should he choose to do so.

In most of the Parliaments under consideration the Speaker does not seem to be deeply involved in matters of administration and, with certain notable exceptions, the staff, including the Clerk of the House himself, are members of the public service. The desirability of keeping the parliamentary establishment separate from the public service is a frequent subject of discussion at Clerks' conferences. Integration with the public service means that the Clerk of the House and his colleagues are subject to transfer to other departments. When this happens Parliament is deprived of the staff continuity so essential to the highly specialised functions associated with the Clerks' profession. Against this it has been argued that in countries where the parliamentary staff is small their avenues of advancement would be severely limited if the right of transferability did not exist. Speaker Khonje of Malawi has spoken of the inconvenience which can be caused when a Clerk having gained experience of the parliamentary milieu is transferred elsewhere and replaced by a newcomer.[37] The fact that parliamentary staff form part of the public service does not necessarily mean that Parliament is certain to lose its staff. In Kenya, for example, the present Clerk of the National Assembly joined the parliamentary establishment as Clerk Assistant in 1961. On the other hand both the Botswana National Assembly and the House of Representatives of The Gambia recently lost their Clerks through transfer to other departments.

Zambia and Zimbabwe both have independent parliamentary establishments. In Zambia the Clerk's status is equated with that of a High Court judge and the Clerk Assistant's with that of the permanent head of a department. Zambia probably goes farther than any other Commonwealth country in its recognition of the prestige of the Clerk's position. In many other Commonwealth Parliaments the Clerk ranks with the permanent head of a government department, but only in Zambia does he rank higher. In Zambia the Speaker is the final authority on all matters affecting administration and personnel, and the constitution provides that the Clerk be appointed under his authority. While much responsibility is delegated to the Clerk, the Speaker's direct involvement is assured through his chairmanship of several crucial committees. In Zimbabwe the constitution provides that the appointment of the Secretary to Parliament and of other staff shall be made by the Speaker in consultation with the President of the Senate. The Speaker is chairman of a management committee which determines administrative policy and considers promotions and appointments at the departmental head level. Other appointments are normally made on the recommendation of the head of the department concerned. Staff below the executive level are represented by a workers' committee.

In Tanzania the Speaker chairs an appointments committee which considers recommendations made by the Clerk of the House. In Kenya the Speaker chairs a committee which looks after the welfare of members and staff, and he is also a member of the catering committee. Speaker Mati has said that he is involved in almost everything that goes on in Parliament, including the provision of facilities for members and security arrangements, but that most of his administrative responsibilities are delegated to the Clerk.[38] In Mauritius the Speaker is responsible for ultimate policy decisions but consults closely with the Clerk and seldom interferes with the latter's administrative jurisdiction. In Malawi, Uganda and Lesotho the Speaker's direct involvement in administrative and personnel matters appears to be much less than in other jurisdictions.

In most African Parliaments the prestige of the Speaker's office is recognized by according him a high place in the official order of precedence. In The Gambia he ranks third, following the President and the Vice-President. In Botswana and Lesotho he ranks fourth following the Chief Justice but ahead of all cabinet ministers except (in Lesotho) the Prime Minister. In Botswana there is no such office as Prime Minister since the President is a member of the National Assembly, but the Speaker precedes the Vice-President. In Kenya the Speaker ranks at fourth place before all the judges but after all cabinet ministers. In Zambia, Tanzania, Mauritius and Sierra Leone he comes fifth after the Chief Justice but ahead of all cabinet ministers except the Prime Minister. In Malawi, although he ranks ahead of the Chief Justice, his place in the order of precedence is relatively low since he is preceded by all office-bearers and members of the national executive of the party and all ministers whether or not they are members of the cabinet.

In some African Parliaments there is a great sensitivity to press criticism and the Speaker may find himself ruling on questions of privilege relating to the conduct of the press. At a conference held in London in 1976 Speaker Mati made the following observations concerning the relations between Parliament and the press:

> Encroachment on the supremacy of Parliament may also come from the Press. I believe that where there has been freedom of the Press, and where the freedom of the Press is a reality, there has been some form of clash, however mild, between the legislature and the Press. We know this should not be so and that the two institutions should aim at the same goal and should therefore be able to co-operate rather than compete; where there is criticism it should be constructive. Instead, we quite often hear of or read about attempts by the Press to undermine the authority and the credibility of Parliament. On the other hand, we also sometimes are subject to tirades of accusations by some Members blaming on the Press every imaginable sin of omission or commission on earth. But I believe that Parliament cannot be truly free if other institutions are not free, and the Press is one such institution. I am, of course, referring to

responsible freedom, not a licence on the part of the Press to disrupt or to attempt to discredit Parliament in the eyes of the public.[39]

Standing Order 165 of the Kenya National Assembly makes provision for the manner of dealing with misconduct on the part of the press and reads as follows:

> Any newspaper whose representative infringes these Standing Orders or any rules made by Mr. Speaker for the regulation of the admittance of strangers or persistently misreports the proceedings of the House, or neglects or refuses on request from the Clerk to correct any wrong report thereof to the satisfaction of Mr. Speaker, may be excluded from representation in the Press gallery for such term as the House shall direct.

Zambia is a country where the press has regularly come into conflict with Parliament. In 1970 the editor of *The Times of Zambia* was adjudged guilty of a breach of privilege and a gross contempt of the House on account of an article criticising the assembly's handling of a bill to amend the constitution. He was ordered to publish an unreserved apology, and the Speaker observed that if the freedom of the press were not respected in Zambia '*The Times of Zambia* would have been banned once and for all, and the Editor imprisoned—if not sent to the gallows.'[40] In 1976 the *Zambia Daily Mail* found itself in trouble because of an editorial published under the heading 'M.P.'s Boob!'. The article had criticised the members who had voted against a certain bill, and the words used were deemed to be irresponsible, provocative and insulting and therefore an affront to Parliament. The editor-in-chief was ordered to apologize to the House. Among the points made by the Speaker in delivering the judgment of the House were that no outsider had the right to say that what the House decided was wrong and that members should not be attacked for exercising their right to vote as they chose. He said that comments and criticisms of whatever is debated in the House were acceptable provided they were constructive.[41] The following year *The Times of Zambia* was again in trouble. The case arose from a speech delivered in the assembly by a member who expressed doubt as to the commitment of some Zambian leaders to a free press because of the appointment of a new editor-in-chief to the newspaper in question. The editor-in-chief responded by quoting a verbatim report of the member's speech from the uncorrected parliamentary debates and publishing an open letter to the member in defence of his appointment. He was adjudged guilty of a breach of privilege and a gross contempt of the House for publishing extracts from uncorrected transcripts and for his letter which was described by the Speaker as scandalous, irresponsible and threatening. The editor-in-chief was called upon to apologize to the House and the Speaker suggested that those who had appointed him to the position might also wish to mete out punishment.[42] Later in the same year the Speaker made a statement in the House in which he ruled that the press was forbidden to report proceedings which had been ruled out of order or expunged from the record. He accused the press of promoting hostility towards Parliament and of trying to create a rift between Parliament and the party.⁴³ In 1980 another editor of *The Times of Zambia* was summoned to the Bar of the House for having criticized the Speaker and the House in two editorials for what he saw as declining standards of conduct and diligence. He was made to publish an apology and to read it to the House, and was also subjected to a severe rebuke by the Speaker. Shortly afterwards he published another editorial on parliamentary privilege and press freedom, to which the attention of the House was also down, but the Speaker declined to take further action. He observed that criticism may be tolerated but not insults, and appealed to members not to be over-sensitive.⁴⁴ It is interesting to note that both *The Times of Zambia* and the *Zambia Daily Mail* are government-owned and their editors appointed by the government. This suggests that Parliament, while taking an attitude very restrictive of press freedom, may to some extent feel itself to be in an adversary situation with the executive and party authorities in protecting its privileges and independence.

Not all African Parliaments are engaged in the kind of ongoing conflict with the press which has been described above, but this may well be that in some countries the press is more compliant, less critical, or more responsive to the susceptibilities of the parliamentarians. In Tanzania, for example, questions of privilege related to press comment are very seldom raised. Occasionally a member might claim to have been misquoted and raise the matter in the chamber with a view to setting the record straight, but there the matter would normally rest.

It will be apparent from this chapter that the Speakers of the African Parliaments of the Commonwealth do not all view their responsibilities in the same way and that the Speaker's role must adapt to the political conditions of the country concerned. The institutions of these countries are still in the process of evolution, the speakership included, and the stresses on the political fabric of the nation are bound to shape that process. In many cases the one-party system is seen as the only means of striving towards national unity and overcoming tribal divisions. In Africa the coup d'état is not a rare occurrence, and in those cases, as in Uganda and Nigeria, where parliamentary government has been restored it becomes necessary to rebuild political institutions from scratch. The importance of the speakership in the parliamentary system seems to be widely appreciated in Africa. The value of continuity and experience in the job has been recognized in most of the countries dealt with in this chapter. In most of them it is regarded as normal that the Speaker should retain his political affiliation, although Botswana, Lesotho and Sierra Leone have opted for the 'non-political' Speaker. In most cases a Speaker who does not represent a constituency seems to be preferred, the exceptions being Nigeria, Mauritius and Malawi. No Commonwealth African Parliament has departed completely from Westminster practices, and Speakers in particular are conscious of the value of retaining the link. In some cases the link remains close, in others it is largely superficial, and there is broad agreement that there should be no hesitation in discarding practices which are inappropriate to the domestic political context. Speakers and other parliamentarians attach great importance to the public image of their Parliaments and seek to ensure that the institution and its practices should be meaningful to the people as a whole and relevant to their culture and traditions.

Notes to Chapter Eight: The Speakership in the African Parliaments of the Commonwealth

1. See H. B. Ndoria Gicheru, Parliamentary Practice in Kenya, Transafrica Publishers, 1976, pp. 18–23.
2. Quoted in Gicheru, p. 67.
3. Proceedings of the Second Conference of Commonwealth Speakers and Presiding Officers, New Delhi, 28 December 1970 to 1 January 1971, pp. 80–81.
4. Gicheru, op. cit., p. 151.
5. Ibid., p. 151.
6. The Parliamentarian, vol. II no. 3, July 1970, p. 232.
7. Gicheru, op. cit., p. 77.
8. See Standing Order 88 (2), National Assembly of Kenya, Standing Orders, 7 November 1969.
9. Fourth Conference of Commonwealth Speakers and Presiding Officers, op. cit., p. 38.
10. Ibid., p. 52.
11. Ibid., p. 52.
12. Report of the Sixth Conference of Commonwealth Speakers and Presiding Officers, Ottawa, April 23rd., 24th and 25th 1981, pp. 120–121.
13. Ibid., p. 121.
14. R. M. Nabulyato, The Speakership in Zambia, The Parliamentarian, January 1978, vol. LIX, no. 1, p. 16.
15. See The Parliamentarian, April 1969, vol. L, no. 2, p. 151.
16. See The Parliamentarian, April 1971, vol. LII, no. 2, pp. 163–164.
17. Report of the Fifth Conference of Commonwealth Speakers and Presiding Officers, op. cit., pp. 50–51.
18. See Standing Orders 121–145, National Assembly of Zambia, 1980.
19. Standing Order 155, House of Assembly of Zimbabwe, 1980.
20. Sixth Conference of Commonwealth Speakers and Presiding Officers, op. cit., p. 48.
21. Fourth Conference of Commonwealth Speakers and Presiding Officers, op. cit., p. 64.
22. See Speaker Khonje's contributions to the Fourth Conference of Commonwealth Speakers and Presiding Officers, op. cit., pp. 63–65, Fifth Conference, op. cit., pp. 44–45 and Sixth Conference, op. cit., pp. 47–48.
23. See A. R. W. Stumbles, Some Recollections of a Rhodesian Speaker, Bulawayo, Books of Rhodesia, 1980, pp. 134–136 and 187–188.
24. See Report of the Sixth Conference of Commonwealth Speakers and Presiding Officers, op. cit., pp. 43–44.
25. Ibid., p. 44.
26. Report of the Fifth Conference of Speakers and Presiding Officers of Commonwealth Parliaments, op. cit., p. 52.
27. See Report of the Conference of Speakers and Presiding Officers of

Commonwealth Parliaments, held at Ottawa and Toronto, Canada, 8th to 12th September 1969, pp. 97–101.
28. Speaker Kolane has been a regular attender at Commonwealth Speakers' Conferences and has recorded his observations on the speakership in Lesotho at the Fifth Conference, op. cit., pp. 45–47, and the Sixth Conference, op. cit., pp. 44–46. See also his article in The Parliamentarian, vol. LIX, no. 1, January 1978, pp. 20–23.
29. See Sir Alieu Jack, The Speakership in The Gambia, The Parliamentarian, vol. LIX, no. 1, January 1978, p. 27.
30. See Report of the Conference of Speakers and Presiding Officers, 1969, op. cit., p. 72.
31. Ibid., p. 75.
32. Ibid., p. 30.
33. Report of the Sixth Conference of Commonwealth Speakers and Presiding Officers, op. cit., p. 58.
34. See Report of the Conference of Speakers and Presiding Officers of Commonwealth Parliaments, 1969, op. cit., pp. 31 and 92–93.
35. Report of the Fifth Conference of Speakers and Presiding Officers of Commonwealth Parliaments, op. cit., p. 47.
36. Report of the Sixth Conference of Commonwealth Speakers and Presiding Officers, op. cit., p. 52.
37. See Fourth Conference of Commonwealth Speakers and Presiding Officers, op. cit., p. 72.
38. Ibid., pp. 66–67.
39. Ibid., p. 39.
40. See The Parliamentarian, vol. LI, no. 3, July 1970, p. 232.
41. Ibid., vol. LVIII, no. 1, January 1977, pp. 64–65.
42. Ibid., vol. LVIII, no. 4, October 1977, pp. 278–279.
43. Ibid., vol. LIX, no. 3, July 1978, pp. 196–198.
44. Ibid., vol. LXI, no. 3, July 1980, pp. 159–162.

Chapter Nine

The Speakership in Sri Lanka, Malaysia and Singapore

Sri Lanka, which was known as Ceylon prior to the adoption of a republican constitution in 1972, became an independent member of the Commonwealth in 1948, one year after India. These two countries may be regarded as the heralds of the new Commonwealth which emerged after the Second World War. Unlike India, which became a republic almost immediately on achieving independence, it was some years before Ceylon found it possible to give expression to its own national sentiment in a similar manner. Nevertheless, by remaining in the Commonwealth along with India, Ceylon greatly assisted the process of transition whereby the former 'white' Commonwealth evolved into the multi-racial association of independent states we know today.

Sri Lanka has a long parliamentary tradition which can be traced back to the establishment in 1833 of the first Legislative Council which was presided over by the Governor. Constitutional advances were implemented in 1910, 1920 and 1923, when the Legislative Council first acquired the power to elect its own Speaker. However, it was not until 1931 that universal suffrage was introduced and the first State Council was elected. This constitution remained in force until 1947 when, in preparation for independence, Ceylon became self-governing and a bicameral Parliament was introduced, consisting of a Senate and a House of Representatives.

The first Speaker of the first State Council was Mr. (later Sir) Francis Molamure whose first tenure of office ran from 1931 to 1934. He was succeeded by Mr. F. A. Obeyesekere who served until the dissolution of the first State Council twelve months later. The second State Council, which lasted from 1936 to 1947, was presided over by Sir Waitialingam Duraiswamy throughout the entire period. In 1947 Sir Francis Molamure returned to preside over the first House of Representatives. He remained Speaker until his death in 1951, thus bridging the transitional period between self-government and independence. Until 1947 there was no organized party system in Ceylon. At the general election for the first House of Representatives Sir Francis stood as a candidate for the party which formed the government, but he resigned from his party following his election as Speaker. He was succeeded by Sir Albert Peries, also a member of the governing party, and he continued in office until 1956. These first Speakers adhered closely to the concept of the British speakership. They remained aloof from party politics, took no part in debate and were diligent in their efforts to promote the independence of the Chair. There had been some discussion of the principle of allowing the Speaker an uncontested election in his constituency and some support for the idea had been expressed but no steps were ever taken to implement it. The result has been that Speakers have not been immune from electoral defeats and have regularly fallen victim to the dramatic political reversals which have characterised the politics of Sri Lanka.

With the election of the government of Mr. S. W. R. D. Bandaranaike in 1956 the speakership entered a new phase. The House elected as Speaker Mr. H. S. Ismail who was both an independent and the first Moslem to occupy the Chair. He presided over a difficult House. On one occasion he called in the police to remove from the Chamber a member who, having been named and suspended from the service of the House, refused to withdraw.[1] In 1960, following the election of a minority government led by Mr. Dudley Senanayake, a contested election for the speakership was won by a candidate jointly sponsored by the opposition parties, Mr. T. B. Subasinghe.* He defeated the government's nominee, Sir Albert Peries, by 93 votes to 61. This Parliament lasted only five months but it marked a departure from the earlier conventions relating to the Chair whereby Speakers had been selected by consensus. Henceforward, there developed a tendency on the part of Speakers to remain more closely attached to their parties and to be more hesitant to remove themselves from the mainstream of politics.

A second election in 1960 was to bring to power Mrs. Sirima Bandaranaike, wife of the former Prime Minister who had been assassinated. The first Speaker elected in this Parliament was Mr. R. S. Pelpola, a member of the party in power. He was elected without a contest, but he became unpopular with the opposition because, in their eyes, his partisanship was reflected in his conduct in the Chair. In fairness to him it must be conceded that he presided over the House of Representatives during a difficult period which saw an attempted coup d'état and a state of emergency which lasted for two years. It was a period in which the classic conditions for a breakdown in parliamentary government and a military takeover were evident, but happily parliamentary democracy survived in Ceylon without interruption. This is not to suggest that the normal freedoms were not restricted. Following the abortive coup in 1962, the Speaker, in answer to a question from a member, stated that the press were not free to publish the proceedings of the House without censorship and that a censor board had been set up in the House.[2]

Speaker Pelpola resigned in 1964 and was succeeded by the Deputy Speaker, Mr. Hugh Fernando, who was elected without opposition. During his brief period of office, which lasted barely a year, he gave greater satisfaction to the opposition than had his predecessor. He was a member of the governing party when called to the Chair but he subsequently changed sides and became a minister in the government of Mr. Dudley Senanayake which was elected in 1965. Mr. Fernando's defection from the Sri Lanka

---

* He subsequently became a minister in the government of Mrs. Bandaranaike but broke with her in 1977 just prior to a general election.

Freedom Party, led by Mrs. Bandaranaike, was symptomatic of the volatile nature of the country's politics during this period. A catholic, he was a member of a religious minority which broke with the Bandanaraike party and transferred its allegiance to the United National Party of Dudley Senanayake. Sir Albert Peries, another catholic, became Speaker once again following the 1965 election. He too presided over an unruly House and like Speaker Ismail before him he called in the police on one occasion to remove a disorderly member. He remained in office until his death in 1967. The Deputy Speaker, Mr. Shirley Corea, was unanimously elected to replace him.

In 1970 Mrs. Bandaranaike's party was re-elected to power with an overwhelming majority. Having won more than the two-thirds majority of seats in the House of Representatives necessary to change the constitution, the government lost no time in setting the process in motion in accordance with the mandate it had sought at the general election. Mr. Stanley Tillekeratne, a government member who openly supported his party's policies and the demand for a new constitution, was elected Speaker. A few weeks later, on 19 July 1970, the House of Representatives was convened as a Constituent Assembly and Speaker Tillekeratne was elected its chairman. In 1971 the Senate was abolished and in 1972 a new republican constitution was proclaimed providing for a unicameral Parliament styled the National State Assembly. Backed by its huge majority the government was able to extend the life of the Parliament elected in 1970 until 1977. The political situation had seriously deteriorated and the popularity of Mrs. Bandaranaike's government was at its lowest point when she was finally forced to call an election following a three-month period during which Parliament stood prorogued.

The 1977 election was as much a triumph for Mrs. Bandaranaike's opponents as the 1970 election had been for her. Under its new leader, Mr. J. R. Jayewardene, the United National Party won 139 of the 168 seats and Mrs. Bandaranaike's party was virtually eliminated. One of the electoral casualties was Speaker Tillekeratne who had presided throughout the Parliament of 1970–1977. Taking advantage of its unprecedented majority, the new government also addressed itself to constitutional reform as a first priority, and in 1978 another new constitution was promulgated providing for an executive president elected by the people.* He heads a cabinet of ministers who are members of Parliament and collectively responsible to Parliament.[3] The first Speaker of the new Parliament was Mr. Anandatissa de Alwis who was shortly afterwards appointed to the cabinet. He was succeeded in 1978 by Al Haj M. Abdul Bakeer Markar who at the time of writing remains in the office.

The republican constitution confers certain powers and responsibilities on the Speaker. Unlike the practice in many other countries, the head of state is not required to give his formal assent to legislation. Instead the Speaker is required to certify that a bill has been duly passed by Parliament and it becomes law

---

* The 1978 constitution also made provision for proportional representation which should obviate the disproportionate majorities which have resulted from some general elections in the past.

when his certificate is endorsed thereon. In the case of a bill requiring a special majority under the constitution the Speaker is required to certify that this provision has been complied with. Certain bills require the approval of the electorate at a referendum following their adoption by Parliament, and in such cases the Speaker's certificate must state that the bill shall not become law until so approved. If such a bill is approved at a referendum it must be endorsed with the certificate of the President of the Republic. The certificate of the Speaker or the President, as the case may be, cannot be questioned in a court of law.[4]

The Speaker has certain duties which relate to the office of President. If the President resigns he does so in writing addressed to the Speaker.[5] In certain circumstances the Speaker performs the functions of the President. Normally the Prime Minister would act during the absence or incapacity of the President, but if the Prime Minister is for any reason unable to act, or if the office of Prime Minister is vacant, the Speaker is the one designated by the constitution to act in his place. If the Chief Justice in consultation with the Speaker comes to the conclusion that the President is unable to perform his duties he communicates this opinion in writing to the Speaker. In such a case the Prime Minister, or if he is not available, the Speaker, would exercise the functions of the office.[6]

The constitution also provides a mechanism whereby any member of Parliament may give notice of a resolution, in writing addressed to the Speaker, alleging that the President is incapable of discharging his functions and calling for an inquiry by the Supreme Court. In entertaining notice of such a resolution the Speaker must ensure that it complies with the conditions set out in the constitution. The notice must be signed by not less than two-thirds of the members, but if signed by not less than one half of the members it may be entertained by the Speaker if he is satisfied that the allegations merit inquiry and report by the Supreme Court.[7] Should such a case be referred to the Supreme Court, the Court must report its determination to the Speaker within two months of the date of reference[8], and if the allegations were upheld a resolution supported by not less than two-thirds of the members would still be required in order to remove the President from office.

Apart from the constitutional powers outlined above, the adoption of a republican constitution has done little to change the nature of the Speaker's office in Sri Lanka. Earlier Speakers, as has been pointed out, were more closely attached to Westminster traditions than later incumbents of the office. But although the speakership has become more party-oriented, the Speaker is usually elected to the Chair without a contest and he does not attend party meetings. If the Speaker's election is contested it is conducted by secret ballot and if three or more candidates are in the field the balloting continues until one candidate secures an overall majority.[9] The constitution and the standing orders provide that the Speaker or other member presiding shall be equipped with a casting vote but not an original vote.

The powers of the Speaker under the standing orders are very similar to those of his Westminster counterpart. He has the same discretion in relation to a closure motion and may refuse to accept it if he believes it to be an abuse of

The Office of Speaker

the rules of Parliament or an infringement of the rights of the minority.[10] If he feels that a dilatory motion is an abuse of the rules of Parliament he may put the question forthwith without debate or decline to propose the question.[11] He may expedite the taking of a vote if he believes a division to have been unnecessarily claimed.[12] The allowance of emergency adjournment debates lies within his discretion but, unlike the British Speaker, he must state his reasons for disallowing an emergency adjournment motion if, having refused his consent, he allows the member raising the matter to read the proposed motion.[13] Standing Order 71 (1) specifically prohibits appeals from any ruling of the Speaker or chairmen of committees in any circumstances. Their rulings may be reviewed by Parliament only upon a substantive motion made after notice.

The Speaker's disciplinary powers follow the same pattern which is to be discerned in most Commonwealth Parliaments. He may 'name' a member for disregarding the authority of the Chair and other offences, but in such a case the Speaker himself puts the question for the member's suspension.[14] There is a provision in the standing orders which empowers the Speaker to take such steps as he deems necessary to compel the withdrawal of a member or members who refuse to leave the chamber after being suspended.[15] Speaker Ismail and Speaker Peries were presumably acting under the authority of this standing order when they called in the police to deal with a recalcitrant member. The Speaker may direct a member who persists in irrelevance or tedious repetition to discontinue his speech.[16] He is empowered to order a member to withdraw for the remainder of the day's sitting (a disciplinary measure which avoids the severer sanction consequent upon 'naming' a member) and in cases of grave disorder he may adjourn the House or suspend the sitting on his own initiative.[17]

The Speaker has a number of important responsibilities relating to committees of which there are several kinds in the Parliament of Sri Lanka. They are variously designated committees of the whole Parliament, standing committees (which deal with legislation), consultative committees, committees for special purposes, and select committees (which are appointed *ad hoc*). At the commencement of every session the Speaker nominates a Chairmen's Panel of not less than four members. From this panel the Speaker appoints the chairman of each standing committee. They also act as temporary chairmen of committees of the whole Parliament.[18] It is interesting to note that the Speaker himself is the principal chairman of a committee of the whole Parliament. In his absence the Deputy Speaker, Deputy Chairman of Committees or a member of the Chairmen's Panel presides.[19] A temporary chairman when presiding over a committee of the whole Parliament possesses the full powers of the Deputy Speaker.[20]

The chairman and members of all select committees are appointed by the Speaker.[21] The Speaker himself chairs a number of committees for special purposes. These are the Committee of Selection, which nominates the members of the other committees for special purposes, the consultative committees and the standing committees, and which also considers the numbers, functions and constitution of the consultative committees and the standing committees; the House Committee, which is concerned with the comfort and convenience of members; the Committee on Standing Orders, which is concerned with procedure and the conduct of business; the Committee on Parliamentary Business, which deals with the allocation of time to the business of the House; and the Committee on Public Petitions.[22]

As chairman of the Committee on Parliamentary Business the Speaker has a responsibility similar to that of his counterpart in India. The committee is a very important one as it is charged with the organization of the parliamentary programme. Its membership comprises, in addition to the Speaker, the other two principal Chair occupants, the Leader of the House, the Leader of the Opposition, the chief whips of government and opposition and five other members.[23] The Speaker's role is essentially that of a moderator. He guides the committee in its discussions, offering suggestions to facilitate the process of negotiation, but it is left to the parties to reach agreement on the allocation of time to the various items of business.

Two standing orders, which appear to overlap, confer on the Speaker a wide residuary discretion. Standing Order 136 empowers him 'to regulate the conduct of business in Parliament in all matters not provided for in these Standing Orders' and Standing Order 142 provides that 'All matters not specifically provided for in these Standing Orders and all questions relating to the detailed working of these Standing Orders shall be regulated in such manner as Mr. Speaker may, from time to time, direct'. Together these standing orders allow to the Speaker a very wide discretion in determining the operation of the rules and practice of the House.

The Speaker is the head of the parliamentary administration and his administrative authority is clearly stated in Standing Order 137 which provides that he 'shall be responsible for the management of buildings, security arrangements and the general administration of the Chamber'. The staff of Parliament are independent of the public service and the Speakers of the Parliament of Sri Lanka have consistently protected this administrative autonomy. Speakers have not hesitated to protest on occasions when ministers have attempted to interfere with the parliamentary estimates by demanding economies. The right of Parliament to decide what its own requirements should be has been jealously guarded in Sri Lanka. Insistence on this principle has never excluded the need to practice restraint, but Speakers have sometimes felt obliged to point out that the estimates of Parliament are carefully prepared to reflect genuine needs, and that restraint will be practised without the need for executive interference.

Under the Parliament (Powers and Privileges) Act the Speaker is empowered to order material to be expunged from Hansard and in such a case to prohibit the publication of such words. The Act was amended in 1980 to confer this power on the Speaker and to provide that the publication of words or statements ordered expunged would constitute a breach of privilege. Sri Lanka's parliamentarians have tended to show great sensitivity towards any words or actions which might be seen as infringing their privileges, and questions of privilege are regularly raised, requiring the Speaker to determine whether or not a *prima facie* case exists. The original Act, adopted in 1953, provided that serious cases involving parliamentary privilege could only be tried and punished by the Supreme Court. An amendment of 1978, while preserving the jurisdiction of the Supreme Court, conferred equal powers in determining such cases on the National State Assembly, which can now impose a fine or prison sentence on an offender.[24] The change contains the potential for conflict between Parliament and the courts which is undoubtedly a matter of concern for the Speaker even though, under the Act, the advice of the Attorney-General is available to him when a question of privilege is raised. Only two days after the amendment of the law Parliament proceeded against two journalists who were found guilty of breach of privilege and ordered to pay a fine. A series of articles, highly critical of Parliament, were subsequently published concerning this case. The author of the articles was tried for breach of privilege by the Supreme Court which found that no offence had been committed and discharged him.[25]

It has been suggested that the Speakers of Sri Lanka, because of their party orientation, tend to favour the government and rarely uphold a point of order raised by the opposition. However, there is at least one occasion on record which does not bear out this assessment. On 19 January 1973 Speaker Tillekeratne upheld an opposition submission on an important constitutional issue and incurred the wrath of the government as a result. One of the parties to the coalition government of that period vowed to move a motion of no confidence in the Speaker but failed to win the support of its coalition partners.[26] Motions of no confidence in the Speaker are infrequent, although one was moved against Speaker Peries on 9 February 1966. The motion accused him of partisan conduct on the occasion when he called in the police to remove a member who had been suspended from the service of the House. It was defeated by 89 votes to 32.[27]

Malaysia is a federation consisting of the eleven states of the Malay peninsular together with Sabah and Sarawak. The federal Parliament is bicameral and each state has its own unicameral legislature. Although parliamentary institutions in this region may be said to date from 1909, the first significant representative body representing the entire country as it existed at the time was the Federal Legislative Council established in 1948. Although entirely nominated, two-thirds of its 75 members were 'unofficial' — that is to say, free of any commitment to support the government in the legislature. The High Commissioner presided over the Council until 1953 when the first Speaker was appointed. The first general elections for an enlarged Council of 98 members were held in 1955 and in 1957 an independent Federation of Malaya came into being. The unicameral Federal Legislative Council continued in being until the elections of 1959 which were held under a constitution providing for a bicameral Parliament consisting of the Supreme Head of State (Yang di-Pertuan Agong),* a Senate (Dewan Negara) and a House of Representatives (Dewan Rakyat). In 1963 the Federation was enlarged to include Singapore, Sabah and Sarawak and was re-styled the Federation of

---

* The head of state is a constitutional monarch chosen on a rotating basis by and from the Conference of Rulers which consists of the sultans of the eleven Malay states.

Malaysia. However, in 1965 Singapore withdrew from the Federation and became an independent state.

Article 57 (1) of the constitution provides that the Speaker of the House of Representatives (Yang di-Pertua Dewan Rakyat) may be chosen from among the membership or from outside the House.* If he is an elected member of the House he is equipped with a casting vote and is required to exercise it 'whenever necessary to avoid an equality of votes'. A Speaker selected from outside the House has no casting vote.[28]

The first two Speakers of Dewan Rakyat were elected members but the others were all non-members at the time of their appointment. All Speakers have been associated with the governing coalition, the United Malay National Organisation, which has governed the country ever since the first elections were held in 1955. Opposition parties have always been weak in Malaysia, both at the federal and state level, and the right of the government to choose the Speaker has never been challenged. The candidate is nominated by the Prime Minister and no Speaker has ever faced a contested election. This does not mean that opposition parties have necessarily approved of the government's methods in selecting the Speaker, but any attempt at resistance would simply underline their lack of strength and possibly expose them to ridicule. The Speakers so far chosen have, nevertheless, usually proved acceptable to those in opposition to the government. They have been men who have distinguished themselves in public life, some having served as diplomats and chief ministers of states, and all of them having had previous parliamentary experience. A trend is also evident on the part of the government to bolster the judicial nature of the speakership and to select legally-trained candidates for the office.

The first Speaker of Dewan Rakyat, Tan Sri Datuk Haji Mohamed Noah bin Omar, was a former magistrate who served from 1959 to 1964. His successor, Datuk Syed Esa bin Alwee, was an educationist who held the office for only six months in 1964. Tan Sri Datuk C. M. Yusuf, the first Speaker to be chosen from outside the House, was a lawyer who served two terms from 1964 to 1974. During the period between 1969 and 1971 when parliamentary government was suspended this Speaker remained in office and continued to draw his salary. Tan Sri Datuk Nik Ahmed Kamil bin Haji Mahmood, Speaker from 1974 to 1977, also had a legal background and died in office. His successor, Tan Sri Datuk Syed Nasir bin Ismail served two terms from 1978 to 1982 and also died in office. He was a non-lawyer, but the practice of choosing a Speaker with a legal background was restored with the appointment of a former judge, Dato Mohamed Zahir bin Haji Ismail in 1982.** Prior to becoming a judge he was a member of Parliament but has not rejoined his party since his appointment as Speaker. His predecessor, on the other hand, was a member of the Supreme Council of the governing party at the time of

---

* At the time of writing Dewan Rakyat consists of 154 members and if the Speaker is elected from outside the House he becomes the 155th member.
** At the time of his appointment a Deputy Speaker of Chinese origin also was elected, the first non-Malay to be chosen as an occupant of the Chair.

his death.[29] In spite of their party associations Speakers never attend meetings of their party caucus, although the Deputy Speaker customarily does so.

If the election of the Speaker were to be contested it would be conducted by secret ballot. Standing Order 4 lays down the procedure for a contested election, and if three or more candidates are proposed the balloting continues until one candidate emerges with an overall majority. Provision is made for lots to be drawn in the event of two candidates receiving an equal number of votes.

As in many other jurisdictions, the standing orders of Dewan Rakyat have much in common with those of the British House of Commons, and a number of the Speaker's powers are virtually identical with those of his British counterpart. No appeal is allowed from the rulings of the Chair, although a decision may be reviewed by the House by way of substantive motion, moved for that purpose, of which two days notice is required.[30] The Speaker's disciplinary powers are similar to those of the British Speaker[31] and although he rarely has recourse to 'naming' a member he does not hesitate to use his power to order the withdrawal of a member for the remainder of the sitting. His powers in relation to closure motions,[32] emergency adjournment motions,[33] allowing urgent questions without notice,[34] and allowing personal explanations[35] also resemble those of the British Speaker. Malaysian procedure, like the British, permits members to raise matters on the daily adjournment motion, the number of members who may do so being limited to two on each sitting day. Members wishing to take advantage of this procedure must give written notice to the Speaker at least seven days beforehand, and the Speaker selects the members to whom the opportunities shall be allotted. He may in his discretion do so by ballot and the standing order requires him to give preference to members who have not previously raised a matter during the session.[36] No petition may be presented unless it has been approved by the Speaker.[37] He may disallow any question which he deems to be an abuse of the right of questioning or which he believes is 'calculated to obstruct or affect prejudicially the procedure of the House, or to promote feelings of ill-will or hostility between different communities in the Federation, or infringes any of the provisions of the Constitution or the Sedition Act, 1948.'[38]

Some of the powers vested in the Malaysian Speaker are somewhat unusual. In certain circumstances he can oblige a minister to answer a question, although this is a power which is rarely invoked. Standing Order 23(4) gives a minister the right to refuse to answer a question on the ground of public interest 'with the approval of Tuan Yang di-Pertua'. If a minister refused to answer a question without giving a reason it is likely that the Speaker would ask him to provide a reason. If, for example, a minister declined to answer a supplementary question on the ground that it was irrelevant to the main question, the Speaker, if he thought otherwise, might rule that it was relevant.

Although the standing orders make no provision for time limits on speeches the Speaker or the Chairman has the right to impose time limits of his own.[39] This power will normally be invoked after considerable discussion of an issue has already taken place. When the occupant of the Chair feels that an appropriate point has been reached, he may announce that all further speeches will be limited to such length of time as he will determine in his discretion. During major debates, such as those on the King's speech and the budget, the Chair allows greater latitude concerning the length of speeches, and special regard is had for the rights of the opposition in determining the limits. Although the business of the House is largely controlled by the government, the Speaker is consulted and there are certain initiatives he can take in deciding how much business shall be taken and how the available time should be allocated.[40] There are circumstances in which he might terminate a debate or postpone an item of business. This would normally be done in consultation with both sides of the House, but he would give equal consideration to a request from the opposition as to one from the government. He is also empowered to disallow a motion or amendment or to terminate a debate if he is of the opinion that breaches of order might result if debate were allowed to take place or continue on the matter concerned.[41] He would normally exercise this power following consultation with the Prime Minister and Leader of the Opposition.

The procedure relating to the questioning of ministers requires that fourteen days notice of all questions is required before each meeting of the House, the questions being divided numerically among the sitting days which constitute that particular series of sittings. The Speaker has taken it upon himself to limit to twenty the number of oral questions and to five the number of written questions which may be asked by any one member. Questions which are not reached for oral answer receive written answers. The Speaker controls the question period by much the same criteria observed by his British counterpart, allowing important issues to be aired at some length, and ensuring that the opposition members receive more than a proportionate share of the supplementary questions. If a member asking a question for oral answer fails to rise when the question is called it is open to any other member to claim the question as his own.[42] However, a recent decision of the Speaker has varied the interpretation of this rule. If the member initiating the question is absent, the Speaker passes immediately to the next question, and not until all the questions set down for that day are disposed of can another member claim to ask the absent member's question.

A motion the object of which is to suspend any standing order may be made with notice, but in other circumstances the consent of the Speaker is required before any business may be embarked upon which would have this effect. If such a motion is made without notice it may proceed with the agreement of the Speaker. If he is of the opinion that any bill, amendment, motion or petition would have the effect of suspending all or any of the standing orders the Speaker's consent is required if such business is to proceed.[43]

The language of Parliament and the official language of the country is Malay and under recent legislation the permission of the Speaker is required if a member wishes to speak in English. Previously, under article 152 of the constitution, a member of Parliament had the right to use the English language if he wished, the main purpose being to accommodate the members from Sabah and Sarawak who were less likely to be fluent in Malay. The

Speaker continues to show tolerance to members from these states although he is likely to refuse permission to a member who is known to be fluent in Malay. It is also unlikely that he would allow an entire speech to be delivered in English. There are occasions when the use of English is necessary in order to deal with a technical issue and in such cases the Speaker can be expected to allow reasonable flexibility.

The Speaker is chairman of four committees, these being the Committee of Selection which is responsible for the nomination of members to committees;[44] the Standing Orders Committee, which is concerned with procedure and all matters relating to the standing orders;[45] the House Committee, which deals with services and amenities and matters affecting the comfort and convenience of members;[46] and the Committee of Privileges.[47] As chairman of the Standing Orders Committee the Speaker plays a prominent role in the area of procedure and does not hesitate to take the initiative in proposing procedural changes. Cases of privilege are very rarely raised in the Malaysian Parliament but if such a matter were to come before the Committee of Privileges, the Speaker might be expected to play a leading role in determining the outcome. The standing order empowers the Speaker to refer a matter to the committee on his own initiative, and he would do so only if he were satisfied that a *prima facie* case had been established.

The Speaker is the head of the parliamentary administration and is co-chairman, together with the President of the Senate, of the Parliamentary Services Advisory Committee which includes government and opposition members of both Houses and representatives of the public service. The committee deals with hiring, promotion, and other matters affecting the personnel who serve Parliament. The Speaker is not directly involved in matters of day-to-day administration, these responsibilities being largely delegated to the Clerk of the House (Setiausaha).

Under article 58 of the constitution, the Speaker's salary, together with those of the Deputy Speaker and the President and Deputy President of the Senate, are charged directly to the Consolidated Fund. Article 68 provides the Senate with a delaying power respecting legislation similar to that of the House of Lords and, as in Great Britain, the Speaker is responsible for certifying money bills and for certifying that the provisions of this article have been complied with in the event that a bill is presented for the assent of the head of state without the consent of the Senate.

One constitutional provision has recently posed a problem for the Speaker. Article 52 provides that leave of absence may be granted to a member by resolution of the House. In 1961 this power was delegated by the House to the Speaker, but the present Speaker has been faced with a situation which has caused him to express reservations about the constitutional validity of this delegation. A cabinet minister was convicted of murder and condemned to death, but he retained his seat in the House pending an appeal, thereby creating the need for a leave of absence. There are precedents for granting leave of absence to members in custody although, following a constitutional amendment adopted in 1981, members granted leave of absence may no longer participate in the proceedings of the House by, for example, submitting notice of questions to ministers. This would appear to be an area where the authority of the Speaker requires clarification.

By the very nature of Malaysian politics, the opposition parties having virtually no muscle to flex, the Speaker is heavily reliant on the government and his political independence is accordingly limited. A Speaker who displeased the government would run the risk of being displaced although this has never happened. In the normal course of proceedings, during the question period and in debate, Speakers have been at pains to be fair to the opposition. Government members are just as likely to be called to order as members of the opposition, and a minister answering a question at great length runs the risk of being interrupted equally with the opposition member who embarks upon a lengthy supplementary. However, a Speaker who took an important initiative without assuring himself of the government's approval might find himself overruled. One Speaker changed the form of the prayer on his own initiative, only to find that the government would not endorse the change because it had not been considered by the Standing Orders Committee.

One Speaker, Tan Sri Datuk Syed Nasir bin Ismail, ordered the chairman of the Public Accounts Committee to desist from making public statements concerning certain evidence received by the committee. The House was in recess at the time and the committee had not made a report. The Speaker invoked Standing Order 85[48] as the justification for his intervention. Some commentators saw this initiative as an assertion of independence on the part of the Speaker as the protector of the privileges of the House. Others, however, took the view that he was under pressure to protect certain government ministers from the suggestion of scandal which the evidence in question had awakened. There is no means of telling which might have been the stronger motivation.

The robes worn by the Malaysian Speaker comprise a gown and the traditional Malayan headdress, the songkok. An embroidered ceremonial gown and songkok are worn for special occasions. A wig once formed part of the costume but this was abandoned in favour of the songkok by Tan Sri Datuk Nik Kamil bin Haji Mahmood. His successor, Tan Sri Datuk Syed Nasir bin Ismail, designed the ceremonial robe with its gold embroidered chrysanthemum pattern.

The Speakers of the State Parliaments are all members of their respective Houses. As at the federal level, the opposition in the State Parliaments is very weak and in some cases non-existent. At the time of writing the Kelantan Legislative Assembly is the only one with an opposition of any strength, while those of Pahang and Johore have no opposition at all. Although several parties are represented in the legislature of Sarawak (Council Negri) they all support the government and there is no opposition in the official sense. It is not surprising in these circumstances that the Speakers are government-oriented and feel that their main responsibility in regulating debate is to the government. There appears to be little attempt on the part of backbenchers to assert their independence so that the protection of the Chair is seldom sought and Speakers, for their part, are not faced with the challenges confronting those who preside over politically divided Houses. Speakers at the state level sometimes go on to become cabinet ministers and conversely they have occasionally been appointed from ministerial ranks. Thus, from every point of view, the Speaker's political detachment is hardly an issue.

A conference of Malaysian Speakers is held annually, the fifteenth conference having taken place in Sarawak in 1983. The Speaker of Dewan Rakyat is the permanent chairman of the conference and the Clerk is its secretary-general. It was agreed at the 1981 conference held in Perlis that the Speakers should seek to promote uniformity in the procedure and standing orders of all the legislatures of Malaysia. Progress towards this goal was made at the 1982 conference in Johore and it appears that the state legislatures are content to accept federal leadership in this area.

Singapore first acquired a Legislative Council in 1946 while still a colony, the Governor being its presiding officer. A Legislative Assembly with a majority of elected members was established in 1955 and a Speaker was appointed for the first time. In 1959 Singapore became internally self-governing and the Legislative Assembly a fully elected body. From 1963 to 1965 Singapore was a constituent state of the Federation of Malaysia, and following its secession from the Federation it became an independent republic within the Commonwealth with a Parliament which since 1981 has consisted of 75 members.

Under article 40(2) of the constitution the Speaker may be chosen from among the members or from outside Parliament, but in the latter case he must have the qualifications required by a member of Parliament. Article 42(2) makes similar provision for the Deputy Speaker who, in contrast to the practice in most other Commonwealth Parliaments, may also be a non-member. Articles 41 and 42(3) respectively provide that the salaries of the Speaker and Deputy Speaker are charged to the Consolidated Fund and may not be diminished during their term of office. Article 57 provides that a Speaker elected from outside the House shall have no vote but that if he represents a constituency he shall have an original vote but no casting vote, this being another interesting departure from the practice usually found elsewhere. The same provisions apply to the Deputy Speaker and to any other member who may preside over the House. In the event of an equality of votes the motion is lost.

The first Speaker, Sir George Oehlers, held office from 1955 to 1963. He was appointed to the Chair in the first instance, continued in office after the dissolution of the first Legislative Assembly in 1959 and elected by the House in 1960, although he did not represent a constituency. He was succeeded in 1963 by Mr. E. W. Barker, an elected member, who resigned in 1964 to become a minister. His successor, Mr. A. P. Rajah, was not a member of the assembly at the time of his election as Speaker, having been defeated in his constituency in 1963. He served until 1966 when he was appointed High Commissioner to the United Kingdom. He was followed by the Deputy Speaker, Mr. Punch Coomaraswamy, a non-member who remained in office until 1970. He too entered the diplomatic field, serving subsequently as High Commissioner to India and Australia and Ambassador to Washington. The present Speaker, Dr. Yeoh Ghim Seng, has represented a constituency ever since he was elected Deputy Speaker in 1968. He succeeded Speaker Coomaraswamy in 1970 and is a medical doctor, the first non-lawyer to become Speaker of the Parliament of Singapore.

Although not a one-party state, the governing party in Singapore is all-powerful and opposition parties command very little support. Between 1968 and 1981 no opposition member succeeded in gaining election to Parliament, but in 1981 a candidate opposing the government managed to win a seat at a by-election. The Speaker's seat is nearly always contested at a general election, but the opposition virtually disappears between elections and the Speaker encounters no problems in maintaining contact with his electors and looking after the interests of his constituency. During an electoral campaign the Speaker deals with local issues and tries to avoid political confrontations. However, opposition candidates tend to fight intensely political campaigns and do not refrain from personal attacks simply because their opponent happens to be the Speaker.

No speaker has ever faced a contest in the House at the time of his election to the Chair, but in such an event a secret ballot would take place. A detailed procedure is prescribed by standing order[49] and if three or more candidates are nominated the balloting continues until one emerges with an overall majority. The Deputy Speaker would be elected in like manner in the event of a contest.[50]

A number of the Speaker's powers are comparable to those of his British counterpart, including those relating to order and discipline. Like the Malaysian Speaker, he can call a member to order for irrelevance and tedious repetition and, if necessary, direct him to discontinue his speech;[51] order a member whose conduct is grossly disorderly to withdraw for the remainder of the day's sitting;[52] 'name' a member whose conduct warrants a severer sanction;[53] and adjourn Parliament or suspend the sitting in the case of grave disorder.[54] His powers relating to closure,[55] the rule of anticipation,[56] emergency adjournment debates,[57] personal explanations,[58] the allowance of dilatory mentions,[59] and urgent questions asked without notice[60] closely resemble those of the British Speaker. His rulings are not subject to appeal but may be reviewed by way of a substantive motion of which two days notice is required.[61]

The Speaker presides in committee of the whole Parliament as well as in the House, and between 1970 and 1972 when the office of Deputy Speaker was left vacant the Speaker himself occupied the Chair for more than 80% of the time during which Parliament sat. Fortunately for the Speaker's endurance, Parliament only sits on average for about 25 days of the year, although committees continue to sit while Parliament is in recess. As in the British House of Commons, a half-hour debate takes place on the adjournment motion at the end of each day's sitting, the opportunity to raise a matter being 'allotted to one Member only for each sitting day, if necessary by ballot, under the direction of the Speaker.'[62] The Speaker normally remains in the Chair himself for the adjournment debate.

Singapore has four official languages, English, Malay, Mandarin and Tamil, and a member may speak in Parliament in any one of these languages.

The majority of members use the English language and Hansard is published only in English. In an interview he gave the author, Speaker Yeoh Ghim Seng referred to a problem for the Chair to which a multiplicity of languages can give rise. An unparliamentary expression when delivered in one language may prove to be perfectly acceptable in translation, and the monitoring of speeches in the interests of maintaining order becomes somewhat complicated when four languages are in use. Speaker Yeoh's approach is to monitor all speeches in the English language, as it is for all practical purposes the common language of Singapore and the most widely used language in Parliament. The Chair is not expected to be conversant with all four official languages and is therefore reliant on the translation when following a speech delivered in a language which he does not understand. Translation can vary nuances of meaning and substitute parliamentary for unparliamentary language and vice versa, with the result that the application of uniform standards becomes difficult in these circumstances.

As in Malaysia, the Speaker is chairman of the Committee of Selection, the Standing Orders Committee, the House Committee and the Committee of Privileges, these committees having functions comparable to those of their Malaysian counterparts. He also chairs the Public Petitions Committee and appoints the chairmen of the Public Accounts Committee and the Estimates Committee.[63] A select committee elects its own chairman but it may, if it chooses, elect the Speaker as its chairman whether or not he is a member of the committee.[64] The establishment of a Committee of Privileges was originally suggested by Speaker Oehlers and the proposal was considered and recommended by the Standing Orders Committee. Most matters considered by the latter committee are referred to it by resolution of the House, but the Speaker will sometimes take the initiative, following consultation with the Leader of the House, in suggesting procedural reforms that the committee might consider.

A Speaker who presides over a Parliament in which there is little or no opposition obviously leads a very different parliamentary life from that of the Speaker of a House where opposition parties are strongly represented. The only period when Singaporean Speakers experienced a difficult time was between 1963 and 1965 when the radical Barisan Socialist Party was represented in Parliament. Their obstructive tactics led to the introduction of fixed hours of sitting. Since their disappearance from Singapore's political scene, the Speaker's life has been relatively peaceful. Speaker Yeoh informed the author that while he is strict in his control of the question period and his application of the rule of relevance, he leans over backward to protect the lone opposition member. Clearly, without some special consideration this member's voice would scarcely be heard; thus, he probably appears to other members to enjoy a privileged status. But it is the duty of the Chair to protect minorities, and to have regard for the intimidating isolation of a member who is a minority of one in a Parliament of 75. Fortunately there is ample time to accommodate all members who wish to speak as the Parliament of Singapore does not face the time pressures encountered in some Parliaments.

Singapore's Speakers have seldom faced challenges to their rulings, but in

1960 a complex procedural situation arose in which a decision of the Chair was questioned. The sequence of events began with an attempt by the Deputy Prime Minister to move without notice a motion to condemn another member for dishonourable conduct and suspend him from the service of the House. Speaker Oehlers ruled that the motion required notice and that, since it contained two distinct propositions, it should be divided. The member against whom the motion was directed claimed, for his part, that it was out of order and gave notice of the following motion: 'That the ruling of the Speaker admitting the motion of the Deputy Prime Minister in regard to the Member for Hong Lim be rescinded and that this Assembly has no jurisdiction to deal with the matters raised therein.' The motion was defeated and the member for Hong Lim resigned his seat before the Deputy Prime Minister's motion could be disposed of.*

Certain responsibilities are vested in the Speaker under the constitution. Should the President or Vice-President resign they do so in writing to the Speaker.[65] If the President is unable to discharge his functions owing to absence, illness or other cause the cabinet may appoint the Vice-President or any other suitably qualified person to act in his place. On at least one occasion the Speaker has been appointed acting President. Speaker Coomaraswamy acted in this capacity for two months in 1968 between a dissolution of Parliament and the election of a new one.[66] The constitution provides for a Presidential Council for Minority Rights, one of whose functions is to draw attention to any legislation which, in the opinion of the Council, is a differentiating measure. In these circumstances a number of specific duties devolve upon the Speaker. He must send an authenticated copy of the bill to the Council before it is presented for the President's assent. He receives the Council's report on the measure, and if it is amended by Parliament as the result of the report, he must send a copy of the amended bill to the Council. The constitution details the procedure to be followed in the case of such bills and the Speaker must certify that these provisions have been complied with before such a bill is presented to the President for assent. The provisions do not apply to money bills and the Speaker is required to certify, in the case of such a bill, that it conforms to the constitutional definition of a money bill. Parliament itself has the right to refer a matter to the consideration of the Council, in which case the reference is made by the Speaker.[67]

The staff of Parliament are not independent of the public service, but the constitution provides that they shall not be eligible for promotion or transfer without the consent of the Speaker.[68] The Clerk of Parliament is appointed by the President after consultation with the Speaker and the Public Service Commission.[69] If he resigns he does so in writing to the Speaker, and he

---

* See Loke Weng Chee, Singapore: Motion for the condemnation and suspension of a member, and its sequels, The Table, Volume XXX for 1961, pages 80–94, for a detailed account of this incident. A motion of condemnation was subsequently adopted by the assembly after a Commission of Inquiry had examined and reported on the member's conduct. The member concerned was re-elected at a by-election and no further move was made to suspend him.

cannot be removed from office except by a two-thirds majority resolution of Parliament or by the President following consultation with the Speaker.[70] The terms of service of parliamentary staff are determined by Parliament on the advice of a commission consisting of the Speaker as chairman, not more than three ministers and a member of the Public Service Commission. In matters of day-to-day administration the Speaker's responsibilities are almost entirely delegated. The Clerk is responsible for the parliamentary administration and he reports to the Speaker.

The Speaker's constume is relatively simple on most occasions. At the opening of Parliament he wears a full-bottomed wig and gown. When presiding over the House he discards the wig and wears the gown over a dark suit.

Notes to Chapter Nine: The Speakership in Sri Lanka, Malaysia, and Singapore

1. See The Table, vol. XXVI for 1957, page 148.
2. See Journal of the Parliaments of the Commonwealth, volume 43, 1962, page 166.
3. See J. R. Jayewardene, Sri Lanka's New Constitution, The Parliamentarian, vol. LX, no. 1, January 1979, pages 1—4.
4. Constitution of Sri Lanka, Articles 79 and 80.
5. Ibid., Article 38 (1) (b).
6. Ibid., Article 37.
7. Ibid., Article 38 (2).
8. Ibid., Article 129 (2).
9. Standing Orders of the Parliament of the Democratic Socialist Republic of Sri Lanka, Standing Order 4.
10. Ibid., Standing Order 41 (1).
11. Ibid., Standing Order 16.
12. Ibid., Standing Order 43.
13. Ibid., Standing Order 17.
14. Ibid., Standing Order 72 (1).
15. Ibid., Standing Order 72 (4).
16. Ibid., Standing Order 73.
17. Ibid., Standing Orders 74 and 76.
18. Ibid., Standing Order 139.
19. Ibid., Standing Order 87.
20. Ibid., Standing Order 139.
21. Ibid., Standing Order 97.
22. Ibid., Standing Orders 121, 122, 123, 124 and 128.
23. Ibid., Standing Order 124.
24. See The Parliamentarian, vol. LIX, no. 3, July 1978, pages 198—199.
25. Ibid., vol. LXI, no. 4, October 1980, pages 276—277.
26. Ibid., vol. LIV, no. 2, April 1973, pages 96—99.
27. Ibid., vol. XLVII, no. 2, April 1966, pages 168—169.
28. Standing Orders of the Dewan Rakyat, 1981, Standing Order 45 (1).
29. See speech of Tan Sri Datuk Syed Nasir bin Ismail, Report of Sixth Conference

of Commonwealth Speakers and Presiding Officers, op. cit., pages 48–49.
30. Standing Orders of the Dewan Rakyat, 1981, Standing Orders 43 and 99.
31. Ibid., Standing Order 44.
32. Ibid., Standing Order 40.
33. Ibid., Standing Order 18.
34. Ibid., Standing Order 22 (1).
35. Ibid., Standing Order 25.
36. Ibid., Standing Order 17 (2).
37. Ibid., Standing Order 19 (1) (d).
38. Ibid., Standing Order 23 (2).
39. Ibid., Standing Order 35 (8).
40. See for example Standing Orders 66 (6) (a) and 67 (7) (a).
41. Ibid., Standing Order 36 (11).
42. Ibid., Standing Order 24 (2).
43. Ibid., Standing Order 90.
44. Ibid., Standing Order 76.
45. Ibid., Standing Order 78.
46. Ibid., Standing Order 79.
47. Ibid., Standing Order 80.
48. Standing Order 85 reads as follows:

> 'The evidence taken before any Select Committee and any documents presented to such Committee shall not be published by any member of such Committee, or by any other person, before the Committee has presented its Report to the House.'

49. Standing Orders of the Parliament of Singapore, 1970, Standing Order 11.
50. Ibid., Standing Order 16.
51. Ibid., Standing Order 54.
52. Ibid., Standing Order 55.
53. Ibid., Standing Order 56.
54. Ibid., Standing Order 58.
55. Ibid., Standing Order 51.
56. Ibid., Standing Order 50 (3).
57. Ibid., Standing Order 22.
58. Ibid., Standing Order 23.
59. Ibid., Standing Order 25 (3).
60. Ibid., Standing Order 19 (1).
61. Ibid., Standing Order 53.
62. Ibid., Standing Order 1 (8) (d).
63. Provision is made for all these committees by Standing Order 95.
64. Ibid., Standing Order 96 (2).
65. Constitution of Singapore, Articles 17 (3) and 23 (3).
66. See Report of the Conference of Speakers and Presiding Officers of Commonwealth Parliaments, 1969, op. cit., page 120.
67. Part VII of the constitution, articles 68 to 92, deals with the Presidential Council for Minority Rights.
68. Ibid., Article 51 (5).
69. Ibid., Article 51 (2).
70. Ibid., Articles 51 (3) and (4).

Chapter Ten

The Speakership in the Smaller Nations of the Commonwealth

Over the past 25 years the Commonwealth has been significantly expanded by the emergence of a large number of small countries in the Carribbean, Pacific and Mediterranean regions as equal and independent partners in the great family of nations. The majority of these countries are islands, in some cases collections of islands, the only two exceptions being Guyana and Belize which are situated respectively on the South and Central American mainland. In most of these countries the constitution adopted at the time of independence was the result of a process of constitutional evolution which reflected the increasing degree of autonomy which developed during the pre-independence period. The institutions of government were strongly influenced by the British system. The speakership was, in most cases, modelled on the British pattern, and the assumption that this was an appropriate example to follow does not seem to have been seriously questioned. It was an assumption which ignored local political realities and failed to anticipate the pressures to which the office was likely to be exposed. In some countries these pressures have been softened by a provision that the Speaker does not necessarily have to be a member of the House over which he presides.

The option of selecting a Speaker from inside or outside Parliament is provided in the constitutions of Malta, Trinidad and Tobago, Guyana, Dominica, St. Lucia, St. Vincent, Belize and the Cook Islands.* The constitution of Kiribati (formerly the Gilbert Islands) specifies that the Speaker must be a non-member. The constitutions of the Solomon Islands and Vanuatu (formerly the New Hebrides) are not specific on the point and one assumes from the wording of the relevant article that the Speaker may be chosen from either inside or outside Parliament. In Tonga the Speaker is appointed by the King.

In Cyprus, where it is less easy to make comparisons because the Westminster model has not been followed, the constitution requires that the President of the House of Representatives be a Greek and the Vice-President a Turk. No mention is made of whether or not they should be members of the House, but in practice the President has always been a member and an active

---

* The Cook Islands, although not fully sovereign in strict constitutional terms, have a special relationship with New Zealand and are for most practical purposes independent.

politician. The division of the island and the resultant political situation has rendered the constitution inoperative from the point of view of Turkish participation but the Greek-Cypriot government is conducting its affairs and holding elections as though the Turks were not in occupation of the northern half of the island.

Among other countries where the Speaker is always a member of the House, either by constitutional requirement or by practice, are Jamaica, Barbados, Bahamas, Fiji, Papua New Guinea, Western Samoa, Nauru, Tuvalu (formerly the Ellice Islands), and Bermuda (which at the time of writing is not fully independent).

There are various reasons why the Speakers in the Parliaments of these small countries find it difficult to detach themselves from party politics. They are usually closely committed to the governing party and the speakership is likely to be regarded as a prize for the victors. In a small assembly where the government has a narrow majority the latter may find itself dependent on the Speaker's casting vote* and the Speaker's political support might well be one of the conditions of appointment. The decisions forced on a Speaker in a small House are likely to involve greater pressures than in a larger assembly where the occupant of the Chair might be able to take a more detached position. Given the political circumstances of the Caribbean countries, where political divisions are often deep and bitter, the Speaker is likely to face a difficult task in pursuing the Westminster path. However good his intentions may be he may not always find it possible to be impartial, and however much he strives he is unlikely to convince everyone of his impartiality. As the holder of one of the plum jobs he must expect to be, like other holders of high office, a target of abuse and resentment. In certain other countries, notably those where the ethnic composition is largely Polynesian, it has been held by some that the party system is unsuited to local traditions and customs. In a tradition-oriented society, such as Western Samoa for example, an individual's prestige is likely to depend more on his standing in the community than on his occupation of the office of Speaker. The substitution of party government for government by consensus has imposed strains, not only on the speakership, but on the entire political structure of these countries.

In those Parliaments where the Speaker is a member of the House there are constituency pressures to contend with. All members in these small countries are close to their constituents, and if the Speaker represents a constituency he will be expected to be no less active than his colleagues in looking after its interests. If he were to abstain, in the interests of impartiality, from taking up issues of importance to his community, he could expect little appreciation from his electors. His contacts with those he represents is likely to be a very personal one. Speaking at a conference in 1978 Speaker Darling of the Bahamas House of Assembly commented:

Politics in the larger countries tend to be rather impersonal when

---

* Although there are some jurisdictions where the Speaker is not equipped with a casting vote.

compared with the politics in the Caribbean, which are very personalised. One knows one's constituents. One knows them very well. One attends funerals and all sorts of social parties and gatherings and it is virtually impossible for a Speaker under our system, once elected by his constituents, to divorce himself totally from active political participation.[1]

Speakers who are elected members are therefore obliged to conduct political campaigns during general elections and this is hardly likely to inspire confidence in their impartiality.

The constitutions of some countries impose duties on the Speaker which require him to rise above his political associations. For example, in Papua New Guinea, the Solomon Islands, Vanuatu, Dominica and, in certain circumstances, Tuvalu the Speaker acts for the head of state in the absence or incapacity of the latter. In Trinidad and Tobago the President of the Senate or the Speaker, in that order, may act for the head of state. The constitution of Cyprus provides that the President of the House of Representatives may act for the President of the Republic. This and the other reasons outlined above have all been cited by various commentators in justification of the principle that the Speaker in small assemblies should be chosen from outside Parliament.[2]

Although this has not been adopted as the universal solution, the practice of choosing a non-member as Speaker is fairly widespread, Speaking at a conference in 1966 Speaker Thomasos of Trinidad and Tobago stated:

> In my opinion it is an urgent necessity that the Speakers of the Commonwealth should cooperate in establishing an image of the Speakership in the tradition of a judge. The main function of a Speakers' Conference is to help bring this about. I myself have taken an active part in my own country in trying to establish this principle and I believe that the Speaker should take the initiative in promoting this idea. I have spoken in public on the role of a Speaker in a democratic society and been widely and favourably reported in the Press. I have taken the line that a Speaker should dissociate himself from politics; that he should be above party; that he should not be the nominee of any one party. He is elected by the House as a whole, and once elected should immediately cease to take any interest in party affairs.[3]

One of the longest serving Speakers in the Commonwealth, Speaker Thomasos was already Speaker when Trinidad and Tobago became independent in 1962. At that time he was an elected member of the House but he was subsequently and continuously re-elected as a non-member until his retirement in 1981. He thus succeeded in setting a precedent for the continuity of the speakership in his Parliament. He was succeeded by Mr. Matthew Ramcharan, a former diplomat, who, lacking the extensive parliamentary experience of Speaker Thomasos, inherited a difficult task. In Trinidad and Tobago the same party has been continually in power for many years and this has engendered in the opposition an attitude of bitterness and a lack of will to co-operate. The new Speaker was immediately regarded as the government's man; his rulings were seen as partisan, and he had difficulty in winning the opposition's confidence. This was no reflection on the capacity of Speaker Ramcharan who faced the problem of any newcomer following in the footsteps of one whose prestige and authority were based on many years tenure and experience.

In Guyana also a tradition of continuity seems to be developing, the present Speaker, Mr. Sase Narain, having been in office since 1971. Speakers in Guyana have not usually been openly affiliated with any political party, although this has not prevented the opposition on occasion from proposing a candidate of their own and thus forcing a contest. According to a former Speaker, Mr. R. B. Gajraj, there was at one time a tendency on the part of the politicians in power to regard the Speaker as the servant of the ruling party. The Chair, through the exercise of its influence and authority, apparently succeeded in changing this concept.[4]

St. Lucia and Dominica are among other Caribbean countries which may elect their Speakers from outside the House. Speaker St. Clair-Daniel of the St. Lucia House of Assembly held office from 1967 to 1979 and returned to the Chair in 1982. He has gained a reputation for impartiality and faithful adherence to Westminster practice which is probably unsurpassed in the smaller countries of the Commonwealth. This nevertheless did not prevent his being replaced as a result of a change of government in 1979. Mr. Clarence Rambally and Mr. Donald Alcee were his successors in the period from 1979 to 1982. In Dominica the speakership has had a rather chequered history. In 1978, when the country became independent, Mr. Fred Degazon was Speaker of the House of Assembly. He was a controversial Speaker against whom the opposition had directed a motion of no confidence. In spite of this he was elected President of the Republic shortly afterwards by the government majority in the House of Assembly. In 1979, while still head of state, he left the country during a political crisis which led to the downfall of the government. His successor in the Chair, Mr. Pershing Waldron, was also caught up in the turmoil and he resigned as Speaker while the crisis was at its height. He was succeeded by Mr. Eden A. Bowers following the formation of a new government. Following a further change of government resulting from a general election in 1980 another new Speaker, Mrs. Marie Davis-Pierre, was elected and with her accession to the Chair its foundations appear to have stabilized. Mrs. Marie Davis-Pierre is a former Clerk of the House and one of the Commonwealth's few women presiding officers. She was chosen unanimously by the House of Assembly because of her experience as Clerk and her knowledge of parliamentary practice and procedure enable her to preside with confidence. Those consulted by the author have acknowledged her fairness and impartiality and have stated that the manner of her appointment did much to promote the independence of the Chair. She is greatly respected and, while firm in her control of the House, is always ready to offer a guiding hand rather than rely too heavily on the imposition of her authority.

Not all Speakers have enjoyed a similar success. The Bahamas, a country with a long-standing parliamentary tradition, provides an example of the dangers which beset a Speaker who decides to take a politically independent course. Until 1967 the reins of government were largely in the hands of the white population. The general election of that year produced a change of government by a narrow majority, the party supported by the majority of the black population gaining power for the first time. The Speaker in the previous Parliament, Mr. R. H. Symonette, was among the defeated candidates. He was succeeded by Mr. A. R. Braynen who had been Deputy Speaker, thus introducing an element of continuity following the change of government, and Mr. Arlington Butler became the new Deputy Speaker. In 1972 Speaker Braynen was defeated at a general election after 37 years as a member of the House of Assembly and Mr. Butler succeeded him as Speaker. Shortly afterwards Speaker Butler placed on record his view 'that a Speaker can retain party membership without party involvement and at the same time remain as an impartial Speaker.' Describing his own case he said: 'I was an elected member; I came in as a party member. I had served as chairman of my own particular political party. When elected, I decided at that time to resign the party whip. I continued to retain party membership of a sort. I have no party involvement at this time, even at the constituency level.'[5]

Later Speaker Butler broke with his own party over the question of disclosure of members' interests and as a result he failed to secure his party's nomination at the following election. He decided to run as an independent, presenting himself as the Speaker seeking re-election in accordance with the British practice. He failed dismally, coming at the bottom of the poll with only a very few votes. This was a powerful demonstration by his electorate of how they saw their priorities. Happening as it did in a country with long experience of parliamentary government, it suggests quite forcefully that the Westminster model is not suitable for export in all its aspects even to countries which are not strangers to British parliamentary tradition. Speaker Butler was succeeded in 1977 by Sir Clifford Darling.

Jamaica and Barbados are also countries where the Speaker is elected from among the membership of the House. Both have deeply-rooted parliamentary traditions and the speakership in both countries has an honourable record of striving to maintain its impartiality in circumstances which are far from easy. Total political detachment is impossible because the Speaker has to get elected like every other member. Close personal contact with his constituency is an element essential to success and he is obliged to fight a campaign on behalf of his party because his opponents are likely to attack him on a party basis. One Jamaican commentator, while acknowledging the generally excellent record of Jamaican Speakers, offered the comment that they tended to become somewhat partisan as a general election approached. Oppositions in Jamaica are inclined to harass and provoke the Chair as a part of their strategy. They will pursue spurious points of order, forcing the Speaker to rule against them, and thus appear partisan. Jamaican Speakers have nevertheless succeeded in surmounting these challenges to their authority. A member of the present Jamaican government, who was in opposition prior to the general election of 1980, spoke very highly to the author of the qualities of Speaker Ripton Macpherson, who held the office from 1972 to 1980, and of his predecessors Speakers Parkinson and Golding. This tribute from a political opponent has been endorsed by other commentators. Given the political circumstances in Jamiaca, a change of government involves a change of Speaker. Speaker Macpherson did not stand for re-election in 1980 but had he done so and won his seat it is highly unlikely that he would again have been chosen as Speaker by the new government majority, in spite of the esteem in which he was held. He was succeeded by Speaker Talbert Forrest, who would probably be the first to acknowledge the strength which a Speaker derives from inheriting a sound tradition. He himself was the target of a vicious verbal attack on 28 July 1981 by a member who was subsequently suspended for the remainder of the session.[6] The incident illustrates the bitter intensity of feeling which frequently colours Jamaican politics.

In a speech he made at a conference in 1978 Speaker Macpherson recorded some observations which shed an interesting light on his own approach to the duties of the Chair. He questioned whether a member's parliamentary immunity should extend so far as to protect him if he wantonly defames individuals or companies under the cloak of privilege.

> I wonder whether there is not a sort of reciprocal privilege to the people so that any Member who abuses privilege in this way could be said to be in breach of privilege and brought before the Committee of Privileges of the House. I am in no doubt that if this privilege is wantonly abused the House will, in due course, find itself in disrepute in the community.[7]

He also suggested that the Speaker should have a role to play in situations where the government withholds information from Parliament without any apparently good reason.

> I question the right of the Executive to decide unilaterally that the representatives of the people have no right to certain information. I think it is the duty and prerogative of the Speaker to decide whether Parliament has a right to receive that information.[8]

In Barbados, as in Jamaica, the Speaker fights an election campaign and has always been chosen from the government side of the House. Sir Arnott Cato, the President of the Senate, expressed the view to the author that, although it has never happened, it is not inconceivable that a well-regarded Speaker might be returned to the Chair following a change of government. The speakership in Barbados can also boast a record of impartiality and Speakers are usually elected to the Chair without a contest. However, the present Speaker, Mr. W. C. B. Hinds, faced an opponent when re-elected to the Chair in 1981, having fallen foul of the opposition in the previous Parliament as the result of a motion of no confidence which had been moved against him. The opposition in the new Parliament used the occasion of the Speaker's election to express what they believed to be their grievances against Speaker

Hinds, who has the reputation of being tough in his control of the House. However, according to those consulted by the author he is just as tough with government as with opposition members.

Like Speaker Darling of the Bahamas, Speaker Hinds has spoken of the close personalised contact which the Speaker must maintain with his constituents and of the need for him to retain his political associations. he stressed, however, that since his election as Speaker he had refrained from attending his party's caucuses. He did not, as some of his fellow Speakers have done, advocate the system of selecting the Speaker from outside parliament.[9] At a previous conference one of his predecessors, Sir Theodore Brancker, spoke strongly in favour of the principle that the Speaker should represent a constituency.[10]

On the other side of the world from the Caribbean is another group of island nations completely different in character. The Caribbean countries of the Commonwealth have a parliamentary tradition extending back to the old colonial period. The parliamentary system is a relatively recent import to the Commonwealth countries of the Pacific region and the process of adapting it to their social and political structures is still continuing. The operation of the modern parliamentary system depends in large measure on the participation of organized political parties, which vie with each other in an electoral battle to obtain power. Reference has already been made to the incompatibility of this system with the long-standing customs of some of the Pacific nations. In Western Samoa, for example, society is based on close family relationships, decisions in the interests of the community are traditionally arrived at through consultation and consensus, and the dissension and bitterness which normally characterise party politics are alien to the nature of the people. The introduction of the Parliamentary system thus underlined a clear need to integrate parliamentary practices with the requirements of local custom and tradition.

Western Samoa became independent in 1962 and a full member of the Commonwealth in 1970. It has an unusual electoral system whereby, except in the case of two special constituencies, the vote and membership of Parliament are limited to the *matais*, who are the representatives of families chosen by the family communities as their political spokesmen. A *matai*, who can be either a man or woman, is not necessarily the senior member of the family. He or she speaks for the family as a whole, casts a single vote on behalf of the whole family and will take his or her place in the hierarchy of matais according to the rank or dignity to which the particular individual is entitled. Holders of high office, such as the Prime Minister or Speaker, are not necessarily of the highest rank. Of the 47 members of the Legislative Assembly, 45 are matais. The remaining two are elected by registered citizens who are not of Samoan origin.

In the context of Western Samoan politics the party system is something of an innovation and until recently it existed only in rudimentary form. The adoption of the parliamentary system led to a measure of party organization among the members of the Legislative Assembly on the basis that a party is needed to support the government in the face of those members who are ranged in opposition to it. The general election of 1982 was won by the Human Rights Protection Party with a majority of one. The previous Speaker lost his seat and a new Speaker, Leulumoega Sofara Nonumalo, was elected from among the party members. He was formerly Clerk Assistant of the Legislative Assembly and thus another of the small group of Commonwealth Speakers who have brought to the Chair an expertise acquired at the Table. Shortly after the general election the Prime Minister and another minister lost their seats as the result of a judicial decision. However, they regained their seats at by-elections and the Human Rights Protection Party remained in power, the former Deputy Prime Minister becoming Prime Minister. When the party temporarily lost its majority Speaker Nonumalo was requested to resign but refused to do so.

The present Speaker's predecessor, Tu'u'u Faleto'ese, was elected to the Chair before the party system had crystallised. He saw his role as that of an impartial arbiter, but as members have become more politically oriented those in the opposition have sometimes questioned his impartiality. Most commentators consulted by the author agreed that Western Samoan Speakers took great pains to preserve a position of detachment, but the office is still in the process of adapting to the evolving political circumstances, and the exercise of the Speaker's authority is sometimes seen as an expression of bias. One particularly strong critic of a former Speaker was said to be a consistent breaker of the rules whom the Speaker was continually obliged to call to order.

Speaker Tu'u'u Faleto'ese, explained to the author that he never hesitated to apply what he described as 'customary methods' in his interpretation of the standing orders. He was flexible in his control of the House, seeking to reach decisions by consensus, and falling back on the standing orders only when he felt a sterner discipline was needed. The Speaker thus attempts to guide debate and act as a mediator who seeks to steer the House away from the built-in potential for conflict between parliamentary practice and the conventions of Samoan society. Whether the successful integration of the two systems can be brought to fruition remains to be seen. What can be stated is that the Speaker has a particularly crucial role to play in the process and his position is regarded as one of special prestige.

One of the Pacific countries where the party system has been seen to have a detrimental effect on political behaviour is the Cook Islands, and this was dramatically reflected in an incident concerning Speaker Marguerite Storey. Sister of a former Prime Minister, her position was compromised by her close identification with the governing party and the nepotism so blatantly practiced by the politicians in control at the time. She eventually fell victim to a scandal which led to the dismissal of a government by judicial process and her own subsequent removal from office after thirteen years as Speaker.

Following the general election of 1978 a number of results were declared invalid by reason of corrupt practices. The Prime Minister himself was tried and convicted on various charges of corruption and the effect of overturning the election results in a number of constituencies was to give the victory to the party which had been in opposition. The Speaker, who is not required by the constitution to be a member of the House, had been elected to the Chair at the outset of the Parliament and was expected to resign after the change in the election results gave the majority to the other party. However, she claimed that, having been properly elected, she was under no obligation to resign. The House then proceeded to adopt a motion of no confidence in her but, amazingly, she still refused to resign. The new government then decided to proceed by way of a constitutional amendment and, having a two-thirds majority in the House, it was able to carry a bill providing that a Speaker against whom a motion of no confidence was carried would be obliged to resign. The matter was afterwards taken to court, where the right of Parliament to dismiss a Speaker in these circumstances was upheld, but Mrs. Storey resigned before the judgment was rendered.

It would be difficult to conceive of a sequence of events more damaging to the prestige and authority of the speakership than these. Mrs. Storey's successor came to the Chair under the shadow of this incident and apparently ran into difficulties in the enforcement of his authority. There was a feeling on the government side of the House that he was too lenient with the opposition, but he was undoubtedly trying, by allowing a reasonable latitude to the members of a demoralised and humiliated former governing party, to restore a measure of equilibrium to the political scene and to promote confidence in the Chair by demonstrating his fairness.

But this was not the end of Mrs. Storey's parliamentary career. In 1983 her party was returned to power and she was again called to the Chair. Furthermore, she found herself once again at the centre of a constitutional issue. The constitution of the Cook Islands provides that a Prime Minister must submit his government to a vote of confidence within seven days of the first meeting of Parliament following a general election. A tied vote was anticipated and the question arose as to whether the Speaker, being a non-elected member, was competent to exercise a casting vote on a constitutional issue. The matter was referred to the courts which ruled that she was not. In the event, she did not take the Chair when the vote was taken. Instead, the Clerk of the House was elected to preside over the proceedings and he was vested with the full powers of the Chair except, of course, the power to exercise a casting vote.

Nauru, a small country with a Parliament of only 18 members, has so far resisted any tendency to form political parties and all its members of Parliament are independents. The President of the Republic is elected by Parliament from among its members. He heads a cabinet consisting of not less than four and not more than five other ministers. The President, who has direct responsibility for certain government departments, attends Parliament where he speaks on behalf of the government and steers government business through the House. On these occasions, he is subject to the authority of the Speaker like any other member. The cabinet cannot always be sure that their measures will be supported by a majority in the House, and the Speaker, being an independent himself, is not in the position of having to maintain the balance between competing factions. It is no doubt easier in a very small Parliament to operate free of the restraints imposed by the party system. From the point of view of the Chair, the protection of the rights of individual members would probably be seen as the paramount duty. In the event of the resignation of the President of the Republic, the constitution provides that he should resign in writing to the Speaker.

The Parliament of Nauru is convened and prorogued by the Speaker on the advice of the President. However, should one-third or more of the total number of members representing at least three constituencies (members being elected by proportional representation) request that a session be held for a specified purpose, the Speaker must convene Parliament within 14 days. The duration of Parliament is three years, but should the President advise an earlier dissolution, the Speaker is required to refer such advice to Parliament within 14 days. Unless Parliament resolves that the President and his cabinet should be removed, the Speaker would dissolve Parliament seven days after the reference of the matter to Parliament. Following a dissolution of Parliament, a general election must be held within two months on a date determined by the Speaker in consultation with the President. A bill becomes law as soon as the Speaker certifies that it has been adopted by Parliament.[11]

One country in which political parties appear to flourish is Papua New Guinea. A former Speaker, Mr. Kingston Dibela, has commented: 'Papua New Guinea has found the Westminster system very relevant to the political situation in our country. Our people have always been politically inclined and seem to enjoy the contest for office.'[12] The Speaker himself is likely to be an active politician who conducts a political campaign like any other member. To quote Speaker Dibela once again:

> Firstly, the means of selection of the Speaker ensure that he must be politically involved. The Government of Papua New Guinea is presently a coalition, and the position of Speaker came under negotiation in the formation of the coalition. I think it would be correct to say that since 1968, when my distinguished predecessor, Sir John Guise, became Speaker, our Speakers have participated actively in politics. The only qualification I would add here is that some Speakers have practised politics more openly than others. Sir John Guise was a master at exerting pressure behind the scenes for development in his electorate. Many times he also resorted to speaking out publicly as John Guise, Member for Alotau, knowing full well, I believe, that his statements would be buttressed by the prestige of his position.[13]

In 1972 Sir John Guise became a minister and his successor, Speaker Kwan, was elected to the Chair by a one-vote majority over his opponent, Mr. Mathias Toliman. A subsequent Speaker, Mr. Barry Holloway, explained that there was great fluidity in the country's multi-party system, and made the following comments in relation to this contested elections:

> ... the Leader of the Opposition in the election for Speaker in 1972 when my predecessor was elected missed being elected Speaker by one vote. We have a secret exhaustive ballot to elect the Speaker. It is a secret

ballot and if there are more than two candidates then there are a succession of ballots until only two candidates remain and the one having a simple majority, which would be an absolute majority in this case, is elected as Speaker. On this occasion in 1972 the Leader of the Opposition agreed to be a candidate and missed out by one vote. It was quite obvious that in the succession of ballots that people had looked at who they really wanted as Speaker and crossed party lines, indicating that they did regard it as being a decision above party politics.[14]

Speaker Holloway was a very active and influential member of his party and went on to become Minister of Finance. He was Speaker when Papua New Guinea became fully independent in 1975. He was succeeded by Speaker Dibela who campaigned as an independent and, having no strong party ties, felt better able than his predecessors to withdraw to some extent from active politics once he was in occupation of the Chair. If he had any thoughts of promoting the continuity of the office, however, his attempt at political detachment was of no avail. Following the 1981 general election he was defeated in a context for the speakership by Mr. Sevese Morea.

During his tenure of office Speaker Dibela found himself in a conflict of interest situation because of his duty to act as Governor-General during the latter's absence. The problem he faced may be described in his own words:

> We share in Papua New Guinea a problem which I would imagine is common to most developing countries, and that is a shortage of skilled legislative drafting staff. Consequently, urgent legislation has often only been finally drafted immediately before the Government wished to introduce it, thus placing the Government in a position where it needed leave to have legislation proceed to the second reading stage — leave which could be denied by one dissenting voice. Members were becoming restive about the hasty and often ill-understood passage of legislation and it became more common for leave to be denied, thus dislocating the government's legislative program. In the end, the remedy the Government sought was to introduce the legislation under standing order 256 as an appropriation measure with a recommendation from the Governor-General. This is standard practice for appropriation measures in many of our countries, but I am sure delegates will realise that, by stretching the point, virtually any measure can be said to obtain appropriation clauses.
>
> Thus, when the Governor-General was absent overseas during a meeting of Parliament, I was placed in the compromised position of signing recommendations to Parliament, as Acting Governor-General. The situation was even more disconcerting when, after the Governor-General had returned, I was forced to read a message from myself, as Acting Governor-General, to myself as Speaker. These recommendations allowed through Parliament without notice and with no procedural hindrance Bills which were not true appropriation measures. This placed me in an embarrassing political situation, where the

impartiality of the Speaker was so clearly called into question. As a result, the Governor-General has given a written undertaking that he will not go overseas during meetings of Parliament.[15]

It is interesting to note that article 108(1) of the constitution of Papua New Guinea delineates the duties of the Speaker, stating that he is responsible 'for upholding the dignity of the Parliament, maintaining order in it, regulating its proceedings and administering its affairs, and for controlling the precincts of the Parliament as defined by or under an Act of the Parliament'.

Fiji is a country where the evolution of the speakership has been beset with problems of considerable complexity. As originally conceived it was oriented towards the practices of Westminster. It may be said to have originated in 1954, sixteen years prior to the attainment of independence, when the Governor, who presided over the Legislative Council, was authorized to appoint a Speaker to act on his behalf. The first two Speakers, Ratu Sir Lala Sukuna and Sir Maurice Scott, were appointed by virtue of this power in 1956 and 1958 respectively. Both were guided by the traditions of Westminster and faithfully observed the principle of political neutrality in the discharge of their duties. These assumptions were not questioned, but it later became clear that their acceptance should not so readily have been taken for granted. In the words of one expert commentator: 'Only gradually was the office exposed to the kinds of pressure with which it would have to come to terms once power was transferred to indigenous leadership.'[16]

A constitutional amendment of 1966 provided that the Legislative Council would henceforth elect a Speaker and Deputy Speaker from among its own ranks. Following the general election of that year Mr. Ronald Kermode, a member of the government party, was called to the Chair and the Deputy Speaker was elected from the opposition, both of them unanimously. In pursuit of the British tradition Speaker Kermode resigned from his party, hoping thereby to lay the foundation for the continuity of the office. He remained Speaker of the enlarged House of Representatives established at the time of independence, but with the first post-independence general election in 1972 his tenure of office came to an abrupt end. Having severed his connection with his party he was unable to secure its nomination in his constituency. He had hoped to be re-elected unchallenged as an independent, and since he had been a popular Speaker he probably had every reason to believe that this would be acceptable to both government and opposition. In the event no party proved willing to forego the opportunity of winning his seat for itself. He was thus left to ponder on the injustice of a situation which found him excluded from the House because of his honest attempt to promote a non-partisan speakership.

The governing party retained its majority following the general election and came to an agreement with the opposition that one of the latter's Members, Mr. R. D. Patel, who had been Deputy Speaker in the previous Parliament, should become Speaker. In accepting the nomination Mr. Patel made it clear that he would not resign from his party and would continue to attend its meetings.* It was not long before he became embroiled in a complex procedural dispute which greatly compromised his credibility as an impartial Speaker.

The details of this remarkable series of events have been admirably chronicled elsewhere[17] and it will suffice for the purposes of this study to give an abbreviated account. In 1973 the government introduced highly controversial legislation to regulate trade disputes which the opposition determined to delay by every means possible. On 4 April the Speaker upheld a claim by the opposition that the second reading of the bill could not be taken on the same day as the first reading. A motion to adjourn the House *sine die* having been defeated, the opposition then claimed that since all the business on the order paper for that day had been completed, the House was obliged to adjourn indefinitely. Although there was no procedural substance to this claim the Speaker, to everybody's surprise, upheld it and set in motion the somewhat farcical train of events which ensued. The members of the governing party decided to ignore the ruling and assembled in the chamber on the following day, but the Speaker forbade the officers of the House to attend the sitting and ordered that the mace be kept under lock and key. The Clerk, accompanied by the mace, did appear later in the day, having been formally summoned, after the Deputy Speaker had taken the Chair, but it was not until the following day that all members took their seats and some attempt was made to legitimize the proceedings. However, procedural wrangles continued and the Speaker twice adjourned the House on his own authority, exercising a power which the standing orders apparently conferred on him, although it is highly doubtful that he exercised it in the manner intended. The deadlock was broken following private negotiations in which the Prime Minister was involved. Speaker Patel announced his intention to stand down for a week and the debate on the trade disputes legislation, which came as something of an anti-climax, was disposed of during his absence with the Deputy Speaker in the Chair.

But the Government had no intention of letting the matter drop. In their view the Speaker, through his abuse of the rules of procedure, had allied himself with the opposition in its obstruction of important legislation. On 16 April the government moved a motion of no confidence in the Speaker, which the opposition had attempted to forestall by petitioning the Supreme Court for a ruling that the sitting of 5 April was unconstitutional. When the motion was moved it was claimed that the matter was *sub judice* because this writ had been issued, but the Deputy Speaker ruled that the court had no

---

* Although when he spoke at a conference in Zambia in 1973 he said: 'Quite frankly, why I kept my membership of the party was only with a view to keeping my options open. Though I have kept my membership of the party alive, I am not taking part in the parliamentary party meetings of my party. I am not taking part in the working committee of the party where the policy decisions of the party are made. I do not take part in their annual conventions, except to make a courtesy appearance for a few minutes. I only make an appearance without speaking a word at the convention'. See Verbatim Report of the Proceedings of the Third Conference of Commonwealth Speakers and presiding officers, op. cit., page 63.

jurisdiction over the internal affairs of the House. The petition was, in fact, subsequently dismissed on these grounds. The vote on the non-confidence motion was eventually adopted on 1 May by 21 votes to 15. However, the constitution required that the Speaker could only be removed by a two-thirds majority of the House, and Patel declined to resign. He continued in office until October 1975 when he resigned both the speakership and his parliamentary seat following a dispute with his own party.

He was succeeded by the Deputy Speaker, Mr. Vijay Singh, whose tenure of office demonstrated that he had a greater affinity for the task than his predecessor. He succeeded in upholding the dignity of the speakership although he had no illusions about the difficulties of doing so. Speaking at a conference in 1976 he observed; 'I do not see how responsibility for order or for the maintaining of dignity can repose solely in the hands of the Speaker because, if the members of the House are determined to bring about chaos and disorder, no Speaker will succeed.'[18] Nevertheless he apparently did succeed and he was subsequently knighted in recognition of his services.

Speaker Singh was succeeded in 1977 by Mr. Mosesa Qionibaravi who remained in office until 1982. He successfully maintained the political detachment of the Chair, adopting what one commentator described as a low key apporach to his task, and discharging his duties with unfailing tact and courtesy. An admirer of the Westminster concept of parliamentary government, he was nevertheless aware of the difficulties of adapting it to the needs of a country such as his own. Discussing this problem at a conference in 1978 he observed:

> Most of the territories that were formerly under British rule have adopted a Westminster-type government, but in doing so they have tried to take account of particular situations in their own countries. We in Fiji have a Constitution which has tried to ensure a balance of the various races in the country and also to ensure the representation of the minority. In certain parts of the Constitution we have tried to ensure that the interests of the indigenous people are protected.
>
> In adopting the Westminster type of government, we have inherited with it the adversary character of a parliamentary two-party system.
>
> . . . .
>
> A two-party system can tend to cause divisions. In countries such as mine such political division tends to fall largely along racial lines. It is therefore difficult to build a national consciousness.[19]

The problems referred to by Speaker Qionibaravi are compounded by the fact that Fiji has a complex electoral system involving three separate voters' rolls, one for Fijians, one for Indians and one for other races. It is designed to protect the representation of the indigenous population who form a minority of the population as a whole.

On 30 April 1982, the last day on which the House of Representatives met prior to the dissolution of Parliament, Speaker Qionibaravi in an address to the House expressed his thoughts on the role of the Speaker and also spoke of some of the measures he felt the House should take to improve its effectiveness. He suggested that the House should expand its committee system, that Parliament should enjoy financial autonomy and that its appropriation should cease to be incorporated with the government estimates, and that a new Parliament building was required in order to improve the facilities of members. In the course of his remarks he also said: 'I have had the advantage in the last five years to visit many Parliaments in the Commonwealth and I can say without any hesitation that our House is one of the most orderly ones that I have had a chance to witness.'[20]

Speaker Qionibaravi was succeeded by Mr. Tomasi Vakatora who, according to a press comment, was elected to the Chair 'under a cloud of open dissent from an unhappy opposition.'[21] However he was not long in office before winning the confidence of the opposition and a warm press tribute at the same time. The Deputy Speaker had ruled that Fijian chiefs were above criticism in the House of Representatives except by way of a substantive motion as their status was similar to that of the royal family, judges and members of Parliament. Speaker Vakatora reversed his colleague's ruling on the ground that chiefs participate actively in politics and are therefore subject to legitimate critical comment. In its editorial comment The Fiji Times observed: 'Mr. Vakatora's action yesterday must have bolstered the confidence of the House, and the nation, in the independence and impartiality of the Chair, which is so important to the conduct of national affairs.'[22]

Among the countries of the Pacific region are four of the most recent adherents to the Commonwealth, all having attained independence since 1978. They are the Solomon Islands, Tuvalu, Kiribati and Vanuatu. The provisions of their constitutions differ significantly, including those which affect the office of Speaker. We have already seen that in Tuvalu the Speaker must be an elected member of Parliament, in Kiribati he may not be, and in the Solomon Islands and Vanuatu he may be chosen from inside or outside Parliament.

In Kiribati the head of state (Beretitenti) is elected by the national electorate, the candidates being members of Parliament (Maneaba ni Maungatabu) nominated by their fellow-members. Once elected Beretitenti continues to sit as a member and is therefore subject to the authority of the Speaker in the course of the proceedings of Parliament. Following a dissolution of Parliament the executive functions of government are vested in a Council of State of which the Speaker is a member together with the Chief Justice and the Chairman of the Public Service Commission. The authority to convene a meeting of Parliament is vested solely in the Speaker although a meeting may be advised by the Beretitenti or one-third of the members. He is also empowered to apply to the High Court for a decision as to the interpretation of the constitution. Together with the Chief Justice he appoints the members of the Public Service Commission. Provision is made for the Maneaba Members' Salaries Commission whose members are appointed by the Chairman of the Public Service Commission in consultation with the Speaker.

In the Solomon Islands the Speaker plays a role in deciding who shall be recognized as the Leader of the Opposition and the Leader of the Independent Members. They are appointed by the Governor-General on the advice of the Speaker who consults with the groups concerned and such other persons as he deems appropriate. The Speaker is the chairman of the Electoral Commission and a member of the committee which appoints the Ombudsman.

In Tuvalu the Speaker would, unless exempted by Parliament, be obliged to vacate his office if he failed to disclose, within thirty days after election, any interest in a government contract. He is also responsible for monitoring the requirement that a member's seat is vacated if he enters a parliamentary debate on a matter in which he has a pecuniary interest without disclosing that interest.

In Vanuatu the Speaker, and also the Prime Minister or a majority of the members, may request an extraordinary session of Parliament. He is chairman of the Electoral Commission, nominates a judge of the Supreme Court and is consulted on the appointment of the Ombudsman. It is of interest to note that the first Speaker to be elected under the independence constitution was a member of the opposition even though the governing party won a two-thirds majority.

It is gratifying to observe that the Speakers from three of these young countries, the Solomon Islands, Kiribati and Vanuatu, were able to attend the most recent conference of Speakers and Presiding Officers of Commonwealth Parliaments held in Canada in 1981.[23]

On the other side of the world in the Mediterranean are two more island nations of the Commonwealth, Malta and Cyprus. Malta's independence constitution of 1964 provides that the Speaker may be either a member or non-member of Parliament. Until 1982 it had always been the practice to look outside Parliament for a Speaker and the choice had invariably fallen on a defeated candidate of the party which formed the government. Mr. Daniel Micallef, elected Speaker on 15 February 1982, was the first since independence to be a member elected at the general election for a constituency. In that same general election, two former Speakers, running as candidates, had been defeated.

From the information available it may be deduced that the speakership in Malta is regarded as a political office and a prize of the party which forms the government. One of the first duties of Speaker Micaleff following his election to office was to declare the seats of all the opposition members vacant because of their action in boycotting the sittings of Parliament. The boycotting of Parliament is a method of protest which has more than once been used by the opposition in Malta and has involved the Chair in decisions inconsistent with the principle of its impartiality and political detachment. In 1982, the members of the opposition having absented themselves for a period of two months following the opening of a new Parliament, Speaker Micallef, having quoted from the constitution and the standing orders, declared 'that the final responsibility of deciding whether a Member's seat in Parliament becomes vacant or not, falls on the Chair which has the power to approve or disapprove the absence of a Member from sittings'. On 26 April, having given the opposition members an extension of time in which to attend Parliament and take the oath, the Speaker declared their seats vacant. He indicated in the course of his statement that he had received a letter from the opposition members informing him that they disagreed with his interpretation of the constitution and appealing to him to help in finding a solution to the problem in the national interest. The problem stemmed from the fact that the opposition party, in spite of having polled a majority of the popular vote, had won a minority of the seats. It is therefore difficult to envisage what the Speaker could have done on his own initiative to resolve the dispute.[24]

In spite of the political associations of the speakership, the Speaker's election is not always opposed. Of the five Speakers who have held office since 1966 three were elected without opposition, although in the case of Speaker Micallef the opposition party had not taken their seats, having decided to boycott Parliament as indicated above. Speaker Alfred Bonnici faced an opponent in 1966. Speaker E. Attard Bezzina and Speaker Nestu Laiviera were both elected unanimously in 1971 and 1976 respectively, and in both cases the nomination was seconded by the Leader of the Opposition. Speaker Laiviera had previously been Deputy Speaker and it may be assumed he had given satisfaction to the opposition in the manner in which he had discharged his duties. He was succeeded in 1978 by Speaker Calcidon Agius who was opposed by the opposition on account of certain articles he had written. The Leader of the Opposition nevertheless expressed feelings of personal friendship towards him and Speaker Agius, acknowledging that he himself had opposed the election of Speaker Bonnici, indicated that his attitude towards the opposition would be in no way affected.

There is no doubt that Maltese Speakers strive to be impartial but, as in other jurisdictions, they are constrained by the political climate in which they are obliged to operate. Speaking at a conference in 1969, Speaker Bonnici observed that there is wide divergence of view between the political parties on domestic issues. 'That is when the Speaker is usually in trouble, when the Opposition try to cling to the minutest objection, to the minutest flaws and to press home their rights on those grounds. It is on such occasions that I, myself, find it very difficult and sometimes rather embarrassing to convince both sides of the House of the impartiality of the Chair.'[25] This comment sheds light, perhaps, on some of the interpretations of procedure rendered by Maltese Speakers. For example, on 26 March 1980, Speaker Agius, explaining his acceptance of a closure motion, gave among other reasons the fact that the Chair was aware that the government wanted the bill concerned to pass within a stipulated time.[26]

Questions of privilege are regularly raised in Malta's Parliament and the Chair sometimes gives a wide interpretation of what can constitute a *prima facie* case of privilege. Unparliamentary language when used in the House has been seen by the Chair as falling within this context. In 1977 a reference to one member by another as 'a coward and a swindler' was ruled by the Speaker to be *prima facie* a breach of privilege, although the ensuing debate on a motion moved by the offended member was defeated on a straight party vote.[27] More surprising, perhaps, was a ruling of 1976 concerning the use of the word 'cockroach' by a reporter. Finding that the use of the word constituted a *prima facie* breach of privilege, the Speaker announced that he did so, not because he was convinced the word amounted to an insult, but because the member concerned felt offended by it.[28] Of interest also is a ruling of 1977 which found that a *prima facie* case had been established as the result of a derogatory remark made by a spectator in the Strangers' Gallery against a minister. The remark was overheard by two persons who reported it to the minister, who in turn raised the matter in the House, which adopted a resolution declaring that the remark constituted a breach of privilege.[29]

Turning now to Cyprus, we find it more difficult to make comparisons between the role of the President of the House of Representatives and the Speakers of the Parliaments of other Commonwealth countries. The system of government in Cyprus is based on the separation of powers as in the United States. Ministers of the government are not members of Parliament and the party of the President of the Republic is not necessarily the party with the largest number of members of Parliament. The President of the House is closely involved in political issues and is likely to be a political leader in his own right. It so happens that the President of the House at the time of writing, Mr. George Ladas, belongs to the party of the President of the Republic, although it is a minority party in the House iself. Two former Presidents of the House of Representatives, Mr. Glafcos Clerides and Mr. Alecos Michaelides, are party leaders in their own right. The latter formed a new party just prior to the general election of 1981 but was defeated together with all his candidates.

Speaking at a conference in 1978 Mr. Michaelides discussed the role of the President of the House of Representatives in his country, pointing out that he could not avoid political involvement and is expected to campaign strongly on behalf of his party at election time. Since the constitution provides that he should act for the President of the Republic during the latter's absence he cannot, suggested Mr. Michaelides, adopt an a-political stance. In substantiation of this assertion one might recall the highly political circumstances in which Mr. Glafcos Clerides acted as President of the Republic in 1974 following an attempted coup d'état and the temporary absence of Archbishop Makarios. Mr. Michaelides illuminated his view of the responsibilities of the President of the House of Representatives in the following words:

> Some countries are facing very serious problems which threaten the very basis of their existence and their identity. Cyprus is one such example. Over the last four years it has faced the consequences of an act of aggression by Turkey. Turkey still occupies 40 per cent of our land and has turned one-third of our population into refugees. Can I, as Speaker of the Cyprus Parliament, play the role of the ombudsman? When a country faces a problem of survival and its very existence is threatened, as in Cyprus, or a country faces some other severe economic or political problem, can the Speaker be simply impartial? I believe that the Speaker must definitely be one of the prime movers in marshalling people's efforts to face the problems of the country. The Speaker can set the standard for the Parliament so that Members think beyond the local

problems of their own constituencies and develop a strong sense of purpose for the country and for the people in general. On these major issues the Speaker can supplement the role of the Executive. I believe that the Speaker can also contribute in other areas such as foreign relations.[30]

President Michaelides was himself very active in the field of foreign relations and it was due to his initiative that Cyprus formed its own branches of the Commonwealth Parliamentary Association and the Inter-Parliamentary Union and recruited the necessary staff to further the participation of the Cyprus Parliament in international activities.

Article 74(3) of the Constitution of Cyprus provides that the President of the House may summon an extraordinary session of Parliament at the request of ten or more members.

With the possible exception of Cyprus, the Parliaments of the countries considered in this chapter have been influenced to a greater or lesser extent by British custom and practice. Most of the Speakers wear robes of office, although in Cyprus, Malta, Nauru, Kiribati and Vanuatu no special costume is worn. In Western Samoa and Tonga traditional dress is worn, although one Western Samoan Speaker was presented with a full set of Westminster-style robes, complete with full-bottomed wig, by the Speaker of the Australian House of Representatives. He allowed himself to be photographed in this costume and apparently wore it once or twice in the House without provoking any objection from other members.

Most of the Speakers dealt with in this chapter are equipped with a casting vote if a division results in a tie, those of the Solomon Islands and Kiribati being among the exceptions. In Fiji, Papua New Guinea and Tuvalu the Speaker has not only a casting vote but also an original vote in certain circumstances. It is normally exercisable on questions requiring a special majority under the constitution but in Papua New Guinea and Tuvalu the Speaker may exercise a deliberative vote on motions of no confidence in the government. Conventions governing the use of the casting vote vary. In Papua New Guinea the Speaker is not obliged to exercise it and if he does not do so the question is withdrawn. In most of the Parliaments considered in this chapter the Speaker would probably use it to sustain the government. Speaker Dibela of Papua New Guinea once used his casting vote in favour of the government on a confidence issue. Speaker Tu'u'u of Western Samoa informed the author that he would probably use his casting vote in such a way as to keep the matter open for further discussion. He said, however, that in the case of the third reading of a bill he would probably make up his own mind with regard to the value of the bill and vote according to his own opinion and inclination.

As in most other Commonwealth Parliaments, the standing orders of the Parliaments considered in this chapter are modelled to a great extent on those of the House of Commons at Westminster. The powers of the Speaker in relation to maintaining order, recognition of members seeking the floor, control of the question period, allowing emergency adjournment motions and closure motions, determining points of order, checking irrelevance and tedious repetition and ruling on whether a question of privilege should be accorded precedence, among other matters, are similar in most of the jurisdictions we are dealing with. There are, however, important variations to be noted.

It is not unusual in small parliaments for the Speaker to share with the Deputy Speaker the duty of presiding in Committee of the Whole House. This is the practice in Jamaica, Trinidad and Tobago, Fiji, Western Samoa, Papua New Guinea, Kiribati, Bermuda and, no doubt, in some of the other countries covered in this chapter. Interestingly enough the Speaker does not preside in committee of the whole in Nauru which has one of the Commonwealth's smallest Parliaments. In some jurisdictions there are other committees in whose activities the Speaker is involved. In Jamaica and Trinidad and Tobago he is the chairman of the Committee of Privileges and of the Standing Orders Committee. In Western Samoa, Papua New Guinea and the Cook Islands he also chairs the Standing Orders Committee. In Bermuda he is chairman of the Rules and Privileges Committee which has the combined function of dealing with matters of privilege and procedure. In some Parliaments he chairs a committee dealing with such matters as accommodation and members' facilities, a committee which in Western Samoa and Fiji is styled the House Committee and in Papua New Guinea the National Parliament Committee. In Papua New Guinea the Speaker also chairs the Private Business Committee and the Committee on Broadcasting of Parliamentary Proceedings. In Malta the Speaker may be appointed to any select committee and presumably may therefore become the chairman of any select committee. In Nauru he chairs various committees while in Tonga he is not obliged to serve on any committee. In Kiribati the Speaker nominates the chairmen and members of all select committees and also determines their size. In Bermuda the Speaker appoints the members of the Public Accounts Committee. In Trinidad and Tobago, if a select committee fails to elect a chairman at its first meeting the Speaker appoints one.

As one would expect, the procedures of these far-flung Parliaments, while influenced by the formal traditions of Westminster, frequently draw upon equally time-honoured practices of indigenous origin. In Vanuatu, for example, a topic may be debated without the presentation of a previously determined motion. The Speaker may formulate a motion in accordance with the shape of the debate, which was the custom in the British House of Commons in earlier centuries before procedure became strictly formalised.

In Papua New Guinea a Speaker's ruling is open to immediate objection and a motion of dissent, if submitted in writing and seconded, may be debated forthwith. On one occasion the Speaker intervened during a member's speech by reason of what appeared to the Chair to be a conflict of interest situation. The ruling was objected to and upheld by a majority vote. Had it been overturned the Speaker would probably have regarded the decision of the House as a vote of no confidence in himself. In cases of disorder the Speaker may suspend a member on his own authority after reporting to the House that the member has committed an offence. If a question of privilege is raised and the Speaker thinks it should be investigated he will automatically refer it to the

The Office of Speaker

Committee of Privileges and this is an area in which he apparently has complete discretion. The standing orders of Papual New Guinea contain no rule comparable to that which is found in most Commonwealth Parliaments regarding emergency debates. The Speaker is therefore never called upon to use his discretion in deciding whether or not to allow such a debate.

In Kiribati the Speaker may on his own authority suspend a member whose conduct is grossly disorderly for periods specified in the standing orders, and the offending member is required to apologise to the Speaker at the first opportunity after retaking his seat. If he declined to apologise he would presumably be again ordered to withdraw from the House. The standing orders also empower the Speaker to suspend a sitting at any time for such period as he shall determine or to adjourn the House until the next sitting day. No requirements are specified as to the conditions in which such action would be warranted.

In Tonga the Speaker, in certain circumstances, has the power to compel the attendance of members. If, on the second attempt to convene Parliament, no quorum is present, the constitution provides that the King or the Speaker may order the members to attend the meeting of Parliament. In Western Samoa the Speaker is vested with what must surely be a unique and, one would assume, unwelcome power. Under the Electoral Act the Speaker may vacate the seat of any member who has sexual intercourse with anyone other than his or her spouse. No information is available as to how the Speaker would make a determination in such a case, or the lengths to which he is expected to go in order to do so.[31]

In some of the countries considered in this chapter the Speaker, in the case of a contest, is elected by secret ballot, and these include Fiji, Papua New Guinea, Western Samoa, Nauru, the Cook Islands and Kiribati. In Kiribati the Chief Justice presides over the election of the Speaker. Where there are more than two candidates the balloting continues until one emerges with an overall majority, except in Fiji where the candidate receiving the greatest number of votes on the first and only ballot is declared elected. Debate on the election of the Speaker is not normally allowed in those jurisdictions where it is conducted by ballot. The election of the Speaker is conducted without debate in Jamaica and Trinidad and Tobago also, although the procedures of their Parliaments adhere fairly closely to those of Westminster in other respects. In some Parliaments the Speaker is removable only by a two-thirds majority and this provision is to be found in Fiji, the Solomon Islands, Tuvalu, Kiribati, and St. Vincent. In Vanuatu the constitution provides for the office of Speaker but is silent with regard to his functions and conditions of tenure. Perhaps it is assumed that a simple resolution expressing no confidence in the Speaker would be followed by his resignation as it is unlikely that the framers of the constitution intended that he should be irremovable.

In small Parliaments it is frequently the case that the staff are members of the public service, the reason being that their avenues of advancement would otherwise be limited. Arrangements are usually made, particularly at the senior levels, to ensure a measure of continuity in the tenure of office of parliamentary staff, otherwise the services which Parliament has the right to expect would suffer. In many of these small Parliaments we find that the Speaker has few direct administrative responsibilities as these are largely delegated. The Parliaments of Papua New Guinea and Western Samoa are among those which employ their own staff independently of the public service. Speaking on this matter at the First Commonwealth Parliamentary Conference of Members from Small Legislatures, Speaker Tu'u'u of Western Samoa indicated that the staff of his Parliament were separated from the public service in 1975. The Clerk and Clerk Assistant are appointed by the head of state on the recommendation of the Cabinet after consultation with the Speaker, the remaining staff being appointed by the Speaker on the recommendation of the Clerk.[32] In Nauru the Clerk of Parliament is appointed by the Speaker under the authority of the constitution and is not a member of the public service.

In many of the small countries considered in this chapter the speakership is not necessarily seen as the summit of a career in public life. Some Speakers are subsequently appointed to cabinet office, as in the case of Speaker Holloway of Papua New Guinea and Speaker Qionibaravi of Fiji. Speaker Degazon of Dominica, as we have seen, became his country's head of state. Speaker Dibela of Papua New Guinea was appointed Governor-General. In bicameral Parliaments it is not unusual for Speakers to be appointed to the upper House. Speaker Rambally of St. Lucia became a senator, as did Speaker Brancker of Barbados who also went on to become President of the Senate. Some Speakers embark on a diplomatic career. For example, Speaker Braynen of the Bahamas became his country's High Commissioner in London and Speaker Bezzini of Malta was appointed ambassador-at-large. Speakers, like other politicians, are subject to the hazards of elections and changes of government and where alternative careers are available it is understandable that they would wish to keep such avenues open.

Finally, this study would be incomplete without a reference to the speakership in a most interesting and unusual legislature, that of the Isle of Man. Although not a sovereign country by constitutional definition, the Isle of Man is self-governing and is not bound by Acts of Parliament of the United Kingdom unless specifically mentioned in them. It claims to have the world's oldest Parliament, the High Court of Tynwald.* Tynwald has existed for over one thousand years, although the earliest record of any allusion to it in a legal document dates from 1417. While it has lost most of its judicial functions it remains the Parliament of the Isle of Man and consists of the Lieutenant-Governor representing the Crown and two chambers, the Legislative Council and the House of Keys, the latter consisting of 24 members elected by popular suffrage from six 'sheadings' and four municipalities. The Speaker is an elected member chosen by the House itself from among their own number.

The Speakership in the Manx Parliament has a dual function which sets it apart from the other speakerships we have been considering and probably makes it unique in the Commonwealth. In the House of Keys the Speaker is the presiding officer and is vested with the usual powers and duties vested in

---

* Derived from the Norse words 'Thing Völlr' meaning 'Parliament Field'.

the Speaker of a popular chamber. But he is also a political leader, and when the two chambers meet together as the High Court of Tynwald under the presidency of the Lieutenant-Governor he sits as an elected member and the spokesman of the Keys. In the House of Keys he has both a deliberative vote and a casting vote in the event of an equality of votes. In Tynwald he votes like any other member and, in fact, has an obligation to vote.* While the members of the House of Keys are largely independents, party politics being far less pronounced than is the case in most Parliaments, they are nevertheless politicians and the Speaker, while himself an independent, is not required to be politically detached like the Speaker of the House of Commons. He represents a constituency and is expected to speak and vote in its interests.

In the House of Keys he has wide discretionary powers and is chairman of the Consultative Committee which considers all matters which come before the House related to government policies. He has the right to speak in the House like any other member but rarely exercises it. In Tynwald he speaks as freely as his colleagues and is the recognized leader of the Keys. He may be referred to in debate as Mr. Speaker although he does not sit in this capacity when the two chambers meet together. In the Tynwald chamber there are special seating arrangements consisting of a 'Floor' and a 'Gallery'. The 'Floor' is occupied by the Keys and the Speaker has a special seat. Members of the Legislative Council sit in the 'Gallery' where the Lieutenant-Governor sits directly above the Speaker and presides over the joint meeting. However, if during a joint sitting a member of the Keys moves that the latter should retire to their own chamber to deliberate separately, it is the Speaker who puts the motion. He reports the results of the votes in the Keys to the Lieutenant-Governor. The Lieutenant-Governor and the Speaker authenticate with their signatures all resolutions of Tynwald and certificates of Royal Assent to and promulgation of bills.

The earliest reference to a presiding officer of the House of Keys dates from the tenure of office of John Stevenson who was designated 'chairman' and who served from 1704 to 1737. The first to claim the title of Speaker was probably Sir George Moore who held office from 1758 to 1780. As in the House of Commons, where the Speaker formally presents himself for royal approbation, the House of Keys present their Speaker to the Lieutenant-Governor following his election. This has become a matter of courtesy, as in Great Britain, but on one occasion they presented two candidates and the Lieutenant-Governor was obliged to make a choice. He selected John Taubman who held office from 1799 to 1822.

On two occasions, in 1934 and in 1959, suggestions were put forward that the Speaker should cease to represent a constituency, the purpose being to relieve him of the responsibility of taking a stand on political issues. On neither occasion was the proposal adopted, and the second time it was the influence of the then Speaker, Sir Joseph Qualtrough, which was largely the determining factor. First elected in 1937 he had seen over twenty years service as Speaker and in the interests of maintaining the prestige and historical

---

* Until 1961 he was required to exercise his vote in the House of Keys also.

tradition of the office he advocated no change and his view prevailed.

In spite of the significant differences of function, the Speaker of the House of Keys has much in common with his Westminster counterpart in terms of his responsibilities as presiding officer and the markedly similar robes he wears provide an outward indication of a shared tradition.[33]

The once mighty British Empire has faded into history. 'The evil that men do lives after them,' said Mark Anthony; 'the good is oft interred with their bones.' But perhaps in the case of the British Empire we might venture to vary this dictum. Hopefully the evils associated with Britain's long imperial supremacy are buried with it and perhaps the good things which came out of it are its true legacy, as reflected in the Commonwealth and its institutions. The parliamentary system has certainly endured, in various forms, in the face of many pressures. In some Commonwealth countries it remains suppressed, and there are others where the framework of democracy within which it operates is fragile or very limited. Yet it is one of the essential common denominators which hold the Commonwealth together in an indefinable fraternity. Every country which gained its independence from Britain set out with a Parliament and a Speaker. Their Westminster origins are, in most cases, instantly recognizable, and the ceremonial trappings were usually retained as well. If there is one thing which, we hope, this book has demonstrated, it is that these widely separated Parliaments have enough in common to enable comparisons to be made of their essential elements. It is submitted that none is more essential than the speakership.

Notes to Chapter Ten: The Speakership in the Smaller Nations of the Commonwealth

1. Report of the Fifth Conference of Commonwealth Speakers and Presiding Officers, 1978, Canberra, page 23.
2. See for example, C. J. Lynch, The Westminster Model in the Pacific, The Parliamentarian, vol. LXIII, no. 3, July 1982, page 142.
3. Report of a Conference of Commonwealth Speakers held at Ottawa on 29th and 30th September 1966, page 15.
4. See speech of Speaker Gajraj, Report of the Conference of Speakers and Presiding Officers of Commonwealth Parliaments, 1969, op. cit., pages 93—95.
5. Verbatim Report of the Proceedings of the Third Conference of Commonwealth Speakers and Presiding Officers, op. cit., page 58.
6. See The Parliamentarian, vol. LXIII, no. 1, January 1982, pages 40—41.
7. Report of the Fifth Conference of Commonwealth Speakers and Presiding Officers, op. cit., p. 77.
8. Ibid.
9. Ibid., pages 55—57.
10. Report of the Conference of Speakers and Presiding Officers of Commonwealth Parliaments, 1969, op. cit., pages 67—69.
11. See K. S. Bhalla, Nauru: A Central Pacific Parliamentary Democracy, The Parliamentarian, vol. LXIV, no. 3, July 1983, pp. 127—133.

12. Report of the Fifth Conference of Commonwealth Speakers and Presiding Officers, op. cit., page 93.
13. Ibid., page 31.
14. Fourth Conference of Commonwealth Speakers and Presiding Officers, op. cit., page 47.
15. Fifth Conference of Commonwealth Speakers and Presiding Officers, op. cit., pages 32–33.
16. John D. Chick, The Speakership in Fiji, The Parliamentarian, vol. LVIII, no. 3, July 1977, p. 218.
17. Ibid., pp. 218–226.
18. Fourth Conference of Commonwealth Speakers and Presiding Officers, op. cit., page 49.
19. Report of the Fifth Conference of Speakers and Presiding Officers of Commonwealth Parliaments, op. cit., pp. 88 and 89.
20. See The Parliamentarian, vol. LXIII, no. 4, October 1982, pages 326–328 for full text of the speech.
21. The Fiji Times, December 11, 1982.
22. Ibid.
23. For details of the constitutions of these four Pacific countries, see two articles by C. J. Lynch published in The Parliamentarian: Three Pacific Island Constitutions: Comparisons, vol. LXI, no. 3, July 1980, pages 133–141; and The Constitution of Vanuatu, vol. LXII, no. 1, January 1981, pages 46–53.
24. See The Parliamentarian, vol. LXIII, no. 3, July 1982, pages 170–173.
25. Report of the Conference of Speakers and Presiding Officers of Commonwealth Parliaments, 1969, op. cit., page 36. This conference, the first of the series, was the only one so far attended by a Maltese Speaker.
26. See The Parliamentarian, vol. LXI, no. 3, July 1980, pages 187–191.
27. Ibid., vol. LVIII, no. 4, October 1977, page 283.
28. Ibid., vol. LVIII, no. 3, July 1977, pages 227–228.
29. Ibid., vol. LIX, no. 1, page 61.
30. Report of the Fifth Conference of Commonwealth Speakers and Presiding Officers, op. cit., page 41.
31. See Fourth Conference of Commonwealth Speakers and Presiding Officers, op. cit., page 42.
32. First Commonwealth Parliamentary Conference of Members from Small Legislatures, Fiji, 1981, Report of Proceedings, page 63.
33. Readers are referred to two articles in "The Parliamentarian" from which much of the information on the Manx speakership was derived: T. E. Kermeen, The Speaker of the House of Keys, vol. LVI, no. 4, October 1975, pages 277–279; and H. C. Kerruish, The Speakership in the Isle of Man, vol. LIX, no. 1, January 1978, pages 28–31.

Select Bibliography

Primary Sources

The primary sources of reference used in the preparation of this book include the parliamentary debates, journals or other records of proceedings, standing orders, constitutional documents and other relevant statutes of the countries concerned, wherever they were available.

Other primary sources include the following:

Report of a Conference of Commonwealth Speakers, held at Westminster on 16th and 17th June, 1965.

Report of a Conference of Commonwealth Speakers, held at Ottawa on 29th and 30th September, 1966.

Report of the Conference of Speakers and Presiding Officers of Commonwealth Parliaments held at Ottawa and Toronto, Canada, September 8th to 12th, 1969.

Proceedings of the Second Conference of Commonwealth Speakers and Presiding Officers, New Delhi, India, Monday, December 28, 1970 to Friday, January 1, 1971. Lok Sabha Secretariat, New Delhi.

Verbatim Report of the Proceedings of the Third Conference of Commonwealth Speakers and Presiding Officers, Monday, 24th September to Friday, 28th September, 1973. Mulungushi Conference Hall, Lusaka, Zambia.

Fourth Conference of Commonwealth Speakers and Presiding Officers 7th to 10th September, 1976, Houses of Parliament, London.

Report of the Fifth Conference, Speakers and Presiding Officers, Commonwealth Parliaments, 28th August to 1st September, 1978. Parliament House, Canberra.

Report of the Sixth Conference of Commonwealth Speakers and Presiding Officers, Ottawa, April 23rd, 24th and 25th, 1981.

Primary sources used exclusively in relation to the speakership in Great Britain include the following:

Chandler, Richard
Debates of The House of Commons, 15 volumes, 1670–1743.

D'Ewes, Sir Simonds
Journals of all the Parliaments during the reign of Queen Elizabeth.

D'Ewes, Sir Simonds
Journal of the Proceedings of the Long Parliament.

Select Bibliography

Grey, Anchitell
Debates of the House of Commons from the year 1667 to the year 1694, 10 volumes, 1763.

Hatsell, John
Precedents of Proceedings in the House of Commons, under separate titles; with observations, 4th edition, 4 volumes, 1818.

House of Commons
Report of the Select Committee on the Office of the Speaker, 1852–3, H.C. 487.
First Report from the Select Committee on House of Commons (Procedure), 1906, H.C. 89.
Report from the Select Committee on House of Commons (Procedure), 1915, H.C. 378.
Special report from the Select Committee on Procedure on Public Business, 1931, H.C. 161.
Report of the Select Committee on Parliamentary Elections (Mr. Speaker's Seat), 1938–9, H.C. 98.
Second Report from the Select Committee on Procedure, 1946, H.C. 58-I.
Third Report from the Select Committee on Procedure, 1946, H.C. 189-I.
Report from the Select Committee on Procedure, 1958–59, H.C. 92-I.
First report from the Select Committee on Procedure: the rule relating to reference in the house to matters considered as sub judice, 1962–63, H.C. 156.
Report from the Select Committee on the Palace of Westminster, 1964–65, H.C. 285.
Report from the Select Committee on Parliamentary Privilege, 1966–67, H.C. 34.
Second report from the Select Committee on Procedure: Standing Order No. 9; urgent and topical debates, 1966–67, H.C. 282.
Second report from the Select Committee on Procedure: Question time, 1969–70, H.C. 198.
Second report from the Select Committee on Procedure: the Process of Legislation, 1970–71, H.C. 538.
First report from the Select Committee on Procedure: Election of a Speaker, 1971–72, H.C. 111.
Fourth Report from the Select Committee on Procedure, 1971–72, H.C. 298.
Report from the Select Committee on Parliamentary Questions, 1971–72, H.C. 393.
House of Commons (Administration): Report to Mr. Speaker by Committee under Chairmanship of Mr. Arthur Bottomley, M. P., 1975, H.C. 624.
Third Report from the Committee of Privileges: Recommendations of the Select Committee on Parliamentary Privilege, 1976–77, H.C. 417.

Parliamentary History of England from the earliest period to the year 1803, 36 volumes.

Rushworth, John
Historical Collections, 4 volumes in 7, 1682–1701.

Further useful sources include the reports and proceedings of conferences and seminars organized by the Commonwealth Parliamentary Association and the various regions of the C.P.A.

Principal books of reference

(This list does not include the wide range of political and historical biographies, autobiographies and memoirs which contain peripheral material relating to the subject of this book.)

The Annual Register.

Anson, Sir William
The Law and Custom of the Constitution, volume I: Parliament, Fifth edition by Maurice L. Gwyer, Oxford U.P., 1922.

Beauchesne, Arthur
Beauchesne's rules and forms of the House of Commons of Canada, Fifth edition, by Alistair Fraser and others, the Carswell Company, 1978.

Bourinot, Sir John George
Parliamentary procedure and practice in the Dominion of Canada, Fourth edition edited by Thomas Barnard Flint, Canada Law Book Company, 1916.

Bradshaw, Kenneth and David Pring
Parliament and Congress, Constable, 1972.

Bowen, Catherine Drinker
The Lion and the Throne: The Life and Times of Sir Edward Coke, Hamish Hamilton, 1957.

Burns, Alan
History of the British West Indies, Allen & Unwin, 1954.

Cambridge History of the British Empire.

Campion, Lord
An Introduction to the Procedure of the House of Commons, 3rd edition, Macmillan, 1958.

Chambers, R. W.
Thomas More, Jonathan Cape, 1948.

Chester, D. N. and Nona Bowring
Questions in Parliament, Oxford U.P., 1962.

Crisp, L. F.
Australian National Government, Longmans, 4th edition, 1978.

Dasent, Arthur Irwin
The Speakers of the House of Commons, Bodley Head, 1911.

Dawson, Robert MacGregor
The Government of Canada, 5th edition, revised by Norman Ward, University of Toronto Press, 1970.

Dawson, William F.
Procedure in the Canadian House of Commons, University of Toronto Press, 1962.

Denison, John Evelyn
Notes from my Journal when Speaker of the House of Commons, John Murray, 1899.

Dictionary of National Biography.

Dube, Maya
The Speaker in India, S. Chand, 1971.

Gicheru, H. B. Ndoria,
Parliamentary Practice in Kenya, Transafrica Publishers, 1976.

Select Bibliography

Graham, Harry
The Mother of Parliaments, Methuen, 1910.

Hanson, A. H. and H. V. Wiseman
Parliament at work: A Case-book of Parliamentary Procedure, Stevens, 1962.

Hulme, Harold
The life of Sir John Eliot, 1592–1632, Allen & Unwin, 1957.

Institute of Pacific Studies
Cook Islands Politics, Polynesian Press, 1979.

Jackson, Robert J. and Michael M. Atkinson
The Canadian Legislative System, Macmillan, 1974.

James, Robert Rhodes
An Introduction to The House of Commons, Collins, 1961.

Jennings, Sir Ivor
Parliament, 2nd edition, Cambridge U.P., 1957.

Kaul, M. N. and S. L. Shakdher
Practice and Procedure of Parliament (with particular reference to Lok Sabha), Metropolitan Book Co., 1968, 3rd Edition 1978.

Keith, Arthur Berriedale
Responsible Government in the Dominions, 2nd Edition, 2 Volumes, Oxford U.P., 1928.

Lal, A. B.
The Indian Parliament, Chaitanya Publishing House, Allahabad, 1956.

Laundy, Philip
The Office of Speaker, Cassell, 1964.

Littlejohn, Charles P.
Speakers' Rulings 1867 to 1980 Inclusive, New Zealand House of Representatives, 1982.

Lloyd, Selwyn
Mr. Speaker, Sir, Jonathan Cape, 1976.

Lucy, Henry
The Balfourian Parliament 1900–1905, London, Hodder & Stoughton, 1906.

Lummis, Edward
The Speaker's Chair, Unwin, 1900.

Macdonagh, Michael
The Pageant of Parliament, 2 Volumes, T. Fisher Unwin, 1921.

Macdonagh, Michael
The Speaker of the House, Methuen, 1914.

Mackenzie, Kenneth R.
The English Parliament, Penguin Books, 1959.

Macminn, E. George
Parliamentary Practice in British Columbia, Victoria, B.C., 1981.

Manning, James Alexander
The Lives of the Speakers of The House of Commons, E. Churton, 1850.

Marsden, Philip
The Officers of the Commons, 1363–1978, H.M.S.O., 1979.

Select Bibliography

May, Sir Thomas Erskine
Parliamentary Practice, 19th Edition, Edited by Sir David Lidderdale, Butterworth, 1976; *20th Edition,* Edited by Sir Charles Gordon, Butterworth, 1983.

Moir, Thomas L.
The Addled Parliament of 1614, Oxford U.P., 1958.

Morris–Jones, W. H.
Parliament in India, Longmans Green, 1957.

Morrison, Lord (of Lambeth)
Government and Parliament, Oxford University Press, 3rd Edition, 1964.

Mukherjea, A. R.
Parliamentary Procedure in India, Oxford U.P., Bombay, 1958.

Namasivayam, S.
The Legislatures of Ceylon, 1928–1948, Faber & Faber, 1951.

Neale, Sir John Ernest
Elizabeth 1 and her Parliaments, 2 Volumes, Jonathan Cape, 1953–7.

Neale, Sir John Ernest
The Elizabethan House of Commons, Jonathan Cape, 1949.

O'Connor, T. P.
Gladstone's House of Commons, Ward and Downey, 1885.

Pettifer, J. A. Editor
House of Representatives Practice, Australian Government Publishing Service, 1981.

Porritt, Edward
The Unreformed House of Commons, 2 Volumes, Cambridge U.P., 1903.

Redlich, Josef
The Procedure of the House of Commons, 3 Volumes, Constable, 1908.

Reser, Clarence
The Speakership in British Columbia, 1970–1979, Thesis submitted to the University of Victoria in 1981.

Roskell, J. S.
The Commons and their Speaker in English Parliaments, 1376–1523, Manchester U.P., 1965.

Shakdher, S. L., Editor
The Commonwealth Parliaments, Lok Sabha Secretariat, 1975.

Smith, G. Barnett
History of the English Parliament, 2nd Edition, 2 Volumes, Ward, Lock, Bowden & Co., 1894.

Stewart, John B.
The Canadian House of Commons: Procedure and Reform, McGill-Queen's University Press, 1977.

Stumbles, A. R. W.
Some Recollections of a Rhodesian Speaker, Books of Rhodesia, 1980.

Taylor, Eric
The House of Commons at work, 9th Edition, Macmillan, 1979.

Thomas, P. D. G.
The House of Commons in the Eighteenth Century, Clarendon Press, 1971.

Select Bibliography

Todd, Alpheus
On Parliamentary Government in England, 2nd Edition, 2 Volumes, 1887–89.
Todd, Alpheus
Parliamentary Government in the British Colonies, 2nd Edition, Longmans Green, 1894.
Ullswater, Viscount
A Speaker's Commentaries, 2 Volumes, Edward Arnold, 1925.
Vulliamy, C. E.
The Onslow Family, Chapman & Hall, 1953.
Walkland, S. A., Editor
The House of Commons in the Twentieth Century, Clarendon Press, 1979. See, in particular, Chapter III: Laundy, Philip *The Speaker and his Office in the Twentieth Century.*
Wight, Martin
The Development of the Legislative Council, 1606–1945, Faber & Faber, 1946.
Wilding, Norman and Philip Laundy
An Encyclopaedia of Parliament, 4th Edition, Cassell, 1971.
Williams, Orlo Cyprian
The Clerical Organization of the House of Commons, 1661–1850, Oxford U.P., 1954.
Winterton, Earl
Orders of The Day, London, Cassell, 1953.
Wright, Arnold and Philip Smith
Parliament Past and Present, Hutchinson, 1902.
Young, Roland
The British Parliament, Faber & Faber, 1962.

Articles, Pamphlets, etc.

Three periodicals in particular are valuable sources of information relating to the subject of this book. These are:

The Parliamentarian
Journal of the Parliaments of the Commonwealth Published by the Commonwealth Parliamentary Association.
Parliamentary Affairs
Journal of the Hansard Society for Parliamentary Government.
The Table
Journal of the Society of Clerks-at-the-Table in Commonwealth Parliaments.

Specific References

Aitchison, James H.
'*The Speakership of the Canadian House of Commons.*' Reprinted from Canadian Issues: *Essays in Honour of Henry F. Angus*, Ed. Robert M. Clark, University of Toronto Press, 1960.
Bhalla, K. S.
Nauru: A Central Pacific Parliamentary Democracy, *The Parliamentarian*, Volume LXIV, No. 3, July 1983.

Select Bibliography

Bolton, Geoffrey
The Choice of Speaker in Australian Parliaments. Parliamentary Affairs, Volume XV, No. 3, Summer 1962.

Briers, P. M.
The Speaker of the House of Commons, Hansard Society Pamphlet No. 3, 1946.

Campion, G. F. M.
Methods of Closure in the Commons, Journal of the Society of Clerks-at-the-Table in Empire Parliaments for 1932, Volume 1.

Chawla, M. C. and K. S. Bhalla
Speakers and Party Membership, Constitutional and Parliamentary Studies, 1968.

Chick, John, D.
The Speakership in Fiji, *The Parliamentarian*, Volume LVIII, No. 3, July 1977.

Combe, G. D.
The Speaker's Vote Topples Governments, *The Table*, Volume XXXIX for 1970.

Commonwealth Parliamentary Association
A Memorandum on the Position, Powers and Privileges of Speakers in Parliaments of the Commonwealth, C.P.A., 1959.

Dawson, W. F.
The Speaker in Canada and Australia, *The Table,* Volume XLVIII for 1980.

Donahoe, Arthur
Procedural change in the Nova Scotia House of Assembly, *Canadian Parliamentary Review*, Volume 4, No. 2, Summer 1981.

Duboy, J. Gordon
Canada: House of Commons: Relations between Chair and Opposition, in 1956, *The Table*, Volume XXV for 1956.

Forsey, Eugene
Constitutional Aspects of the Canadian Pipeline Debate, *Public Law*, Spring 1957,

Hegde, K. S.
The Speakership in India, *The Parliamentarian*, Volume LIX, No. 1, January 1978.

Hinds, W. C. B.
The Speakership in Barbados, *The Parliamentarian*, Volume LIX, No. 2, April 1978.

Jack, Sir Alieu
The Speakership in the Gambia, *The Parliamentarian*, Volume LIX, No. 1, January 1978.

Jackson, Keith
Parliamentary reform in New Zealand, *The Parliamentarian*, Volume LX, No. 4, October 1979.

Jayewardene, J. R.
Sri Lanka's New Constitution, *The Parliamentarian*, Volume LX, No. 1, January 1979.

Jerome, James
The Speakership in Canada, *The Parliamentarian*, Volume LIX, No. 2, April 1978.

Jerome, James
Televising the House of Commons: A Retrospective, *Canadian Parliamentary Review*, Winter 1981–82.

Kashyap, Subhash
The role of the Speaker — some random thoughts, *Journal of Constitutional and Parliamentary Studies*, October–December 1968.

Kermeen, T. E.
The Speaker of the House of Keys, *The Parliamentarian*, Volume LVI, No. 4, October 1975.

Kerruish, H. C.
The Speakership in the Isle of Man, *The Parliamentarian*, Volume LIX, No. 1, January 1978.

King, Horace
The Impartiality of the Speaker, *The Parliamentarian*, Volume XLVII, April 1966.

Kolane, John T.
The Speakership in Lesotho, *The Parliamentarian*, Volume LIX, No. 1, January 1978.

Laundy, Philip
Conferences of Speakers and Presiding Officers, *The Parliamentarian*, Volume LII, No. 4, October 1971.

Laundy, Philip
The Speaker of the House of Commons, *Parliamentary Affairs*, Volume XIV, No. 1, Winter 1960–1.

Lavoie, Jean-Noël
New Standing Orders for the National Assembly of Quebec, *The Parliamentarian*, Volume LIV, No. 4, October 1973.

Levy, Gary
Speakers of the House of Commons, *Library of Parliament*, Ottawa, 1983.

Littlejohn, C. P.
New Privilege Rules in New Zealand, *The Table*, Volume XLIX for 1981.

Livingston, William S.
The Security of Tenure of the Speaker of The House of Commons, *Parliamentary Affairs*, Volume XI, No. 4, Autumn 1958.

Lynch, C. J.
The Consitution of Vanuatu, *The Parliamentarian*, Volume LXII, No. 1, January 1981.

Lynch, C. J.
Three Pacific Island Constitutions: Comparisons, *The Parliamentarian*, Volume LXI, No. 3, July 1980.

Lynch, C. J.
The Westminster Model in the Pacific, *The Parliamentarian*, Volume LXIII, No. 3, July 1982.

MacMinn, E. George
Legislative Procedure Review Act: *The Speaker and the Legislative Assembly of British Columbia*, 1982.

Mahajan, Des Raj
Evolution of Speaker's Office, *Journal of Constitutional and Parliamentary Studies*, October–December 1968.

Nabulyato, R. M.
The Speakership in Zambia, *The Parliamentarian*, Volume LIX, No. 1, January 1978.

Notestein, Wallace
The Winning of the Initiative in the House of Commons (*Raleigh Lecture on History*, 1924); Published for the British Academy by O.U.P., 1949.

Pannell, Charles
Article in *The Times*, 4 March, 1972, page 12.

Pannell, Charles
Under Big Ben: Mr. Speaker, Broadcast on the English Service of the B.B.C. 30 30 May 1958.

Powell, Enoch
A Speaker before the "The First": Published in *Parliamentary Affairs*, Volume XVIII, No. 1, Winter 1964-5.

Robert, Charles
Ringing in Reform: An Account of the Canadian Bells Episode, *The Table*, Volume LI for 1983.

Shakdher, S. L.
Powers and Functions of Speakers, *Journal of Parliamentary Information*, October 1973.

Singh, Dalip
Depoliticizing the Indian Speaker, *Journal of Constitutional and Parliamentary Studies*, January-March, 1971.

Singh, Sardar Hukam
The Speaker in India, *The Parliamentarian*, Volume XLVIII, No. 1, January 1967.

Smith, Denis
The Speakership of the Canadian House of Commons: Some Proposals. A paper prepared for the Special Committee on Procedure and Organization, April 1965. Appended to the Votes and Proceedings, 2 June 1965.

Snedden, Sir Billy
The Speaker of the Australian House of Representatives, *The Parliamentarian*, Volume LIX, No. 4, October 1978.

Snedden, Sir Billy
The Westminster Convention and the Speaker, *The Parliamentarian*, Volume LX, No. 3, July 1979.

Thomas, George
New Order, Old Standards, Article in *The Times*, 13 June 1983, page 10.

Thomas, George
Parliamentary Privilege at Westminster, *The Parliamentarian*, Volume LXI, No. 4, October 1980.

Thorne, Peter
Ceremonial and the Mace in the House of Commons, London, H.M.S.O., 1980.

Watkins, Alan
The Fix for the Speakership, *New Statesman*, 18 December, 1970.

Yadav, J. N. Singh
The Speaker and the Money Bills, *Journal of Parliamentary Information*, Volume 22, No. 3, July-September, 1976.

Yadav, J. N. Singh
Term and Vacancy in the Speaker's Office, *Journal of Constitutional and Parliamentary Studies*, July-September, 1980.

Index

Abbott, Charles, 46–7
Abdul Bakeer Markar, Al Haj M., 220
Abercromby, James, 49–50
Addington, Henry, 45, 47, 63
'Addled Parliament', 29
Agius, Calcidon, 252
Aitchison, Professor James H., 109, 111, 119
Alberta (Canada), 136–8
Alcee, Donald, 239
Algie, Sir Ronald, 173
Amerongen, Gerard, 137–8
Amin, Idi, 194–5
Anguilla, 10
Anne, Queen, 40–1
Antigua, 4, 6
Arundel, Archbishop, 16
Aston, Sir Willam, 174, 155
Attlee, Clement, 74
Audley, Sir Thomas, 22
Australia, 3, 5, 143–61; State legislatures, 157–61
Ayyanga, M. A., 176, 178, 179

'Bad Parliament', 13
Bahamas, 4, 6, 237, 239–40, 257
Baker, Sir John, 23
Baldwin, Stanley, 69
Bandaranaike, S. W. R. D., 219
Bandaranaike, Sirima, 219, 220
Bangladesh, 10
Barbados, 4, 6, 237, 240, 241, 256
Barbuda, 4, 6
'Barebones Parliament', 36
Barker, E. W., 230
Beauchamp, Sir Walter, 20

Beaudoin, René, 110–19, 122, 134
Beaumont, Henry, 12
Belize, 4, 236
Bell, Robert, 26
Benn, Anthony Wedgwood, 85–6
Bermuda, 6, 237, 255
Bezzina, E. Attard, 252, 257
Bhagat, B. R., 187
Black Prince, 12–13
Bolingbroke, Henry, 15
Bonnici, Alfred, 252
Botswana, 193–4, 198, 207, 208, 212, 213, 215
Bowers, Eden A., 239
Boyd-Carpenter, John, 76
Bradlaugh, Charles, 54–5
Brancker, Sir Theodore, 242, 257
Brand, Henry Bouverie William, 52–5, 93
Braynen, A. R., 240, 257
British Columbia, 136–9
British Virgin Islands, 9
Brockelbank, John, 137
Bromley, William, 41
Buckingham, Duke of, 30–1
Burghley, Lord, 26
Bussy, Sir John, 14–15
Butagira, Francis, 206
Butler, Arlington, 240

Caicos *see* Turks and Caicos Islands
Calwell, Arthur Augustus, 149
Cameron, Archie, 147–50, 152, 155
Cameron, Colin, 114–15
Canada, 2, 3, 5–8, 103–39; continuity of Speakership, 107–11, legislature in provinces, 136–9; Pipeline

debate, 112–19; procedure in, 119–36
Caribbean, 236–42
Catesby, William, 20
Cato, Arnott, 241
Cavendish-Bentinck, Sir Ferdinand, 199
Cayman Islands, 9
Ceylon *see* Sri Lanka
Charles I, 22, 30–4
Charles II, 37
Charlton, Sir Job, 38
Chaucer, Thomas, 18
Cheyne (Cheney), Sir John, 16
Church of England, 22, 29, 97; *see also* Protestants
Churchill, Gordon, 114
Churchill, Winston, 70, 74, 82, 97
Chute, Chaloner, 36
Civil War, 35
Clerides, Glafcos, 253
Clifton-Brown, Douglas, 69, 73–5, 80, 82, 87, 89, 95, 98
Cockburn, James, 107
Coke, Edward, 27–8
Colonial Office Conference 1927, 8–9
Commonwealth Parliamentary Association, 2, 5
Compton, Sir Spencer, 41
Conference of Speakers and Presiding Officers, 4–5, 187
Conteh, W. N. S., 210
Cook Islands, 236 243–4, 255, 256
Coomaraswamy, Punch, 230–1
Cooper, Sir Daniel, 158
Cope, James, 152

270

Corea, Shirley, 220
Cornwall, Charles Wolfram, 45
Council, Canadian CPA, 5
Crewe, Randolph, 29
Crewe, Sir Thomas, 30
Crisp, Professor L. F., 150
Croke, John, 28
Cromwell, Oliver, 35–6
Cromwell, Richard, 36
Cunningham-Reid, Captain, 74
Cust, Sir John, 44
Cyprus, 2, 236–8, 251, 253–4

Daby, Ajay, 207
Darling, Sir Clifford, 237
Davies, Glen, 158
Davis-Pierre, Marie, 239
De Alwis, Anandatissa 220
De Freitas, Geoffrey, 77
Degazon, Fred, 239, 257
De Keighley, Henry, 11
De la Mare, Sir Peter, 12–13
De Montfort, Peter, 11
De Montfort, Simon, 11
Denison, John Evelyn, 51–2
De Shareshull, William, 12
De Thorpe, William, 12
Devlin, Bernadette, 83
Dewan Negara (Malaysian Upper House), 4, 224
Dewan Rakyat (Malaysian Lower House), 5, 224–5
D'Ewes, Sir Simonds, 34
Dhillon, G. S., 178, 179, 187
Dibela, Kingston, 245, 246, 254, 257
Diefenbaker, John, 108, 109
Dominica, 236, 238, 239, 257
Dorewood, John, 16, 18
Dowding, Gordon, 137, 139
Dudley, Edmund, 20
Dunning, John, 44
Duraiswamy, Sir Waitialingam, 218
Durham, Earl of, 7–8
Dyer, Sir James, 23

Eastick, Dr, 158
Edward II, 12
Edward III, 12
Edward VI, 23
Eliot, Sir John, 30–1
Elizabeth I, 24–8

Elizabeth II, 63, 103, 105, 153, 165
Empson, Sir Richard, 20
Esturmy see Sturmy, Sir W.
Ezeoke, E., 211

Falkland Islands, 9
Fell, Bryen, 8
Fellowes, Edward, 9
Fernando, Hugh E., 219
Fiji, 4, 237, 247–50, 254–7
Finch, Sir John, 30–1, 35
Fitzroy, Edward Arlington, 68–70, 76, 81, 82, 88, 89, 97
Fleming, James, 116
Flower, Roger, 16
Foley, Paul, 40
Forrest, Talbert, 241
Fraser, Malcolm, 153

Gaitskell, Hugh, 80
Gajraj, R. B., 239
Gambia, The, 193–4, 198, 208–9, 210, 213
Ganoo, Alan, 207
Gargrave, Sir Thomas, 25
George I, 41
George II, 43
George III, 44
Ghana (Gold Coast), 10, 194, 211–12
Gibraltar, 9
Gicheru, H. B. Ndoria, 199
Gilbert Islands see Kiribati
Gladstone, William, 52–4, 80
Glanville, Sir John, 32
Gold Coast see Ghana
Golding, T. N., 241
'Good Parliament', 12, 13
Goulburn, Henry, 50
Green, Henry, 12
Gregory, William, 39
Grenada, 10
Grenville, William Wyndham, 45
Grey, Earl, 48
Grimston, Sir Harbottle, 37
Groom, Sir Littleton, 146, 153
Gujarat Assembly, 190
Guildesborough, Sir John, 13–14
Guise, Sir John, 245

Gully, William Court, 56–7, 68, 73, 87, 88
Guyana, 236, 239

Hailsham, Lord, 81
Hanmer, Thomas, 41
Hardie, James Kier, 87
Hare, Sir Nicholas, 23, 24
Harley, Robert, 40
Harrison, Sir Richard, 168, 169, 172, 173
Haskins, J. G., 207
Hatsell, John, 43, 63–4
Haxey, Thomas, 14
Hegde, K. S., 178, 188
Heigham (Higham), Sir Clement, 24
Henry IV, 16–18
Henry V, 18–19
Henry VI, 19
Henry VII, 20
Henry VIII, 20–2, 23
Higham see Heigham
Hinds, W. C. B., 241–2
Hodges, Nancy, 139
Holder, Sir Frederick, 147
Holloway, Barry, 245–6, 257
Horne, Sir W. H., 199
Hong Kong, 9
Hume, Joseph, 51
Hungerford, Sir Thomas, 12
Hungerford, Sir Walter, 19, 20
Hylton-Foster, Harry, 70, 75–6, 80, 82, 85

India, 2, 5; Central Legislative Assembly, 175–6, 185; under Republican Constitution, 176–88; Speakers' Conference, 188–9
Indian State Legislative Assemblies, 3, 189–91
Ireland, 52–5, 57, 81, 84, 93
Ismail, H. S., 219

Jack, Sir Alieu, 208–10
Jack, Sir Roy, 167, 172
Jackson, Professor Keith, 173
Jakhar, Dr Bal Ram, 178, 186
Jamaica, 4, 237, 240, 254, 256

Index

James I, 28–9, 32
James II, 39
Jayewardene, J. R., 220
Jeewoolall, R., 207
Jenkins, Dr Harry, 146, 150
Jennings, Ivor, 69
Jerome, James, 108, 111, 121, 124–5, 129–31, 134–5
John of Gaunt, 12–13
Johore Assembly, 229
Joynson-Hicks, Sir William, 73–4

Kelantan Assembly, 229
Kenya, 9, 193–201, 212–14
Kenyatta, Jomo, 199
Kermode, Ronald, 247
Khonje, N., 203–4, 212
King, Horace Maybray, 55, 67, 76, 80, 82–6, 89, 91, 98
Kingston, G. S., 159
Kiribati (Gilbert Islands), 236, 250, 251, 254–6
Knowles, Stanley, 109, 110, 113–15
Knyvet, Sir John, 12
Kolane, J. T., 208
Kwan, P., 245

Ladas, George, 253
Laiviera, Nestu, 252
Lambert, Marcel, 110, 120, 131
Lambton, Lord, 86
Lamoureux, Lucien, 107–11, 121–2, 131–3
Lansbury, George, 69, 70
Latimer, Lord, 12
Laucke, Sir Condor, 3
Laud, Archbishop, 32, 33
Leeward Islands, 6
Le Marchant, Sir Denis, 49
Lemieux, Rodolphe, 107
Lenthall, William, 21, 33–7
Le Scrope, Geoffrey, 12
Lesotho, 193, 197–8, 208, 210, 213, 215
Littleton, Sir Thomas, 38, 40
Lloyd, Selwyn, 64, 66, 70, 72, 76, 77, 80, 82, 83, 85, 86, 89, 94, 98
Lloyd George, David, 69, 70
Lock, Rev. Albert, 207–8, 209
Lok Sabha (House of the People), 176, 178–88
London, 5, 6, 36, 40, 213, 257

Lord Chancellor, role of, 2, 3, 63, 83
Lowther, James William (Viscount Ullswater), 73, 80, 85, 87, 89, 98
Lucy, Henry, 57
Luke, Mr Justice, 210

McAndrew, Sir Charles, 75
McCready, Robert, 136
MacDonald, Sir John A., 104
MacDonald, Ramsay, 69
Macfarlane, R. M., 167
McIlraith, George, 126
McLeay, Sir John, 147, 150, 153
Macmillan, Harold, 83
Macnaughton, Alan, 104, 111, 126, 129, 131
NcNeill, Ronald, 73–4
Macpherson, Ripton, 241
'Mad Parliament', 11
Makarios, Archbishop, 253
Malawi (Nyasaland), 193, 196–9, 203–4, 210, 213, 215
Malaya, Federation of, 224
Malaysia, 4, 5, 224–30
Malta, 236, 251–3, 254, 255, 257
Man, Isle of, 257–9
Manipur Assembly, 190
Manitoba (Canada), 136, 137
Manners-Sutton, Charles, 46–50
Maoris, 171
Margai, Sir Albert, 210
Mary I, 23, 24
Mary II, 39–40
Mary, Queen of Scots, 26
Mati, F. M. G., 199, 200, 213
Mauritius, 193–4, 197–8, 206–7, 210, 213, 215
Mavalankar, G. V., 176–80, 184–9
Maxwell-Hyslop, Robin, 76
May, Erskine, 89, 124
Mediterranean region, 251
Melbourne, Lord, 48–9
Melville, Lord, 46–7
Menzies, Robert, 88, 147
Merriweather, Dr Alfred, 207
Metcalfe, Sir Frederic, 9
Micallef, Daniel, 251–2
Michaelides Alecos, 253–4

Michener, Roland, 107–9, 111
Milner, James, 74–5
Mitford, Sir John, 45
Mkwawa, Adam Sapi, Chief, 205
Mohamed Noah bin Omar, Tan Sri Datuk Haji, 225
Mohamed Zahir bin Haji Ismail, Dato, 225
Moi Daniel, arap, 196
Molamure, Sir Francis, 218
Monk, General, 36–7
Montserrat, 9
Moore, Sir George, 258
More, Sir Thomas, 20–3, 25
Morea, Sevese, 246
Morrison, Lord 96
Morrison, William Shepherd, 67, 70, 74, 75, 82, 88
Moyle, Sir Thomas, 23
Mundia, Nalumino, 196–7
Murray, W. H., 139
Mutasa, Didymus, 205

Nabulyato, R. M., 201, 202
Nairn, W. M., 146
Narain, Sase, 239
Nauru, 237, 244–5, 254–7
Neale, Sir J. E., 25
Nehru, Jawaharlal, 189
Nehru, Pandit, 180
New Brunswick (Canada), 8, 136–7
New Hebrides *see* Vanuatu
New South Wales (Australia), 143, 157–60
New Zealand, 5, 164–73
Newfoundland (Canada), 136–7, 139
Nigeria, 4, 9, 193–4, 198, 210–11, 215
Nik Ahmed Kamil bin Haji Mahmood, Tan Sri Datuk, 225, 229
Niue, 9
N'Jie, Momodou, 209
Nkumbula, Harry, 202
Nonumalo, Leulumoega Sofara, 243
Northcote, Sir Stafford, 53
Northern Rhodesia, 9, 204; *see also* Zambia
Northern Territory (Australia), 143
North-West Territories (Canada), 136
Norton, Sir Fletcher, 44

272

Index

Nova Scotia (Canada), 8, 136–7, 139
Nyasaland, 9; see also Malawi

Obeyesekere, F. A., 218
Oehlers, Sir George, 230, 232–3
Oldhall, William, 20
Onslow, Arthur, 41–3, 64, 65
Onslow, Sir Richard, 25–6, 41
Ontario (Canada), 136–7, 139
Ottawa, 5, 137, 139, 207

Pacific region, 242–57
Page, T. S., 201
Pahang Assembly 229
Pannell, Lord Charles, 74–6, 81–3, 86
Papineau, Louis-Joseph, 7
Papua New Guinea, 237–8, 245–7, 254–7
Pardoe, John, 77
Parkinson, E. C., 241
Parnell, Charles Stewart, 52
Patel, Narendra, 194–5
Patel, R. D., 247–9
Patel, Vithalbhai, 175–6, 179, 180, 184, 191
Pearson, Lester, 120
Peel, Arthur Wellesley, 55–6, 57, 87
Peel, Sir Robert, 48–9, 50
Pelpola, R. S., 219
Peries, Sir Albert, 218–20
Perrers, Alice, 13
Phelips, Sir Edward, 29
Pickering, Sir James, 13
Pipeline Bill, Canada, 112–19
Pitt, William, the younger, 63
Popham, John, 26
Powell, Enoch, 11
Powle, Henry, 38–9
President of the Upper House, role of, 2, 3, 4
Prince Edward Island (Canada), 136
Protestants, 24–5, 28; see also Church of England
Puckering, Sir John, 26–7
Punjab Assembly, 178, 190
Puritans, 24–5, 27, 29

Qionibaravi, Mosese, 249–50, 257
Qualtrough, Sir Joseph, 258
Quebec (Canada), 136–8
Queensland (Australia), 3, 143, 159–61

Rajah, A. P., 230
Rajya Sabha (Council of States), 3–4
Rambally, Clarence, 239, 257
Ramcharam, Matthew, 238–9
Ratu, Sir Lala Sukuna, 247
Reddy, Dr N. Sanjiva, 177–8, 189
Redford, Sir Henry, 17
Reformation Parliament, 22
Rhodes, E. N., 107
Rich, Sir Richard, 22–3
Richard II, 13–15
Richard III, 20
Richardson, Sir Thomas, 29–30
Roman Catholic Church, 7, 22–5, 28, 39, 46, 48, 220
Rosevear, J. S., 148, 153
Rushworth, John, 34
Russell, Lord John, 49–50

Sabah, 224, 227
St. Clair-Daniel, W., 239
St. Helena, 9
St. Lucia, 3, 4, 236, 239, 257
St. Vincent, 236, 256
Samuel, Sir Herbert, 69
Sarawak, 224, 227, 229
Saskatchewan (Canada), 136–7
Sauvé, Jeanne, 106, 108, 111, 122–3, 124, 135, 142
Savage, Sir Arnold, 16–17
Scholes, Gordon, 150, 152
Scotland, 29, 32, 96
Scott, Sir Maurice, 247
Senanayake, Dudley, 219
Senegal, 194
Senegambia, 209
Seychelles, 10
Seymour, Sir Edward, 24, 38
Shaw-Lefevre, Charles, 50–1, 54
Shroeder, Harvey, 138
Sierra Leone, 193, 198, 210, 213, 215

Simon, John, 69
Singapore, 91, 224–5, 230–4
Singh, Hukam, 176–8, 186, 188
Singh, Vijay, 249
Slade, Humphrey, 194, 199
Smith, Professor Denis, 104, 109, 121
Smith, Ian, 205
Smith, John, 41
Smith, D., 138, 139
Snedden, Sir Billy, 146, 150–1, 155–6
Solomon Islands, 236, 238, 250, 251, 254, 256
Soskice, Sir Frank, 75
South Australia, 143, 159–60
Southern Rhodesia, 5, 204, 205; see also Zimbabwe
Speakership: in Chair, 88–96; continuity of, 68–80; history, to Mary I, 11–24, Elizabeth to Cromwell, 24–37, Restoration, 37–45, Nineteenth Century, 45–57, Twentieth Century, 62–80; statutory duties of, 96–9
Sri Lanka (Ceylon), 218–24
Stanfield, Robert, 104, 110
Stanford, W. P., 208
Stevenson, John, 258
Stevens, Dr Siaka, 210
Stewart, Alistair, 114
Storey, Marguerite, 243–4
Stott, T. C., 159
Strafford, Earl of, 33
Stokes, Jack, 136–7
Strutt, H. W., 158
Stourton, William, 18
Stumbles, A. R. W., 205
Sturmy, Sir William, 17
Subasinghe, T. B., 219, 220
Suffragettes, 81
Swaziland, 4, 193, 198
Syed Esa bin Alwee, Datuk, 225
Syed Nasir bin Ismail, Tan Sri Datuk, 225, 229
Symonette, R. H., 240

Tamil Nadu Assembly, 190
Tanganika, 9
Tanzania, 193, 197–8, 205–6, 210, 213, 215
Tasmania (Australia), 143, 157–60

Index

Taubman, John, 258
Thatcher, Margaret, 84
Thomas, George, 64–7, 70, 80, 83, 85–7, 92, 99
Thomasos, C. A., 238
Thorpe, Thomas, 20
Tillekeratne, Stanley, 220, 224
Tobago *see* Trinidad
Tiptoft, Sir John, 17, 20
Toliman, Mathias, 245
Tonga, 236, 254–6
Tranmire, Lord, 81
Tresham, Thomas, 20
Tresham, William, 20
Trevor, Sir John, 39–40
Trinidad and Tobago, 4, 236, 238, 255, 256
Trussell, William, 12
Turks and Caicos Islands, 10
Turner, John, 136–7
Turnour, Sir Edward, 37
Tu'u'u Faleto'ese, 243, 254, 257
Tuvalu (Ellice Islands), 237–8, 250–1, 254, 256
Tynwald, 257–8

Uganda, 9, 193–5, 198, 206, 213
Ullswater, Lord *see* Lowther, J. W.

United States of America, 4, 6, 194, 210

Vaghjee, Sir Harilal, 206–7
Vakatora, Tomasi, 250
Van Dieman's Land (Tasmania), 8
Vanuatu (New Hebrides), 236, 238, 250–1, 254–6
Victoria (Australia), 143, 157, 160
Victoria, Queen, 50
Virginia (USA), 6

Waldegrave, Sir Richard, 14
Waldron, Pershing, 239
Wales, 80
Walton (Wauton), Sir Thomas, 20
Wars of the Roses, 19–20
Weatherill, Bernard, 77
Wedd, W. G., 158
Wellington, Duke of, 48
Wenlock, Sir John, 20
Wentworth, Paul, 26
West Bengal Assembly, 190
Western Australia, 143, 157, 159–60
Western Samoa, 237, 242, 254–7
Whitelaw, William, 76
Whitlam, Gough, 152–3

Whitley, John Henry, 67, 73–4, 81, 87–8
Whyte, Sir Frederick, 175
Wight, Martin, 8
Wilkes, John, 44
William III, 40
William of Orange, 39, 40
Williams, Thomas, 25, 201
Williams, Sir William, 39
Willis, Henry, 157
Wilson, Sir Harold, 76
Wingfield, Sir Thomas, 22
Winterton, Lord, 88
Wolsey, Thomas, 21–2
Wray, Christopher, 26
Wycliffe, John, 16

Yelverton, Christopher, 28
Yeoh Ghim Seng, 230, 232
York, Duke of, 15
Yukon (Canada), 136
Yusuf, Tan Sri Datuk C. M., 225

Zambia (Northern Rhodesia), 5, 193, 196–9, 201–2, 212–15
Zimbabwe (Southern Rhodesia), 4, 193, 197–8, 203–5, 212